# THE OFFICIAL HONEYMOONERS TREASURY

# The Official Honeymooners Treasury

**PETER CRESCENTI & BOB COLUMBE**

*Co-founders of RALPH* ™

Published in 1989 by

Galahad Books
A division of LDAP, Inc.
166 Fifth Avenue
New York, NY 10010

By arrangement with The Putnam Publishing Group.

Stills from The Honeymooners provided courtesy of Viacom Enterprises.

Library of Congress Catalog Card Number: 85-16891

ISBN: 0-88365-739-2

Printed in the United States of America.

# CONTENTS

# *ACKNOWLEDGMENTS*

We'd like to thank the following people, without whose help this book could not have been written:

Jackie Gleason
Allen Dubois, CBS Inc.
Irene Mizwinski and Lynn Fero, Viacom Enterprises
Richard Green, Esquire

We'd also like to thank the following people for their support and their contributions to this book: Leslie Barrett, Howard Bender, Hal Bowden, Joan Reichman Canale, Art Carney, Brian Carney, Alexander Clark, Phil Cuoco, Humphrey Davis, Irving Deutsch, Ed DeVierno, Bullets Durgom, Jim Engel, Herb Finn, Arthur Forrest, Ken Geiman, Val Irving, Jay Jackson, Coleman Jacoby, Charles Kaplan, Seymour Kaplan, John Langton, Bill Mark, Frank Marth, Doreen Marx, Myron Marx, George Mathews, Donna McCrohan, Bob McGee, Audrey Meadows, Leo O'Farrell, James Oliver, George Petrie, Jack Philbin, Rosalie Poznachowski, Joyce Randolph, Ralph Robertson, Freda Rosen, Joe Ruskin, A. J. Russell, Frank Satenstein, Abbie Lewis Seymour, Anne Seymour, John Seymour, George Silano, Sydell Spear, William Spiegler, Fredrica Stalter, Leonard Stern, Walter Stone, Roberta Weir, Jerry Yarus, Cora Zelinka, Bill Zuckert.

Special thanks to our editors, Judy Linden and Lee Ann Chearneyi, for their enthusiasm, encouragement, and good judgment. Sweet kids.

# audrey meadows six

May 28, 1985

Messrs. Peter Crescenti
         Bob Columbe
RALPH
C. W. Post
Greenvale, New York 11548

Dear Peter and Bob:

Congratulations on all your hard work.  There is
no tribute too great, or praise too lavish, for me
to express concerning the magnificent talent of
Jackie Gleason.  I treasure the years that I worked
with him.

As I look back now at the old shows and see the
brilliance of his timing and the wonderful
characterizations of all the characters that he
played, I marvel at his talent.  With practically
no rehearsal, he can be whatever character he wishes.
His instincts as an actor are always right.  He can
break your heart in a scene as quickly as make you
laugh.

And, as the man, he is a kind, warm, loving, caring
and sensitive human being.  I love and admire him,
and I value his friendship.

                    Fondly,

                    Audrey

AMS/lh

# INTRODUCTION

*The Honeymooners* figures . . . to be the part of Gleason's bag of tricks most destined to succeed over the long pull.
—Steve Allen, 1955

When Morley Safer, in a *60 Minutes* interview, asked Jackie Gleason why *The Honeymooners* was still so popular so many years after its debut on television, Gleason had a simple answer: "It's funny."

Gleason was right. *The Honeymooners* is funny; many people think it's the funniest TV show ever made. But after three decades of reruns, after the formation of RALPH (Royal Association for the Longevity and Preservation of the Honeymooners), a fan club that has grown to include thousands of members from Bensonhurst to Britain, and after 5,000 people from all across the United States and Canada attended two Honeymooners conventions on Long Island in 1984, people begin to wonder, *"What makes it so funny?"*

Since Bob Columbe and I founded RALPH in 1982, if we've been asked that question once, we've been asked it a thousand times. Each time we answer it, we give what we think are the obvious answers: First, the uncommon chemistry between Gleason and Art Carney, and between Gleason and Audrey Meadows. Next, Gleason and Carney are superb comic actors; the two *became* Kramden and Norton—viewers forgot they were watching actors at work.

Then there is the writing. Gleason's writers—head writer Marvin Marx, Walter Stone, Leonard Stern, Syd Zelinka, Andy Russell, and Herb Finn—were among the best in the business. People are still laughing at their material thirty years later. And doing the show before a live audience in a theater gave *The Honeymooners* an edge and an intensity that would never have happened in an empty studio. And so on.

Art Carney and Audrey Meadows have their own ideas about the show's appeal. "It was funny, period," Carney says. He elaborates: "It was a comic strip come to life. It was broad—there was nothing subtle about it. But somehow or other, everybody, from Park Avenue to downtown, could relate to *The Honeymooners*. People believed these two guys existed. They believed that he [Gleason] was a bus driver, and they believed I was a sewer worker."

Audrey agrees and adds, "Naturally, none of us dreamed it would still be going on. But the power of it, to me, the power of that comedy, was that every single situation was based on truth. They were legitimate, real people. Every problem they had—now, I had friends that were in a different economic bracket, but they had the same kind of fights, and they'd say to me, 'My wife and I fight the same way you do with Kramden,' because the problem has nothing to do with how much money a bus driver makes, or a lawyer, or a doctor, or whoever. The problems were all the universal kinds that we all deal with.

"We never put the characters in a situation that wasn't totally believable. Very often, you see a show that's funny, and you can laugh like mad, but you don't remember it because it's just gags—no identification. The reason people like the feeling of the tremendous bond between Ralph and Alice, that real love, is because it is so truthful. You know that she really loves him and he really loves her—so he could say almost anything he wanted and get away with it."

These are all good reasons, and there are more. But you could line up all the good reasons from one end of Madison Avenue to the other, and when you've finished, somehow all those reasons fall a teensy-weensy (or is it itsy-bitsy?) bit short of really answering the question, "Why is *The Honeymooners* still so funny?" And that's because those classic thirty-nine half-hour shows possess that magical "something," that indefinable, elusive quality separating "the greatest" from the great.

The Honeymooners began in 1950, as just another sketch on Gleason's first TV show, *Cavalcade of Stars*. The idea, in itself, wasn't so original. Put a husband and a wife together, and let 'em go at one another. Walter Stone, recruited for the *Cavalcade* writing staff by Marvin Marx shortly after the Honeymooners was conceived, confirms that it was meant to be nothing more than an occasional sketch. There was no intention at the beginning of creating characters who would appear on the show week after week.

"The first one was about four, five minutes. He comes home from work, she's steaming. She says, 'Go to the store,' or something. Just five minutes of that. Then, the second or third one, they needed a neighbor, and Carney, a very good actor they had used in other things, became the upstairs neighbor. We didn't plan that to be permanent or anything. Bring in a neighbor. . . ."

"I said, 'Give me a crack at 'im,'" says Carney. "I think I got an idea of the type of guy he is. I used the hat, vest, and T-shirt. That was my idea. Great originality."

Carney had been introduced to Gleason earlier that season by two of Gleason's writers, Coleman Jacoby and the late Arnie Rosen. The pair worked with Carney on television and in radio, and when they had a part to cast in a Reggie Van Gleason III sketch, they thought of Carney.

"We told Gleason we had this wonderful actor," says Jacoby. "He played the part of a society photographer in the sketch, and from that week on, he was on the show forever."

"They told Gleason that I was a capable actor," says Carney, "a comedic actor, could do dialects and characters, and things like that. Gleason and I shook hands—we had never seen each other before."

The Honeymooners, then featuring Pert Kelton as Alice Kramden, gradually became more popular—with the writers, because it was easy to write; with Gleason, because he liked playing Ralph Kramden; and with the audience, because the sketches were funny and because viewers identified with the Kramdens' antics. By the time Gleason moved from the Dumont Network to CBS in 1952, and replaced Kelton with Audrey Meadows, Ralph Kramden had found his niche in Gleason's large and diverse cast of characters.

By 1955, the Honeymooners was taking up more and more time on *The Jackie Gleason Show;* Gleason was even doing hour-long Honeymooners. Gleason fans were seeing less and less of his other characters—Reggie Van Gleason III, The Poor Soul, Fenwick Babbitt, Joe the Bartender, Charlie Bratton, Rudy the Repairman, and others—and more and more of Ralph Kramden. And they loved it!

"Gleason Is Signed to $6 Million Pact," read the *New York Times* headline announcing Gleason's deal with Buick to produce seventy-eight half-hour Honeymooners for the 1955–56 and 1956–57 television seasons. As Jack Philbin, executive producer for *The Honeymooners,* put it, Buick wanted to "buy Gleason for something." *The Honeymooners* is what they bought.

Philbin says it was Mike Kirk, of the Kudner advertising agency, who came to him one afternoon with the idea of Gleason doing a new half-hour show sponsored by Buick, one of Kudner's clients.

"Kirk and I were in the back of the theater during a rehearsal for a Honeymooners skit," says Philbin, "and he told me his agency was looking for a half-hour show. One of us, I don't know which one—it could have been Kirk—said, 'Why don't we do a half-hour Honeymooners show?'

"He said, 'What would it cost?' And I said, 'It will cost you well over $10 million, I'll tell you that.' And he said, 'You're not scaring me, because the sponsor will be Buick.'

"So I said, 'Let's go up and talk to Gleason,' and we did, and that got it on the track."

The original deal called for seventy-eight filmed episodes—two seasons of thirty-nine shows each—with an option for a third season. During the first season, Buick would pay Gleason Enterprises $65,000 per show and half that amount for thirteen summer reruns; the second season, the figures would jump to $70,000 and $35,000. (Had *The Honeymooners* run for three years, Gleason Enterprises would have been paid over $3 million during the third year.)

It was decided that *The Honeymooners*—television's first spin-off— would air from 8:30 to 9 PM on Saturday nights. The 8 to 8:30 PM spot occupied by Gleason's variety show for three years would now be filled by *Stage Show,* a variety show featuring the Dorsey Brothers band, the June Taylor Dancers, and guests. It would also be produced by Gleason Enterprises. (CBS would have preferred to schedule *The Honeymooners* in the 8 PM time slot. But it had an agreement with the P. Lorillard Tobacco Company to schedule Lorillard's popular quiz show, *Two for the Money,* after any Gleason show. Since Gleason insisted on running *Stage Show* back to back with *The Honeymooners,* CBS had no choice but to run *The Honeymooners* at 8:30.)

*The Honeymooners* was filmed twice a week—Tuesday and Friday nights at 8 PM in the Adelphi Theater on 54th Street in Manhattan. More than 1,000 people attended each show, filmed on the then-revolutionary Electronicam system for broadcast at a later date. The show was usually in the can in about forty minutes. The action stopped only for set changes, and to allow film magazines on the three Electronicam cameras to be changed. Gleason would not allow the action to stop for any other reason.

"When we started," Audrey remembers, "Jackie said, 'If any major mistakes take place while we're taping with the audience, we will continue on with that audience, but we will *not* use the shot. We will not do anything over—we won't stop and go back and pick up anything and repeat it in front of the audience. If anything major happens that we have to do over, we'll put the show aside for at least five or six weeks, and then come back and do it so it's brand-new again in our minds.' We never did anything over."

*The Honeymooners* was one of New York's hottest tickets, but the scheduling of *Stage Show* at eight o'clock, before *The Honeymooners* at eight-thirty, proved to be a ratings blunder—and *The Honeymooners'* undoing.

"We were on against Perry Como," says Stone. "Gleason wanted *Stage Show* on at eight. We were on at eight-thirty. *Stage Show* never really caught on. If you had a choice of music, you'd probably watch Como. It was tough coming in [with *The Honeymooners*] at the half hour.

"It's funny. We were in Lindy's, I think it was, and we met the Como writers just before the season started. The guys said, 'We give up! Forget it! We got no chance!'"

With a weak lead-in, *The Honeymooners* never got a foothold in the ratings battle against *The Perry Como Show.* Halfway through the season, *The Honeymooners* and *Stage Show* switched time periods, but it was too late. *The Honeymooners* finished the season ranked twentieth in the ratings.

Just the season before, *The Jackie Gleason Show* was the number two show in the country, right behind *I Love Lucy*. Oddly enough, Como finished only one notch ahead of *The Honeymooners*, at number nineteen.

Gleason canceled his deal with Buick after the first season—that's why there are only thirty-nine *Honeymooners* episodes. A year later, Gleason, whose agreement with Buick called for Gleason Enterprises to retain ownership of the thirty-nine shows, sold them to CBS for $1.5 million. The following year the show went into syndication. Today, in many cities around the country, you can watch *The Honeymooners* five, six, or seven nights a week—and that's been the case for nearly thirty years.

And Kramden, Norton, and company have made an impact not only on the public, but on the entertainment industry as well. Warner Brothers, in the mid-fifties, produced two cartoons featuring "The Honey Mousers," and in one of its Bugs Bunny cartoons Bugs finds himself on a train with two hoboes who are dead ringers for Ralph and Norton.

References to *The Honeymooners* and its characters regularly pop up in prime time, too; *Remington Steele* and *Kate & Allie* are the leaders in plugging the show. And those who saw the feature film *Alligator* will never forget that the monster gator gobbled up a sewer worker named Ed Norton.

That brings us to RALPH, and this book.

Chamfort once said, "The most thoroughly wasted of all days is that on which one has not laughed." By the beginning of 1982, the year Bob and I founded RALPH, *The Honeymooners* had been off the air in New York for two years. There were lots of wasted days during that time. Growing up in the New York metropolitan area we had been spoiled; a TV station in New York had been showing *Honeymooners* reruns since 1958 and always seemed to have the show on its schedule. Sometimes the show went off the air, usually for only a few months. But two years?!

Kramden and Norton were out of sight, but they were never out of mind. When telephone calls and letters to the TV station begging for the reinstatement of *The Honeymooners* failed, what else could we do but what every special-interest group does these days: organize, and form a lobby!

Through persistence—we learned that from Kramden, who kept chasing that high note—we appeared on *The Joe Franklin Show*, a late-night/early-morning talk show that's been on television in New York longer than *Honeymooners* reruns. Franklin, the undisputed King of Nostalgia, loves old-time television. He called us crusaders and compared us to "knights of old." RALPH was just a couple of weeks old at that point, and with a buildup like that how could we quit until we brought home the grail (or at least a trophy from the Racoon Lodge's bowling tournament)?

Exactly ten days after our appearance on *The Joe Franklin Show*, *The Honeymooners* came back to New York television viewers on Sunday nights. Station officials called the timing coincidental. Maybe so. But a couple of

*The Honeymooners.* COURTESY RALPH.

months later, *The Honeymooners* was running seven nights a week, presumably to cash in on the furor RALPH created in its pursuit of what we believed to be an authentic Ralph Kramden bus driver's uniform. (Yes, the same one Alice fell in love with, and married Ralph for.)

It was the summer of '83, and RALPH's membership had grown to over 200, largely because of an article about the club that appeared in a student magazine at Long Island University's C.W. Post Campus and a mention in the TV guide of *Newsday*, a Long Island daily newspaper.

A Long Island woman who joined RALPH sent some of the club literature (at that time, the membership kit consisted of a hand-pressed RALPH button, welcoming letter, quiz, and a one-sided photocopied newsletter) to her son, Tom DuBocq, a reporter for the *Miami News* and a devoted fan of *The Honeymooners*. A short time later, Tom was assigned to cover the auction of a Miami mansion formerly owned by Gleason (the house had changed hands twice since Gleason owned it). Some of the contents of the house were going to be auctioned as well; among them, a uniform purported to have been worn by Gleason/Kramden. Tom called us in New York and told us about the auction and the uniform. "Would the club bid for it?" he wanted to know. Would Ralph Kramden pass up the chance to buy stock in a uranium mine in Asbury Park?

Tom wrote a story about the auction, the uniform, and RALPH that appeared on the front page of the *Miami News* and was soon picked up by the wire services. Soon we were giving interviews to reporters from all across the country.

We scrambled to raise some money so we could at least submit a competitive bid. Some old eccentric in Florida would probably bid a couple of thousand bucks and walk away with the uniform, but we were still determined to get our noses right in the middle of the action.

We raised $600. Peanuts! Peanuts! What were we gonna do with peanuts? Win the uniform, that's what! We couldn't have been more surprised if you told us Jane Russell was throwing a party and couldn't get started until we got there.

We won the uniform, but we never even saw it. The auctioneer we called our bid into the night before the auction assured us that if we had the highest bid he would hold the uniform until we collected all the money pledged to us. But right after the auction the man quit the auction company and his employer, for whatever reason, refused to honor the agreement we'd made with his auctioneer. A doctor's report telling us we had arterial monochromia would have been better news!

These events were monitored in Florida by Gleason's secretary, Sydell Spear, daughter-in-law of Gleason's former music director, the late Sammy Spear. Even before the auction Sydell told us she couldn't confirm the authenticity of the uniform, but that she'd do anything she could to help us. When the deal for the first uniform fell through, she kept her promise. She went straight to Gleason with the news.

We'd heard from various sources that Gleason was fed up with hearing about the Honeymooners. Anyway, what could we expect him to do, call the auction company president and threaten to bend him into a pretzel unless he gave us the uniform? But if Gleason had grown cool toward the Honeymooners over the years—and we suspect this was never the case—he did a sudden about-face. He gave us a Ralph Kramden uniform right out of his wardrobe.

The letter accompanying the uniform read:

Dear members of RALPH:

I understand you had difficulty in receiving a supposed Ralph Kramden uniform.

I have sent you the absolute genuine article, and want to take this opportunity to wish you all the best. Thank you, from the bottom of my heart, for your valued support!

How sweet it is!

Your friend,
Jackie Gleason

*Rare Honeymooners memorabilia from RALPH's archives.*
COURTESY SAMUEL LOWE COMPANY.

Largely because of the media's coverage of this strangely Kramdenesque affair, RALPH's membership multiplied from a couple of hundred to a couple of thousand. As mail poured in—from kids, housewives, college professors, politicians, doctors, entertainers, athletes, company presidents, and rank-and-file you-name-its—we realized a fan club for *The Honeymooners* was not a crazy harebrained scheme after all, but an idea long overdue.

RALPH's first Honeymooners convention, held in March 1984 at Long Island University's C. W. Post Campus, sold out in three weeks. (The Racoons held conventions, we gotta hold conventions.) After mailing the last ticket, we still had close to a thousand ticket requests left unfilled. We hastily scheduled another convention for May and that one sold out too. Nearly 5,000 people attended the conventions, and we still hear from people who twice missed getting tickets.

Not long after RALPH started, we thought about writing a trivia book. Honeymooners fans love trivia like Norton loves pizza. We live in a time, though, where everybody seems to love trivia. An astute editor at Perigee Books figured fans of *The Honeymooners* must be like everyone else, and so we have this book.

Yes, there's trivia—*everything* you ever wanted to know, about all thirty-nine episodes. Never again will you be stumped by such questions as, "What was Trixie's brother-in-law's name?" (Harvey); "Who blew the whistle on KranMar's Delicious Mystery Appetizer?" (Mr. Peck); and "What are Ralph's twenty-two bad points?" (Look them up in the back of the book!) *But there's so much more!*

You will find comments from and interviews with dozens of people who worked on the Classic 39: Jackie Gleason, Art Carney, Audrey Meadows, Joyce Randolph, Walter Stone, Leonard Stern, A. J. Russell, Herb Finn, Jack Philbin, George Petrie (Freddie Muller, Joe Munsey, Dick Gersh, Danny, etc.), Frank Marth (Bibbo, Grogan the cop, Dick Prescott, Mr. Martin, etc.), Jay Jackson (Herb Norris), Freda Rosen (Rita Weedemeyer), George Mathews (Har-veee!, a lovely name), Leslie Barrett (George), Alexander Clark (Andre, Herbert J. Whiteside), Ralph Robertson (Tommy Manicotti), the writers, the cameramen, and others.

Next, the photos and illustrations, most of which appear in print for the first time. Thanks to Mr. Gleason, CBS, and Viacom Enterprises, this book contains thirty-nine frame blowups, one from each of the episodes. You'll also enjoy seeing rare publicity stills from the fifties of Ralph, Norton, Trixie, and Alice. The illustrations are a regular riot: Ralph, Alice, and Norton, from coloring books, children's books, and a doll pop-up book published in the fifties; caricatures of Norton and the Kramdens done by noted cartoonist Preston Blair for an aborted Honeymooners cartoon series, and more.

Finally, the pot of gold! The bag full of money on the bus! Fortune! The high note! *"Lost" material from the original scripts!* Deleted scenes and dialogue. Rewritten beginnings and endings of episodes. Never-before-told facts about the characters. Characters you never knew existed. All—thanks to Mr. Gleason, CBS, the writers, and their families—published here, for the first time anywhere.

Where do we begin to tell you about the amazing, the amusing, the unbelievable information we found in the scripts? How about Ralph's favorite dinner: pot roast and potato pancakes (from "The Babysitter"). Have you often wondered where Ralph got the money to do the commercial for the Handy Housewife Helper? It's in the script, but Gleason left out the line: Ralph borrowed the money against his life insurance!

How about this: The original title for "$99,000 Answer" was "$88,000 Answer." The title "Dial J for Janitor" was a takeoff on the popular Broadway show, *Dial "M" for Murder*. And, from "A Matter of Record": After seeing *Murder Strikes Out*, Ralph planned to take Alice to the penny arcade to play pinball.

Did you know Alice has a brother, Frank? Or that another of Alice's pet names for Ralph is "Poopsie"? Did you know "Leave it there, the cat'll get it" was an ad-lib? So was, "Don't call me Norton. Call me Eduardo." (The script reads, "Call me Edward.")

We were as surprised as Ralph was when he came home and discovered his surprise birthday party had been canceled, at the wealth of deleted material, rewritten portions of episodes (sometimes more than half the show), and unknown facts about the characters contained in the scripts. We had seen a couple of scripts long before we began working on the book, but they scarcely hinted at what we would find the day we visited the CBS script library. "Eureka!" we cried, and it wasn't because our garbage cans were full!

We also discovered things about the writers and the way the three writing teams wrote, from a study of the scripts. Stern and Zelinka's scripts were skimpy on stage directions. Marx and Stone, on the other hand, not only put the words in the characters' mouths, they choreographed their movements, their manner of speaking, and even their facial expressions.

We found lots of writers' code words and expressions too: "macaroni," for Ralph's what-a-moax-I-am look; "beached whale," when Ralph's supposed to faint; and, at the end of many episodes, "Kissville."

We were also surprised at two words we *didn't* find in any of the scripts: "Bang! Zoom!" Gleason probably stuck that in whenever he felt it was appropriate.

Some of the writers had favorite jokes they kept putting in the scripts and Gleason kept crossing out. There were also lots of threatening remarks from Norton about belting Trixie that were almost always cut out. Ralph, too—as sneaky and incorrigible as he is in the shows—is even more so in the scripts.

Reading all this stuff—which appears in boldface in each chapter—will give you the same thrill you'd get from watching a fortieth episode. And that's always been every Honeymooners fan's dream.

PETER CRESCENTI

*Huntington, New York*

# TV OR NOT TV

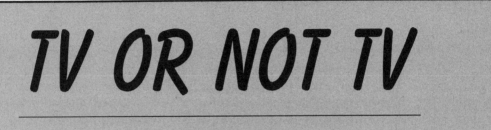

October 1, 1955 · Marvin Marx and Walter Stone

*As travelers part, camera holds on establishing shot of the Kramden kitchen. There is a clothes basket filled with wet wash on table. Standing up in sink is washboard. Impression around sink is that Alice has just finished doing wash in sink. Stage is bare for a split when Alice enters hurriedly from bedroom carrying plumber's-friend plunger. She is dressed housework-style. She crosses quickly to sink and puts plunger over drain and starts pumping. After a couple of pumps, she releases plunger and we hear accentuated sound of drain opening and water going down, regurgitating-style. It is done Mel Blanc—style. She then puts plunger over drain again and pumps a couple of more times. As she is doing this, door opens and Trixie enters.*

TRIXIE: Hi'ya, Alice.

ALICE (*turns but continues pumping as she speaks*): Oh, hello, Trix. This darn sink is stopped up again. It's always either stopped up or backin' up.

*At this point Alice stops pumping and removes plunger. We again hear hokey draining sound. It is prolonged. At conclusion of sound Alice leans over cautiously and looks into sink and then steps back quickly as geyser of water shoots up into air from drain. After quick shot of water it subsides.*

TRIXIE (*slightly alarmed*): What was that?

ALICE (*sarcastically*): Oh, don't get scared, Trix. It's just "old faithful"!

TRIXIE: Gee, you better call a plumber.

ALICE (*sarcastically*): Oh, Ralph wouldn't call a plumber. He says this is a "do-it-yourself" age.

TRIXIE: Well, has Ralph tried to fix it?

ALICE (*sarcastically*): You don't understand, Trix. "Do it yourself" means me!

1. What "routine" is Trixie going to use on Norton to get a new TV set?

ALICE: Gee, here you are getting your second set and we haven't even had our first one yet.

*Alice, a little steamed, starts shelling peas.*

ALICE: Boy, I'd give anything if Ralph'd get me a set.

TRIXIE: Well, I don't see why you don't get a set. You can buy one on time. It only costs five dollars down and a dollar and a quarter a week.

ALICE (*flatly*): Ralph doesn't believe in buying things on time.

TRIXIE (*trying to understand*): Well, you can't blame him for that. A lot of people only believe in buying for cash.

ALICE (*sarcastic*): Oh, he doesn't believe in that either. He wants to win 'em on quiz shows!

*Trixie laughs a little at this.*

ALICE: It's not funny, Trix. I've begged Ralph for a television. I've pleaded with him. But he won't spend a dime on anything for this house. And I know why. He's never home. He's out at work all day, and then when he comes home all he does is gulp down a fast supper and then run out again to the pool hall, or the bowling alleys or some lodge meeting or something. He doesn't care that I have to spend twenty-four hours a day in this dump, staring at the four walls. And that's about all I've got to stare at.

TRIXIE: Look, Alice, you're never gonna get anything out of Ralph by begging. Husbands just love to see us beg. Whenever I want to get something out of Ed, I just use the old pipe-and-slippers routine.

ALICE: What's that?

TRIXIE: Well, when Ed comes home, I get him his pipe and slippers, flatter him a little, wait on him, make him comfortable. And then when I got him in a good mood, I spring it on him. And it never fails, Alice. He's just like putty in my hands.

ALICE (*dubiously*): Well, I don't think it'll work with Ralph, Trix. He's an awful big blob of putty!

Joyce Randolph will never forget the night of the premiere of *The Honeymooners*: it was the eve of her wedding day.

On October 2, 1955, Joyce married Dick Charles, a friend of the late Peggy Morrison, costume designer for *The Honeymooners*, who introduced Joyce and Dick at The Cordial Bar, a favorite hangout of the *Honeymooners* crew.

"We used to go to Sam's on Saturday night," says Joyce, "and one night Peggy and her husband, Dave, brought this handsome guy over to meet some of the girls. Five months later we got married."

*Joyce Randolph, today.* COURTESY BRUCE BENNETT/BRIAN WINKLER AND RALPH.

2. Ralph: "Who's 'sweetums'?" Alice: "You're 'sweetums.'" Ralph: "You're _____."
3. What is Ralph's favorite drink?
4. Why won't Ralph buy a TV set?

RALPH (*hurt*): Cheap? That's why you think I ain't buyin' a television set? Cause I'm cheap? Well, that's how much you know. That ain't the reason at all.

ALICE (*disgustedly*): Then what is the reason?

RALPH (*groping*): Well, it's 'cause, uh . . . It's 'cause . . . uh . . . uh . . . I'm waitin' for color!

ALICE: Are you waitin' for color refrigerators too? Let's face it, Ralph. You're just too cheap to get me a set.

RALPH: Stop sayin' that, Alice! Stop sayin' that! I ain't cheap. There's a big difference between bein' cheap and bein' thrifty. I have to look after my money, Alice. It don't grow on trees for me. I got to work for it. I didn't inherit it from no rich father. I wasn't born with no silver spoon in my mouth, you know!

ALICE: No, you were born with a fork in your mouth and you've been eating ever since!

5. True or false: Norton's salary is $75 a week.
6. What appliances do the Nortons own?
7. How much money is in the Kramdens' bank account?
8. The Kramdens' last electric bill was:
   A. Sixty-five cents.
   B. Sixty-two cents.
   C. Eighty-nine cents.
   D. Thirty-nine cents.
9. How long ago did the Kramdens last blow a fuse?
10. Before they were married, Alice told Ralph she'd be happy to live with Ralph in:
    A. A tent.
    B. A tent with a small snake.
    C. A tent with a big snake.
    D. A home on Long Island.
11. How long have the Kramdens lived in their apartment without a stick of furniture being changed?

RALPH: I can see you still don't see the light, Alice. You still don't understand. It ain't just the money in the bank. It's everything else. Do you realize that if Norton misses one payment on any of his stuff, the man he bought it from will come over and take it back. We don't have that worry. They can never come and take this stuff back.

the floor above their drab Brooklyn apartment lives Ralph's best pal-o'-mine, Ed Norton, in far spiffier surroundings.

Naturally the first show of the season finds Battling Kramden locked in conflict. The arena —the Kramden apartment. Point of argument —clash of artistic opinions. Subject of argument—television.

Though *The Honeymooners* is on film this year, the Electronicam method of filming is used. This means that the show is staged like a live telecast. Gleason believes he has preserved the spontaneity for which the comedy sketches were noted during past seasons.

**DEBUT** Gleason is back with a 30-minute show devoted entirely to *The Honeymooners*, the saga of bus-driver Ralph Kramden, full of wild money-making schemes, and his everloving but quick-on-the-retort wife Alice. On

**Cast**

Ralph Kramden ......................Jackie Gleason
Ed Norton .........................................Art Carney
Alice Kramden ....................Audrey Meadows
Trixie Norton............................Joyce Randolph

**TV GUIDE**          A-7

The Honeymooners *debuts, and* TV Guide *features the new show in its October 1–7, 1955 issue.* REPRINTED WITH PERMISSION FROM TV GUIDE® MAGAZINE. COPYRIGHT © 1955 BY TRIANGLE PRODUCTIONS, INC., RADNOR, PENNSYLVANIA.

ALICE: You're darn right they can't. The man we bought it from died fifteen years ago!

12. Alice doesn't want to look at the stove, the sink, the icebox, or the walls. She wants to look at:
    A. Basil Fomeen.
    B. Captain Video.
    C. Liberace.
    D. Charlie Chan.

RALPH: Look, Alice, it ain't just the money. There's another reason I don't want no television in this house. It changes people. They stop usin' their brains. They just look. When people get television, they stop readin' books.
ALICE (*sarcastic*): Well, it can't change us. We don't even have a book!
RALPH (*grasping straw*): All right. All right. I'll get you a book!

13. How many credit accounts does Norton have going? What is Norton's latest credit purchase?
14. Ralph and Norton decide to purchase a TV set jointly, and they flip a coin to see in which apartment the set will stay. How does the coin come up, and who loses the flip?
15. Norton: "I hope I don't insult you, Ralph, but would you mind giving me back my _____."

5

"Flip a kern. That broke Gleason up once in rehearsal," Art Carney says. "I said, 'All right, we'll flip a kern.' And he started to laugh. It broke him up. He had a relative that said kern instead of coin."

*Ralph takes coin out of pocket thinking madly how he can cheat Norton. Idea hits and he speaks.*

RALPH (*hopefully casual*): Okay, Norton . . . heads I win. Tails you lose.
*Ralph looks at Norton out of corner of his eye and Norton nods assent. Ralph flips and then displays coin to Norton.*

RALPH: There it is. Tails you lose!
*Ralph starts to put coin back in pocket when Norton speaks.*

NORTON: Wait a minute, Ralph. Wait a minute.
*Ralph looks weakly at Norton, feeling he's caught.*

RALPH (*weakly*): What's'a matter, Norton?

NORTON (*hopefully*): What'da'ya say we make it two out of three!

RALPH (*relieved*): Oh, sure. Sure.
*Ralph's about to toss when Norton speaks again.*

NORTON (*happily*): You know, Ralph, this sharin' the television set is just gonna work out great. You and me, we just get along fine.

RALPH (*Oliver Hardy–style*): We certainly do. And just to show you what a sport I am, we'll make it three out of five.
*Norton looks gratefully at Ralph and as Ralph flips we DISSOLVE from scene.*

Scene Two in the script opens with Ralph coming home from work carrying a bag full of snacks. Alice is in front of their new television, hypnotized.

RALPH: Hi'ya Alice.
*Alice, entranced with the movie, pays no attention to him. Ralph crosses to table and puts grocery bag down. Ralph then leans toward Alice, digging what's going on, and speaks louder.*

RALPH: I said, "Hi'ya Alice!"
*Alice, still entranced with picture and without looking up, speaks absently.*

ALICE: Huh!

RALPH (*steamed, shouts at her*): Alice, I'm home!
*Without looking at Ralph, Alice puts her finger to her mouth shhhh-style and then speaks.*

ALICE: Shhhhhhhhh!
*She then points toward set. Ralph just looks at her steamed and then crosses to stove looking-for-supper-style. Quickly seeing that there are no pots on top of stove he opens oven door and looks in. Seeing nothing inside, he slams oven door angrily. He then crosses steamed to Alice.*

RALPH (*steamed*): Alice, I'm hungry!

ALICE (*absently as before*): Huh?

*Ralph, exasperated, crosses to set and angrily snaps it off.*

RALPH (*steamed*): We interrupt this program for an important announcement. Where's my supper!

ALICE (*coming out of daze*): Oh, Ralph, you're home.

RALPH (*mimicking Alice*): Oh, Ralph, you're home. (*Then steamed*) I been home for an hour! Now would you mind tellin' me where my supper is.

ALICE (*weak defense*): I didn't make it yet. I didn't realize it was so late. I sat down to watch the movie around four o'clock and I got so interested I, uh . . . What time is it now, anyway?

RALPH (*steamed*): You want to know what time it is? I'll tell you what time it is. It's exactly six o'clock.

*Ralph puts his fist under Alice's chin threatening-style.*

RALPH: Moon time!

ALICE (*sheepishly*): I'm sorry, Ralph.

RALPH: I knew this would happen, Alice. We've had that set three days now, and I haven't had a hot meal since we got it. Every night I come home and you're sittin' there like this.

*Ralph does eye bulge, mimicking TV watcher.*

RALPH: One night it was tuna fish. The next night it was cold cuts. Tonight nuthin'.

ALICE (*a little annoyed*): I said I was sorry, Ralph.

RALPH: "Sorries" don't help, Alice. *Pointing to stomach.* I can't fill this with "sorries."

ALICE: Then try helium. That's what they fill most blimps with!

RALPH (*eyes bulge with anger*): Oh boy, Alice, are you gonna get yours! Before this night is over are you gonna get yours! Now just for that I ain't gonna eat your cold supper tonight. So start gettin' dressed and go down to the Hong Kong Gardens and pick me up some Chinese food.

*With this Ralph turns and crosses to table and starts opening mouth of bag he brought. Alice, who just stood there watching him cross, speaks.*

ALICE: What'a you got in the bag, Ralph?

RALPH: Well, I figured on stayin' home tonight so I picked up a few snacks to nibble on while I'm watchin' television. Now, hurry up and get the Chinese. Chop chop! Do you understand?

*Ralph goes back to opening bag. Alice sticks her tongue out at Ralph's back.*

RALPH: Cut that out!

*Alice registers mild surprise and then crosses into bedroom. Ralph starts emptying contents of bag. It's loaded. He takes out big bag of potato chips, pretzels, popcorn, Fritos, Cheetos, a couple of quart bottles of beer, a big box of Ritz crackers, several Tastee cakes and Nabs, a big pie, bananas, oranges, apples, a bag of peanuts, etc. He places all this on side of table nearest television. He then takes chair and places it next to table, facing*

*Norton the Space Cadet.*
COURTESY HOWARD BENDER. COPYRIGHT
© 1985 HOWARD BENDER.

*television, and goes through motions of lining it up very carefully, flying Steinhart-teeterboard-style. After he's satisfied with this, he sits down in chair and by reaching over to table makes sure that all snacks are within reaching distance. He does this by moving arm from one bag to another. While doing this, though, his face is watching television. Set is not on. This is merely a dress rehearsal. Satisfied with this he gets up and surveys whole setup.*

RALPH (*happily, with Reggie headshake*): Perfect. I'm set for the night.

16. True or false: Captain Video's space rangers all have space helmets and denaturizers.

RALPH (*Hardyish*): Whaaat is that?

NORTON (*stands up and gives hokey salute*): This is my official Captain Video helmet. I'm off to outer space!

RALPH: You're off, all right. I'll tell you that much.

NORTON (*in joking attitude pulls out gun*): Careful what you say, earthling. I may be forced to disintegrate you. *He looks Ralph up and down fat-joke-style.* It'll be the biggest pile of ashes the world has ever known!

17. Captain Video is blasting off. Where is he headed?
18. Recite the Captain Video ranger pledge.
19. What rank does Norton hold in the Captain Video space academy?
20. What has Norton watched in the three days he and Ralph have owned their TV set?
21. Ralph wants to watch a movie. He tells Norton that if he dares to make a sound while he's watching the movie, he'll cut off his _____.

*Norton just looks hurt. Ralph lets go of hose and snaps set on and changes channel. He looks at Norton smugly as sound comes up on set. First we hear soft violin music followed by a few lines of dialogue.*

MAN (*suave-style*): Julia.

WOMAN (*sexy-style*): Yes, Harry?

MAN: It's awfully warm in here. Let's go out on the terrace.

*We hear music for a couple of seconds and then Norton speaks.*

NORTON (*sulking*): It's a lot of silly mush.

*Ralph shoots him steamed look.*

NORTON: Well, I got my rights too, Ralph, and I wanna watch Captain Video.

*Norton snaps dial. Immediately we hear dialogue.*

CAPTAIN VIDEO: Yes, Rangers, and now we are approaching the inner atmosphere.

*Ralph, steamed, snaps dial back. We again hear violin music followed by dialogue.*

MAN: Oh, sweetheart, your kisses are heavenly.

WOMAN: Oh, Harry.

MAN: Your lips are like rubies . . . and your mouth . . . your mouth is like . . .

*Norton snaps dial.*

CAPTAIN VIDEO: A giant crater filled with boiling lava! . . .

*Ralph looks at Norton, steamed.*

CAPTAIN VIDEO: And now, Rangers, let me remind you of the drink that builds healthy bones and strong muscles. The drink that Captain Video drinks . . .

*Ralph snaps dial.*

WOMAN: A double scotch on the rocks! Certainly, darling.

*Norton snaps dial.*

CAPTAIN VIDEO: Yes, Rangers. That's the drink that makes Captain Video fly high!

*Ralph snaps it, steamed.*

WOMAN: Oh, sweetheart, you're my everything. Tell me what to do, and I'll do it. Tell me where to go and I'll go.

*Norton snaps it.*

CAPTAIN VIDEO: You're going to the moon!

RALPH (*snaps set off, steamed*): And you're gonna be on the moon waitin' for him when he gets there!

NORTON (*belligerently*): Oh, yeah? And what if I was to send you to the moon?

RALPH (*I-dare-you-style*): Go ahead and try.

*Norton, not wanting to strike blow, looks Ralph up and down fat-joke-style.*

NORTON: In fact, if I painted you yellow, you could be the moon!

22. Who are the characters in the movie Ralph wants to watch?

23. Who's in the cast of the movie *Rhythm on Ice*?

24. Ralph and Norton agree to watch:
    A. Fights of the World.
    B. Fights of the Universe.
    C. Fights of Kelsey's.
    D. Fights of Bayonne.
25. Who are the fighters in the boxing match Ralph and Norton are going to watch?
26. Norton comes down to the Kramdens' at one in the morning to watch:
    A. *Rhythm on Ice.*
    B. *Dead Men Tell No Tales.*
    C. *Ready, Willing and Able.*
    D. *The Galloping Ghost of Mystery Gulch.*

*Norton is dressed in nightshirt, slipper socks, and hat. He looks around is-Ralph-out-of-sight-style, and then crosses over and snaps set on. He then sits down in chair that Ralph occupied. As he looks at set, music on set starts. It is* Late Show *theme, "Syncopated Clock." Norton shakes his head in rhythm to music. After a few bars, voice on set is heard. The voice is Stanley R. Sogg. Jackie could do this on offstage mike, or it can be pre-recorded.*

STANLEY R. SOGG: Hello there, friends, and welcome to *The Late, Late, Late Show,* brought to you by my sponsor, Mother Fletcher. Mother Fletcher, manufacturer of toys for Japan made in the United States. We'll get even with them! And now, friends, on with *The Late, Late, Late Show.* Tonight we bring you a chiller entitled *Charlie Chan in Pittsburgh.* Let it roll, Harvey.

*At this point, "Syncopated Clock" music fades and we hear mysterious background music. As Norton watches intently for a split, mysterious music builds suspense-style and then suddenly we hear two gunshots and several long sustained shrieking female screams from set. This is followed by several more screams. Suddenly bedroom door bursts open and Ralph comes tearing out like wild bull. Ralph, not seeing Norton, races over to window like terrified madman, flings it up, and shouts out.*

RALPH (*shouting*): Help! Police! Somebody's bein' murdered!

*Norton looks at Ralph what's-going-on-style. Ralph is still looking out window wildly when we hear voice from set. This comes almost on top of Ralph's speech.*

WOMAN'S VOICE: Help! Police! Somebody's being murdered!

*Ralph, not digging, turns toward set and speaks.*

RALPH: Yeah! Somebody's bein' . . .

*Realization comes over Ralph as his eyes bulge and he looks from set to Norton. As Ralph stands there, eyes akimbo, Norton speaks jovial-style.*

NORTON (*jovial-style*): Hey, Ralph, you thought somebody was bein' murdered, huh? Ha, ha, the joke's on you!

*Ralph's panic turns to a boiling within. He walks slowly to set and all the while looking at Norton. He snaps set off. He then crosses to Norton and speaks in steamed calm.*

RALPH (*calmly steamed*): Oh no, Norton. The joke's on you . . . cause somebody is gonna be murdered. And it ain't gonna be on film. It's gonna be live before your very eyes!

After a few minutes of arguing:

RALPH: You're impossible, Norton. You are really impossible. I should have known better than to start anything with you, because you don't think of anybody but yourself. It was bad enough to make me watch all them kid shows. Spacemen! Cowboys! Puppets! But now, to come down here at one o'clock in the morning and wanna start watchin' television . . . that's the end! All right, Norton, I'm washin' my hands of this whole affair. I'm gonna pay you for your half of the set, and I'm gonna keep it here. And I don't want you ever to come down here to watch it.

NORTON: If that's the way you want it, Ralph. We paid a hundred and forty dollars for that set. Hand over seventy.

*Norton extends his hand.*

RALPH (*amazed*): Seventy? Seventy? I'll give you thirty dollars. That set is secondhand!

NORTON: All right. In that case I'll give you thirty dollars, and I'll take the set.

Then, after Alice wakes up and scolds Ralph and Norton for being a couple of babies:

RALPH (*meekly*): I guess Alice is right, Norton. We have been acting like babies.

NORTON (*sheepishly*): Yeah. I guess she is right.

RALPH: After all, we're good friends, Norton. We shouldn't be fightin' over a silly thing like this. Friendship is just a matter of give and take.

NORTON: You're right, Ralph. It's just a matter of consideration.

RALPH: We ain't gonna fight no more.

NORTON: No more.

RALPH: Good night, pal.

*Ralph gives Norton friendly squeeze on arm.*

NORTON: Good night, buddy boy.

*Norton gives Ralph friendly clip on chin. Ralph crosses and goes into bedroom. Norton watches him go in. After he's in, Norton speaks to himself.*

NORTON: There goes one sweet kid.

*Norton then immediately crosses to television set, snaps it on, and crosses back to chair and sits down to watch. After a split we hear two gunshots and female scream again from set. A second after this, Ralph comes charging out of bedroom. Ralph just stands there wide-eyed, staring at Norton, unbelieving-style. Norton notices him and speaks friendly-style.*

NORTON: Hey, buddy boy. I see you're still up.

RALPH: What are you doin'? What are you doin'? I thought you went upstairs.

NORTON: What do you mean, "went upstairs"? When you said about give and take I thought you meant I could watch the set!

RALPH: But when you said consideration, I thought you were gonna get out of here and let me get some sleep.

NORTON (*annoyed*): Wait a minute, Ralph. Half that set is mine. If I get out of here, it goes with me.

RALPH (*steamed*): Oh no it don't, Norton. It stays right here.

NORTON: Well, if it stays here, I'm watchin' it here.

RALPH (*pointing to door*): You're goin'.

NORTON (*pointing to floor*): I'm stayin'.

*As they stand there yelling at each other, music comes up and we DIS-SOLVE from show.*

Marvin Marx and Walter Stone, who together wrote sixteen of the thirty-nine half-hour Honeymooners episodes, were Jackie Gleason's senior writers during the fifties. Marx joined Gleason in 1951, while Gleason was still hosting *Cavalcade of Stars* for the Dumont Network. Marx had worked with Stone on *The Jack Carter Show*; when Carter's show went off the air, Marx asked Stone to join him at Dumont.

"It was funny," says Stone, "because Gleason at Dumont was changing writers every week. It was like they hired you and they already had your replacement.

"Marvin told me, 'I'm working on this Gleason thing.' I told him I thought he was nuts. He said, 'You're not working. You want a week's salary?' So I did it, but in the meantime they fired Marvin. Then after they fired him they realized he was a good writer. They said, 'What did we fire him for? Because we had his replacement—we had to fire him.' But they brought him back.

"After they hired Marvin back, the week after I started, Gleason went into Doctor's Hospital to lose weight. He was bored, so we worked with him there—Marvin, Harry Crane, and myself. We'd go in and write three sketches and a monologue with Jackie. It was easier to write with him, because immediately he'd say no, or yes. That was the relationship.

"We'd go in every day, and we'd do the show on Friday. Gleason would check out Friday morning, do the show, and check back in. We'd meet him again Saturday morning and start working on the next show. This went on about two or three weeks.

*Left to Right:*
*Walter Stone, Jackie*
*Gleason, Marvin Marx.*
COURTESY DOREEN MARX.

"Marvin and I went up one day and told the nurse we wanted to see Gleason. The nurse said, 'I'm sorry, but Gleason went home.' We asked what happened. She answered, 'He got sick.' He checked out of the hospital and went home because he got sick."

Both Marx and Stone were from New Jersey, which is why the names of so many New Jersey cities pop up in their scripts. Marx, who was married, developed plots and situations; Stone, a bachelor, wrote most of the one-liners. When they wrote the Honeymooners scripts—both the sketches on the hour-long Gleason show and the half-hour episodes—Marx, whom a writer in *Collier's* magazine once described as "an amiable fellow with a blissful choirboy expression," took on Kramden's personality and Stone became Norton.

"It was a good relationship," says Stone of his years working with Marx. "I've worked with other guys, and we've gotten along all right, but that was just a relationship that worked.

"Marvin was a good plot guy. I wrote a lot of the dialogue, though he wrote his share, too. It's hard with two people, but it's better with two because you balance things off."

Just like Kramden and Norton.

# FUNNY MONEY

October 8, 1955 · Marvin Marx and Walter Stone

1. Boss thinks the counterfeit money he's cutting is terrible. According to his crony, what is wrong with it?
2. How much counterfeit money is Ziggy picking up at Boss's apartment?
3. What happens to the money on its way from the apartment to Boss's basement hideout?
4. A cop gets on Ralph's bus at which of the following streets?
   A. Madison Avenue.
   B. Thirty-fourth Street.
   C. Forty-ninth Street.
   D. Park Avenue.
5. "Supposing somebody leaves something on a bus, say a suitcase. What does he gotta do to get it back?"
6. If after thirty days nobody claims something left on a bus, who gets it?
7. Alice's mother, Mrs. Gibson, comes for a visit. She complains that things in the Kramden apartment are always broken, and that Ralph should buy Alice some new things. She says "Just because you're married to a horse _____."
8. Mrs. Gibson begins insulting Ralph. He remembers that in the past she used to "start slow" with a couple of what?
9. Alice wants to know why Ralph and her mother can't get along. Ralph counters, "I didn't start this, _____ did."
10. Ralph wants Alice to give him some money. How much does he need, and why does he need it?
11. Mrs. Gibson tells Alice not to give Ralph the money. He tells her that one day she's going to push him too far. True or false: she says the only thing that could push Ralph is a steamroller.
12. What job did Alice quit to marry Ralph?
13. Alice refuses to give Ralph the money he's asked for because:
    A. His lodge dues are supposed to come out of his allowance.
    B. He spent his lodge dues on pizza.
    C. He spent his lodge dues on salad.
    D. He lost his lodge dues to Norton shooting pool.
14. All the guys at the Racoon Lodge are Ralph's pals, buddies, and friends. What will they do if Ralph doesn't pay his dues?
15. Do you know how embarrassing it would be to be thrown out of the Racoon Lodge?
16. Alice says she won't give Ralph the money she has stashed away because she's saving it to buy something. What?
17. True or false: The Kramdens' furniture was a wedding present from Ralph to Alice.
18. What does Norton suggest Ralph do to raise his lodge dues?

*Boss and Ziggy.* COURTESY JIM ENGEL.

NORTON: What's in the bag, Ralph? You takin' a trip?

RALPH: Oh, that . . . no. I found it on the bus about thirty days ago and nobody claimed it so it's mine.

NORTON: What's in it?

RALPH: I don't know. I ain't even opened it yet. Now, never mind the bag, Norton. You gotta help me. I need fifteen dollars desperately!

NORTON: What'a you need it for?

RALPH: I'm behind in my Racoon dues. If I don't get it up they'll throw me out.

NORTON: Ah, I wouldn't worry too much about that, Ralph. I got a feelin' the Racoon Lodge is gonna fold up soon anyway.

RALPH: What do you mean?

NORTON: I'll tell you what I mean. The members are losin' interest. A lot of the guys sold their Racoon hats during the Davy Crockett craze.

19. Ralph opens the suitcase he found to see what's inside. He finds money; enough, says Norton, to keep Ralph in _____ for the rest of his life.

20. Ralph figures a millionaire must have left the money on the bus. Norton says he hopes so, because he'd hate to think the money was left on the bus by:
A. A courier from Merrill Lynch, Pierce, Fenner & Ziggy.
B. Some poor person who could really need it.
C. Mary Monahan's butler.
D. The Grand High Exalted Mystic Ruler.

RALPH: I know what it is . . . it's one of those new kind of quiz shows. It's probably called "Find the Money on the Bus" or something. You know how they're all crazy in television. *Then definite.* That's it, Alice, it's a quiz show. I remember one day a guy on the bus asked me how do you get to the public library. That probably was the $64,000 question.

ALICE: Ralph, stop being ridiculous. Don't you think something is phony?

RALPH: No, I don't. What's the matter with you, Alice? Every time we have a little good luck you think there's something phony about it. I'll bet that if right now you went over to the sink and turned on the hot water and oil came out, you wouldn't believe it!

ALICE: If I went over to that sink and turned on the hot water and hot water came out, I wouldn't believe it!

RALPH: Boy, Alice, you kill me. You really kill me. You're always talkin' about your ship comin' in. Well, look, the *Queen Mary*. Well, I believe it, Alice. I believe it. And you know what I'm doin' first thing tomorrow mornin'? I'm goin' down and I'm quittin' my job. And I ain't just quittin', Alice. I'm lettin' that Marshall know how he's made me suffer for the past fourteen years. I'm tellin' him off good. I might even punch him in the nose!

ALICE: Ralph, you're not quitting your job until you find out what this is all about.

RALPH: Boy, Alice, I can't understand you. You know what's your trouble? You're just like your mother. Why couldn't you take after your father a little? He quit his job just because your mother won fifty dollars playin' bingo.

21. Why does Grogan the cop show up at the apartment?

22. How much does Ralph usually give to the annual children's party at the Youth Center?

23. Now that Ralph's a "millionaire," how much does he give for the children's party?

24. Ralph begins spending the money all over town. He hires Norton as his chauffeur and sends him out to buy some new clothes and other things. What is the specialty item Norton tells Ralph he has to wait for?

25. Ralph has telephones installed in the apartment. How many does he order, and where are they installed?
26. Why does Ralph have a phone installed on the fire escape?
27. Ralph decides to test the phone before the installer leaves. What does Norton suggest?
28. Who does Ralph call, and what does he say?
29. Ralph has one minor complaint about the phone. What is it?
30. How much does Ralph tip the installer to make sure he takes care of the problem?
31. Ralph takes a drag on his cigar and begins hacking and gagging. He looks the cigar over and says, _____.
32. Since the news got out that Ralph's got money, who's been after him?
33. Boss and Ziggy are looking for Ralph. Ralph figures Boss is the head of some investment firm that wants him on the board of directors. The name Ziggy rings a bell with Norton. Where does he think Boss and Ziggy are from?
34. Now that Ralph's got some cash, his mother-in-law becomes a real sweetheart. What is her new nickname for her "favorite son-in-law"?
35. How much money does Alice's mother want from Ralph, and what is she going to do with it?
36. Ralph wants to buy a motorboat. What unusual "option" does he want?
37. Who takes Ralph's suit to the cleaners, how much does Ralph tip him, and what happens to him when he spends the money?

Tommy Doyle's mother is one of many characters written into the scripts who never made it to the stage at the Adelphi. She comes to the Kramden apartment, furious because her son's been thrown in jail on account of the counterfeit money Ralph gave him. In the following excerpt, Ralph walks in as Mrs. Doyle is talking to Alice.

*At this point front door opens and Ralph enters. He is wearing a very loud checked sport jacket away-we-go-style and smoking a long cigar.*

RALPH (*pompously*): Hello, Alice. . . . Oh, hi'ya Mrs. Doyle. Boy, Alice, wait'll you see the new motorboat!

ALICE: Ralph!

WOMAN (*with contempt*): You snake!

*Ralph turns slowly and looks a little bewildered.*

ALICE: Ralph, that hundred dollars you gave Tommy was counterfeit. He's in jail.

RALPH (*bewildered*): In jail? Counterfeit?

ALICE: You don't understand, Ralph. That explains everything . . . why nobody claimed it. It must be all counterfeit. It's no good.

*Boss, alias Boris Aplon.*
COURTESY BORIS APLON.

**RALPH:** But Alice, I been spendin' that money all over town. That means that I . . . I . . . I. . . . What am I gonna do?

**WOMAN:** Never mind what you're gonna do. What about my Tommy?

**RALPH** (*in daze*): Gee, I'm awfully sorry, Mrs. Doyle. Look. . . . *Ralph pulls bill out of pocket.* Here's a hundred dollars. Go down and bail him out!

38. Boss and Ziggy come to claim their money and Ralph thinks they're the police. What does Norton tell Ralph to do with the money so the police can't use it as evidence against him?

39. The counterfeiters become impatient when Ralph doesn't answer the door. What does he say to stall them?

40. How long does Ralph have the money before he discovers it's phony?

41. Ralph's money came easy and it went _____.

42. Alice reminds Ralph that everything he bought has to go back to the store, except for one thing. What?

# THE GOLFER

October 15, 1955 · A. J. Russell and Herbert Finn

"The Golfer" is one of the funniest of *The Honeymooners,* for at least two reasons: Kramden's outlandish golfing outfit and inept attempts to swing a golf club, and Norton's "Hello, ball" salutation. Herb Finn thinks it's the best of the bunch. As he recalls, "They came away from the screening still laughing. The cast was laughing. Everyone was laughing. We knew it was a funny show, and when it went on the air, we saw how funny it was."

But "The Golfer" was almost the show that wasn't, according to A. J. Russell, Finn's writing partner.

"This particular script we took to Jack Philbin [the show's executive producer], and Philbin said no. He didn't like the idea. But I said, 'This is such a good idea.' So we went back and we persuaded Philbin to let us give it a try. Of course when Jackie saw it, once he saw what the possibilities were, he ran with it. Jackie dreamed up that crazy costume and really went to town with it."

1. The hot rumor at the Gotham Bus Company is that Ralph's going to be the new assistant traffic manager. Whom does Cassidy hear it from, and whom does he tell?
2. Who's glad he doesn't have stock in the bus company?
3. What does Ralph give the guys to celebrate his "promotion," and what does he promise them after work?

NORTON: Boy, wait'll the boys in the sewer hear about this. There's gonna be some celebratin' goin' on down there!

RALPH: The boys in the sewer? Why should they celebrate? They don't even know me.

NORTON: So what? They don't know Little Orphan Annie either. But when Daddy Warbucks found her—boy, what a celebration we had!

4. What does the sign in the bus company locker room say?
5. Who doesn't believe the rumor that Ralph's going to be assistant traffic manager?
6. Where did Reilly hear about Ralph's "promotion"?
7. Who is the traffic manager at the bus company?
8. Why does Freddie doubt that Ralph's going to be assistant traffic manager?
9. What rumor does Norton tell Ralph he should have started?
10. You can know the encyclopedia backward and forward, says Ralph, but if you don't have _____ you get nowhere.
    A. Mr. Harper's telephone number.
    B. Golf clubs.
    C. Connections.
    D. Membership at Silver Oaks.

11. Ralph wants to talk to Mr. Harper. What does Norton advise Ralph to say to him?

12. Where did Ralph read about how to influence people?
    A. In a book.
    B. In the papers.
    C. In comic books.
    D. In *American Weekly*.

13. According to Ralph, what is the best way to influence people?

14. Mr. Harper's married to _____ and they have _____ children.
    A. Shirley; four.
    B. Agnes; two.
    C. Mrs. Harper; no.
    D. None of the above.

15. You put a golf club in Ralph's hands and he's:
    A. A moax.
    B. A mope.
    C. A clam.
    D. Dynamite.

16. Where does Ralph tell Mr. Harper he plays golf?

17. Where does Mr. Harper play golf?

*Mr. Harper.* COURTESY JOHN F. LANGTON, JR.

18. Norton tries to arrange a game between Ralph and Mr. Harper for which day of the week?

19. Why can't Mr. Harper play golf with Ralph that day of the week?

20. When and at what time does Mr. Harper propose they play?

21. What's going to happen when Ralph gets to the golf course? He doesn't even know where _____ is.

22. Norton says he will go with Ralph to the golf course. What does he know about playing golf?

23. How long has Norton worked in the sewer?

24. Ralph comes home dying to tell Alice about his "promotion." What does she want him to do first?

25. Ralph tells Alice he won't be needing his lunch box much longer. Why not, according to Alice?

26. Ralph admits to Alice that his "promotion" isn't official yet. Alice sighs an I've-heard-this-all-before "ohhh." What three things does Ralph think Alice means by "ohhh"?

27. When Alice hears that Mr. Harper made a golf date with Ralph, she tells Ralph that Harper doesn't need an assistant, he needs:
    A. A keeper.
    B. An assistant plumber.
    C. To bring doctors down from the moon to have his head examined.
    D. The key to Bellevue.

28. Ralph figures he can always break the golf date once he gets the job. What excuse does Alice suggest he use?

29. How does Alice get messages to Ralph during the day?

30. Mr. Harper changes the golf date. What's the new plan?

31. Norton doesn't know how Ralph is going to do with the golf clubs he borrowed, but in the borrowed outfit, Ralph is _____.

"Everybody else on the show would dress for the dress rehearsal, but Jackie would dress only for the show," says Joan Reichman Canale, production assistant for *The Honeymooners*. "When he came out wearing that outfit . . . It was just priceless! Even though we were working, we were always laughing."

Not letting anyone see him in costume before showtime was typical Gleason; he was always looking for that comic edge. In fact, it was in the script for Norton to wear the golfer's outfit; it was Gleason's idea to have Ralph dressed up instead. (It was an unusual switch: Gleason usually gave a lot of the funny lines and bits to Carney.)

32. What does Norton give Ralph to use as a practice "ball"?

33. Complete the sentence: "What did you expect to find in a pin cushion, _____?"

34. You don't swing a golf club ordinarylike, you've got to do it _____ like.
35. How long does Ralph have to learn how to play golf?
36. Norton tries to teach Ralph golf by the book. What is the book's dedication?

"We reasoned that if they were going to learn how to play golf and they didn't know anything about it, what would these guys do? They would go out and buy a book about golf," says Russell. "So we went out and bought a rudimentary book on how to play golf, and there it was, all laid out for us— what you do, how you walk up, how you address the ball, all those terms that helped so much with the jokes were all there in the book.

"Kramden and Norton used it, but it was also a primer for anyone in the audience who did not know anything about golf."

NORTON: I'll start from the beginning.
RALPH: All right. But make it fast, Norton. Please, I only got two days to learn.
　　*Norton does warm-up bit, clears his throat while Ralph controls his temper.*
NORTON: Golf. Chapter one, page one. The game of golf is believed to have originated in Scotland around the year 1440. It enjoyed great popularity at that time. King James himself was an ardent golfer.
　　*Ralph shifts his weight from foot to foot with controlled patience.*
NORTON: Archery, which was the popular sport of the day, began to suffer, because so many people were enthusiastic about golf. *Norton looks up from book to Ralph.* Interesting, ain't it, Ralph? Imagine! All this happened before Columbus discovered America! *Norton looks down at book again and reads. Ralph is about ready to explode.* However, it wasn't until the year 1457. . . .
　　*Ralph explodes and gives Norton a shot on the shoulder.*
RALPH: Whattaya readin' that for?
NORTON: I was just fillin' you in with a little background!
RALPH: Get to the part where I swing at the ball. I don't need to be filled in with any background!
NORTON (*looks slyly in the direction of Ralph's posterior*): Your point is well taken.

37. Name the three steps preceding the golf swing.
38. Who does Norton cite to Ralph to encourage him to continue practicing?
　　A. Jane Frazee.
　　B. Willie Mays.
　　C. Dizzy Dean.
　　D. Bobby Jones.

39. How does Norton address a golf ball?
40. In golf, it don't mean a thing, _____.
41. After Norton sees Ralph take a practice swing and whack himself in the neck, what does he say is the biggest thing Ralph did wrong?

RALPH: It's no use, Norton! I can't learn how to play a good game of golf in two days. It'd take me at least a week!

NORTON: That don't sound like my Ralph talkin'. You can't give up! Where would Bobby Jones be if he gave up before he started? Ben Hogan! Sammy Snerd!

"He was very sensitive, Gleason was," Finn says. "We had a line in there about 'Sammy Snerd,' for Sammy Snead. He changed that; he wouldn't have it. We had to put in Sammy Snead. He'd never say a derogatory thing about a performer. Never. Which is to his credit."

42. What does Ralph think he should do in order to play a great game of golf?
43. Norton has Ralph practice uphill shots by standing on a book and then a pot. Next he wants Ralph to imagine he's hit a ball on a mountain. Ralph wonders, "Who am I playing golf with, Mr. Harper or _____?"

NORTON: Hold the phone! You ain't through yet. You been doin' it with the right foot. Now do it with your left foot on the garbage pail.
RALPH: All right.
NORTON: All right, shoot!
RALPH: Wait a minute! What am I doin' now?
NORTON? Whattaya think you're doin'? You're shooting downhill.
RALPH: Oh.

44. Alice comes home and finds Ralph practicing his swing. What sport does she say she thinks he's practicing?

ALICE: Can't I stay and watch?
RALPH: You ain't watching!
ALICE: I won't get in the way.
RALPH: You ain't watching!
ALICE: What's the matter? Are you afraid I'll laugh?
RALPH: No, I ain't afraid you'll laugh. Because I know that you know that if you laugh, I might get just steamed enough to mistake your head for a golf ball.

45. According to Ralph, why do people play golf?
46. What does Norton insist is essential to a good game of golf?

47. What does Ralph offer to do to prove to Norton he's relaxed enough to practice?
48. Why does Ralph get himself into fixes like having to play golf?
49. Who comes to visit Ralph the morning before he's supposed to play golf? What news does he bring?
50. Who's going to take Mr. Harper's place?

*Douglas exits. Ralph walks around as Alice glares him down.*

ALICE (*mimicking Ralph*): I'm never gonna brag again. So help me, Alice, I'm never gonna shoot off my big mouth again.

RALPH: Why didn't you remind me!

ALICE: Remind you! If I'd reminded you any harder you wouldn't have a shirt on your back. All right, champ. What're you going to do now?

RALPH: There's only one thing to do—what I shoulda done all along! I'm gonna go down to the office and tell Mr. Douglas I'm a liar and a four-flusher. That'll take care of the promotion! They ain't gonna give a promotion to a liar and a four-flusher. But I don't care. I'm gonna go down and tell him everything.

ALICE: You're going to do nothing of the kind!

RALPH: Huh?

ALICE: You're not going down there and tell Mr. Douglas everything. You're going to tell him the truth! Tell him you can't play golf. Tell him you never had a golf club in your hand in your life.

RALPH: Wait a minute! That ain't exactly true. I ain't been doin' so bad with the golf clubs. I got the uphill shot and the downhill shot and—

ALICE: Ralph!

*He stops cold, looks sheepishly at her.*

ALICE: The truth!

RALPH: Baby, you're the greatest!

*KISSVILLE.*

A. J. Russell and Herb Finn were the last of the six writers who would write the Classic 39 to be hired by Gleason.

Russell was the only one in the bunch who hadn't written comedy, but Gleason didn't hire him to write jokes. The pair first met in the early fifties when Gleason starred in a *Studio One* drama called "The Laughmaker," which Russell had written. Gleason liked Russell, and promptly hired him to develop story lines.

"I told him I wasn't a joke writer," says Russell, "and he said, 'Look, I don't need a joke writer. I need somebody that comes up with story ideas. I got guys that can write jokes.' So for about two or three years, I used to work on the premise of the show, like when he thinks he's going to inherit forty million dollars. Things that had the human value.

"Jackie wanted ideas that could happen to a regular guy. Ralph Kramden was a regular guy. He wanted to better himself, to move up, to do nice things for his wife. Gleason could make the situation funny, but the situation had to be real. It was just a slight exaggeration of the human situation. Ralph Kramden and Ed Norton were real people, people that you knew. Slightly exaggerated, but based on truth."

When Gleason's six writers paired off for the Classic 39, the "newcomers," Russell and Finn, a comedy writer who had done shows such as *Amos 'n' Andy* and *Duffy's Tavern,* wound up together.

"When they teamed me up with Herb, I learned a lot about writing jokes," Russell says in admiration of his former partner. "Herb Finn was great for the funny parts—the jokes and the lines and the little things."

By the time Finn joined the Gleason crew, he was already a veteran comedy writer. His first television job, writing for *Duffy's Tavern,* was a perfect training ground for writing for *The Honeymooners,* because it was a show that demanded scripts jam-packed with jokes.

Finn got a call from his agent on a Friday to be in New York that Sunday for a job with Gleason. He left his family in Hollywood and flew to New York, and found he'd been booked into a two-bedroom, two-bath suite in the Park Sheraton.

"Monday there was a story meeting, and Gleason was having a manicure there. We shook hands, and everybody looked. It was the first time he shook hands with a writer, apparently. A famous first. He'd gotten so he didn't want to talk with writers."

Finn says that when Gleason did communicate with the writers, he did it in a typically unorthodox way.

"We'd get a call—'Jackie wants to see you.' And we'd say, 'Uh oh, what now?'

"We'd go down to his office and he'd be sitting at his desk, looking out the window, and Philbin, his producer, would be sitting on the couch, *very* serious face. Gleason would say, 'All here?' And he'd look at Philbin and say, 'We didn't have to have that set. The doctor could have come to the apartment.'

"And he would bawl Philbin out for something we had done. *Never* look at us, always at Philbin. And Philbin would take it and take it.

"Walter Stone had a funny line. Walter said Gleason had a dream, and a voice said, 'Jackie! Jackie!' And Gleason says, 'Who's that?' And the voice says, 'Charles Dickens.' And Gleason says, 'You know I never talk to writers.'"

# A WOMAN'S WORK IS NEVER DONE

October 22, 1955 · Marvin Marx and Walter Stone

*As travelers part, camera holds on establishing shot of the Kramden kitchen. After a split Alice enters from bedroom. She is dressed working-around-the-house-style. She is carrying a pair of Ralph's pants folded over her arm. They are a very large brown pair of pants, khaki-style. She holds them up, pulling them taut in order to get as much size value as possible. She looks at seat of pants for a second and then shakes her head isn't-this-ever-gonna-stop-style. Front door opens and Ralph enters. He is dressed in bus uniform, carrying lunch box. He slams lunch box on bureau. Ralph now crosses toward bedroom and as he does he spots khaki pants on table in heap. He does not recognize them as his pants. He stops and comments.*

RALPH (*can't-you-do-anything-style*): Alice, we been back from the campin' trip for two weeks now. Don't you think it's about time you put that tent away?

ALICE (*sarcastic*): It's not the tent. It's your pants. I'm letting them out again.

RALPH (*sheepishly*): Oh.

*Ralph picks up pants and holds them tautly as Alice had done before. As he looks at them, he's a little shocked by the size.*

RALPH: Well, don't you think you let 'em out a little too much?

ALICE (*flatly*): I haven't started yet.

RALPH (*slightly embarrassed*): Well, you can do that after dinner. Get the food on the table. Me and Norton are bowlin' tonight.

ALICE: If I wait'll after dinner, I'll have to let 'em out more!

1. When Ralph comes home from work, he wants to eat quickly and go bowling. He's immediately aggravated because Alice didn't do something he asked her to do. What was it?
2. What is the name of Ralph's bowling team?
3. If Ralph doesn't wear his team shirt, how are people going to know he's a Hurricane?
4. Alice makes a wisecrack about Ralph's big mouth; he warns her to be careful. "The life you save," he cautions, "_____."
5. What else did Ralph ask Alice to do that she didn't get around to doing?

RALPH: There you go with the sorries again. You're always sorry, Alice. Why don't you do something for a change so you won't have to be sorry? Now, what am I supposed to do tonight? Go bowlin' without my bowlin' socks? And don't tell me to wear another pair of socks 'cause it don't make no difference. When you're bowlin', Alice, everything counts. Your socks and shirt are just as important as the ball, no matter how unimportant you think they are.

ALICE (*you-big-baby-style*): Well, I can't see where a pair of socks can make any difference.

RALPH (*dramatically*): Oh, you can't. Well, might I remind you of an old saying, Alice. For want of a nail, the shoe was lost. For want of a shoe, the horse was lost. For want of a horse, the battle was lost. And, for want of a battle, the war was lost!

ALICE (*laying it in*): Oh, why don't you get lost!

*Ralph, steamed, just glares at her and puts his fist under her chin threatening-style.*

RALPH (*threatening*): You're goin' to the moon, Alice. Right to the moon!

ALICE: Yeah, and you're just the blimp to take me!

A reporter for *The New York Times* once wrote of Audrey Meadows, "Ad-libbing is an important part of the Gleason show. Members of its staff say that Miss Meadows' ability to go along with ad-libs and occasionally insert one of her own is a secret of her success on the show. She has also won respect for her comic timing."

If Audrey Meadows' performance in *The Honeymooners* is overshadowed by Gleason's Kramden and Carney's Norton, it's only because she worked opposite one of the greatest comedy teams in entertainment history—not because she didn't make her own contribution. Audrey can take satisfaction in knowing she created television's most memorable female character—Alice Kramden.

Sure, Gleason's writers wrote some of the funniest one-liners ever written, but can anyone picture another actress delivering them better than Audrey? They called her "The Rock" during the years she worked on Gleason's shows, and she earned the title by keeping Gleason and Carney honest. She'd never step on their ad-libs, but at the same time she'd hold fast to the written script—and make sure Gleason and Carney got back to it too. Gleason came to depend so much on Audrey's ability to keep the show on course that he instructed the writers never to write a long scene for him unless Audrey was also on stage.

She is a smart actress as well. Alice is exactly what Audrey wanted her to be. Yes, writers put the words in her mouth, but everything else—expressions, tone of voice, *lack* of mannerisms—were Audrey's inventions.

"I built the character the way I did because of the way Jackie and Art worked," Audrey says. "The reason I was never physical—you never see Alice waving her hands around or doing a big take—was because *they* were physical. I decided that even if I was off camera, if Jackie paced up and down, I stayed put—because he would always come back to me. A lot of people will follow an actor because they're so nervous they won't be on camera.

"The camera would be on me when it was time. I realized the way to develop something interesting—the only way I would be able to do it—was to be as quiet as possible physically. And it worked out well."

6. Ralph figures he knows why Alice didn't do the chores he wanted done. He suspects she was:
   A. Taking mambo lessons.
   B. Taking cooking lessons from Herman Gruber.
   C. Sitting in the kitchen fooling around.
   D. Helping Mr. Faversham put on a play.
7. Right after Ralph left the house that morning, Alice got into one of those silly moods of hers. Name the jobs she did during the day.
8. Alice is the only girl in town with an atomic kitchen. What does it look like?

RALPH (*sarcastic*): Oh boy, Alice, you really got it tough, ain't you. I could really cry for you. Look, I'm cryin'! You don't know how soft you got it. But things are gonna be different from now on, Alice. You're gonna start doin' a little work around here. 'Cause I'm puttin' in a little system that'll make sure you do. From now on you're workin' on the demerit system. I'm gonna ask you to do something in the morning, and if when I come home, it ain't done, you get one demerit. And every time you don't do somethin' I tell you, it's another demerit. And you know what happens when you get ten demerits?

ALICE (*defiantly*): What?

RALPH (*fist under Alice's chin*): Right to the moon!

ALICE: Oh, shuuut up!

RALPH (*calm and deliberate*): That is one demerit.

*Alice does following in rapid succession, baby-style.*

ALICE: Shut up! Shut up! Shut up! Shut up! Shut up! Shut up! Shut up! Shut up! Shut up! I'm off to the moon!

*On "off to the moon" Alice puts both her hands over her head in upright-stick-up-style, but joins fingers of both hands so they form a point like front of rocket ship. As she stands there like this she looks at Ralph I-dare-you-style.*

RALPH (*backing out*): It don't start till tomorrow.

9. Ralph works an eight-hour day. How long is Alice's day, and when was the last time she had a day off?
10. Alice recites an old saying to Ralph about women and work. What is it?
11. Why is a woman's work never done?
12. Alice is sick and tired of men who yell, scream, give orders, and act like they own the world. Ralph says women have one avenue of revenge. What is it?
13. Where do the Kramdens go to hire a maid?
14. What are Ralph's instructions to Alice when they arrive at the employment agency?

15. Ralph decides he's going to go on *The $64,000 Question,* because he's an expert in which one of these categories:
    A. Popular songs.
    B. Aggravation.
    C. Wisenheimers.
    D. Blabbermouths.
16. True or false: The Kramdens go to the agency during Ralph's lunch hour.
17. Who's the director of the agency?

Mr. Wilson was played by Frank Marth, who ranks second to George Petrie in the number of different roles played on *The Honeymooners.* Gleason liked Marth because he was versatile and dependable. When the woman who was supposed to play the head of the employment agency didn't work out in rehearsal, Gleason asked for Marth.

"We had a woman, a friend of the producer," recalls Stone. "The idea was, she'd walk in and say, 'Oh, you must be the couple . . .' because she thinks they're there for a job. So Gleason says, 'Don't say the line until you reach the desk, when you walk in.' But she'd say it walking.

"Gleason says, 'I don't want to embarrass her, but she's a lousy actress. Get Frank Marth.' So you'll notice Frank does the first line and then he sits down and works looking at his notes, because he didn't really have time to learn the lines. He came in in the afternoon and we were going on that night, and he had quite a few lines."

18. The agency director thinks Ralph and Alice are looking for work. Where does he want to send them?
19. What question does the director ask that causes Ralph to laugh?
20. Ralph says Alice is a "career girl." What is her career, and where does she work?
21. Who is the secretary at the agency?
22. Describe the outfit Ralph thinks all maids wear.
23. The Kramdens hire Thelma, but she can't do heavy work because she's _____.

Thelma was played by Betty Garde, an actress who in the fifties and sixties played in lots of "B" movies, and on TV shows such as *The Twilight Zone* and *The Abbott and Costello Show.* Walter Stone remembers that she, like many other actors and actresses who did *The Honeymooners,* had a tough time adapting to Gleason's no-rehearsal policy.

"It could have been better, that show," Stone asserts. "These people come in, see, and they don't realize that Gleason doesn't really rehearse. So she really stumbled on a couple of lines.

*Mr. Wilson, alias Frank Marth.*
COURTESY FRANK MARTH.

"See, real actors and actresses are used to learning everything perfectly. Gleason would go over it like once with them, then somebody else would go over it with them, then he'd be gone, and a stand-in—the producer or someone—would read the lines. It threw them."

"Audrey got upset with me many times 'cause I didn't rehearse," Gleason once told a reporter. "I'd come in, go through it once, and say, 'Okay, see you tonight.' And that's gotta disturb people. But once they realized they had to learn the script and really know it, it gave them a spontaneity they wouldn't have had if we'd dragged out the rehearsals for hours. The funny thing about 'The Honeymooners' is, you can't tell when a fluff is made 'cause they're all going crazy. Ralph is talking off the top of his head. Many of those long speeches I gave weren't written. I knew where I had to go, and I'd start and I'd try to get there. Like at the end we'd make those speeches to Alice. They were never written."

24. What jobs won't Thelma do, and what are the ground rules she lays down before accepting the job as the Kramdens' maid?
25. Thelma says Ralph looks like he eats:
    A. Plenty of late snacks.
    B. Three kinds of pizza.
    C. Chicken chow mein and potato pancakes.
    D. Hot dogs, mashed potatoes, lima beans, and spaghetti.
26. Thelma threatens to quit if Ralph doesn't do something before they leave the agency. What is it?

27. Where does Ralph get the bell he uses to ring for Thelma?
28. Norton wants to know if Thelma looks like the maid he and Ralph once saw where, doing what?
29. How does Ralph describe Thelma?
30. Ralph decides to show off Thelma by having Norton knock on the door so she can let him in. When Thelma doesn't answer the knock, where does Norton say she must be?
31. What does Ralph want Thelma to say to people when she lets them into the apartment?
32. What will Thelma say when someone calls Ralph on the telephone?
33. Thelma keeps saying "okay." But what does Ralph want her to say?
34. Norton thinks Ralph has reached the height of gracious living by hiring a maid, and he places him into an exclusive group. What group?
35. How much sugar does Norton take in his coffee?
36. What does Thelma threaten to give Norton if he keeps ringing the bell?
37. Thelma describes Norton and Ralph as the _____ and the _____.

NORTON: With my coffee I'd like one lump.

THELMA: You'll get one lump all right!

NORTON (*thinking he's making a point*): That'll be "You get a lump very good, sir!" *To Ralph.* She got a lot of class, Ralph. Reminds you a lot of Jake La Motta in his prime.

*Ralph picks up bell and rings it.*

THELMA: Yeah?

RALPH: Would you mind comin' into the dinin' area again, Thelma?

THELMA: What do you want this time?

RALPH: Instead of cake with my coffee, I think I'll have a sandwich. Will you see what kind of cold cuts we got in the icebox?

*Thelma lumbers over to icebox, opens door and looks in.*

THELMA: You got liverwurst, pressed ham, and salami.

*Ralph ponders for a second and then rings bell. Ralph motions Hardy-style for Thelma to come over to dining area. Thelma gives a ceilingward glance and lumbers over.*

RALPH: Liverwurst.

THELMA (*to Norton*): And what do you want, gracious living?

NORTON (*picks up bell, gives it a couple of tinkles and speaks*): Salami.

*Thelma crosses back to icebox. As she reaches it, Ralph rings bell again. Thelma crosses back to table.*

RALPH: I changed my mind. I'll have salami, too.

THELMA: Oh, you changed your mind, did you? Well, I got news for you. I changed mine, too. I ain't makin' the sandwiches. I got enough trouble cleanin' up this jungle without feedin' the animals besides!

RALPH: Just watch your step, Thelma. You'll keep a civil tongue in your head and do as you're told. You have a very funny attitude. I've had a lot of experience with maids but I never met one like you.

THELMA (*in disbelief*): You've had a lot of experience with maids?

NORTON: That's right! His mother used to be one.

38. Thelma quits, but Ralph tells her she can't. What does he threaten to have taken away from her if she leaves?
39. Thelma leaves the apartment and Ralph screams after her to come back. What does Norton do?
40. How many maids does Ralph hire after Thelma, and why can't he hire any more?
41. Norton only remembers three maids. How come?
42. Ralph enlists Norton to help him with the housework. How much does Norton charge him, and what job won't he do?

RALPH: Now look, Norton, there's a couple of jobs left to do yet. I'll finish scrubbin' the floors and you iron that wash there.

NORTON: Very good, sir.

*Ralph goes into bedroom and reappears with ironing board and iron. He crosses and places ironing board on table and then starts trying to open folded ironing board. He tugs at it several times and then Norton speaks.*

NORTON: Havin' a little trouble, Ralph?

RALPH: It seems to be a little stuck.

NORTON: Hey, Ralph, Trixie got an ironing board just like that. I opened it hundreds of times. *Pointing.* All you gotta do is reach right in there, lift that little catch and then pull.

*Ralph follows instructions, gives tug, and as ironing board opens, he goes into pain bit. At conclusion of pain bit he turns to Norton and speaks in steamed manner.*

RALPH (*steamed*): You idiot. I thought you said you did it hundreds of times.

NORTON: I did . . . and that always happened to me too.

RALPH: Look, Norton, I ain't gonna get steamed, 'cause we got a lot of work to do. But just don't talk to me. Just do your work.

NORTON: Very good, sir.

43. Ralph needs Norton's help to move the bureau. What is the signal to lift it?
44. Why doesn't Norton lift?
45. The bureau is too heavy for Ralph and Norton to move. What does Norton do to make it lighter?

46. What piece of clothing is burned by the iron while Ralph and Norton are moving furniture?

47. According to Norton, what does a woman fall for better than anything else? According to Ralph?

48. What did Alice call Ralph before they were married?

49. Ralph used to be a little cup of butter. Now he's:
    A. A whole tub of lard.
    B. A blimp.
    C. A simp.
    D. 1,053,622 pounds.

50. Ralph thinks he can flatter Alice by "mistaking" her for what famous sex symbol?

NORTON: Hey, hey, Ralph. I got an idea.

RALPH: Keep your stupid ideas to yourself.

NORTON (*indignant*): Stupid? Stupid? And whose idea was it to take the drawers out of the bureau to make it lighter?

RALPH (*reluctantly*): Well, all right, go ahead. What is it?

NORTON: Look, the main reason Alice wants to keep her job in Steinhardt's Bakery is 'cause she thinks the work there is easier than if she was here doin' housework. So all you gotta do is make her job there harder.

RALPH: How'm I gonna do that?

NORTON: By startin' a run on jelly doughnuts. You start buyin' jelly doughnuts. Night and day. All week if necessary. You buy thousands and thousands of doughnuts. Meanwhile, the work is pilin' up down at Steinhardt's. They got Alice workin' night and day. All she's doin' is stuffin' jelly. Finally it gets too much for her and she quits.

RALPH: Wait a minute. Wait a minute. How can I afford to pay for all them jelly doughnuts?

NORTON: Uh . . . uh . . . I got it. Alice can go out and get a job and help you pay for 'em!

*Ralph just stands there for a second looking at him you-nut-style.*

NORTON: Well, what do you think, Ralph?

RALPH (*blowing up*): Oh, shut up!

NORTON: I got another idea, Ralph.

RALPH: I don't want to hear it. You just stand there quietly, Norton. I'll do the thinkin'.

NORTON: All right, Ralph. If you want to waste all that time standin' there thinkin' by yourself. . . . But remember, I'm gettin' paid a dollar an hour!

51. Alice got a promotion. What does she do now?

52. Why does Thelma come back to the Kramden apartment?

53. Who does Thelma go to work for after the Kramdens?

RALPH (*Fenwick*): Please, Alice, come home and do the housework.

ALICE (*reluctantly*): Well . . . do you admit it's hard work, Ralph? Harder than even your job?

RALPH (*Fenwick*): Yes, I do.

ALICE (*slowly*): All right, I'll come back.

RALPH (*grateful*): Oh, Alice, thanks. Thanks a million!

ALICE: But there are a few conditions.

RALPH: Conditions?

ALICE: I want Thursdays and Sundays off, through for the day after I do the supper dishes, I don't scrub the floors—that's man's work—we send the laundry out. . . ."

*As she is enumerating these conditions, Ralph is nodding meekly. Music comes up and we DISSOLVE.*

© PRESTON BLAIR PRODUCTIONS.

# A MATTER OF LIFE AND DEATH

October 29, 1955 · Marvin Marx and Walter Stone

1. What kind of dog does Alice's mother own, and what is its name?
2. How much does the vet charge to examine Alice's mother's dog?
3. How much does the Kramdens' doctor charge for a checkup?
4. Ralph and Norton come home from work; Ralph gets a kiss from Alice, but Norton is stiffed by Trixie. What are her two reasons for not kissing him?
5. What are the Kramdens having for dinner?
   A. Soup.
   B. Pot roast.
   C. Pizza and salad.
   D. Lasagna.
6. What did Ralph's doctor do for Callahan the plumber?
7. Ralph went to the doctor for:
   A. A wrenched back.
   B. Listlessness.
   C. Sleepwalking.
   D. Measles.
8. A messenger delivers the vet's report and Ralph intercepts it before Alice can see it. What does Ralph tell the messenger when he puts his hand out for a tip?
9. What disease does Ralph think he has, and what are its symptoms?
10. What kind of dog usually contracts the disease Ralph thinks he has, and how is it contracted?
11. True or false: Ralph thinks he has six months to live.

RALPH: Imagine me gettin' a disease boxers get. I knew I was gettin' punchy. It's that poundin' I take, drivin' that bus every day. Well, Norton, I guess there'll be no more bus rides for me. I've come to the end of the line. I'm goin' to that big bus depot in the sky. It's a one-way trip with no transfers. You know, Norton, I never thought I'd check out like this. I haven't even tasted life yet. Boy, what a tough life I've had when I think back on it. When I was a kid, I had to sell newspapers. Then when I got out of school, I delivered orders for an A&P. Then came the Depression. I had to shovel snow to eat. That's when I met Alice. She used to hand out the shovels. *He mulls this over fondly, then speaks.* She always used to give me a small shovel with a long handle. And then after me and Alice got married, I had to struggle some more. Then I got this job drivin' a bus. That was fourteen years ago and I'm still strugglin'. Yeah, Norton, my life's been no bed of roses. Forty years ago I came into this world with a pair of strong lungs, pink cheeks, and a lot of big ideas. And what'll I have to show for it when I'm leavin'. A blue tongue . . . a bald head . . . and a saucer of milk with a pill in it.

*Norton blows nose loudly. At this point door opens and Alice enters. She is carrying clothes basket filled with wash. As she enters, she crosses to table to put laundry there, and she is singing "Live Till I Die" as she crosses. As Ralph hears Alice singing song he does eye-bulge reaction.*

RALPH: Will you stop singin' that song.

ALICE (*amazed*): Ralph, what's the matter with you?

RALPH: What's the matter with me? Nothin' at all. I just don't like that song, that's all.

*Alice now notices Norton, who is looking very downcast.*

ALICE (*to Norton*): What's the matter with you? You look like you lost your best friend.

*Norton lets out loud wail of anguish and despair. Alice looks at him like he's crazy and Ralph speaks quickly to cover.*

RALPH: Will you stop askin' questions, Alice. Ain't you got anything better to do?

*Alice shrugs her shoulders and crosses to stove. She looks at soup and stirs it a little. Ralph crosses to bureau and takes hand mirror and sticks tongue out and looks at it in mirror. . . .*

ALICE: Sit down, Ralph, and I'll give you your dinner.

*Ralph quickly puts mirror down so Alice doesn't see what he's doing.*

RALPH: I don't want any dinner. I ain't hungry.

ALICE: Don't you want anything?

RALPH: Well, maybe just somethin' light. I know . . . I think I'll have a saucer of warm milk.

ALICE: A saucer of what?

RALPH: You heard me. A saucer of warm milk! And if you don't mind I'll have it in the bedroom.

ALICE: Ralph, I think you're blowing your top. One of these days they're going to come and take you away!

*Norton lets out another wail of despair and anguish. Ralph looks at him you-understand-don't-you-pal-style.*

RALPH (*sadly*): Yes, Alice, one of these days they will take me away. And that's why I'd like to have a little talk with you.

NORTON (*still crying*): You want me to leave, Ralph?

RALPH: No, you can stay, Norton. Look, Alice, if anything ever happened to me, would you get married again?

ALICE (*sarcastic*): Don't be silly, Ralph. I think I learned my lesson.

RALPH: It's no time for cracks, Alice. I'm talkin' seriously. Now, would you get married again?

ALICE: Well, I don't think so. But I guess if I got lonely and the right guy came along, who knows?

RALPH: Well, I guess I can't blame you, Alice. You're young and in the prime of life. I can see it all now. For a little while after I'm gone, you'll miss me. Then you'll meet some guy and the two of you'll hit it off fine. Then you'll marry him. He'll move in here. Living in my apartment, with my furniture, and with my luck he'll be just my size. And he'll probably wear the new overcoat I bought last winter. Alice, you got to promise me one thing.

ALICE: What's that?

RALPH: If anything ever happens to me, I want you to bury me in my new overcoat.

ALICE: Look, if it'll make you happy, I'll bury you in your bathing suit. Now what are you talking about? Nothing's going to happen to you. You're as strong as a horse.

RALPH: So what? Haven't you ever seen a dead horse?

ALICE: Now that you mention it, there is a resemblance.

NORTON (*crying*): Watch your tongue, Alice. You don't know what you're sayin'.

RALPH (*covering*): Look, Alice, would you mind just gettin' me my saucer of milk, please.

ALICE: But Ralph—

RALPH (*steamed*): Just get my saucer of milk.

*Alice crosses to icebox. She opens door, looks in, and then turns to Ralph.*

ALICE: We don't have any milk. Will Pepsi-Cola do?

*Ralph takes letter from pocket, shields it from Alice. . . . He shoves it quickly back into pocket.*

RALPH: No, it's got to be a saucer of warm milk.

ALICE (*annoyed*): All right, I'll go up to Trixie's and borrow some.

*Alice exits. Boys watch her as she does this.*

NORTON (*crying*): All women are beasts!

12. Norton had a friend whose doctor gave him six months to live. The guy made a monkey out of the doctor by living for _____ months.

13. Name three jobs Ralph had before becoming a bus driver.

14. How did Ralph and Alice meet?

15. Ralph came into the world with pink cheeks, a healthy pair of lungs, and a lot of big ideas. How does he think he's going out?

RALPH (*thinking*): Now let's see. . . . *Then looking up at Norton.* You know, I'm gonna take care of you too, Norton. I'm gonna leave you my bowling shoes.

NORTON (*overwhelmed*): Gee, that's mighty nice of you, Ralph. I was just about to go out and buy myself a new pair. Boy, I'm tellin' you, this couldn't have happened at a better time.

*Norton chuckles with delight. As he keeps chuckling Ralph looks at him with expression which says, "Don't you realize you're laughing at a dying man?" Norton digs this reaction and quickly wipes smile from face.*

*Norton then reverently removes hat from head and holds it over his heart, Flag Day–style. Ralph nods that's-better-style. And looks again toward paper. As Ralph starts thinking, Norton puts hat back on. Ralph speaks with authority as if dictating to lawyer.*

RALPH: Now, to my wife Alice, I leave all my worldly goods. I leave my, ah . . . I leave my, ah. . . .

*Ralph then does a slow realization he has nothing to leave Alice. And big-man tones and expression leave him.*

RALPH (*weakly*): I leave my, ah. . . . Norton, I ain't got no worldly goods. *Ralph gets up in panic.* I got nothin' to leave Alice. Here I am about to die and I got nothin' to leave my wife. A man's got to leave his wife something.

NORTON: Look, I tell you what, Ralph. You leave Alice the bowling shoes. I'll just borrow them when I need them.

RALPH: Shut up. Bowlin' shoes . . . that's nothin' to leave your wife. She'll need money, Norton, and lots of it. After I'm gone, I want her to be able to go on livin' in the manner to which she's accustomed.

NORTON: Well, then she could always sell the bowlin' shoes and live off the money she gets for that!

16. Since Ralph claims he has nothing to leave Alice, Norton suggests he sell his body to science. Why?
17. Norton has a friend who sold a story to a magazine. What was his story, which magazine bought it, and how much did they pay for it?

NORTON: Hey, Ralph, I just got a thought. You know, you got a pretty interestin' story here, ah, how it feels to be a man doomed to six months to live. Well, maybe you could do what a friend of mine did. He had an interestin' story and sold it to a magazine and got five thousand dollars for it. Very similar to yours.

RALPH: You mean he had only six months to live?

NORTON: He didn't have six months—he got six months! You may remember readin' the story in *Confidential* magazine. It was called "Two Screwballs Try to Break into Vassar Dormitory." One of the screwballs escaped and got away.

*Norton chuckles devilishly, knowing that the other screwball was him. Ralph looks at Norton amazed.*

18. Ralph wants to sell his story to a magazine. What does he imagine the title of the first installment will be?
19. Norton thinks Ralph's title is too long. What's Norton's headline?
20. Who's the publisher of *American Weekly* magazine, and what's his office's room number?

21. What's the publisher's secretary's name?
    A. Miss Reynolds.
    B. Miss Evans.
    C. Thelma.
    D. Shirley.
22. True or false: Ralph thinks his story about dying would be even better than *American Weekly*'s story "I Was a Mambo Dancer for the CIA."
23. What does *American Weekly*'s publisher threaten to do to Ralph if his story is a fake?
24. How much does *American Weekly* pay Ralph for his story, and what does Ralph do with the money?

PUBLISHER: Shirley, call the shop and tell them to get set up. We've got a new lead story for this issue.
*Publisher clicks off intercom and then puts arm around Ralph's shoulder.*
PUBLISHER: Well, we're going to do your story.
RALPH (*gratefully*): Thank you very much. *Ralph then takes quick glance at watch, Fenwick-style.* Oh, I beg your pardon, but it's time for my pill. Would anybody happen to have a saucer of warm milk?

25. Alice laughs at the vet's report because she knows it's about Ginger and not about Ralph. Ralph is perturbed, and says, "Aren't you the _____!"

ALICE: What's this crazy story about you having six months to live?
RALPH: It ain't crazy, Alice. I only wish it was. It's true. I got less than six months to live. Pretty soon I'll be gone up there.
*Ralph does this last line very dramatic and as he says it he puts finger up next to his temple, but pointing straight up.*
ALICE: You've been gone up there ever since I've known you!
*As Alice does this line, she points in manner similar to way Ralph did, but crooks her finger so it points to her temple.*
ALICE: And this proves it. Ralph, there's nothing wrong with you.
RALPH: There's nothin' wrong with me? And which one of the Mayo brothers are you?!

26. Who's the vet that examined Ginger?
27. When Ralph learns he's not going to die from arterial monochromia, where does he want to go to celebrate?
    A. The Hong Kong Gardens.
    B. The Colonnade.
    C. Salvatore's Pizzeria.
    D. Every Chinese restaurant in town.

28. Ralph faints and Norton thinks he's dead. In his sorrow Norton laments
    that Ralph won't be driving the Madison Avenue bus anymore. What
    "heavenly" bus does he think Ralph will be driving?

NORTON: You poor little kid! You poor little fat kid! But this isn't goodbye
forever, Ralph. Maybe we'll meet again. Maybe there is such a thing as
reincarnation. Who knows, maybe you'll come back as an elephant! And
then on Sundays we can go visit you at the zoo.

A couple of minutes later, after Alice has revived Ralph:

ALICE: For goodness' sake, Ralph, don't think up any more crazy ideas. You'll
only get yourself in trouble.
RALPH: Did you hear that, Norton? I got a choice of either dyin' in six months or
goin' to prison for twenty years and she says I'm liable to get myself in
trouble! Look, Alice, there's an old saying, "If you can't be constructive,
don't be destructive!"
ALICE (*sarcastic*): And there's another old saying, Ralph. I remember seeing it
in a Charlie Chan picture once. . . . Number one husband like chicken
noodle . . . always in hot water!
*Alice then turns and crosses to bedroom.*
NORTON: Hey, Ralph, I got an old sayin' you could hit her with. When in Rome,
do as the Romans do.
*Ralph nods in agreement, Hardy-style, and shouts loudly toward bedroom
door.*
RALPH: When in Rome, do as the Romans do!
*Ralph then freezes and does slow realization that saying made no sense.*
RALPH (*to Norton*): What has that got to do with it?
NORTON: I didn't know it had to have anything to do with it. I just thought you
were thinkin' of old sayings.

Later, when Ralph decides his only way out of a jail term for fraud is to
find a "doctor" who can "cure" arterial monochromia:

*Both boys gradually get realization it's Norton and they look slowly toward
each other. As their eyes meet realization is shown in their eyes.*
NORTON (*singing* **Dr. Kronkite***-style*): Take off the coat, my boy. Take off the
coat!
*Ralph puts arm around Norton and both boys sing next line together.*
RALPH AND NORTON (*singing*): The coat is off!
*As they hold this pose we DISSOLVE from scene.*

Then, at the *Confidential* magazine office (it was later changed in the script to *American Weekly*):

SECRETARY: If you and the doctor wait right here, Mr. Kramden, Mr. Gersh will be with you in a moment.

NORTON (*professional manner*): Thank you very much. I hope he won't be long. I'm due in surgery at three. I've got to remove a tattoo.

(Another Norton line, also later deleted, was, "Thank you very much. And good health to all from Rexall!")

*Ralph smiles meekly at her like "The doctor's a great kidder." She looks at them both a little strangely and exits. Norton looks after her and speaks.*

NORTON: Va va va voom!

RALPH: Will you cut it out! Norton, for once in your life will you please act sensible. Do you realize if they find out you're a phony doctor, I could get twenty years for fraud!

NORTON: Will you stop worryin', Ralph. I told you this ain't the first time I ever been a doctor. I was a doctor once in a school play. Everybody said I was just like a real doctor.

RALPH: Yeah?

NORTON: Say, what do you say I use the same name I used in the play?

RALPH (*annoyed*): I don't care what name you use.

NORTON: Okay, then from now on just call me Doctor Kangaroo!

RALPH (*what-the-hey-style*): Doctor Kangaroo?

NORTON: Yeah. This was a play about animals. I took a burr out of a lion's foot. He was grateful to me for the rest of his—

RALPH (*interrupting exasperated*): Your name is Doctor Norton!

NORTON (*little scared*): Okay, okay. You don't have to get sore.

*Ralph just looks down toward floor and shakes his head if-only-there-was-somebody-besides-him-I-coulda-picked-style. As he does this, Norton removes his hat and smooths sides of his hair with palms of hand. He has plastered-down-parted-in-the-middle-Clem-Finch-style hair. On finishing hair, Norton puts hat back on and then reaches in breast pocket and takes out pair of thick horn-rimmed glasses and puts them on. Ralph just looks at him and after Norton starts straightening his tie, feeling that he's all set, Ralph speaks, Oliver Hardy–style.*

RALPH (*Hardy-style*): Doctor Kangaroo!

NORTON (*with a little salute*): At your service, Mr. Chipmunk!

29. Where did Norton go to school, and where did "Dr. Norton" study medicine?

*Art Carney or Ed Norton? "Don't touch me, I'm sterile."* COURTESY RALPH.

30. Why didn't Dr. Norton know Oxford was in England?
31. Where does Dr. Norton practice medicine?

PUBLISHER: Doctor Norton, do you know what I think? You're no doctor. You're a phony! This whole thing is a hoax!

RALPH: Habba, habba, habba.

PUBLISHER (*to Norton*): It's bad enough to come in here and try to dupe our magazine with this phony story. But to give false hope to poor Mr. Kramden here who only has six months to live is unforgivable.

*Ralph does sudden realization that they think only Norton is a phony, not him.*

PUBLISHER: How anyone can stoop low enough to take advantage of a doomed man just to get a little cheap publicity is beyond me.

*Publisher looks at Ralph sympathetically and Ralph looks back martyr-style.*

PUBLISHER: You know where you belong, Mr. Norton? In jail. And that's where I'm going to send you, if possible, for the rest of your life.

*Norton shoots panicky look at Ralph. Ralph in panic picks it up quickly.*

RALPH (*in panic*): Uh, uh, you're absolutely right, Mr. Gersh. *To Norton.* How could you do such a thing to me, you cad! Don't worry, Mr. Gersh. I'll see that he goes to prison for the rest of his life. You don't have to do a thing. I'll take him there right now.

*Ralph crosses to door and then looks back at Norton and speaks.*

RALPH: Come on, Doctor Norton, or whatever your name is.

*Norton just stands there looking pathetically from Gersh to Ralph.*

RALPH (*exasperated, pleading through teeth*): Well, come on.

NORTON (*crying*): But Ralph, I don't want to go to prison for the rest of my life!

RALPH (*panicky*): Come on!

NORTON (*crying*): Please, Ralph! Don't take me to jail! I didn't try to pull no hoax. I was only tryin' to help!

*Ralph looks ceilingward during Norton's speech, and then realizes that Norton doesn't dig this is the only way out. Then he decides to level.*

32. Why won't Dr. Norton sit on the couch at the *American Weekly* office?

33. What did *American Weekly* want from Ralph in return for not pressing charges against him for selling them a bogus story?

34. What does Alice give Ralph to eat when he comes home from *American Weekly*?

© PRESTON BLAIR PRODUCTIONS.

# THE SLEEPWALKER

November 5, 1955 · A. J. Russell and Herbert Finn

"The Sleepwalker" is one of several *Honeymooners* episodes that underwent major revisions before it was filmed. To begin with, the show was written to open in Norton's apartment, not Ralph's. And later, Ralph is supposed to go to Detroit with one of the Gotham Bus Company executives to examine some new buses the company considers buying. Ralph wants to go because this is a chance for him to impress one of the big shots and move up in the company. At the same time, he doesn't want to leave Norton to "walk off a buildin' or somethin'." So what does Ralph do? Take Norton along, of course.

Most likely, the script was rewritten because Gleason liked to keep set changes to a minimum. The set would have to be changed four times as originally written: the Norton and Kramden apartments, the hotel in Detroit, and the hospital where Norton ends up after a sleepwalking escapade.

1. How many nights has Norton been sleepwalking?
2. Trixie spots Norton sleepwalking on the roof of:
   A. The Hong Kong Gardens.
   B. Krauss's.
   C. 728 Chauncey Street.
   D. McCloskey's building.
3. What is Norton eating while he's sleepwalking?
4. True or false: Norton slips on a banana peel.
5. Norton visits the doctor from the Sanitation Department. What does the doctor say is causing Norton's sleepwalking, and what does he recommend Norton do about it?
6. What does Norton eat for supper every Wednesday night?
7. True or false: Ralph gives Trixie rock candy to sprinkle around her bed to discourage Norton from sleepwalking.
8. Alice says Norton's sick; Ralph says he never had it so good because he _____, _____, and _____ all at the same time.
9. "Setter" is the answer to what question in a crossword puzzle Ralph's doing?
10. Norton visits the Sanitation Department doctor a second time. What does the doctor give him to calm his nerves?
    A. A saucer of warm milk with a pill in it.
    B. A sleeping pad.
    C. Some aspereen.
    D. A tonic.
11. If nervousness caused sleepwalking, where would Ralph be right now?

> *There is a knock on the door.*
> ALICE: Who can that be?
> *Ralph gets up, goes to door and opens it. A Western Union boy enters.*
> BOY: Kramden? Telegram. Sign here.

*He gives Ralph book and pencil to sign. Ralph does, gives book and pencil back, takes telegram. The boy holds out an open hand for a tip. Ralph starts away, notices this. He looks down at boy's hand.*

RALPH: You got a nice long life line there. Congratulations!

*He shuts the door.*

ALICE: Who is it from?

RALPH: Who d'ya think it's from? Your brother Frank's been pinched for running a crap game again—and I ain't gonna pay his bail!

ALICE: Oh, Ralph, open it.

*Ralph opens telegram, reads it, his face lights up.*

RALPH: Alice! Alice, it's from Mr. Cooper! The vice-president of the Gotham Bus Company!

ALICE: The vice-president! What does he say?

RALPH: Listen to this! *Reads.* "Am leaving for Detroit noon tomorrow to purchase fleet of new buses. Would you like to accompany me and give bus driver's opinion regarding maneuverability, performance, and so forth of new models. Sorry to give you such short notice. Signed, Gregory Cooper."

ALICE: Ralph, that's wonderful! But I wonder why he picked on you?

RALPH: Why? It's obvious. Because I'm an expert on these things. Because I've got opinions and I ain't afraid to express them! Because I've shown that I got the mechanical ability to spot what's wrong with a bus!

ALICE: Ralph, writing an anonymous letter to the boss saying his buses are broken-down pieces of junk is not my idea of showing mechanical ability!

RALPH: Well, I musta impressed Mr. Cooper, because here's the telegram and I'm leavin' tomorrow. *He paces, waving telegram.* Boy, oh boy, do you know what this means? Mr. Cooper's a good man to get next to. This is how careers are made. I'll be close to him, giving him advice, tellin' him what to do. And first thing you know, he'd be dependin' on me. So he makes me his assistant! Yessir, this is it, Alice! This is the break I've been waitin' for. For years I've been tryin' to get ahead, and I couldn't make it. But this time I've rung the bell!

*From offstage we hear the ringing of a small cowbell. The door opens and Norton walks in, sleepwalking, with the bell tied around his wrist.*

The next scene opens with Ralph packing for the trip to Detroit.

*Ralph has a suitcase on top of the table and is struggling mightily to get it closed. The snap locks are facing him. He tries one, then the other, but is unsuccessful. He turns the suitcase around so that snap locks are facing away from him. He now leans on suitcase with his elbows and manages to get it shut. Just as he finishes Alice enters from bedroom.*

ALICE: Now, have you got everything? Money?

RALPH: Yeah. *He slaps pocket at his thigh.*

ALICE: Handkerchief?

RALPH: Yeah. *He slaps back pocket.*

ALICE: Tickets! What about your tickets?

RALPH: Right here. *He reaches into breast pocket and brings out train ticket in envelope.* Nice of Mr. Cooper to send them over by messenger, wasn't it? *He puts tickets back into breast pocket.* Well, I'm all set. How do I look, Alice?

*Ralph stands before her. He is wearing gray sport jacket with blue trousers.*

ALICE (*appraising him*): All right, I guess.

RALPH: I didn't ask you to take a guess. I asked you to tell me how I look!

ALICE: Well, Ralph, I thought you were going to wear the blue jacket that goes with those pants.

RALPH: I was. But I figured this is a little more sporty. Y'know, there's a club car on the train.

ALICE: But Ralph, this is a business trip. I'm sure Mr. Cooper won't be wearing a sport jacket.

RALPH (*worried*): He won't? But my blue jacket is in the suitcase. Why didn't you tell me before I locked it!

ALICE: Well, can't you open it?

RALPH: No, I can't!

ALICE: All right, then. Don't bother.

RALPH: That's just like you, Alice. First you make trouble and then you say "don't bother." *He grunts and opens suitcase.* I wish you'd make up your mind.

*He takes off sport jacket, takes blue jacket out of suitcase, puts it on. Then he puts sport jacket into suitcase. He is about to lock it when Alice speaks.*

ALICE: Ralph, the tickets! You forgot the tickets!

*Ralph feels foolish but he's not going to admit it.*

RALPH: I didn't forget 'em, Alice! I didn't forget 'em. I ain't such a dope to forget my train tickets.

*He opens suitcase, reaches into pocket of coat, gets tickets. He puts them into breast pocket of blue jacket he is now wearing. Then he locks the suitcase. Norton enters. He is fully dressed and wide awake.*

NORTON: Hi, Alice. Hi, Ralph.

RALPH: Oh, it's you. I didn't recognize you without your nightshirt!

ALICE: Ralph, you won't be leaving for a while yet. I'm gonna run up and see Trix. *Alice exits.*

NORTON: I got you a little goin'-away present, Ralph.

RALPH: You did?

NORTON: This is somethin' I gave a lot of thought to. Since you're goin' on a business trip, I wanted it to be just the right thing. I got you somethin' so that when people look at ya, they'll say, "There's an important businessman! There's a man with an eye to the future! There's a man who reads the *Wall Street Journal!*"

RALPH: Gee, Norton. What did you get me?

NORTON: A copy of the *Wall Street Journal!*

*He gets a copy of the* Wall Street Journal *from his back pocket and presents it to Ralph. The newspaper has a large ribbon tied around it. Ralph holds it up, looks at it, obviously disappointed.*

NORTON: I had it gift wrapped!

RALPH: Thanks, Norton. That's very thoughtful of you.

NORTON: So you're all set to go, eh? Let's take a look at you. *He appraises Ralph's clothes.* Uh-hm . . . uh-hm. . . . Ralph, do you mind if I make a suggestion?

RALPH: What is it?

NORTON: Whattaya wearin' that jacket for? Where's your new sport jacket? You look great in that.

RALPH: Norton, ain't you got any sense? I'll wear the sport jacket at night, when I'm seein' the sights. But this is a business trip. Nobody wears a sport jacket on a business trip. Mr. Cooper won't be wearin' one.

NORTON: Whattaya care what anybody wears? Ya gotta wear what you like! Believe me, Ralph, I know big businessmen. They like a man who shows a little individuality. They like a man who stands out, not just one of the herd. Believe me, if you wear that sport jacket, Mr. Cooper'll admire you for it!

RALPH (*thoughtfully*): I knew Alice didn't know what she was talking about. But I ain't gonna change it now. The sport jacket is in the suitcase and it's locked.

NORTON: Well, can't ya open it?

RALPH: No, I can't!

NORTON: All right, then. Don't bother.

*Ralph looks at him, grunts, and then opens the suitcase.*

RALPH: Everybody around here is a fashion expert.

*Ralph takes off blue jacket, puts it over chair. Then he gets the sport jacket from suitcase, puts it on. This done, he packs away the blue jacket, the one that has his train tickets in it. He locks suitcase.*

NORTON: There! Now you look like somethin'. Now you got individuality!

*The door opens and Alice enters.*

ALICE: Ralph, Trixie said that when you're ready to leave, just yell up to her and she'll telephone for a cab. *She notices that Ralph has changed his jacket.* Ralph, where's your blue jacket?

RALPH: It's in the suitcase, Alice! And it's stayin' there. I'm wearin' this one.

And don't give me an argument. I don't wanna be one of the herd. I wanna show a little individuality. I wanna stand out!

*Alice lowers her head and looks at his stomach.*

RALPH: Don't say it, Alice. Don't say it!

ALICE: All right, Ralph. Wear what you like. Now, are you all ready? Have you got your money, your handkerchief, your train tickets?

RALPH (*exploding*): Will ya cut it out, Alice! If you asked me once, you asked me a million times! Now I'll tell you once and for all. Yes, I've got my money. I've got my handkerchief, and I've got my tick . . . tick. . . .

*He pats breast pocket of jacket and suddenly realizes that he forgot the tickets in his blue jacket, which is now in suitcase. For a moment he is trapped. But then he makes a sudden switch to the casual.*

RALPH: Y'know, Alice, I think you're right. I think I'll wear the blue jacket.

*He goes to suitcase and opens it.*

NORTON: What about your individuality?

RALPH: Shut up! *He takes off sport jacket and puts on blue one, packs the sport jacket away.* There! And I ain't openin' that suitcase again until I get to Detroit!

NORTON: Ralph, before you leave, there's a serious matter that I'd like to take up with ya. It's about my sleepwalkin'.

ALICE: Ralph! We never thought of that. Who's going to take care of Norton while you're away?

RALPH: Now wait a minute, Alice. I know what you're leadin' up to, and it's no go. This is the chance of a lifetime, and I ain't gonna miss it just because he walks in his sleep!

NORTON: He's right, Alice. Don't worry about me. I ain't been hit by a truck—yet. I ain't fallen off a roof—yet. And even if I do, that don't mean I'm gonna get killed. You go to Detroit and have a good time, Ralph. Don't worry about me.

*Ralph turns and looks at Alice. She stares accusingly.*

RALPH: Alice, don't look at me like that! I'm goin' to Detroit!

ALICE: You can go, Ralph. But can't you take Norton with you? Then you can keep your eye on him.

NORTON: Wait a minute, Alice. That's askin' too much. Besides, I'm financially embarrassed at this time. I don't even have the fare to Detroit.

RALPH: You see, Alice. It won't work.

ALICE: Ralph, we've got a little extra money. We can buy him a train ticket.

RALPH: All right, Norton. I guess Mr. Cooper won't mind. But hurry up. We ain't got much time. Run upstairs and pack a suitcase!

*Norton takes one step toward door, stops, comes back.*

NORTON: It's no good, Ralph. So I get to Detroit. But where'll I sleep? I got no money for a hotel room.

RALPH: You see, Alice. It's absolutely out of the question!

ALICE: No, it isn't, Ralph. How much can a hotel room cost? Five dollars a night? You'll only be there two days.

RALPH: Okay, Norton, we'll pay for your hotel room. Now hurry up! Go upstairs and pack a suitcase!

*Norton takes one step toward door, stops, comes back.*

NORTON: Wait a minute, Ralph. I just thought of something. I'm in Detroit and I got a hotel room. But what am I gonna eat? I got no money for food.

RALPH: All right, Norton! We'll pay for your food, too.

*Norton grabs Ralph's hand and pumps it.*

NORTON: Ralphy boy, I ain't never gonna forget this! Never, as long as I live!

RALPH (*freeing himself*): Never mind, Norton! We ain't got time for that. We gotta leave in a few minutes! Run upstairs and pack a suitcase!

NORTON: Okay, Ralph.

*Norton dashes out. Ralph and Alice let out a sigh of relief. Suddenly the door opens and Norton enters again.*

NORTON: Ralph, I just thought of somethin'. I ain't got a suitcase!

*DISSOLVE. END OF ACT THREE.*

12. Ralph wants to lend Norton money so he can go to the hospital. How much do the Kramdens have in the bank?

13. How many nights has Trixie gone without sleep?

14. According to Alice, Ralph couldn't waste away if he stayed awake for
    A. Nine years.
    B. Three days.
    C. A hundred years.
    D. Fifteen years.

15. Where does Norton go sleepwalking on Thursday nights?

16. Ralph and Norton use the same color toothbrush. What color is it? How does Norton choose the one he uses?

The scene in which Ralph sleeps with Norton upstairs in his apartment was written to take place in a hotel room in Detroit. Ralph has just discovered that Norton mistakenly used his toothbrush, and it's put him in a foul mood.

*Ralph grunts, goes back into bathroom. Norton goes to telephone and picks it up. Ralph enters from bath as he does.*

NORTON: Gimme room service, please.

RALPH: What are you doin'?

NORTON: I thought I'd order a little snack.

RALPH (*takes receiver from him, puts it in cradle*): Gimme that! Look, Norton, I wanna remind you that I'm payin' for all this!

NORTON: What're you kickin' about? The company gave you an expense account!

RALPH: Sure, for myself! But not for you! This whole trip wouldn't cost me a nickel if it wasn't for you!

NORTON: Oh, I don't know, Ralph.

RALPH: Whattaya mean ya don't know! If I was by myself, I wouldn't need two train tickets, would I?

NORTON (*thoughtfully*): N-no.

RALPH: I wouldn't need two meals every time I sat down to eat, would I?

NORTON (*thoughtfully*): N-no.

RALPH (*pointing to bed*): I wouldn't need a double bed, would I?

NORTON (*brightening*): That's the one I was waitin' for!

RALPH (*holding up fist*): This is the one you're waitin' for, Norton! This is the one you're waitin' for!

*Norton backs away scared. There is a knock on the door. Ralph gives Norton a disgusted look, then goes to door and opens it. Mr. Cooper enters.*

RALPH: Oh, hello, Mr. Cooper.

COOPER: Hello, Ralph. I just wanted to tell you that we have a nine o'clock appointment with the plant manager tomorrow.

RALPH: Oh, I'll be ready, Mr. Cooper.

COOPER: Fine. Norton, I hope you can find something to interest you tomorrow while Ralph and I are working.

NORTON: Don't worry about me, Mr. Cooper. I got a tour arranged. I intend to see every foot of Detroit.

COOPER: All in one day? Detroit's pretty crowded, you know. Kind of hard to get around.

NORTON: Not the way I travel. I got a courtesy card that gives me entry to every sewer in the city!

*Ralph gives him an elbow.*

RALPH: Thanks for droppin' by, Mr. Cooper. I'll see you in the mornin'.

COOPER: Good night. *Cooper exits.*


17. What foods does Norton have on hand for his late-night snack?
18. Where does Ralph first hide the key to Norton's bedroom?
19. What magazine does Norton read before going to sleep?
20. What's hanging on the wall above the Nortons' bed?
21. What famous fictional detective couldn't solve the problem of lifting Ralph up to get to the bedroom key he hides under his pillow after Norton guesses its original hiding place?

RALPH: Wait a minute! How did you know I hid the key under my pillow?

NORTON: Simple deduction. I don't read Dick Tracy just to pass the time, you know.

RALPH: That does it! *Ralph points to straight-backed chair.* Sit down in that chair.

NORTON: Whattaya gonna do, Ralph?

RALPH: I'll show you what I'm gonna do! Sit down!

*Norton sits in chair. Ralph goes to window, yanks the cord off the drapes.*

RALPH: Maybe you learned somethin' from readin' Dick Tracy, Norton. But I learned somethin' from watchin' Hopalong Cassidy!

*He starts to tie Norton to chair with drape cord. DISSOLVE.*

Later in the script Norton has freed himself from the chair—in his sleep, yet. We find him in the hospital, after the police have picked him up sleepwalking in the street.

*The door opens and Norton enters. He is seated in a wheelchair, pushed by a pretty nurse. Norton is still in his nightshirt and hat, happy as a lark. Once in the room, the nurse releases the wheelchair. Norton propels it himself for a moment, going around in a circle.*

NORTON: That's Detroit for ya! Even the wheelchairs have power steering!

RALPH: Look, Norton, this is no time to be funny. You got me in a mess with Mr. Cooper. I'm supposed to be with him right now, not chasin' after you.

DOCTOR: Mr. Kramden, please, don't excite the patient.

NORTON: Yeah, don't excite the patient.

22. What time do Ralph and Norton go to sleep?
23. What time does Norton wake up and begin sleepwalking, and what does he take with him "for the road"?
24. True or false: Ralph calls the Sanitation Department doctor because of the bump on Norton's head.
25. The doctor is going to inject Norton with _____.
26. The doctor injects Norton and tells him to count backward from 100. What numbers does Norton count off?
27. What grave disappointment did Norton suffer when he was twenty-one years old?
28. Norton once had a dog named Lulu. How did he lose her?
29. What does Ralph want to get Norton to solve his sleepwalking problem?
30. It's midnight, but Trixie's going out shopping. For what?

31. What does Ralph want to drink to celebrate what he thinks will be a night of uninterrupted sleep?
    A. A small cup of black coffee.
    B. Lemonade.
    C. Cold grape juice.
    D. A glass of warm milk.

ALICE: Ralph, are you sure Mr. Cooper wasn't angry about you missing that appointment?

RALPH: Not a bit, Alice. He said that under the circumstances I couldn't do anything else but take care of Norton. He was very nice about it. He even paid me a compliment.

ALICE: What'd he say?

RALPH: He said, "Kramden, when I took you to Detroit with me, I doubted that I was doin' the right thing. But after spending two days with you, there's no doubt in my mind whatsoever."

COURTESY
SAMUEL LOWE
COMPANY.

# *BETTER LIVING THROUGH TV*

November 12, 1955 · Marvin Marx and Walter Stone

1. What dress material is Norton allergic to?

NORTON: Look, Trixie, you expect me to get back up on that chair after my best friend comes in here and finds me wearin' a dress?
TRIXIE: Oh, don't be such a baby.
NORTON: A baby, huh? Look, Trix. You see these puffed sleeves?
TRIXIE: Yeah.
NORTON: Well, one more crack outta you, and you're gonna have puffed eyes to match!

2. Ralph is always going to Norton with chances to make a fortune. Why can't Norton stand to make a fortune again?

"Kramden's a dreamer," says Stone. "He always wants something better. He's always trying. He doesn't want to stay a bus driver. He's always hoping he can find some way to get out of that job and better himself, either by getting a better job with the bus company, or going into some business, or finding an invention or something that he can capitalize on. His basic problem was that he was always looking. . . .

"Norton was the happiest man in the world. He loved his job. He was content. Ralph would talk him into these things, and he would go along with Ralph because he was his friend.

"One guy was the world's dreamer, and the other guy was happy as a lark just to be where he was."

3. Ralph admitting that some of his money-making schemes "went a little sour" is the biggest understatement since General Custer said what?
4. Name the eight things Ralph tells Norton the Handy Housewife Helper has or can do.
5. Where did Ralph get the Handy Housewife Helper?
6. How many Handy Housewife Helpers does Ralph want to buy, how much will they cost, and how much does he plan to sell them for?
7. Ralph once had another money-making scheme that "couldn't lose." What was it?
8. How does Ralph plan to sell the Handy Housewife Helper?
9. How much will it cost Ralph and Norton to do a TV commercial?
10. Ralph and Norton will do their commercial during:
    A. A movie.
    B. *$99,000 Answer.*
    C. *Dragnet.*
    D. *Medic.*

11. True or false: Norton's uncle sold his TV set because he was sick of watching commercials.

12. When Norton finds out Ralph hasn't gotten his money from Alice to buy the Handy Housewife Helpers, he thinks his TV debut will be on which program?

13. In Ralph Kramden's castle, Alice is just a:
    A. Peasant girl.
    B. Lowly third-class seaman.
    C. Private.
    D. Slave.

14 . Ralph is boss in his house—he's just like:
    A. George Washington.
    B. Richard the Lionhearted.
    C. King Henry VIII.
    D. Billy the Kid.

15. Ralph has just bragged to Norton that he can get all the money he needs for his scheme from Alice. But when the moment of truth arrives, he backs down. Alice calls him:
    A. The Blimp.
    B. Three hundred pounds of blubber.
    C. Billy the Goat.
    D. Richard the Chickenhearted.


RALPH (*steamed*): All right, Alice, you want to be so stubborn? Well, I can be stubborn too. I wouldn't stay in the same room with you another minute. I'm sleepin' out here! *Ralph waits a second, expecting her to give in.* I ain't kiddin', Alice. Either you give me that money, or I'll never talk to you again. Never, Alice . . . never!
*He waits again, boiling inside as he does.*

RALPH: This is your last chance, Alice! Think it over!
*At this point pillow comes sailing out of bedroom and hits Ralph smack in face.*

ALICE (*from bedroom*): You forgot your pillow!

RALPH (*calm, deliberate*): All right, Alice, I'm callin' your bluff.
*Ralph, steamed, picks up pillow and crosses angrily to table. He then grabs two of the straight-backed chairs and arranges them so they are a little apart and facing each other, bed-style. He then picks up blanket and by putting it around shoulders and holding corners, folds it around him Indian-style with one arm inside. He then sits down angrily in one chair, and with great effort swings his legs up onto other chair. He wiggles, getting himself comfortable for a second and then calls smugly into bedroom.*

RALPH (*smugly*): A few nights of this, and you'll change your tune!
*He then notices that he left pillow on table. He tries to reach it, still holding*

*onto blanket. He can't reach it, so with steamed burn he gets up, dropping blanket on floor. Takes pillow from table. He folds pillow in half and then balances it on top of back of chair. It is an uneven balance, so that the minute he lets go it falls to floor backward behind chair. He picks up blanket and wraps it around himself Indian-style again. He sits down and swings feet up on other chair. He then puts his head back heavily, expecting to hit pillow, and, instead, hitting his head on back of chair. He winces.*

RALPH: Owwww!

*Still steamed and folded in blanket, he looks around and sees pillow on floor behind chair. Without getting up he tries to reach around and get pillow. By reaching and turning so completely in chair, he falls off chair onto floor. He then gets up off floor slowly, slow-burn-style. He tries to calm himself down for a second, and then in fit of temper kicks pillow across room. He then wheels on chair and gives chair kick. From kicking chair, he immediately goes into pain bit. At conclusion of pain bit he storms over to bedroom door and hollers in.*

RALPH (*steamed*): You give up, Alice? You give up?

*Alice comes out.*

ALICE: Ralph, are you gonna come to bed and stop this nonsense? Not only won't you let me sleep, but you're gonna wake up the whole building.

RALPH (*livid*): I don't care if I wake up the whole world! I want that money, Alice. I want that money and I'm gonna get it.

ALICE (*defiantly*): Over my dead body!

RALPH (*threatening finger in Alice's face*): That can also be arranged!


16. Ralph claims the Handy Housewife Helper is the key to his future. Alice looks it over and figures there must be an attachment on it that opens the door to _____.


RALPH (*eyes bulge livid-style*): You're askin' for it, Alice. You're really askin' for it! And you're gonna get it, too! I don't know the exact minute, but before this night is over, you're gonna get yours!

ALICE (*right in his kisser*): Why don't you shut up!

RALPH: You have just picked the exact minute!

*Ralph puts his fist up belt-style. Alice leans in with her chin.*

ALICE (*defiantly*): Go ahead and hit me!

RALPH (*wide-eyed*): You'd like that, Alice. You'd really like me to belt you, wouldn't you? Would you like a little belt, Alice? Would you like one?

ALICE (*defiantly*): What are you waitin' for?

*Ralph stands there for a second frustrated and controlling his fist. He then lets it fall to his side.*

RALPH: I wouldn't give you the satisfaction!

17. How long would it take a guy to sell 2,000 Handy Housewife Helpers if he went selling them door-to-door?
18. What crazy harebrained scheme of Ralph's did Alice hear before she married him?

RALPH (*mock defeat*): All right, Alice, I give up. I give up. I can see it's no use talkin' to you. You don't want to be rich. That must be the whole thing . . . you don't want to be rich.

ALICE: Rich? I'd be satisfied just to be poor! We're not even that!
*Ralph looks at her what-are-you-a-wise-guy-style.*

ALICE: Now you listen to me, Ralph Kramden. I'm getting pretty tired of this. Every week you come home with some new crazy harebrained scheme. That's all I've heard for fourteen years now, one crazy harebrained scheme after another. That's all I've heard since the day we got married.

RALPH: You heard one crazy harebrained scheme before we got married. Remember, Alice . . . I proposed to you!

ALICE (*you've-gone-too-far-style*): What did you say, Ralph?
*Ralph realizes he shouldn't have said it and tries to back out without losing face.*

RALPH (*false bravado*): I don't chew my cabbage twice.

ALICE (*dead serious*): You ever say that again, Ralph, and you won't have any teeth to chew your cabbage once!

19. How long have Ralph and Alice been married?
20. What three things does Ralph tell Alice she can buy with the profits from the Handy Housewife Helper?
21. Name three money-making schemes of Ralph's that have failed.

"Kramden was stupid," says Finn. "Actually *stupid* is too harsh a word. He was gullible. Norton would say a stupid thing, and Ralph would recognize it as stupid. But if Norton said, 'Hey, I know a guy who wants to sell glow-in-the-dark shoelaces,' Ralph would say, 'Hey, that's good. There's money in that.' That way Kramden was stupid, and Alice would always have to bring him back down to earth."

22. Ralph feels betrayed because Alice won't give him money to invest; he even accuses her of not loving him, nor having ever loved him. Why does he think Alice married him?
23. How many times do Ralph and Norton rehearse their TV commercial?
24. What are Ralph's and Norton's names in the commercial?
25. What old-fashioned gadgets does Norton have on hand for the commercial?

26. What is Norton's a—mazed response when Ralph "cuts" a hair with the Handy Housewife Helper?

"I think we worked that bit out ourselves," says Carney of the hair-cutting bit. Norton's "old-fashioned implement" can't make a dent in the hair, while the Handy Housewife Helper cuts through it like a machete. "I don't want to take any credit away from the writers, but a lot of that stuff Gleason and I would work out between the two of us."

27. What is the Handy Housewife Helper proof of?
28. While Ralph and Norton are rehearsing, a piece of the Handy House-wife Helper flies off. What a—mazing new task does Ralph want to add to the gadget's repertoire?
29. What part of the Handy Housewife Helper does Norton tell Ralph to get rid of?

One of the favorite pastimes of Honeymooners fans is "spot the ad-lib." One of the most famous ad-libs, in a show replete with them, is Gleason's "Maybe we ought to say something about spearfishing." The genius and quick wit of Carney are evident here, too. Never nonplussed, he tells Ralph, "Get rid of the skate key."

"These two guys just understood each other," says Russell. "There was some kind of symbiotic relationship back and forth, and they kind of knew what the other guy was going to do and how to respond. If anything ever went wrong, they would keep going until they found themselves, and they would be right on track again. The cues would be right, and the jokes would be right.

"There was no throwing them. They were real pros, and you could always depend on either one to come up with an ad-lib that was good, and that brought them back to home base in the script. It really was a study in professionalism."

30. Ralph and Norton have the _____ commercial break.
31. Can it core a apple?

NORTON: First I will core this apple the slow old-fashioned way. Then the Chef of the Future will show you how easy it is the modern way with the Handy Housewife Helper.
   *Norton sticks corer in apple and gives two quick turns and removes core.*
NORTON: That was the old-fashioned way. Slow and difficult. Show us the modern way, Chef of the Future.
RALPH (*nervous-style*): The modern way—zip, zip, and it's out.

*Ralph picks up apple which has not been precored and attempts to remove core with Handy Housewife Helper. It is difficult even getting corer into apple. He mauls apple as he keeps jabbing at it to get it in. Ralph then tries turning it to remove core. He's struggling and sweating quite a bit. After a few seconds Norton starts to feel a little self-conscious because it's taking so long. As he watches Ralph he speaks. Ralph slips out of his TV nervousness because of his frustration with the apple.*

NORTON (*I-better-do-something-style*): Amazing. Zip, zip, and it's . . . uh . . . amazing. Zip, zip, and it's uh. . . .

*Ralph is still struggling. Every time Ralph makes a move Norton does a zip.*

NORTON: Zip—zip, zip . . . zip, zip, zip . . . zip—zip—zip, zip—zip, zip, zip—zip, zip—zip!

*Ralph is getting panicky. Norton, realizing it ain't goin' so good, tries to help Ralph. He offers Ralph old-fashioned corer.*

NORTON: Here, Ralph, you want to try it with this?

*Ralph gives Norton panicky look and shot with elbow. Norton shrugs shoulders and goes back to zip-zips.*

NORTON: Zip. Zip—zip, zip, zip—zip, zip, zip—zip!

*Ralph, who has now hacked the apple to bits, holds up core, which is about all that's left of apple. He weakly tries to look successful.*

RALPH (*weakly*): There. The modern way.

NORTON: More proof of better living through television!

RALPH (*weakly*): And this is not all the Handy Housewife Helper does. It is also a can opener. Again, the test. The old versus the new.

*He snaps head from camera to Norton. Norton picks up old pump-style can opener and can. He immediately goes to work, and since can is half opened already it doesn't take Norton but a few seconds to open it. Ralph watches him doing this with panic. Norton holds up can when finished.*

NORTON: The slow way!

RALPH (*sink inside*): You sure you got the whole can open, O Chef of the Past?

NORTON (*not digging Ralph's fright*): It is all open, O Chef of the Future. Now go ahead, show 'em the fast way!

*Ralph looks into camera and weakly tries to show confidence. Ralph now takes Handy Housewife Helper and can—not precut. He goes about job of opening it. Because of nervousness he fumbles, knocks can over, etc. He starts trying to turn key but can't. As Norton watches he starts in with zips again.*

NORTON: Zip—zip, zip—zip, zip, zip—zip, zip—zip—zip—zip, zip—zip!

*The zips are getting Ralph even more nervous. As he's trying to open can he keeps shooting Norton steamed looks as Norton continues with zips. He finally slams can down and gives Norton a shot with his elbow, shutting him up, and then picks up can and goes back to trying to open it. He's getting more and more steamed; the more steamed he gets, the harder it is. Norton, out of desperation, looks into camera and speaks.*

NORTON: The phone number to call in New York is Bensonhurst 5–6832! Hurry, hurry. Don't get shut out!

*Ralph, now in real panic, turns back to camera and struggles with can and can opener tremendously. Norton watches him, tapping-foot-style. He then looks into camera and speaks.*

NORTON: In case you ain't too impressed with the Handy Housewife Helper, all these slow old-fashioned utensils are for sale, too!

32. What's the number to call to order a Handy Housewife Helper?
33. What's Norton gonna do to Trixie if she says "I told you so"?

NORTON: If my wife Trixie is watchin', and when I get home she says 'I told you so,' I'm gonna belt her right in the mouth!

*Ralph, who is still struggling with back to camera, just turns head and looks into camera and speaks.*

RALPH (*steamed*): Yeah, and Alice'll get hers, too!

*Ralph now turns and slams can down on table. He turns can over, steamed, and tries to open other end. He's so steamed he don't know what he's doin'. Norton watches and speaks.*

NORTON: Watch out for your finger there, Ralph.

*Ralph has finger between "V" of can opener.*

RALPH (*steamed*): Will you leave me alone!

*Ralph gives twist of key and then goes into pain bit. It is wild pain bit with eyes akimbo. As he pulls hand up from can, can opener clings to finger. He can hold it tight with his other finger. He goes around set in wild enlongated pain bit and as he does Norton stands there in attempt to cover, and speaks into camera.*

NORTON: This is not on film. This is live before your very eyes!

*Ralph goes out swinging door and back in again. Norton, panicky, holds up cheese grater and speaks.*

NORTON: This cheese grater can be yours for only fifty-nine cents!

*Ralph knocks table with utensils on it over.*

NORTON (*nervously*): Remember the phone number, friends. Bensonhurst 5-6832! And now back to Mae Busch!

34. Ralph and Norton do their commercial during a movie about:
   A. Jane Frazee.
   B. Charlie Chan.
   C. Mammy Yokum.
   D. Captain Video.

Honeymooners fans have long wondered whether the ending of this episode, where Ralph knocks over the mock wall on the set, was planned or whether it happened unexpectedly. Gleason, who shows no surprise at all as he's going down, makes it look as if the whole thing was part of the script—it wasn't. The script called for him to knock over the table upon which he and Norton were working.

"As I remember, he bumped into it—it was just a fragile set—and it went over," says Carney, who—though he may have been startled to see Gleason go down—handled it as if he was expecting it to happen. "Down he went. It happened, and it was left in, naturally, because it was funny."

Irving Deutsch, who supervised the Electronicam camera system, remembers that scene as well. "The wall wasn't supposed to go over, but they handled it beautifully. Anybody else would have stopped right there, but they just left it in and ad-libbed around it."

© PRESTON BLAIR PRODUCTIONS.

# PAL O' MINE

November 19, 1955 · Leonard Stern and Sydney Zelinka

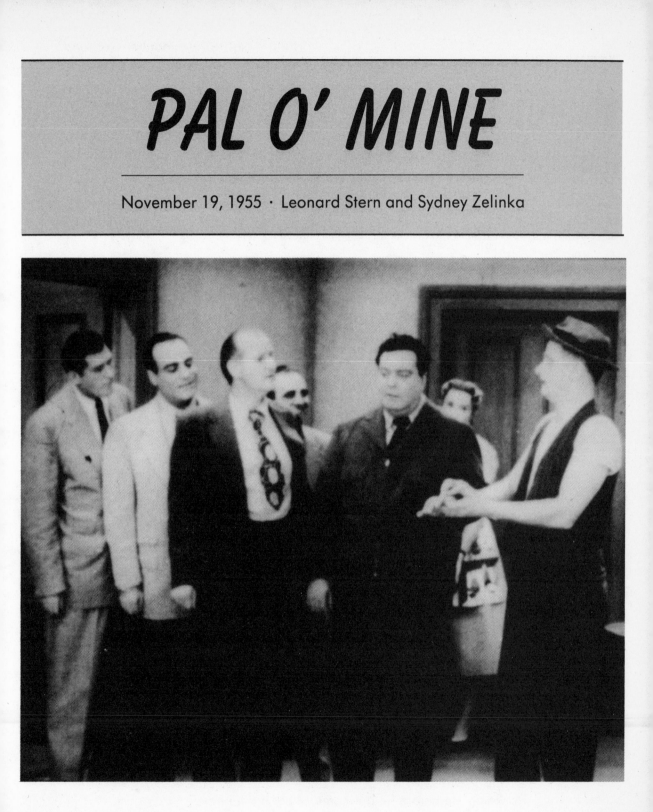

1. Norton's throwing a party and Alice is making punch for him. What's the main ingredient?
2. Who's the party for, and who's invited?
3. What's the occasion?
   A. America won the Davis Cup.
   B. Pierre François de la Briosche's birthday.
   C. Captain Video landed on Pluto.
   D. Jim McKeever was made foreman.
4. What outfit did Norton originally want each of his guests to wear to the party?
5. True or false: Ralph's invited to the party but Alice isn't.
6. What new piece of clothing is Norton wearing to the party?
7. True or false: Norton wears 100-percent cotton T-shirts.
8. Norton is short one item for the party and he has to borrow it from the Kramdens. What is it?
9. What gift is Norton giving to the guest of honor at the party, and what's inscribed on it?
10. What gift did Norton originally want to give Jim McKeever?
11. Who gave Norton his start in the sewer?
    A. Morris Fink.
    B. A wholesale butcher.
    C. Pierre François de la Briosche.
    D. Jim McKeever.
12. Why didn't Norton have Jim McKeever's gift wrapped at the store?
13. True or false: Norton asks Alice for a pair of Ralph's white shorts to use as a tablecloth.
14. Ralph comes home dead tired. Why is he exhausted?

RALPH: You know, Alice, when you drive a bus at night, you meet a whole different class of people. Like tonight . . . this fellow gets on at Thirty-ninth Street. To look at him you wouldn't think he was an important man at all. Just a nice, plain-looking fellow. Well, one word leads to another, and who do you think he turns out to be—he's the head busboy at the Copacabana. It's a swell place, and we oughta go there some time.

ALICE: Yeah, with a contact like that, it's a shame not to take advantage of it!

RALPH: Yeah, he'd treat us real good. Not that I expect him to pick up the check or anything, but we'd be sure to get extra clean dishes.

15. True or false: Ralph is so tired he says he wouldn't leave the apartment even if Jane Frazee was throwing a party and couldn't get started until he arrived.
16. Ralph ate before he got home. What did he have?

17. Ralph gets the ring stuck on his finger. What does Alice give him to help him get it off?

"People used to ask me, 'How come you don't break up?'" says Audrey. "I'd say, 'Because the funnier a line is written, and as funny as it is in the performance, it's not funny at the moment you're delivering it, because you're not making a joke.' You're telling somebody something, either in anger or whatever the emotion is. Like the time Ralph burned himself and said, 'Don't we have any lard around here?' and Alice said, 'About 300 pounds of it.' If you're the character, it isn't funny. It's funny to me, Audrey, but it isn't funny to Alice in the moment she's saying it."

18. How much does butter cost?
19. To what does Norton liken Ralph putting on Jim McKeever's ring?
20. Ralph claims the ring is a "trick" of Norton's. Nobody could get the ring off, Ralph says, including _____.

RALPH: Now I get it. Boy, do I get it. I always knew that Norton was a schemer! What a crumb! Jim McKeever's made foreman, so he plays up to him just like he used to play up to me. Well, it's all over, Alice. Those days are over. He ain't gonna take advantage of me anymore. That fellow living upstairs is one of the lowest creatures on this earth. He just uses his friends for what he can get out of them.
ALICE: What's Norton ever gotten out of you?
RALPH: Plenty. That's what, plenty!
ALICE: Name one thing.
RALPH: I'll name one thing. . . . I'll name one thing. . . . (*Stuck.*)
ALICE: Well?
RALPH: He knew that through me he could get to my wife, who's good at gift wrapping!
ALICE: That's why he posed as your friend?
RALPH: That's right!
ALICE: He sure played it cagey. He waited fourteen years to take advantage of you.

21. Jim McKeever's nickname is:
    A. The Bensonhurst Bomber.
    B. Ol' Muck 'n' Mire.
    C. Twinkles.
    D. Buttercup.
22. How long has Jim McKeever worked in the sewer?
23. Name everything Norton borrowed from the Kramdens for the party.

69

NORTON: Well, this is everything you lent us for the party last night. Let's take a fast inventory. The eight coat hangers—we put them back in the bedroom. Plates, glasses, silverware, tablecloth, bottle of Alka Seltzer, and one chair.

ALICE: Yes, that's everything, Ed.

NORTON: Oh, about the chair, Alice. It's a little wobbly. I don't know what happened, but I'll bring some glue home tomorrow and tighten it up.

ALICE: Don't worry about it. I'm glad your party turned out so well last night.

NORTON: That party, Alice, was the talk of the sewer. But good as it was, it's the last one I throw for a long time.

ALICE: Why?

NORTON: Because no matter how careful you are with the invitations, you make enemies. Now there's a couple of guys, they don't even work in my sewer—they hear about the party and now they're insulted because they weren't invited. I'm telling ya, they act like babies. After all, you can't invite everybody. Now, take Ralph. He's my best friend, lives in the same house. I don't invite him, and does he get sore? Not Ralphy boy. He don't even say a word about it. Alice, you're married to a mature, understanding man.

ALICE (*mystified*): Norton, have you seen Ralph since last night?

NORTON: Nope. Oh, but before I forget, Jim McKeever was saying that he told his wife about the ring and she's real anxious to see it. Do you think it'd be all right if the McKeevers dropped over here on Sunday afternoon and Ralph showed it to her?

ALICE: Well, I don't think it's such a good idea. You know how he felt last night about showing the ring.

NORTON: Yeah. But I promised Jim his wife could see it. After all, it is Jim's ring. Hey, suppose I get Mrs. McKeever to stand on Madison Avenue tomorrow and when Ralph goes by in the bus he can stick his hand outta the window! She'd only get a quick look, but it's better than nothing! With a little luck, she might catch a red light and get a good long look.

When Ralph comes home and sees the broken chair:

RALPH: Look at that!

ALICE: Oh, Ed told me about that. He's going to fix it tomorrow.

RALPH: Fix it, nothing! He's gonna get us a new chair—one exactly like this. I'm not gonna let him get one that don't match, and ruin the beauty of this set! And what's more, he's gonna get it tonight!

ALICE: But Ralph, the junkyards are closed at night. Besides, that chair was about to fall apart when he borrowed it.

RALPH: What proof have you got of that?

ALICE: That's the chair you always sit on! I rest my case!

ALICE: Hello, Ralph.

RALPH: 'Lo.

ALICE: What about the ring?

RALPH: First thing this morning, I go to the head mechanic. I tell him my problem, and he comes up with an idea. He puts my finger in a big vise. He turns the handle until the vise is real tight against the ring. Then, while he keeps it tight, he says I should pull my finger as hard as I can until it's outta the ring. So I pull as hard as I can.

ALICE: In a vise? I hope you didn't try it.

*Ralph takes hand out of pocket and extends pinky, which is well bandaged.*

ALICE: Oh, that's too bad. But at least you got the ring off.

RALPH: It's still under the bandage! My one consolation is, when this ring is off, I'll never have to see that Norton again.

24. Norton wants to bowl with Ralph, but Ralph has a new partner. Who is it?

25. What does Ralph's new friend do for a living?

26. Ralph's new friend and Norton both use water on their jobs. According to Ralph, what's the difference between them?

27. What alley do Ralph and Norton usually bowl on?

28. What does Ralph swear never to do again with Norton?
   A. Play punchball, stickball, and pool.
   B. Shoot golf balls uphill and downhill.
   C. Dance the Hucklebuck.
   D. Go to the Racoon convention.

29. Norton is asked to report to work because there's an emergency in the sewer on:
   A. DeKalb Avenue.
   B. 225th Street.
   C. Himrod Street.
   D. Park Avenue.

ALICE: I'll put the bowl in the bedroom closet. Bring in another chair.

RALPH: Never mind. *Takes punch bowl from Alice.* I can get it up on the shelf without a chair.

*He goes into bedroom. She takes dishes and puts them on sink. Ralph comes out.*

ALICE: Did you push it far enough back on the shelf so it won't fall off?

RALPH (*annoyed*): What do you think?

*Sound of crash as punch bowl falls and breaks into a hundred pieces.*

ALICE: I think you didn't!

*Ralph goes to bedroom, peers inside. Comes back to table.*

RALPH: Norton owes us fifteen dollars for a new punch bowl!

ALICE: Why should he pay for it? You broke it!

RALPH: I knew you'd find some way of blaming me. Yesterday, that punch bowl was up on the shelf in one piece. If Norton hadn't borrowed it, it'd still be there. It wouldn't be broken. It's his fault, and I'll leave it to a thousand judges.

*Alice, brush and pan in hand, looks at him as if he is crazy.*

RALPH: If you think I'm wrong, just tell me. I've got an open mind.

ALICE: Well, you'd better close it before the rest of your brains fall out!

30. Ralph and Teddy Oberman are bowling against:
    A. Trixie and her old lady.
    B. The Bayonne Bunch.
    C. A couple of guys at the alley.
    D. Mr. and Mrs. Manicotti.

31. Ralph tells Teddy Oberman he wouldn't care if Norton was in:
    A. Weehawken.
    B. Africa.
    C. New Zealand.
    D. Tibet.

32. Norton is hurt in an explosion in the sewer. What happens to him, and where is he taken for treatment?

33. Complete this line from Ralph: "What I say about Norton is one thing; _____."

34. What occupational hazard in the sewer has happened to Norton hundreds of times?

35. How does Norton bid his attending physician goodbye?
    A. *Hasta la vista.*
    B. *Gasa mañana.*
    C. *Semper fidelis.*
    D. Rx.

*Teddy Oberman.*
COURTESY
JIM ENGEL.

"Jackie and Art would always ad-lib in character," says Stern. "One time Norton was in the hospital and Ralph comes to give him blood. In the scene where Norton leaves, he wanted to say something to the doctor. We didn't write this, but he said, in character, 'Rx.' I remember standing in the back of the theater and breaking up."

"I did that while we were right on the air; I don't think I even did that in a rehearsal," Carney says of Norton's ad-libbed farewell. "For some reason or other it came to me: What would Norton say, when he was saying goodbye to a doctor, to give the doctor the impression he was in the know? What would he say? Rx! That was a goodbye.

"When Norton said goodbye to a teacher or something, I said 'E plu-ribus unum.' Just to make an impression."

36. Who treats Norton?
37. Who is the doctor attending the patient who occupies the room Norton vacates when he checks out of the hospital?
38. Ralph arrives at the hospital to visit Norton, and in a mix-up thinks Norton needs a transfusion. What is Ralph's blood type, and who is the doctor who gives him a blood test?

Dr. Hyman, one of the physicians at Bushwick Hospital, was played by stage and radio actor John Seymour. He also played butlers in "Opportunity Knocks But" and "Ralph Kramden, Inc." His wife, Abbie Lewis Seymour, made her only appearance in the Classic 39 as the nurse in "Pal O' Mine."

"John was more or less a regular, and because of him I got the part of the nurse," says Abbie. "We had known Jack Hurdle [producer of *The Honey-mooners*] in radio, and he brought quite a few actors to Jackie.

"We rehearsed in the theater where the show was done live. I was ready to rehearse and Jackie walked on, took one look at me, and turned and left. So Jack Hurdle came down and said, 'I'll rehearse with you, Abbie.' So he did, and then he said, 'Abbie, if you want to be in the show, step back and follow the money, and don't wait for a direct cue.'

"So I said yessir, and I thought about it. 'Follow the money.' That would mean Gleason. What he was trying to say was if Jackie changes the business, if I want to be in the show, get as close as possible to Jackie because they photograph Jackie. Follow the money.

"The second thing—don't wait for a direct cue—meant Jackie was not rehearsed, nor would he rehearse. He was going to play the scene without rehearsal. That meant I'd better learn the whole scene, and if Gleason needed help with his lines, I ought to be ready. In other words, don't just learn your speech, Abbie. Get that script and memorize the whole scene. So I did and I was prepared.

"Then we got into our clothes. The set was rolled out and we took our positions. I stepped onto the nurse's platform, which was a roll-in. I was at my position at the desk and Jackie made his entrance. I busied myself at the desk, and I was aware that Jackie had made his entrance. I turned and looked at him, and as I moved close to him, I looked in his eyes and they were the kind of eyes that actors get when they don't know their lines. It's a very special look that comes over their face.

"So I waited for him to speak—the first line was his. I looked at him to see if he was going to say the line, and he definitely was not, so I knew I would not be stepping on his lines and said, 'Yes, may I help you?' And he looked at me with that face and said, 'Ah, a friend, a friend,' because I gave him the key words to his speech.

"Then he gave his speech and started to move, and I had sense enough to follow the money—wherever he went, I went with him, but I made it look natural.

"We finished the scene and it was time for me to leave the desk. I turned to leave and the whole trolley moved. Now, if you watch that episode closely, you'll see it move. It darn near upset me—I almost fell down because I didn't expect the floor to roll."

39. What does Norton forget to take with him when he checks out of his hospital room?
40. When Norton discovers that Ralph was going to donate blood because he thought Norton was seriously hurt, Norton says Ralph is:
    A. A simp.
    B. A mope.
    C. One of nature's noblemen.
    D. One of the hippiest critics he's ever seen.

NORTON: Ralph! Ralphy boy! What's the matter? . . .
RALPH: Norton! What are you doing there? I thought you—
*Doctor and attendant appear from room and take hold of Ralph.*
DOCTOR: Mr. Kramden! We need you now! We must start!
RALPH: But doctor, I thought he. . . .
*As they are getting him back into room, Ralph's speech is interrupted. Door closes on doctor, attendant, and Ralph.*
NORTON: Ralph! Ralph! *Norton turns to nurse desperately.* Nurse! You gotta tell me what's wrong with my pal. Even if it's the worst, you gotta tell me!
NURSE: There's nothing at all wrong with him. He just offered to give a transfusion to a patient who needs it.
*After it sinks in, Norton pauses and speaks reverently.*
NORTON: Nurse, there is the finest human being of all time. And I want you to do me a favor.
NURSE: Certainly.
NORTON: When he's through in there, just tell him his pal, Ed Norton, wants him to keep the ring.
*Norton blows his nose as he heads toward elevator. FADE-OUT.*

41. What does Norton want the doctor to do with Ralph while Ralph is giving blood?

# BROTHER RALPH

November 26, 1955 · Marvin Marx and Walter Stone

1. Ralph puts a suggestion in the bus company's suggestion box. What was his suggestion, and how did the bus company reward him for it?
2. Norton says Ralph eats, drinks, and sleeps buses. "He's even _____ like one."
3. How many bus drivers were laid off by the bus company as a result of Ralph's suggestion?
4. How many years has Ralph driven a bus?
5. How come the mail is always delivered, even in rain, snow, and sleet?
6. True or false: This is the first time Ralph's been laid off at the bus company.
7. Somewhere in the world there is a _____ waiting for Norton.
8. What does Alice want Ralph to stop spending money on while he's not working?
   A. Pool.
   B. Bowling.
   C. Pizza.
   D. Lodge dues.

ALICE (*amazement*): High livin'??

RALPH: That's right. We're gonna have to give up a few luxuries. For instance, you're gonna have to cut out the movies and those Friday-night five hundred rummy games with Trixie.

ALICE (*disappointed*): Oh, gee, Ralph. I don't mind givin' up the movies, but I really love those rummy games with Trixie.

RALPH (*reluctantly*): Well, all right. But cheat a little. We need the money. And there are a few other things we're gonna have to give up, too.

ALICE: Wait a minute, high livin'. I've already given up the movies. What are you givin' up?

RALPH: Well, I'm givin' up . . . uh . . . uh . . . uh . . . uh . . . I'm givin' up the pleasure I get from havin' you out of the house when you go to the movies!

9. How much in bills do the Kramdens owe?

RALPH: Hey, Alice. This is great. The interest is all paid on the icebox. Now we can start workin' off the principal!

10. How much money do the Kramdens have in war bonds, in the bank, hidden around the house, and in their Christmas Club?
11. The Kramdens' savings include _____.
12. Why doesn't Alice know how to handle money?

RALPH: You're supposed to handle the finances in this family. The money is your department. Well, where is it? I'll tell you where it is. You spent it! You're extravagant!

ALICE (*amazed*): I'm what?

RALPH: You heard me . . . you're extravagant! You're always buyin' things you don't need. You're always buyin' useless things.

ALICE: Why should I buy useless things? I've got them already—that stove and sink and that icebox!

RALPH: That ain't what I'm talkin' about, and you know it. You know where you spent the money, Alice—on clothes. Every time we get a little bit ahead you go out and start buyin' clothes. That's all you ever think of—buyin' things for your back!

ALICE (*coldly*): The only thing I ever bought for my back was a mustard plaster.

RALPH: Yeah! That's all you bought was a mustard plaster? I'll show you your mustard plaster.

*Ralph crosses to bureau steamed. As he crosses he waves threatening finger at Alice.*

RALPH: You'll need that mustard plaster for your eye when I get through with you!

*He flings open one long drawer and ruffles up ladies' clothes and underclothes which fill it almost to top.*

RALPH: This is your drawer, Alice. Look at it!

*He then shuts drawer. He then opens another long drawer. He points toward open drawer and speaks.*

RALPH: And this is my drawer! You know what's in there? One pair of my pants!

ALICE: That's all that'll fit in there!

*Ralph's eyes bulge livid-style.*

ALICE: While you're over there, Ralph, why don't you open my drawer again and look at some of the stuff I got. Oh, it's all beautiful. And it's all very modern. I was the first girl in town with a shortie nightgown . . . 'cause I'm still wearin' the one I had when I was a kid!

RALPH: All right, Alice, if you didn't spend the money on clothes, you spent it on something else. Money burns a hole in your pocket. You gotta always be buyin' things. Anytime anybody in this building gets somethin', you want it. Mrs. Manicotti gets somethin', you want it. You know what your trouble is, Alice? You want to keep up with the Joneses. That's all you got on your mind, keepin' up with the Joneses.

ALICE (*laying it in*): The only Jones I keep up with is Spike Jones.

*Alice reaches behind her and pulls washboard out of sink. She quickly runs her finger down it, Spike Jones–style. She then displays it to Ralph.*

ALICE: Isn't it beautiful, Ralph? It's the latest thing. And don't think I'm not grateful. It's a wonderful time-saver. I mean if I didn't have this, you know what I'd have to do? I'd have to run all the way down to the Gowanus Canal and beat the clothes against a rock!

RALPH (*threatening Alice with fist*): I'll beat you against a rock!

13. What's Ralph's salary?
14. Alice wants to get a job during Ralph's layoff. Where did she learn shorthand and typing?

**RALPH:** Don't start that again, Alice. No wife of mine is gonna work. I got my pride. You know, no Kramden woman has ever supported her husband. The Kramden men are the workers in the family.

**ALICE:** Wait a minute, Ralph. What about your father? For a long time there he didn't work at all.

**RALPH** (*proudly*): But neither did my mother. At least he kept his pride, Alice. He went on relief!

15. Alice works and Ralph cooks. What does he make for supper?
16. How many times in a week has Ralph made hot dogs for supper?
17. What does Alice have to do after dinner? Why does it upset Ralph?
18. Who's Tony?
19. Who are the guys at the office where Alice works?
20. True or false: Alice's boss thinks she's single and that Ralph is her brother.
21. Norton has a single cousin who works, and her boss doesn't ask her out. Why?
    A. She looks like the real Karloff.
    B. She wears false faces to work.
    C. She is the ugliest woman who ever lived.
    D. She looks like an orangutan.
22. Ralph wants to discourage Alice's boss from trying to make a date with her, so Ralph tells him Alice is dating:
    A. A wholesale butcher.
    B. The Grand High Exalted Mystic Ruler.
    C. A prizefighter.
    D. Kingfish Lavinsky.

*Tony Amico.* COURTESY JIM ENGEL.

23. Ralph offers to go with Alice and her boss to their office so he can bring her home on the subway when she's finished working. How long will it take them?
24. Alice's boss offers to drive her home after work in his convertible. Ralph: "I'm going with you, _____."
25. Alice wants Ralph to have his head examined, and he's ready to oblige by seeing doctors in the United States and in Vienna. He's even willing to import doctors from _____.
    A. Bayonne.
    B. The moon.
    C. Pluto.
    D. Utica.

ALICE (*plenty steamed*): How could you embarrass me like that? What's the matter, don't you trust me?

RALPH: Oh, I trust you all right. It's just that I don't trust him! I don't trust no man that wears patent leather shoes to work!

26. What will the doctors who examine Ralph's head find in there?
27. Who brings Ralph the good news that his layoff's over?
28. True or false: Ralph's going back to driving the Madison Avenue bus.
29. How long have Ralph and Alice been married? (That is, according to this episode!)

How Audrey got the part of Alice Kramden is one of the great show business stories. One wonders how the course of TV history might have been changed if Audrey hadn't been the plucky young actress she was that fateful day in 1952.

"The story's been told the wrong way a number of times," says Audrey. "The actual story is, Jackie's manager, a man called Bullets Durgom, ran into my manager, Val Irving. Bullets was going crazy because they had just about two weeks before [the Gleason show] went on the air and no one to play Alice. He was talking to Val and Val said, 'I'm on my way to see Audrey. We'll go ask her for suggestions.'

"Now, I'm in a hit show on Broadway, *Top Banana*, and neither one of them thought of me. They told me the problem and I started suggesting names. Every actress I suggested they had seen—or didn't bother to because Gleason would say 'She's too old' or 'She's too straight an actress' or 'She isn't funny.' There was something wrong with everybody, and I was giving them some pretty good names.

"I was racking my brains, and then it came to me—I wasn't that serious about it, but I said, 'We're so dumb. I thought of the perfect person.' They said, 'Who? Who?' 'She's just marvelous,' I said, and kept going on and on.

They said, 'Who?' I said, 'Me!' They said, 'Oh, come on, Audrey.' I said, 'Well, what's wrong with me? He's seen everybody else in New York and Hollywood, and the only one he *hasn't* seen is me. Let me go up and see him.'

"They said okay, and Bullets set it up for the next day.

"*Life* magazine was doing an interview with Jackie, and they held up the interview for a while and I went in with Bullets and Val and chatted a bit. Jackie was very nice, very noncommittal."

But Gleason wasn't so nice to Durgom later. "Jackie called me," Durgom recalls, "and said, 'Are you crazy or something, wasting my time with this girl? She's not Alice—she's too attractive.' He turned her down."

"Now, I was *not really serious* about it . . . until I heard that," Audrey says. "And I was so disappointed. I thought, I would take that from a producer who's not a performer, but not from an actor. This guy should know I can play that. Play it with my eyes closed. It would be very easy. I wouldn't have to worry about a good makeup, or false eyelashes, nothing. So we said goodbye to Bullets and walked out of the Park Sheraton.

"Then I said to Val, 'Listen, they have to make a decision pretty fast. *Top Banana* is going on the road, and I've *been* on the road—I don't want to go. Let's get a photographer who can come first thing in the morning. I won't even get up until you ring the bell. It has to be a photographer who can take the pictures right back and develop them and get the prints to us in the afternoon. We'll send them to Jackie with no name on them.' So Val got hold of Bill Mark to take the pictures."

For better than three decades, Bill Mark has been one of New York's busiest show business photographers. He recalls the photo session that helped dispatch Audrey Meadows from Broadway to Bensonhurst.

"It was about three o'clock in the morning, and we were at Toots Shor's at a party. Val Irving comes over to me and says, 'Bill, I need you seven o'clock tomorrow morning to take some pictures of Audrey.' I said, 'You can't get any pictures of Audrey looking sexy [at 7 AM]. She's got to go to the hairdresser, have makeup, this and that. Push it back to noon.' He says, 'You don't understand. I need these pictures by twelve. I gotta show them to Jackie, and Audrey may end up being Mrs. Ralph Kramden.'"

"When I went back to my apartment that night," Audrey continues, "I thought, What will I wear? I had an old blouse and I tore the sleeve so it hung off a little bit. I got an apron. And I thought, What will I do with my hair? Jackie'd said I was too young, too pretty, so I pulled my hair back with combs, all ratty, and I thought, That doesn't look too bad, especially if I sleep on it. Then I pulled little side pieces down."

"At seven o'clock I was at Audrey's house," Mark recalls. "She lived in a brownstone right across the street from the Stork Club, on Fifty-third Street,

COURTESY PERSONALITY PHOTOS, INC.

off Fifth Avenue. Val was there, Audrey and her sister [Jayne Meadows], and their mother.

"Just when I'm ready to shoot, Audrey's mother would come in and say, 'Audrey! Audrey! You look awful! Let me fix your hair.' And she kept dressing her up. Finally, Jayne—who really had a cold—went to her room, after we made up a signal: As soon as Audrey and I were ready, Jayne would say, 'Mother! Mother!,' and mom would go off to take care of Jayne so I could take a picture of the healthy daughter."

"The next day Val brought me the pictures," recalls Durgom, "and I walked into Jackie's office and said, 'What do you think of this girl?' He looked at the pictures and said, 'That's the girl, that's the look. Who is it?' I said, 'Audrey Meadows.' And he said, 'You're kidding—get her!'"

81

"And that's how come I never had to read the part for him," Audrey says. "Imagine the chance he took. Then I had to get out of *Top Banana*. I figured I had to give them two weeks' notice, but that would have taken me through the Saturday matinee and Saturday night. So I had to get Phil Silvers' permission to get out of the show. I took the pictures of me as Alice to the theater and I told Phil the story.

"I said, 'Phil, what am I going to do? They go on the air Saturday night. What are you going to do about the matinee and evening performances?' He answered, 'That's my problem. Don't you worry about it. I wouldn't stand in your way.' Phil's a real pro and a fine person.

"Well, I was hired, and I went up to Jackie's office each day. I'd get there and they'd say, 'Mr. Gleason left. He had an appointment.' That's when I got to know Art Carney—I'd see him every day. No rehearsal, so we'd go home. Tuesday. Wednesday. Thursday. Now the fright is really building up because he'd never had me read the part for him. He didn't know whether I could do it or not, and I was always a rehearsal-happy kid—and always worked with people who *wanted* to rehearse.

"Friday came, and I went up there. No Gleason. Saturday my call was one or two o'clock in the afternoon. I sat there. We went through it once, without costume, without props. And I said to Art, 'When do we do our next run-through?' He said, 'You just did it.' I said, 'How about the blocking?' He said, 'You just did it.' I said, 'How about dress rehearsal?' He said, 'You just did it.'

"I sat in that theater with my manager beside me and I just looked straight ahead, and the tears started down my face. My manager was saying, 'Don't cry! Don't cry! Your eyes will swell up bright red. You'll be a mess.' I went up to my dressing room, thinking, I don't know what's going to happen with this show.

"I knew my lines. I had learned all of Jackie's and all of Art's as protection—which is what I used to do in summer stock. If you *don't* know the other person's lines and they go blank, it looks like *your* mistake. You're waiting for them to say something.

"In that night's show, Ralph sits down and asks what he's going to get for dinner, and I say steak. It was supposed to be a frozen steak, and he yells and screams about being served a frozen steak. I hadn't seen the steak until I got on the air, and it was just a piece of wood painted to look like a steak. I brought it over to the table, and he grabs it and starts banging it on the table. It broke right in half, and half of it flew off the set.

"He says, 'That's what you're going to serve me, a frozen steak?' I said, 'No, I'm going to serve you *half* a frozen steak.' I went to make my exit to the bedroom, and the door stuck for a minute. I couldn't make the angry exit I wanted to. So I said, 'And how many times have I told you to fix this door!'

*The beautiful Audrey Meadows.*
COURTESY PERSONALITY PHOTOS,
INC.

And just as I said that the door opened. And in the control room they're all looking at each other saying, 'Where's that in the script?'

"As soon as the sketch was over—it was like a fourteen-minute sketch in those days—Gleason had other sketches to do, and a guest singer—I went up to my dressing room and got dressed as fast as I could, and went downstairs and got in a cab. I was home before the show was over, crying the whole way. My sister, Jayne, was there, and I told her I'd never been so nervous in my whole life.

"Then the phone rang and I answered and said, 'Who is it?' He said, 'This is The Greatest.' He always called himself The Greatest. The World's Greatest Comedian. Always had that marvelous, wonderful ego. I said, 'Okay, who is it?'—knowing full well who it was. He said, 'You were very upset earlier tonight. I'm giving a party and I want you to come.' I said, 'No, thank you. I don't need any parties.' I was still in a state of being hurt in a way very strange to describe. A kind of professional hurt. I didn't feel I'd been able to do my very best. I probably did without knowing it.

"He carried on and said, 'No, no, no, you've got to come.' He said everyone was going to be there. I said, 'Okay, I'll come on one condition: I have a new puppy, and I'm going to bring my sister and the new puppy, and the puppy's going to make mistakes all over your rug and you deserve it.'

"But I finally told him, 'As long as you don't want to rehearse, I will call the rehearsals every week. We'll all rehearse and you can come in Saturday and wherever there's a space for you to stand, you fill in there.'

"We've been great, close friends ever since, with a great mutual respect. I love the man."

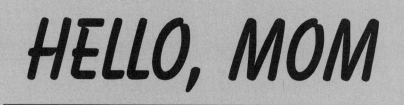

# HELLO, MOM

December 3, 1955 · Marvin Marx and Walter Stone

1. What are the Kramdens having for dinner, where did Alice find the recipe, and whose favorite dish is it?
2. Alice is letting out a pair of Ralph's pants. What does he think she's doing?
3. Where is Ralph going after supper?
   A. The Racoon Lodge.
   B. Bowling.
   C. The pool hall.
   D. Out on the fire escape to spy on Alice.
4. Alice asks Ralph to thread a needle for her. He can't do it but Norton can. How fast does he do it?
5. Norton's doing a crossword puzzle. What does he write as a four-letter word for place of dwelling?
6. What's an eight-letter word for incognito?
7. The Kramdens get a telegram from "Mother," who's coming for a visit. When is she arriving?

"The absence of a telephone was a dictum of Jackie's," says Stern. "He was very fearful that all the plots' exposition would be on the phone if it existed. He was very astute in that observation and realization. It ultimately led to the Honeymooners receiving more telegrams than I think any show or couple conceivably could."

8. Alice's mother once made a "short visit" to the Kramdens'. When did she arrive and when did she leave?

RALPH: Now look, Alice. You call your mother and tell her she ain't comin'. That woman is nothin' but a troublemaker. She never caused me anything but trouble!

ALICE: Just a minute, Ralph. You're forgetting that she's my mother. Remember, she brought me into this world.

RALPH: That's what I mean. She never caused me anything but trouble!

9. Alice's mother is always whining about the things "poor Alice" doesn't have. What are they?
10. Why can't Alice call her mother and tell her not to come for a visit?
11. True or false: Ralph and Alice's mother are natural enemies, like a boa constrictor and a polo pony.
12. What joke did Alice's mother tell everyone at Ralph and Alice's wedding?
13. What three-letter word for insect does Ralph misspell for Norton's crossword puzzle? What's the correct word? Why does Norton go along with Ralph's spelling?

14. Which two of Alice's suitors does her mother always bring up to needle Ralph, and what could each have given Alice had she married one of them?
15. Why did the girls at the beach used to crowd around Ralph?
16. "Out" is a three-letter word for _____.
17. Alice calls the Kramden apartment Disneyland. What three "lands" of Disneyland does she say the Kramdens have, and how does she describe them?
18. What is the one thing missing from Alice's Disneyland, and how does Ralph propose to give it to her?
19. Ralph says he's going to move out if Alice's mother comes for a visit. Where will he go?
    A. Fred's Landing.
    B. Mr. Marshall's.
    C. Fred's gasoline station.
    D. Norton's.

RALPH: Look, Norton. You go to bed. I'll set the cot up. I don't want to be any trouble to you.

NORTON: Don't be silly, Ralph. It'll only take me a second.

RALPH: Please, pal, I insist. I don't wanna be a burden.

NORTON: Well, okay, Ralph.

*Norton steps away from cot and Ralph steps up to it, grabbing it. He tugs at it, trying to pull it apart several times.*

RALPH: Whatsa matter with this thing? It's stuck or somethin'.

NORTON: It ain't stuck, Ralph. I done it hundreds of times. All you gotta do is lift that little bar there and pull.

RALPH: Oh.

*Ralph then lifts locking bar and pulls. Cot opens but catches Ralph's finger as it does and Ralph goes into pain bit. Ralph, holding finger in pain, rants and raves around room doing pain bit. At conclusion of pain bit Ralph wheels on Norton steamed-style.*

RALPH (*steamed*): I thought you said you did it hundreds of times.

NORTON: I did—and that always happens!

RALPH (*controlling self*): Norton, if you weren't in uniform, I'd punch you right in the mouth!

*At this point bedroom door opens and Trixie comes out. She is wearing robe over nightie and her hair is in curlers.*

TRIXIE: What's going on here? Ralph, what are you doing here?

NORTON: He's gonna stay with us a couple of days.

RALPH: Yeah, I had a fight with Alice. Her mother's comin' for a visit.

TRIXIE: Ralph, do you mean that you left Alice just because her mother's coming?

RALPH (*amazed*): Just because her mother's comin'! Don't take this so lightly, Trix. Did you ever get a load of that woman? You remember when they had that picture playin' over at Loew's Pitkin—*The Beast from 20,000 Fathoms*? Well, her mother won a free pass to it in a look-alike contest!

20. Name another Racoon who lives at 328 Chauncey Street.
21. At the lodge meeting, Ralph has an idea to promote international good will. What is it?
22. What spoils attendance at the Racoon Lodge?
23. Name one thing worse than Ralph's mother-in-law coming for a visit.
24. Norton doesn't care for his mother-in-law either. Compared to her coming, _____ would be a boon to mankind.
25. In *Ring* magazine, who's the number two contender for the Marciano title?
26. Is Trixie's mother fat! From the front she looks _____.
27. Norton insults Trixie's mother, so Trixie spends the night with Alice. The next day, what groceries does she pick up for Alice?
    A. Piccalilli and chowchow.
    B. Milk and a pound of margarine.
    C. Celery and onions.
    D. Chicken chow mein and potato pancakes.

TRIXIE: Do you want anything else at the store besides milk, Alice?
ALICE: You better get a pound of margarine, too.
TRIXIE: Okay, Alice.
    *As Trixie starts toward door, it opens and Ralph enters. Ralph is wearing Racoon pants and shirt. Trixie and Ralph exchange glowering glances. Alice notices Ralph and speaks.*
ALICE: Maybe you won't have to get the margarine, Trix. Four hundred pounds of lard just walked in!
RALPH (*steamed*): You have just said the secret word, Alice. You have just won yourself a trip to the moon!

28. If Trixie's mother was a contestant on *The $64,000 Question*, what would her category be?
29. If she ever made it to the last question, who would she have to bring along as an expert?

NORTON: Take my mother-in-law, for instance. Eeeeeee! Trixie's mother's a real beast!
    *Trixie looks at Ed a little on the steamed side.*
NORTON: I mean I don't know what you're complainin' about. Your mother-in-law's a doll compared to mine. At least when your mother-in-law comes

you can introduce her as a member of the family. When mine comes I got to tell everybody we got a new cocker spaniel! Ain't that right, Trix?

*Trixie just glowers at him. Norton, not digging, continues to Ralph.*

NORTON: And what a personality Trixie's mother's got. You think your mother-in-law's mean? My mother-in-law watches *Strike It Rich* just for laughs!

TRIXIE (*steamed*): Just a minute, Ed.

NORTON (*ignoring her, to Ralph*): You know how you said your mother-in-law won the look-alike contest for *The Beast from 20,000 Fathoms*? Trixie's mother played the part.

*Trixie is livid and looks ready to explode. Norton, not digging yet, looks at Trixie and speaks.*

NORTON (*loud aside to Trixie*): I think it's goin' great, Trix. *He looks back to Ralph.* You complain about your mother-in-law. You don't know how great you got it. If you're playin' Twenty Questions with Trixie's mother, believe me, she's all animal. Except one ear . . . that's vegetable. It's cauliflower!

TRIXIE (*exploding steam*): Ed Norton! How dare you talk about my mother like that?!

NORTON (*sotto to Trixie*): Hey, that's good thinkin', Trix. Make Ralph think you're steamed! *Norton turns back to Ralph.* And I ain't makin' this up about Trixie's mother. These are facts! And what a build she's got. *Norton laughs.* Boy, is she fat! From the front she looks like you from the back!

*Norton then turns to Trixie for support.*

NORTON (*to Trixie*): Go ahead, tell him, Trix. Ain't this the truth!

TRIXIE: Ed Norton, I wouldn't stay here with you another minute. I'm packing a suitcase and going down with Alice!

*Trixie turns and storms into bedroom. Norton looks after her perplexed. Then he looks at Ralph bewildered.*

RALPH (*amazed*): What did you do that for?

NORTON: Don't ask me. This whole thing was her idea!

RALPH: Don't you realize what you did? Now she's gonna leave you.

NORTON (*shrugging, also smiles*): Well, at least some good come out of this!

RALPH (*shaking head*): Norton, you could qualify for the bughouse easy.

*At this point there is a knock on the door.*

NORTON: Come in.

*Door opens and male neighbor enters. He is dressed in pajamas and robe, having-been-asleep-style.*

NORTON: Oh, hiya, Fogerty.

FOGERTY (*angrily*): Why don't you guys pipe down in here? You woke up me and the wife. She's gotta go to work in the morning!

RALPH (*annoyed*): Okay, okay.

FOGERTY: What's the beef anyway?

NORTON: Ralph's stayin' up here with me for a couple of days. He had a fight with Alice. His mother-in-law's comin'.

FOGERTY (*knowingly*): Oh.

> *At this point woman appears in doorway. She is dressed in nightgown and robe, with hair akimbo, having-just-gotten-up-style.*

WOMAN: Joe, will you come back to bed? It's two o'clock in the morning.

FOGERTY: Okay. So long, Ralph. And believe me, you got my sympathies.

> *Fogerty starts for door, when his wife stops him by speaking.*

WOMAN (*concerned*): Sympathies about what?

FOGERTY: Ralph's mother-in-law's comin' for a visit. I really feel for you, Ralph. I remember when her mother came.

> *Fogerty shakes his head what-a-blow-that-was-style, and starts heading for door again.*

WOMAN (*dead serious*): What do you mean, you remember when my mother came?

FOGERTY (*nasty*): Well, let's face it, Gladys. Your mother is one person I can do without!

WOMAN (*steamed*): Oh, she is, is she? And just what's wrong with my mother? You never made any cracks about her when she was here.

FOGERTY: How could I? She never shut up long enough for me to get a word in!

WOMAN: How dare you!

FOGERTY (*disgusted*): Come on. Let's go to bed.

> *Fogerty walks out door followed by wife. As wife exits she starts in on him. After wife's first line we hear argument out in hall as Ralph and Norton stand there looking at open doorway.*

WOMAN: Joe Fogerty, how dare you talk about my mother like that!

> *After Fogerty and wife exit, Trixie comes out of bedroom carrying packed suitcase. Without saying a word, she crosses quickly to front door and exits. After she's out door, Ralph crosses to doorway and shouts out after her.*

RALPH (*steamed*): And you can tell Alice, before this is over is she gonna get hers. Boy, is she gonna get hers!

> *Ralph comes in and slams door behind him. Immediately a male voice hollers from offstage.*

MAN'S VOICE: Hey, Kramden. Kramden.

RALPH: Oh, that's that troublemaker Garrity. Probably wants to complain about the noise down here. I'll fix him. *Ralph crosses, steamed, to window, flings it open, looks up and yells.* Whatta you want, Garrity.

MAN'S VOICE (*offstage*): Don't get sore, Kramden. I just wanted to call you and tell you this is one time I'm on your side.

WOMAN'S VOICE (*offstage and angry*): Oh, you are, are you?

> *This is followed by sound of immediate crash offstage, such as flower-vase-over-skull-style. Ralph is still looking upward when we hear man's voice again.*

MAN'S VOICE (*offstage*): Set up another cot. I'll be right down!

> *As Ralph pulls his head in and shuts window, front door opens and Fogerty*

*enters. Norton and Ralph turn and look at him and he speaks controlling-steam-style.*

FOGERTY (*controlling steam*): You guys got room for one more?

NORTON: Sure. Glad to have you aboard. Welcome to Boys Town!

30. What does Ralph want Alice to tell her mother if she asks why Ralph isn't home?
31. Ralph says Alice resembles a famous clown. Who? What part of the clown's outfit or makeup is Alice missing?
32. Whose mother actually visits the Kramdens?
33. Where is Ralph's father?
    A. Away for a couple of days.
    B. At Kelsey's Gym.
    C. On the *Ile de France*.
    D. Visiting Bill Davis in Chicago.

MOTHER: Oh, I didn't realize. . . . I hope I didn't cause any trouble.

*Ralph crosses Fenwick-style to mother.*

RALPH (*Fenwick-style*): Trouble? Don't be silly. How could you cause any trouble, Mamma? Ain't that right, Alice?

*Ralph looks at Alice meekly and wrinkles his nose embarrassed-rabbit-style. Alice just glares at him. Ralph speaks to break tension.*

RALPH: You know my mother, don't you, Alice?

ALICE (*boiling inside*): Hello, Mother Kramden.

RALPH (*Mamma's-boy-style*): Boy, I bet you're tired from your trip, Mamma. If you wanna change or anything, I'll take you in the bedroom.

MOTHER: Thanks, Sonny.

RALPH: Boy, I hope you can stay for a while, Mom.

MOTHER: Thanks, Sonny. You're so considerate. *Then to Alice.* You know, you're lucky to have a boy like Sonny, Alice!

*Ralph just looks weakly at Alice, wrinkling nose again. Ralph then starts walking toward bedroom with suitcase. Mother follows him and as she does she speaks.*

MOTHER: I think you need some of your mother's cookin', Sonny. You've lost a lot of weight!

*They go into bedroom. Alice just holds her position and stands there glaring at bedroom door. After a split Ralph comes out of bedroom. He immediately sees Alice's glare and doesn't know what to say. He goes over to Alice as if to say something, then, digging her attitude, can't find words and starts walking around room doing arm motions trying-to-talk-style, but not knowing where to start. He keeps pacing this way for a few moments with Alice glaring at him. He looks down at table, unable to look her in face. He sees newspaper there and picks it up trying to make conversation.*

COURTESY GLEASON ENTERPRISES.

RALPH (*weakly, trying-to-break-ice-style*): Boy, look at this, Alice. They're building a new superhighway in Tibet!

*Alice just continues to glare and Ralph puts newspaper down weakly. He paces a little while again before speaking. He tries to laugh his way out of it.*

RALPH: My mother, and I thought it was your mother! Funny, ain't it?

*She continues to glare, Ralph paces a little more, and changes tack.*

RALPH: Look, Alice. I know you're steamed. And you got every right to be. Here I am happy to see my mother, but I didn't want your mother to come. If you never talked to me again I wouldn't blame you. Gee, now seein' my mother, I know how you must feel about yours. I had no right. . . .

*Ralph sticks his chin out.*

RALPH: Go ahead and hit me, Alice. I deserve it.

*Alice just looks away from him and at floor.*

RALPH: Go ahead. Hit me. Hit me. I deserve it.

*Alice turns and gives him a quick shot in stomach. He holds his stomach and gives quick howl of pain.*

RALPH: What did you do that for? I didn't think you'd hit me.

ALICE (*smiling*): Oh, Ralph, I love you.

RALPH: Baby, you're the greatest!

*EMBRACE AND KISSVILLE.*

34. Alice asks Ralph to read a letter about mothers-in-law. Who wrote it, and when?

"That letter he read, it's awful," Stone says about Ralph's schmaltzy letter. "Some guy, I forget who he was, brought that in from Toots Shor's. Don't ask me who gave it to him at Toots Shor's.

"It's like that 'What Is a Mother' Jack used to do when he first started. Somebody had this 'What Is a Mother-in-law' thing, so Jackie threw it in. It wasn't our fault. The show was good up until then."

# THE DECIDING VOTE

December 10, 1955 · A. J. Russell and Herbert Finn

NORTON: Hi'ya, Alice. Mrs. Manicotti asked me to give you this. Must be an anniversary present.

ALICE: I wonder what it is. *Alice opens the box. She is pleased and surprised.* Oh, Ed! Ralph's going to like this. It's a his and hers towel set!
*She picks a small towel out of box. "Hers" is written in big letters on towel. She holds it up. Norton reaches into box for the other towel. It is a huge one, many times the size of the other. "His" is written on it. Norton holds it up. He has to stretch his arms out wide to do so.*

NORTON: His!

1. What do the Nortons buy Ralph and Alice for their anniversary, where do they buy it, and how do they pay for it?
2. Alice has a bowl on the kitchen table and Norton tastes what's in it. What does he think he's eating, and what's really in the bowl?
3. Ralph gives Alice an anniversary present he says she's wanted all her life. What is it, where did he buy it, and what did it cost?

RALPH: Keep guessing. You'll never get it, but keep guessing. Go ahead, take another guess.

ALICE: It's a bridge lamp!

RALPH: A bridge lamp! When do we ever play bridge?

NORTON: It's a poker lamp! You play poker!

4. What can Alice do with her new vacuum cleaner?
5. What home furnishings has Ralph been promising to buy Alice?
6. What test does Ralph give the vacuum? When the vacuum fails the test, Norton says the motor needs _____.
7. The vacuum fails a second test, too. What does Norton propose Ralph do?
8. Did the salesman who sold Ralph the vacuum cleaner demonstrate with the one he sold Ralph? What does Alice tell Ralph to do with the vacuum?
9. Norton is always ready with a helping hand or expert analysis. What is his explanation of what's wrong with the vacuum?
10. Who visits Ralph with news that he's going to be elected convention manager at the Racoon Lodge?
11. Who is opposing Ralph in the election?
12. Who in the lodge is eligible to vote for convention manager? Whose votes does Ralph think he's going to get?
13. Where is the Racoon convention being held that year, and what two benefits of being convention manager does Ralph look forward to?
14. Where does Norton go, and with whom, the night of the Kramden's anniversary?

15. Ralph wants to treat Norton to dinner the night of the vote, but Norton isn't around. What did Ralph want to buy him for dinner?

RALPH: Hi, Norton! *He speaks sourly to MacGillicuddy.* Hi, MacGillicuddy. *He turns to Norton again.* Why didn't you come home tonight, old pal? I was waitin' for you. I was gonna blow you to a big Chinese dinner.

MACGILLICUDDY (*belligerently*): Norton had dinner with me! He had steak, right, Norton?

NORTON: That's right! A three-pound steak smothered in mushrooms, mashed potatoes and French fries, corn on the cob, four vegetables, a tossed green salad with Thousand Island dressing. . . .

MACGILLICUDDY: Then he had dessert. Three pieces of mince pie with chocolate fudge on top and two pots of coffee. Then he had dinner mints.

NORTON: Then I had another steak!

RALPH (*to MacGillicuddy*): Boy, are you sneaky! But it ain't gonna do you any good because Norton ain't votin' for you. Are you, Norton?

NORTON (*cold-style*): Brother MacGillicuddy, would you inform this person that me and him ain't no longer on speakin' terms.

RALPH: What's the matter with you, Norton? You're not sore because I threw you outta the house last night, are you? I've thrown you out before! I've thrown you out at least a million times. I throw out all my friends. There was nothin' personal in it!

MACGILLICUDDY: Why don't you leave him alone, Kramden? He don't wanna have nothin' to do with you!

RALPH: That's what you say! Me and Norton've been pals too long to have anything come between us! We've been through thick and thin together. We may have an argument once in a while, but when an emergency comes we're right there to help each other. Am I right, Norton? Remember the time we were playin' baseball and you got hit in the head with a bat? Who took you to the hospital in a cab? I did! Who came to see you every day? I did! Who brought you candy and cigarettes? I did!

NORTON: Who hit me over the head with the bat? You did!

RALPH: That's the trouble with you, Norton. You always remember the bad things. You never remember the good things.

MACGILLICUDDY: You're not kiddin' anybody, Kramden. You're just trying to make up with Norton because you're afraid you won't get his vote.

RALPH (*making it big*): I'm afraid I won't get Norton's vote? Har de har har har! If there's anything I'm sure of, it's Norton's vote. And when you hint that he might not vote for me because we had a little argument, you're saying he's spiteful! You're saying that he's a low, miserable double-crosser. You're saying he's a rat that would stab his best friend in the back! *Ralph turns to Norton.* Norton, I'm surprised at you! How could you have dinner with a guy who says things like that about you!

MacGILLICUDDY: All right, Kramden. Be smart. You'll be singing a different tune when the votes are counted. Am I right, Norton?

*Norton starts a long sneeze.*

NORTON: Ahhhh . . . choo!

MacGILLICUDDY (*very solicitous*): Norton, you sneezed! Do you want an aspirin? Should I get a doctor?

NORTON: No, it's just a little cold I caught workin' in a sewer on Park Avenue. I always catch a cold when I work in a Park Avenue sewer!

RALPH: Why, what's so different about a Park Avenue sewer?

NORTON: It's air-conditioned!

RALPH: It's probably those two-for-a-nickel cigars you're smoking.

*He takes cigar out of Norton's mouth, tosses it aside. He gets one from his pocket, puts it in Norton's mouth.*

RALPH: Here, try a good one!

MacGILLICUDDY: Listen, Kramden, I gave him that cigar, and they ain't two for a nickel.

RALPH: Oh, I beg your pardon. The cigars you buy are three cents straight!

MacGILLICUDDY (*to Norton*): Get rid of that rope!

*He takes the cigar out of Norton's mouth and tosses it aside on the floor. Then, just as Ralph did, he rams another cigar into Norton's mouth.*

RALPH: Oh, no you don't!

*He takes cigar out of Norton's mouth, tosses it aside, gets another one from his pocket and rams it into Norton's mouth.*

RALPH: He's smokin' mine!

MacGILLICUDDY: Oh, yeah?

*MacGillicuddy repeats the bit.*

RALPH: Yeah!

*Ralph repeats the bit.*

MacGILLICUDDY: Oh, yeah?

*He repeats the bit.*

RALPH: Yeah!

*He repeats the bit with a fresh cigar.*

MacGILLICUDDY: Oh, yeah?

*He repeats the bit. Ralph grabs the cigar out of Norton's mouth, tosses it aside.*

RALPH: Yeah!

*Now he starts fumbling through his pocket. He has no more cigars. Mac-Gillicuddy triumphantly opens his jacket. He is wearing a light vest and we can plainly see that all his vest pockets are filled with cigars.*

MacGILLICUDDY: Still wanna play, Kramden?

RALPH: You dirty old—

NORTON: MacGillicuddy, I think I'm ready for that soda pop now.

*MacGillicuddy is worried now. He doesn't want to leave Norton alone with Ralph.*

MACGILLICUDDY: Now? Well, okay, Norton. I'll be right back. *He points to Ralph.* Remember you're mad at him!

*MacGillicuddy goes off in a rush to get back quickly. Ralph looks at the departing MacGillicuddy and shakes his head.*

RALPH: Boy, what a hypocrite! I've seen some hypocrites in my time but he's the hypo-crittiest hypocrite I've ever seen. Now look, Norton, I know you're mad at me. But all I ask is that you listen to me for one minute. Will you listen?

NORTON: All right, Ralph, go ahead.

RALPH: As you well know, I ain't the kind to butter you up.

NORTON (*lifts up cigar*): Match, please.

RALPH: Oh, yeah! Sure! *Ralph quickly gets a match from his pocket, lights Norton's cigar.* Like I was sayin', I ain't the kind to butter you up.

NORTON: Excuse me. Would you get a pillow for my back?

RALPH: Sure thing, pal.

*Ralph goes to chair, gets pillow, returns to couch and places it under Norton's back.*

RALPH: Comfortable now? If you ain't, I'll get you another pillow.

NORTON: No, I think this'll do.

RALPH: Now let's see . . . where was I?

NORTON: You were sayin' that you're not the kind to butter a guy up.

RALPH: Oh, yeah. I ain't the kind to butter you up.

NORTON: On second thought, maybe I would be more comfortable with another pillow.

*Ralph controls his temper, goes to chair, gets another pillow, returns and places it under Norton's back.*

NORTON: A little more to the left. *Ralph starts to move pillow.* Too far—a little to the right.

RALPH: Look, I can get you another pillow. You sure you wouldn't be more comfortable with three pillows?

*Norton squirms comfortably into pillow.*

NORTON: No, I think two are enough.

RALPH: Okay! Now, like I was sayin'—

*Norton holds up his cigar again.*

NORTON: My cigar went out!

*With monumental patience Ralph takes out his matches and lights the cigar. Then he starts to speak again as Norton puffs contentedly at his cigar.*

RALPH: Norton, I'm gonna level with ya. Sure, I want your vote. But I ain't askin' you to vote for me because we've been very close friends for thirteen years. I want you to vote for me on my own merits. The man who becomes convention manager is gotta be intelligent. He's gotta be capable. He's gotta be a good organizer. You can't just elect anybody to the job. You gotta elect the right man. And I don't mind sayin' that I'm the only guy in this club who could handle such an important job. That's why I'm askin' you to vote for me. Because I'm the best man. Now you just think it over a minute and give me your answer.

*Norton chews reflectively on his cigar, then takes it out of his mouth and studies it as he speaks.*

NORTON: Ralph, I've been thinkin' over what you said, and I come to the conclusion that you're right.

RALPH: I am?

NORTON: Yeah. I would be more comfortable with another pillow!

RALPH (*steamed*): You want another pillow? You want another pillow? Here! Here's another pillow!

*Ralph pulls pillow out from behind Norton's back and hits him with it several times before Norton gets off the couch and away from him.*

NORTON: Just as I thought! You're insincere, Ralph. You'll never be no different. A leopard can't change its spots!

RALPH: I'll give ya spots, Norton. I'll give ya spots. I'll give ya spots all over!

*Norton starts to back away from him. MacGillicuddy comes dashing in with a bottle of Coke.*

MACGILLICUDDY: Here's your soda pop, Norton. I had to run all the way down to Kosciuszko Street for it.

*Norton takes the Coke and hides behind MacGillicuddy, as Ralph advances toward him.*

NORTON: Thanks, MacGillicuddy! You are a true friend!

16. What does Norton eat that evening, and whom does he eat with?
17. Norton sneezes; he thinks he must be catching a cold. Why?
18. MacGillicuddy runs to get Norton:
    A. A tissue.
    B. An aspirin.
    C. A glass of water.
    D. A hero sandwich.
19. Ralph is upset by MacGillicuddy's attentiveness to Norton. He says "I've seen some hypocrites in my day, but he is _____."
20. Norton once got hit in the head with a bat while playing softball. Who got a cab and took him to the hospital; who visited him every day; who brought him cigarettes and candy; who hit him with the bat?
21. What office does Norton hold in the lodge?

PRESIDENT: Brother Racoons, you all know why we're here—to elect this year's convention manager. I can't tell you how important it is to elect the right man. Don't vote for anybody just because he's popular. You all remember what happened last year. The convention manager you elected took the club money and eloped to Chicago!

*At this point Ralph jumps up.*

RALPH: Mr. President, I'd like to remind the members that I'm a happily married man. In fact, next Saturday is our anniversary. I even bought Alice a vacuum cleaner!

PRESIDENT: All right, Kramden.

*Ralph sits down, then jumps up again.*

RALPH: I would also like to remind the members that Frank MacGillicuddy is a very popular bachelor!

PRESIDENT: Kramden, will you please sit down!

22. Who is the last Racoon to vote?

*All the members are quickly writing down their vote and folding the paper, Ralph included. Norton collects all the ballots, places them on desk before president.*

PRESIDENT: All right, Brother Norton. Now fill in your ballot.

*Norton sits upstage side of desk, ballot before him. He goes through warming-up-the-old-soup-bone routine as everyone waits impatiently. Finally Ralph explodes.*

"That hand business—before signing something—I got from my father," Carney says. "One day in rehearsal, Gleason asked me to sign something. This was in New York, years ago. And from out of the blue, I thought of my father, who had passed on a number of years before.

"Whenever I'd bring home my report card for him to sign, he would start to sign it, and he'd take forever. My father was very, very neat, and a lint-picker. And all I wanted him to do was sign the report card and let me get back to school, because the marks were not too good.

"And I thought of him, with the big fat Waterman pen and everything. He must have said, 'Do this.'

"Gleason said, 'What the hell are you doing?' And I said, 'I'm just warming up the old soup bone.' And that became a business. That, and the thing with the handkerchief."

RALPH: Will you hurry up!

NORTON: All right, all right!

*Norton, shielding the ballot from all eyes with his cupped hand, writes something. Then he erases it and writes again. Then he again erases and writes again. Then he folds it very deliberately and hands it to the president. The president lets out a sigh of relief.*

"That was typical kid stuff," says Carney. "Norton was like a kid. Anything to make Kramden irritated."

23. Which Racoons are in arrears in their dues the night of the vote?
24. Who wins the election for convention manager?
25. How do the Racoons celebrate the election?
26. Ralph gets a letter of reference for Norton from Morgan's, the furniture store. There are three questions in the letter. What are they, and how does Ralph answer each one?
27. Trixie wants to borrow something for Norton. What?

NORTON'S VOICE (*offstage*): Hey, how about sendin' some water up here!
*Ralph sticks his head out the window and shouts.*
RALPH: Stay dirty!
*He sticks his head in again and stands in front of sink so Alice can't turn off water.*
ALICE: Ralph, you're making a fool of yourself. You're acting like a five-year-old!
RALPH: Yeah? Well this five-year-old is gonna teach that two-year-old that he can't double-cross me.
ALICE: Oh, you're beautiful, Ralph. Just beautiful! A minute ago you said you were going to forgive and forget. You said you weren't going to be bitter. You said you weren't going to carry a grudge against Norton. That's what you said a minute ago!
RALPH: Sure, but a minute ago I had no way of gettin' back at him!

28. Alice tells Ralph that Norton voted for him. Ralph accuses Alice of being gullible: "You're the type that would bend way over to pick up a pocketbook on April Fool's Day. I wouldn't," he tells her. "_____," she tells him.
29. Who was supposed to vote for Ralph and didn't, and why not?

# SOMETHING FISHY

December 17, 1955 · Leonard Stern and Sydney Zelinka

1. Ralph and Norton are playing Ping-Pong at the lodge. What's the score, and what are the stakes?
2. How many Ping-Pong balls have they lost?
3. All Racoons are brothers under the _____.
4. Why is Ping-Pong the only game played in the sewer?
5. True or false: Last month Ralph volunteered to spearhead the Racoons' old-clothes drive.
6. Which Racoons are behind in their dues?
7. How many new members are the Racoons trying to recruit?
8. What happened during last year's Racoon membership drive?
   A. Frank Brady left and joined the Elks.
   B. Anthony Eden joined.
   C. They lost three of the old members.
   D. Stanley Saxon got married.
9. What are the requirements for becoming a Racoon, and where are they found in the Racoons' rules and bylaws?
10. Who couldn't become a Racoon because of the lodge's residency requirement?
11. Which of the Racoons works at a brewery?
    A. Cassidy.
    B. Andrews.
    C. Dribbin.
    D. Muldoon.
12. What does Dribbin do for a living?
13. What day of the week are the Racoons going fishing?
14. As with last year's fishing trip, _____ will bring the beer and _____ will bring the knockwurst.


PRESIDENT: For the past five years, we have had a trophy for the member who catches the biggest fish. But this year, the trophy will be given to the member who catches a fish!
   *Another cheer of approval.*
PRESIDENT: I'm glad to report that, like last year, Brother Muldoon is bringing the beer, and Brother Havemeyer is supplying the knockwurst.
   *Ralph raises hand.*
RALPH: Point of information. Is Brother Norton supplying the worms again?
NORTON: That is my intention.
   *Ralph ignores Norton, speaks to president.*
RALPH: And is he supplying the potato salad again?
NORTON: I certainly am.
RALPH: I make a motion that this year he packs them separately!

ANDREWS: Second the motion!

*An enthusiastic wahoo from the members. President raps gavel.*

PRESIDENT: Motion is passed.

15. How many Racoons vote not to bring their wives fishing, and how many years have they taken the same vote?
16. Every time the Racoons say yes to their wives, Ralph says they're saying no to their _____.
17. What do the Racoons do as a declaration of independence from their wives?
    A. Drink grape juice.
    B. Dance to Spade Cooley records.
    C. Play poker.
    D. Shoot pool.
18. Who pays for the beer and pretzels at the Racoons' celebration?
19. If Ralph was _____ pounds lighter, the Racoons would have carried him out of their meeting on their shoulders.
20. Why doesn't Ralph stick around to play poker?
21. What do fishing trips and Turkish baths have in common?
22. Ralph to Alice: "I _____ the fish, you _____ the fish. The only time we're together is when we _____ the fish."
23. Whose car does Ralph borrow to drive to the pier, and what time are the Racoons meeting at Ralph's for a ride?

Joe Ruskin had a nonspeaking part as one of the Racoons in "Something Fishy." He was recommended for the part by Joan Reichman Canale, the show's production assistant. Canale and Ruskin were friends, but, says Ruskin, "Joan threatened to thrash me to within an inch of my life if I broke up. My mouth was raw by the end of rehearsal.

"I never understood why they didn't hire actors for that show. They'd hire vaudevillians. I found out the reason was that they needed people to be able to work without everybody laughing all over the place.

"The day I was there was marvelous. I'd had a script all week, and what I saw going on in rehearsal was the story line, but there weren't any of the lines that I read in the script. When they did it on the air, it pretty much held to what they had done in rehearsal, and not what was written."

"It was very compelling for us to watch the rehearsal and then the real show, because during the rehearsal Gleason and Carney were doing all sorts of wacky things," says George Silano, an assistant cameraman for *The Honeymooners*. "Then when we did the show, we wondered what they were going to do.

"It was amazing to me to see a guy like Gleason come in and be able to do this thing 'high diving,' because he really didn't do much in the afternoon. But at night he would be able to hit his marks and do the lines."

"I would see the other cameramen laughing off to the side, and the tears would be coming down their faces at the things we didn't know were going to happen," adds Ken Geiman, one of the three *Honeymooners* cameramen. If you listen to the shows, you'll hear a lot of our laughter in the background."

"In the run-through, if Jackie had a great joke he would never read it," says Arthur Forrest, the stage-right cameraman. He would say, 'Blah, blah . . .' because he didn't want us to hear some of the funny lines he was doing. So when it came time for the show, we were laughing along with the audience. We enjoyed it as much as they did."

24. True or false: Norton was going to tell Trixie she couldn't go on the fishing trip, but he chickened out because she was standing too close to the pots and pans.
25. Where are the Racoons distributing mimeographed copies of Ralph's emancipation speech?
26. Alice buys new gear for the fishing trip. How did she get the money to buy it?
27. Alice and Trixie are going to be ready to go fishing at 6 AM. What time do Ralph and Norton plan to sneak out without them?
28. What time do you have to get up to put one over on Ralph?
29. What's in the bag Norton puts in Ralph's icebox?
30. Ralph can't start the car. What does Alice use to start it?

COURTESY
GLEASON
ENTERPRISES.

# 'TWAS THE NIGHT BEFORE CHRISTMAS

December 24, 1955 · Marvin Marx and Walter Stone

1. Alice wants to hide Ralph's Christmas gift. In what two places does she almost hide it before finally putting it under the icebox?
2. What Christmas decoration is on the Kramdens' door?
3. When do the Nortons and the Kramdens give their Christmas gifts to one another?
4. What does Norton give Trixie for Christmas?
5. Where does Ralph hide Alice's Christmas gift?
   A. In the stove.
   B. In the bureau drawer.
   C. In the closet, behind the hatbox.
   D. Under the icebox, behind the drip pan.

In the filmed episode, when Alice wants to see if Ralph's going to sneak a peek at his present, she tells Ralph she's going up to Trixie's and then hides next to the bedroom door. In the script, while Ralph is supposed to be washing his hands in the bathroom, Alice slams the door as if she's gone out, and stands in front of the icebox:

*After a split, bedroom door opens, and Ralph sticks his head out. He does not look straight ahead toward the icebox, but has his head cocked sideways and is looking toward the front door to make sure Alice does not come back and catch him. He starts crossing toward icebox tippy-toe-style in Indian fashion. He crosses room in this manner until he is almost at icebox. Just as he is a few feet from icebox he turns his head and glances toward icebox. On seeing Alice, Ralph, without missing a beat, breaking stride, or doing a big reaction, and still in tippy-toe-style, veers to the left toward the sink. He quickly picks up bar of soap out of sink. He then turns and starts back in the same Indian fashion, tippy-toe-style. As he passes Alice, still not missing a beat and not stopping his tippy-toe walk, he holds up bar of soap and speaks as he does so in passing.*

RALPH: I forgot the soap!

*He then continues on his way tippy-toe-style and Alice lets him get to center stage before she speaks.*

ALICE: All right! Hold it, twinkletoes!

6. Where does Alice hide Ralph's present after she moves it from its original hiding place, and what booby trap does she set for Ralph?
7. What do Ralph and Norton give each other for Christmas?

NORTON: Hey, I see you're trimmin' the tree there.
RALPH: That's right.
NORTON: I just finished trimmin' our tree. I did it a little different this year. I

didn't use no bulbs or ornaments or nothin' like that. I got a lot of them little candles, and I fixed them on the tree and I lit 'em.

RALPH (*looks at him a little amazed*): You put candles on the tree and you lit 'em. Well, ain't that a little dangerous? It might catch fire.

NORTON: So what if it does . . . the tree only cost us a buck and a half!

RALPH: Norton, during the holiday season, don't get too close to any nutcrackers, 'cause somebody might nail you!

8. Norton's gift to Ralph didn't come from his heart; it came from the _____.

9. Norton finds something in the Kramden kitchen and mistakes it for Ralph's present for Alice. He finds:
    A. A vacuum cleaner from Dowser's.
    B. A dictaphone.
    C. A kitchen thermometer.
    D. A drip pan.
10. What does Ralph buy Alice for Christmas?
11. Where was Ralph's gift to Alice made, and who was supposed to have originally owned it?
    A. Japan; the Emperor of Japan.
    B. Bayonne; the Bayonne Bunch.
    C. Utica; Uncle Leo.
    D. Fred's gasoline station; Fred.

Ralph tells Norton that the box he bought Alice for Christmas was smuggled into the United States; what he didn't add, from the script, was that it was smuggled into the country by Adolphe Menjou's houseboy! And later, when Norton's trying to convince Ralph not to wait until Christmas morning to give Alice the box, he says, "Tomorrow may be too late. The emperor may have spies on the trail of this thing right now. I never did believe that Shirley Yamaguchi came over here just to be in the movies."

12. Who does Norton think is on the trail of Ralph's gift for Alice?
13. Who stops by to give Alice a present, and where is she headed?
14. What gifts do she and Alice exchange?
15. Where did the neighbor buy the present she gives Alice?

One of Norton's endearing qualities is his innocence; sometimes, though, he's downright naive. It never crosses his mind that Ralph's present for Alice didn't come from the Emperor of Japan's house after all. And one never suspects Norton of malice when he's trying to console Ralph about something and ends up delivering a zinger to his pride:

RALPH: Don't you understand, Norton? I was cheated. That never came from the emperor's palace. I know that now. That guy just made up that story to sell it to me. I was cheated.

NORTON: Well, why don't you just tell Alice that?

RALPH: Oh, sure. That'd be just great. Then not only won't her gift be a big surprise, but she'll find out her husband is an idiot.

NORTON: Yeah. It won't be much of a day for her. That ain't gonna be no surprise to her either!

16. It's Christmas Eve and Ralph is grouchy and depressed. Norton: "Compared to you, _____ was a holiday playboy."

"I remember one Christmas show where we were decorating the tree, and I had some tinsel," Carney says. "I went like that," he says, mimicking Norton's patented behind-the-back toss, "and the tinsel landed right on the top. Just perfect, like there was a magnet up there. Lucky."

17. Ralph had some money stashed away, but instead of spending it on Alice he spent it on himself. How much did he have, and what did he buy?

NORTON: Wait a minute, Ralph. Maybe that's your answer. Why don't you give Alice the bowling ball for Christmas?

RALPH: What would Alice want with a bowling ball? She don't bowl.

NORTON: Don't tell her it's a bowling ball. Tell her it's something else. *Ralph looks at Norton bewildered-style.* Well, like for instance, you know them things women use when they're darnin' socks. You know, them little round pieces of wood they put inside the sock when they're mendin' them?

RALPH (*bewildered*): Yeah?

NORTON: Well, you could tell her the bowlin' ball is for when she's mendin' your pants!

RALPH: You know, Norton, when they mended your head, they put a block of wood in there, and they forgot to take it out!

18. What does Norton want Ralph to do with a "do not open until Christmas" label?

19. Whose relative visits the Kramdens, and what does he bring them?

Somewhere between Marvin Marx's typewriter and the stage, Alice's uncle's name changed from Matt to Leo. His scene was also shortened from this: Uncle Matt has just handed Ralph a gift certificate, but before he goes he wants to wash his hands because on his way to the Kramdens' he had to

*Uncle Leo.*
COURTESY HOWARD BENDER.
COPYRIGHT © 1985
HOWARD BENDER.

change a flat tire. While he's in the bathroom, Ralph gets the bright idea to use the gift certificate to buy Alice another present:

RALPH: Wait a minute, I just thought of something. We got to get Uncle Matt out of here before Alice gets back. If she sees him here, I'm dead. And we got to work fast. Alice is liable to be back any minute.
NORTON: Hey, I got an idea how we can get rid of him, Ralph. I'll go out in the hall and start yelling, Fire! Fire!
RALPH: What about all the other people in the buildin'?
NORTON (*hesitating*): Well, uh, then I'll just yell, Fire, Uncle Matt!

Uncle Matt finally comes out of the bathroom, and Ralph tries to give him the bum's rush:

UNCLE: Well, I wasn't goin' yet. I was going to wait and see Alice.

RALPH (*panicky*): Alice!? Ah, bah, ah, but, ah, Alice may not be back for hours.

UNCLE (*bewildered*): But you said she just went out to the store.

RALPH (*flustered*): I did? Ah, yeah, but she went to a store way up in the Bronx!

NORTON: No, she didn't, Ralph. She just went across the street to Krauss's Delicatessen! *Ralph gives Norton a shot with elbow. Norton, exaggerated-style, then digs.* Oh! Oh! Oh! Yeah! Up in the Bronx!
*Norton now gives Ralph large wink, I'm-in-on-it-style, holding hand up to shield wink from Uncle Matt. Ralph gives ceilingward glance, then picks it up again.*

RALPH (*covering*): Ah, yes, you see, first she went to Krauss's and then she went up to the Bronx. You know Alice, Uncle Matt, she's always tryin' to save money. She heard they had chuck roast up there for twenty-nine cents a pound!

NORTON (*helpful*): Yeah . . . chuck roast!

RALPH: I'll tell you what, Uncle Matt. If you leave now and start drivin' up that way, you'll probably bump into her on her way back.

UNCLE: But I'll be in my car . . . she'll be in the subway.

RALPH: No, she won't. I told you how she's always savin' money. She's probably walkin'.

UNCLE (*bewildered*): From the Bronx!?

20. Which neighbor of the Kramdens is home from the navy for Christmas?
21. What is Ralph's scheme to buy Alice a second Christmas gift, and how much money does he think he can raise?

RALPH: I'm goin' out and pawn the bowlin' ball while there's still time. Then I'll get enough money to buy Alice's present. Why didn't I think of this before? You know, Norton, this is gonna be a merry Christmas after all. And you know that sayin' about Christmas? It's absolutely right . . . it's much better to give than to receive.

NORTON: How true, Ralph. And you know there's another old sayin' about Christmas that my grandfather used to say that fits this situation: You can lead a horse to water but you can't make him drink.
*Ralph nods his head in agreement and starts toward the door when he suddenly stops and thinks saying over.*

RALPH: What has leading a horse to water got to do with Christmas?
*Norton thinks it over for a moment and then speaks.*

NORTON: All right . . . then make it a reindeer!

22. What does Alice's mother give Ralph for Christmas?
23. What do Ralph and Alice give each other for Christmas?

# THE MAN FROM SPACE

December 31, 1955 · A. J. Russell and Herbert Finn

1. Ralph is meeting Norton for lunch. He yells into the sewer for Norton to come up. When Norton pops out of the manhole in full sewer regalia, he gives Ralph a fright. Norton asks him who he expected to come out of the sewer:
   A. The man from space.
   B. Captain Video.
   C. Uncle Leo.
   D. The man in the gray flannel suit.

In Russell and Finn's original script, the episode begins this way:

RALPH: Norton. . . . Hey, Norton!

SEWER WORKER (*butler-style*): Yes? . . . Who do you wish to see?

RALPH: Norton. Ed Norton.

SEWER WORKER: Do you have an appointment?

RALPH (*amazed*): Appointment? No!

SEWER WORKER: Who shall I say is calling?

RALPH: Kramden! Ralph Kramden!

SEWER WORKER: Wait here. I'll see if he's in.

*The sewer worker ducks down behind the shield. Ralph, alone for a split, reacts to what just happened. Then Norton appears and comes out to meet Ralph.*

NORTON: Hi'ya Ralph!

RALPH: Hey, what's goin' on? You guys in the sewer are gettin' pretty hoity-toity!

NORTON: We have to, Ralph. It's the only way we can keep out the riffraff!

2. Why doesn't Norton have his lunch, and where does he think it is?
3. Ralph offers Norton his lunch. When that happens, it means one of two things: _____.
4. What has Ralph brought for lunch?
5. What is the first prize at the Racoon Lodge's costume ball?
6. What costumes do Cassidy and Reilly usually wear to the ball?
7. Who is Reilly dressing as for the party this year?
   A. Brutus.
   B. Marc Antony.
   C. Julius Caesar.
   D. Cleopatra.
8. How much money does Ralph want to borrow from Norton, and what does he want to do with it?
9. Why does Norton think Ralph's a genius?
10. Norton's costume is in a package in the sewer. Who tosses it up to him?

11. Ralph begrudgingly gives Norton credit for having an original idea. What's the idea?

Ralph accuses Norton of stealing his idea to rent a costume to wear to the Racoon Lodge's annual costume party, and declares war between himself and Norton. The scene ends like this:

**SEWER WORKER:** What's goin' on, Norton?
**NORTON:** You're just in time, Flaherty! Kindly show this gentleman to the curb. And the next time he calls, tell him I'm not in!

This is how Russell and Finn wrote the beginning of scene two, back at the Kramdens':

**ALICE** (*singing "I Got Plenty of Nuttin'"*): Hi, Ralph.
*Ralph turns his head dramatically away from her. Alice is confused.*
**ALICE:** Ralph, is something the matter?
*He does not answer. Now Alice is concerned. She goes to him, puts her hand on his arm.*
**ALICE:** Ralph, darling, is something the mattter?
*He draws dramatically away from her.*
**RALPH:** Don't touch me!
**ALICE** (*quietly*): All right, Ralph.
*She goes back to table to set the knives and forks, paying no attention to him. Ralph remains silent in a dramatic pose for several beats.*
**RALPH** (*suddenly shouting*): I'll tell you what's the matter! I'm ashamed, Alice! I'm embarrassed! Of all the guys down at the bus depot, I'm the only one that never has any money at the end of the week. Take tonight, for instance. Joe McCloskey had twenty bucks! Pete Crowley had thirty-five bucks. And Frank Willis had even more than that! Of all the bus drivers, I'm the only one that ain't got a dime!
**ALICE:** Well, don't feel too bad, Ralph. You're the only bus driver that's got a uranium mine in Asbury Park!
**RALPH:** Don't get cute, Alice! Don't get cute because I ain't in the mood. I need ten bucks, and you're gonna give it to me! Every time I ask you for money you say no. No, no, no!
**ALICE:** That's right.
**RALPH:** But this time before you say no, I'm gonna tell you somethin'. I work hard for my money. I'm the man of the house, and I got a right to enjoy what I make. And at the moment, I'm after a little enjoyment!
**ALICE:** Now can I say no?
**RALPH:** I ain't through yet!
**ALICE:** Sorry. I'll wait till you're finished!

RALPH: Get ready for the takeoff, Alice! You're goin' to the moon!

ALICE: Ralph, what do you need ten dollars for? What crazy scheme have you got in mind now?

RALPH: It ain't no crazy scheme! I need the money to rent a costume for the party tomorrow night!

ALICE: Rent a costume? I thought you were going to do what you did last year—wear a torn undershirt, talk out of the side of your mouth and go as Marlon Brando!

12. What are Ralph's first and second choices for costumes for the party, and what will each cost to rent?
13. What piece of "costuming" does Alice offer Ralph?
14. Why doesn't Ralph use his brains to make a costume?
15. Who does Norton plan to go as to the party?
16. What is the English translation of the immortal words of Pierre François de la Briosche?

Norton's gaudy costume is totally unlike what one would expect from a man who works, bowls, and eats in a hat, T-shirt, and vest. Here's how Russell and Finn describe Norton's outfit as he models it for the Kramdens for the first time:

*He is dressed in the costume of a court dandy, Louis-the-XIV-style, with satin breeches, silk stockings, buckled shoes, silk waistcoat, frilly jabot. On his head is a powdered wig, and on his cheek is painted a mole. At his side is buckled a rapier-type sword. A lorgnette is fastened to a chain which hangs around his neck.*

Russell and Finn were equally imaginative in their construction of Ralph's man-from-space getup:

*It consists of a saucepan which he is using as a hat, the handle protruding from the back of the neck. On top of the saucepan is a light bulb which is going on and off. The icebox door is strapped around his neck and chest like a shield. It is studded with knobs he took off bureau and three small flashlight bulbs, which also keep going on and off. Also on the icebox door is the kitchen faucet, which is attached up high with the spout facing Ralph's chin. Beneath all this paraphernalia he wears a sweatshirt with a turtleneck collar. For pants he wears the bottoms of a pair of striped pajamas. These are tucked into shin-high galoshes. On his hands he wears a pair of thick gardening gloves. In his right hand he carries a homemade ray gun, which consists of a funnel attached to the handle of a compass saw. Over his eyes he has a huge pair of dark goggles. Ralph has a wide motorcycle rider's belt around his waist, from which flares a knee-length tunic made out of plastic shower curtain.*

17. Alice wonders out loud what kind of costume Ralph could be making with the icebox door. Norton's stymied, too. He says that if Ralph took the whole icebox he could go as a _____.

18. Ralph decides he'd rather wait a couple of hours to eat than sit at the same table with Norton. Norton says if Ralph doesn't eat it'll be tough on:
    A. The farmers.
    B. Freitag's.
    C. Krauss's.
    D. Kraussmeyer's.

19. What does Ralph want for his costume that he can't find in the bureau?

20. Name four things Ralph takes from the kitchen for his costume.

21. Ralph says his costume is going to make Norton's look like a piece of:
    A. French bread.
    B. French cheesecloth.
    C. French toast.
    D. French cheesecake.

In the original script, this scene ends with Ralph and Norton dueling:

*Ralph goes to spot near sink, gets a broom. Holding the handle baseball-bat-style, he advances on Norton, swinging wildly. Norton evades his wild swings, meantime nimbly darting about and making playful thrusts with his sword at Ralph. DISSOLVE. END OF ACT ONE.*

22. Why can't Alice wash up in the sink, play the radio, or open the window?

RALPH: Now look, Alice! I worked for two days on this costume! You certainly ought to have something to say about it! Now say it!

ALICE: Are you AC or DC?

RALPH: Never mind the cracks, Alice! Just tell me—do you like it or don't ya?

ALICE: Well . . . it certainly is original.

RALPH: You bet it's original! And it didn't cost me a cent either! I only used things we had around the house!

ALICE: Yes. Just think what you could have done if we had a furnished apartment!

23. What part of Ralph's costume falls off as he's modeling it for Alice?
24. Alice isn't up on current events because she doesn't read:
    A. The papers and comic books.
    B. *Universal* magazine.
    C. *American Weekly.*
    D. The civil service newspaper.

Between the time Ralph models his costume for Alice and the time Norton comes downstairs, sees Ralph, and thinks Brooklyn's being "invaded" by Sherman tanks was a scene that was dropped from the script before the episode was staged. As usual, Ralph's scheming: This time he's conspiring with Hap from the poolroom to ensure that Norton doesn't enter the costume contest. And to make matters worse, just before Hap shows up, Ralph denies to Alice that he's planning anything sneaky:

ALICE: I wish you luck. But don't be too confident. Norton looked pretty cute in that outfit!

RALPH: He looked cute! Look, Alice, if there's one thing I'm sure of, it's that Norton ain't gonna win. I'm takin' care of that!

ALICE (*suspiciously*): What do you mean 'you're taking care of that'?

RALPH: Huh? Nothin'. Nothin' at all!

ALICE: Ralph, you wouldn't do something underhanded, would you?

RALPH: Whattaya mean, underhanded?

ALICE: You know what I mean—like hiding Norton's costume or something!

RALPH (*phony-hurt-style*): Alice, that's an awful thing to say! How could you think such a thing of me? I admit that I've done some mean things in my time—but I wouldn't stoop that low! I wouldn't do anything to harm Norton—the best friend I have in the world!

ALICE (*contritely*): I'm sorry, Ralph.

RALPH: No, no, no, Alice! Just sayin' you're sorry ain't enough. You really hurt me this time. What you just said shows that you really don't know me! You've been married to me for fourteen years and you really don't know me!

ALICE: Ralph, I really am sorry. *She kisses him on cheek.* Please forgive me.

RALPH (*small macaroni*): Okay, hon.

ALICE: I've got to hurry and get into my costume!

> *Alice exits into bedroom. As soon as she is out there is a knock on the door. Ralph opens it. Hap from the poolroom enters. Ralph grabs his arm and pulls him inside.*

HAP: What'd ya want me for, Ralph?

RALPH: Hap, we gotta get rid of Norton!

HAP (*bewildered*): What's the matter with you, Ralph? Whattaya doin' in that crazy getup?

RALPH: I'm goin' to a costume party. A costume party at which Mr. Ed Norton must not appear! And you're gonna see to it that he don't!

HAP: Wait a minute, Ralph. I ain't goin' in for kidnapping. A thing like that could hurt my business at the poolroom!

RALPH: It ain't nothin' like that! Here's what I want you to do. Go down to the drugstore and call Norton's apartment. Say you're the foreman at the sewer. Say there's an emergency at the 225th Street sewer in the East Bronx. Say that Norton's gotta get there right away! If he don't show up, he's gonna lose his job!

HAP: Ralph, I can't get away with that. Norton'll recognize my voice. He'll know I'm not the foreman.

RALPH: Don't worry about that. I'll get Norton outta the apartment. You give the message to Trixie! If you do it right, I'll give you two bucks.

HAP: I don't know, Ralph. This don't sound like no legitimate proposition.

RALPH: Three bucks!

HAP: I don't know. It still don't sound very legitimate.

RALPH: Four bucks! And that's as legitimate as I'm gonna get!

HAP: It's a deal! I'll go call him.

*Hap exits. Ralph goes to window and calls up.*

RALPH: Norton! Oh, Norton!

NORTON (*offstage*): Whattaya want, Ralph?

RALPH: C'mon down here. I wanna see you about somethin' very important!

NORTON: I can't now, Ralph. I'm powdering my wig!

RALPH: This'll only take a minute! C'mon down!

25. What shocking fact does Norton uncover about Pierre François de la Briosche?

26. Who are Alice and Trixie going as to the party?

NORTON: My, my, my, what a cute little girl! How old are you, little girl?

ALICE (*shy-girl-style*): I'm twelve, going on twelve and a half!

NORTON (*normal*): Don't kid me! No twelve-year-old girl ever had knees like that! Va va va voom!

"As far as I know, I'm the first one to use the expression 'va va va voom,'" says Carney. "The first time I did a 'Norton' character was on a Joe and Ethel Terp series, a fifteen-minute radio show. And the character's name was Philly Ohlman. He was really the first 'Norton' character I did. And on that show Philly was, you know, kinda dopey, like Norton, and whenever a good-looking girl would go by or anything like that, it was 'va va va voom!' I don't know where I got that. It was just the sound of it. . . .

"That carried through until I worked with Morey Amsterdam. I first started with him in 1948 in radio and then in television, when I was Newton, the waiter. And I kept the 'va va va voom.' And from Newton, the next time I did the 'Norton' character was Norton in *The Honeymooners*.

"To me, Norton was just a Bronx–Brooklyn combination, and I played it like that. I felt, This is it. I'm that character, and I know what he's like. I know how he reacts. I always felt comfortable doing Norton.

"There was a friend of mine, an actor named Larry Haynes. We went to school together, and we used to ad-lib and give our impressions of these guys like Norton just leaving a movie.

"Remember that part where he jumped over the cliff with a horse?" says Carney, sliding into the dopey-sounding voice of one of his early characters. "And Larry would say, 'Yeah, but he wasn't killed, because if he was, he wouldn't be in no more movies.' That kind of humor.

"We made a record, and we called the two characters Bobo and Gigi. We did it just for the hell of it, all this talk by two guys who talked like two kids coming out of a movie, giving their impressions of what they saw.

"That's where the Norton character came from, I guess."

27. What happens that prevents Norton from going to the party with Trixie and the Kramdens?

When Hap calls with the news that Norton has to report for work, Norton reacts as you'd expect him to: He bawls. Ralph, wanting to cover up his pleasure in seeing his scheme to keep Norton out of the costume contest succeed, gives Norton a pep talk:

RALPH: I know exactly how you feel, Norton. The same thing happened to me last year during the bowling tournament. Remember? We were just about to leave for the big game when the boss calls me and tells me I gotta work the night shift! Of all the nights to tell me I gotta work, he hadda pick the night of the big game! You remember!

NORTON (*reminiscing*): Yeah . . . that's the night we won!

RALPH: That ain't the point!

TRIXIE: What're you going to do, Ed?

NORTON: Well, if duty calls, I guess I gotta go. Looks like this is one of those days. First I find out that Pierre François de la Briosche is a phony—and now this! I knew I shoulda taken my father's advice! This wouldn'ta happened if I'd gone into the diplomatic service!

When Hap shows up at the Kramdens' door to collect his four bucks, Alice realizes Ralph has lowered himself to new depths to keep Norton away from the lodge:

ALICE: How could you do it, Ralph? How could you do such a thing? To Ed Norton—your best friend?

RALPH: He stole my idea!

ALICE: Stole your idea! Look, Ralph, Ed may not be the brightest man in the world, but he's too smart to steal any idea of yours. You were jealous of him, that's the trouble—jealous of Ed Norton, who wouldn't do a thing to harm you!

RALPH (*contritely*): Yeah. You're right, Alice.

ALICE: You bet I'm right! Not only wouldn't Ed hurt you, but he goes out of his way to help you every time you need him—like last year when you hurt your back and were out of work. He went out and borrowed money to help you pay your doctor bills!

RALPH: Yeah. You're right, Alice.

ALICE: Do you know how long Ed's been looking forward to this party tonight? For months. And just because you were jealous of him, you spoil everything. I hope you're ashamed of yourself!

RALPH: I am, Alice. I really am ashamed of myself. I'm nothin' but a low-down heel! I shouldn'ta done this to Ed. I realize that now. All the good things he's done for me—he didn't deserve it. I spoil an evenin' of fun that he's been lookin' forward to for months. I'm nothin' but a low-down heel! *Ralph stands and starts for the door.*

RALPH: Well . . . let's go!

ALICE: Go? Go where?

RALPH: To the party, of course!

ALICE: You mean that after what you did you still want to go?

RALPH: Alice, you must have a pretty low opinion of me. I spoiled Ed Norton's evening! I ain't gonna spoil yours too!

28. True or false: Nobody does the hesitation waltz like Ralph.
29. The two judges at the lodge think Ralph is dressed as:
    A. A Handy Housewife Helper.
    B. A Sherman tank.
    C. A man from space.
    D. A pinball machine.
30. Who is a cofinalist with Ralph in the contest, and what is his costume?

*Pete Woodruff.*
COURTESY
JIM ENGEL.

An ironic twist to this episode was changed by the time the show was filmed: Originally, Pete Woodruff's costume was supposed to be nearly identical to Norton's:

*Pete Woodruff comes forward through the crowd. When he is clear we see that he is wearing a Louis XIV costume very similar to Norton's de la Briosche. When Ralph sees him he does an eye bulge.*

*Ed Norton and sewer workers. The old soft shoe.* COURTESY PERSONALITY PHOTOS, INC.

31. Norton arrives at the party late, in full sewer regalia. He may be too late for the eats, but what isn't he too late for?

For those of you who want to dress as Norton the sewer worker for Halloween, Russell and Finn provide a list of components: "gas mask; miner's-type hat with lamp; Mae West–type life preserver; tool belt with an assortment of odd tools, including a short-handled plunger; hip boots; long-handled mud scope."

# A MATTER OF RECORD

January 7, 1956 · A. J. Russell and Herbert Finn

1. What's the name of Norton's stickball team, and who's team captain?
2. What does Norton promise to the kids on his team who hit a home run?
3. Where does Norton get the apples?
   A. At Freitag's.
   B. At Krauss's.
   C. From Alice.
   D. From Trixie.
4. How many home runs do Norton and his team captain hit?
5. When did Ralph promise Alice he'd take her to a Broadway show?
6. What show does Ralph have tickets for, and where did he get them?
7. Where does Ralph want to go after the show?
   A. Every Chinese restaurant in town.
   B. Salvatore's Pizzeria.
   C. The Colonnade.
   D. The Hong Kong Gardens.
8. Alice can't go to the show because her _____ is coming from _____ for a visit.

ALICE: You mean the tickets are for tonight? But Ralph, Mother's coming tonight! She'll be here any minute. I can't go! It's impossible!

RALPH: Nothing's impossible, Alice! Nothing's impossible! Even goin' to the moon ain't impossible! And if you spoil this evening for me, I'll prove it to you.

9. Why is Norton reluctant to go see *Murder Strikes Out*?
10. If there's anything Ralph hates it's a nosy _____.
11. How many minutes does Ralph predict it will take for Alice's mother to start a fight with him?
12. How far do the Kramdens live from the subway station?
13. True or false: Alice's sister Agnes lives a short block away from the subway.
14. Alice's mother liked only one of Alice's boyfriends. Who?
15. Alice's mother has a neighbor who saw *Murder Strikes Out*. Who is she?
16. Who committed the murder in *Murder Strikes Out*?
    A. The uncle.
    B. The butler.
    C. Bibbo.
    D. The husband.
17. True or false: Ralph and Norton don't go to the play.

Scene one was originally written to end this way:

*The alarm clock goes off loudly, and continues to ring. Ralph freezes. Then he does a skull toward Mother, then toward Alice. He puts the cards down. Then deliberately, Oliver–Hardy–style, he reaches out and shuts off the alarm with a flick of his finger. Slowly and quietly he stands up and goes and stands over Mother.*

RALPH (*quietly*): You are a blabbermouth! *Voice rising.* Blabbermouth, blabbermouth, blabbermouth!

ALICE: Ralph!

RALPH (*to Alice*): Yeah, I said blabbermouth! You can leave with her like you said, and you can stay away forever, but that don't change it! She's still a blabbermouth!

ALICE: Ralph, you're going to be sorry you said that!

RALPH: There's only one thing I ever said that I'm sorry for, Alice! Know what it is? Fifteen years ago when you first introduced me to your mother I said, 'I'm happy to know you.' That's the only thing I ever said that I'm sorry for. *He goes to door. Exits, slamming it. DISSOLVE.*

Scene two in the script begins in Norton's apartment, with Norton playing chess—with himself:

*Norton is seated at the table with a chessboard set up before him. He studies the board a moment, then makes a move with an air of confidence. He throws a superior smile at his imaginary opponent across the table. Then he quickly goes to the opposite side of the table and assumes his "opponent's" seat. He rubs his chin.*

*He surveys the board in this-is-a-tough-spot-style, then looks toward his imaginary opponent, nods as if to commend him.*

*Now he makes several hesitant attempts at making a move. He finally makes a move but quickly retracts it.*

NORTON: I didn't take my fingers off!

Finally Ralph enters.

RALPH: I didn't know you knew how to play chess.

NORTON: I don't. *Points to imaginary opponent.* But he does!

18. How long is Alice gone before Norton suggests that Ralph make a record apologizing for kicking Alice's mother out of the apartment?

RALPH: It's awful, Norton. I'm goin' outta my mind. I never thought I'd miss anybody so much!

NORTON: Yeah, I know what you mean, Ralph. I went through the same thing myself. Nobody to greet ya at the door and kiss ya when ya come home. Nobody to share your supper. Nobody to sympathize with ya when ya tell 'em your troubles. Believe me, Ralph, I know what it means to miss your better half. Yes sir!

RALPH: Yeah. When did Trixie ever leave you?

NORTON: Trixie? I'm talkin' about Lulu, my cocker spaniel!

NORTON: Look, Ralph, if you miss her so much, why don't ya call her up and apologize?

RALPH: I tried that! But she won't talk to me! I tried sixteen times!

NORTON: Well, don't be a quitter. Try again!

RALPH: It's no use, Norton! Her mother had the phone disconnected. *He paces.* I guess I've got this comin' to me. Alice was right. Even though her mother gets me steamed, I've got no right callin' her a blabbermouth—at least not to the old blabbermouth's face!

NORTON: Yeah, you oughta be careful what you say around women, Ralph. You oughta take a lesson from that old sayin': You can lead a horse to water but you can't make him drink.

RALPH: A horse? What kind of a lesson can I take from that?

NORTON: Plenty! Did'ja ever hear of a horse with mother-in-law trouble? *Ralph looks at him disgusted. He turns away and paces.*

RALPH: What am I gonna do, Norton? I even tried writin' her a letter. I know what I wanna say, but when I start to put it on paper it don't come out right!

NORTON: Afraid I can't help you there, Ralph. I ain't much at writin' letters. In fact, the last letter I wrote was to Santa Claus. And that was, oh, four, five years ago!

19. Norton wants to give a schmaltzy introduction to Ralph's recording to Alice. What song does he play, and what instrument does he play it on?

20. Ralph blows his top making the first record and begins screaming into the microphone. Norton asks if he's pouring out his _____ or his _____.

21. What are Ralph and Alice's pet names for each other?

22. In the words of the immortal bard Shakespeare, what are the three times in a man's life when he wants to be alone?

23. Finish the sentence: "P.S., _____."

Russell and Finn wrote Ralph's apology speech this way.

RALPH: Dear Bunny. *He looks toward bedroom to make sure he is not overheard, then speaks.* This is Poopsie! Gee, it's been a long time since I called you Bunny—way back when we were first married. Remember those days, Alice? The world was before us. We were young and full of dreams. We never used to fight then. Why can't things be like that again? You're still the same Bunny and I'm still the same Poopsie. Please come back. Home is a lonely place without ya. Everything reminds me of you. I look at your apron hanging on the chair, and it reminds me of you. I look at the dirty dishes stacked in the sink, and it reminds me of you. I look at our old beat-up icebox, and it reminds me of you. And when I look at myself I see what a fool I was to do anything to hurt ya. What I'm tryin' to say, Alice—I mean Bunny—is that I can't live without ya. Please come back. Your loving husband, Ralph. P.S. Say hello to your mother.

Norton comes back into the room:

*As Norton enters he blows his nose, just-had-a-good-cry-style, and furtively wipes away a tear. Ralph watches him and steams as he goes to the console and removes the record.*

RALPH: You were listenin'!

NORTON: I couldn't help it, Ralph. Ya got me right here (*touches heart*) and when ya came to that part about "come back to your Poopsie" it was all I could do to keep from rushin' into your arms!

A few minutes later:

RALPH: Hey, what about this first record I made?

NORTON: Oooosh! We better get rid of that! If Alice ever heard what you said in that she wouldn't come back in a million years! Put it on the sink, Ralph, so I won't forget to throw it out with the trash!

RALPH: Well, I guess I'll be goin'. Be careful of that, Norton. My whole future's in that record.

*Norton holds up record, waving it confidently.*

NORTON: Don't worry, Ralph. Your future's in good hands.

*He bobbles record and catches it before it hits floor.*

RALPH: Norton!

NORTON: Hee, hee, hee! It's unbreakable!

RALPH: Just like your head!

Ralph leaves, and Trixie comes in with a bag of groceries.

TRIXIE: Hi, Ed. I got a four-pound pot roast for dinner. Okay?

NORTON: Sure, fine. Whatta you gonna eat?

*The Nortons.*
COURTESY
PERSONALITY PHOTOS, INC.

24. What is Alice's maiden name?
25. What is Alice's mother's address?
26. What precaution did Norton take when he mailed Alice the record of apology Ralph made?

RALPH: Just the same, somethin' musta gone wrong. Look, you got a cousin workin' in the post office. Why don't ya call him and ask him to check up on it?

NORTON: Can't do that, Ralph. My cousin ain't with the post office no more. Too bad, too. He was very popular. The post office'd do anything to get him back.

RALPH: Yeah?

NORTON: Sure. Go to any post office in the country, and there's his picture on the wall! And right above it, it says 'Wanted'!

RALPH: Keep it up, Norton! Keep it up and you'll be like your cousin. Only you won't be on the wall—you'll go through it!

NORTON: I shoulda known you wouldn't appreciate that! It's a family joke!

27. Ralph's in a tizzy because Alice hasn't come home, even though she should have listened to his record of apology. Where does Norton think Alice is?

Norton tells Ralph that Alice must have been so overwhelmed with emotion after hearing the record that when she tried to return home she accidentally got on the wrong bus. In the episode, Norton figures Alice wound up in Bayonne; in the script Russell and Finn dropped her in Hohokus. Regardless, here is Ralph's reaction to Norton's explanation:

*Ralph just looks at him. He is too stunned by this stupidity to speak. Norton goes on.*

NORTON: There's your answer, Ralph. While you're here waitin' for her, Alice is wandering around Hohokus lookin' for this apartment!

RALPH (*deadly sarcasm*): Hohokus, huh? Hohokus! You really think that Alice is wanderin' around Hohokus, New Jersey, lookin' for this apartment! *Ralph lifts his arms hopelessly in the air and turns away from Norton.* How could anybody be so stupid!

NORTON: Don't be too hard on her, Ralph. After all, anybody could take the wrong bus!

In the original script, Norton urges Ralph to clean up the apartment before Alice returns. He says the apartment "looks like hurricane Annie, Betty, Cora, and Dora held a sorority meeting" there. This is the way it was supposed to happen:

*Norton marches into bedroom. Ralph now gets busy. He goes to the bureau, opens the top drawers. Then with one motion sweeps everything that is on the top of the bureau into the drawers. He slams the drawers shut. Moving at an accelerated pace he goes to the sink, takes one quick look at the dirty dishes stacked there. Then he opens the oven door and quickly shoves all the dirty dishes into the oven. He shuts the door. He takes a look at the stack of dishes on the table, decides what to do with them. He opens the icebox door, goes to table, scoops up dishes, shoves them into the icebox, shuts the door. He goes to table, quickly turns the tablecloth other-side-up, then reaches over to the top of the icebox, gets a small vase, places it with a quick flourish on the table centerpiece-style. He then gets broom from corner near sink. He goes to right stage near bureau. He places broom on floor, then takes quick steps to sink without lifting broom from floor, hurry-up-style. . . .*

Norton has another brilliant idea: Decorate the room with flowers, for "the sentimental touch." When Johnny Bennett comes to the Kramden apartment, they decide to send him to the florist:

NORTON: Run down to the corner and buy some flowers. How much should he spend, Ralph?

RALPH: I don't know. But let's not skimp on a thing like this. *He reaches into pocket for a coin.* Here, Johnny, get a dime's worth.

NORTON: A dime's worth? Boy, when it comes to sayin' it with flowers you've sure got laryngitis!

28. Who's the second baseman on Norton's stickball team, and why can't he play in the big game?

29. Norton: "The life of a coach ain't all _____ and _____."

30. True or false: Johnny Bennett wants Norton to oil his baseball glove.

31. Ralph to Norton: "You're a menace to society. You're a menace to me. And _____."

32. When Alice comes back to Ralph, what has she brought home to cook for supper?
    A. Knockwurst.
    B. Pot roast.
    C. Steak.
    D. Spaghetti and meatballs.

33. The doctor who visits the Kramden apartment is:
    A. Dr. Hyman.
    B. Dr. MacDonald.
    C. Dr. Folsom.
    D. Dr. Glockner.

34. Which members of the Cougars have the measles?

35. True or false: Ralph and Norton get the measles.

36. Ralph tells the doctor Alice has been away for:
    A. Three weeks.
    B. Three days.
    C. Seven days.
    D. A month.

37. Ralph to Alice: "Don't touch me, I'm _____."

*Johnny Bennett.*
COURTESY
JIM ENGEL.

In the original ending, Ralph doesn't get to play hero and send Alice away until he recovers from the measles because Dr. Folsom quarantines the apartment and refuses to let Alice enter:

RALPH: Please, doc. My wife's been away from me for three weeks!

FOLSOM: All the more reason! I can't let her be exposed now! This place is quarantined for two weeks!

RALPH (*with outstretched arms*): Bunny!

ALICE (*with outstretched arms*): Poopsie!

*The doctor shuts the door, cutting himself and Alice off from view. As Ralph turns to Norton for the reckoning, we DISSOLVE.*

# OH MY ACHING BACK

January 14, 1956 · Leonard Stern and Sydney Zelinka

1. Trixie is going to her sister's house for a visit. How long is she staying, and how is she getting there?
2. While Trixie is away, what favor does she want Alice to do for her? Why can't Norton do it instead?
3. Alice says she can't have Norton to dinner because she's going somewhere, too. Where, and why?
4. How many years has Ralph been driving a bus?
5. Ralph doesn't want to go out with Alice. Name the three parts of the act he puts on when he comes home.
6. What is Ralph supposed to do the next morning, that he uses as an excuse to stay home?
7. Ralph is really planning to sneak out to go bowling with Norton and the guys from the Racoon Lodge. What's the occasion, and who's the opposing team?
8. The opposing team has already beaten Ralph's chapter of the Racoons at some other competition. What was it, and how did they win?
9. Norton was once supposed to play pool with Ralph on a night Trixie wanted him to go with her to her mother's. What happened that night?
10. What emblems appear on the front and back of the Racoons' bowling jackets?
11. Alice returns to the apartment and finds Ralph dressed to go bowling. Why does she return?
12. What does Alice fear will happen to Ralph if he goes bowling?
13. Who does Ralph tell Norton to get to replace him for the bowling match? Why can't that guy bowl in Ralph's place?
14. Whose bride-to-be is attending the match?
15. Who's preparing the victory feed for the team, and what is he serving?
16. Who's coming to watch Freddie bowl?
17. What finally changes Ralph's mind about going bowling?

Scene two of this episode was originally written to take place at the athletic club where the Racoons hold their annual tournament. It opens with a club attendant and club member in conversation:

ATTENDANT: Didn't you bowl tonight, Mr. Whitney?

WHITNEY: How can you bowl with all those—what do you call them—Racoons running wild out there.

ATTENDANT: I know how you feel, sir. But the club lends them the alleys once a year for their big tournament.

*A cheer is heard from offstage.*

WHITNEY: Once a year is too often. *Notices cabinet.* What's that reducing cabinet doing out here?

ATTENDANT: We're sending it back. There's something wrong with the wiring. *Whitney nods, and goes offstage. Attendant goes off through archway. Suddenly Norton spins into room trying to regain his balance. The impression is that he was just the recipient of a good shove. Ralph comes through swinging door with bowling ball in left hand. He is angry.*

NORTON: Watch who you're pushin'. You're gettin' a little too free with your hands!

RALPH: You are stayin' in here until I finish my game!

NORTON: I was only tryin' to help.

RALPH: I've bowled a hundred and ninety points so far without your help. I can get the last two pins the same way.

NORTON: But those two pins mean everything. If you get 'em it means we beat Bayonne for the championship.

RALPH: Don't you think I know that? But I don't need you tryin' to show me how to make the shot with those crazy motions of yours.
*Ralph does his version of Norton's bowling movements.*

NORTON: Don't exaggerate. I was showin' you the only way you can knock down both those pins and I wasn't usin' any crazy motions. It was like this.
*Norton goes into weird bowling demonstration. Ralph shoots him a scathing look.*

RALPH: You're stayin' here!
*Wilson, a Racoon, sticks his head in.*

WILSON: Come on, Kramden. If you don't bowl, you'll be disqualified!

RALPH: I'm comin'. *To Norton.* I don't even want you sticking your head out the door until I'm through.

NORTON: Okay, okay. Just make that shot.
*Ralph goes out. Norton waits a moment. Sneaks up on door and starts to push it open. He bends over and sticks his head through door and peers out. At the same time Ralph peers into room. His head is above Norton's. He looks down into Norton's face and speaks.*

RALPH: I told you to stay in there!
*Norton jumps back as Ralph's face disappears and door closes.*

NORTON: EEEEEEEEEEEEE! What a grouch!
*Norton starts to pace. He talks out loud.*

NORTON: Ralph, it's up to you. You gotta make it, Ralph. Please make it. Just give it that little twist.
*Norton goes through bowling motion. Over scene comes a big cheer. A throaty roar of approval. "Yea, Kramden" is screamed many times. Wilson comes charging into room.*

NORTON: He heard me!

WILSON: He made it! He made it! We beat Bayonne!
*Norton and Wilson start dancing up and down. Suddenly the cheering changes into a crowd groan. Norton and Wilson stop short.*

WILSON: What's that?

NORTON: Maybe it's a foul. Maybe he stepped over the line!

*The two men are immobilized at the horror of the thought.*

NORTON: I ain't got the nerve to go out and see what's happened.

*The swinging door opens and Mulloy, a doleful-looking member of the team, comes through. He holds door open and shakes head as if he's just witnessed a great calamity.*

NORTON: Didn't we win?

MULLOY: Yeah, we won, all right.

*Mulloy shakes his head, Norton and Wilson exchange puzzled looks. Over scene we hear a series of groans that get louder and louder until doubled-over Ralph appears in doorway with a team member on each side supporting him. They carefully lower Ralph into a chair. He gives one big groan as he is seated.*

18. Ralph hurts his back bowling. What does the doctor advise him to do for it?
19. Norton takes Ralph's temperature, but he can't see the red line. What does he use to read the thermometer?
20. What does Norton think Ralph's temperature is?
21. Ralph wants to sleep up at Norton's so he can put the heating pad on his back. What scheme does he concoct so Alice will let him sleep upstairs?

RALPH: If I sleep on a heating pad, Alice'll know there's something wrong with my back and right away she'll know I been bowlin'.

NORTON: But if you can't use the heating pad on accounta Alice, what are we gonna . . . *Norton spies reducing cabinet.* Eeeeeyyyyyyy! What about that thing over there? They give off plentya heat.

RALPH: I gotta get home before Alice does. I can't sit in that thing all night.

NORTON: Ralph, a half hour in that thing and you'll get more heat than a heating pad'd give you all night.

RALPH: If anybody else said that I'd swear it was a good idea.

NORTON: It is. Just a half hour, you'll get out feeling fine and you get home aheada Alice.

RALPH (*after thoughtful moment*): Help me get up.

*Norton helps Ralph to his feet and walks him to cabinet. He opens it and Ralph gets in. Closes it. This is all done with great care and caution, plus an occasional groan.*

NORTON: There. Now to plug it in. Put it on medium and you'll be okay in jig time!

RALPH: I wonder how long this'll take?

NORTON: In a little while I'll stick a fork in you and see if you're done. *Laughs it up.*

*Ralph glares at Norton.*

NORTON: Okay, okay. But you gotta admit it, this is one time I come up with a pretty good idea! Maybe I better put it on full.

*Norton turns dial. At this moment, a flash pot placed at safe distance behind cabinet goes off. The sides fall from the cabinet and there is smoke. As Norton stands there frozen in terror, Ralph steps out. His pants from knees down are in shreds, poor-beachcomber-style. As Ralph stands there they stare at each other as we DISSOLVE.*

22. Ralph's back hurts so much he can hardly move. He tries to straighten up and "look natural" so Alice won't know he's been bowling. What two things does Norton say he looks like?

NORTON: I got it! I got it! Trixie's away overnight. Be my guest. Stay up at my place and you can keep the heating pad on all night.

RALPH: Are you outta your mind? What excuse can I give Alice for sleeping upstairs?

NORTON: Just say it's accounta me. Say I'm afraid to sleep alone . . . I'm scared of the boogey man.

RALPH: Norton, your parents musta sure loved children to bother bringing you up!

23. What's the signal for Norton to come down to Ralph's to put Ralph's scheme into action?

24. Uncle Leo stops in to see Ralph. How long has it been since they last saw one another?

25. When does Uncle Leo want Ralph and Alice to come for a visit?
   A. At New Year's, and then stay until Christmas.
   B. The Fourth of July.
   C. The day of the Racoon fishing trip.
   D. Around Christmas.

26. Uncle Leo is married to:
   A. Aunt Sarah.
   B. Aunt Shirley.
   C. Aunt Agnes.
   D. Aunt Thelma.

27. Uncle Leo slaps Ralph on the back three times. When Uncle Leo leaves, Ralph bellows in agony. What does it sound like to Alice?

*. . . The front door opens and Norton in his nightgown, slippers, and perennial hat enters, sleepwalking. Alice and Ralph turn.*

ALICE: Ed, what's the—Ralph!

RALPH: Shh, Alice, he's walking in his sleep.

ALICE: Oh, this is terrible. He did this once before, remember?

RALPH: No . . . oh, yeah. Trixie should never leave him alone.

ALICE (*abstractedly*): Yeah.

RALPH: I better wake him up.

*Alice, watching Norton, doesn't answer.*

RALPH: Alice, I said I better wake him up!

ALICE: No. It's dangerous to wake up a sleepwalker.

RALPH: I didn't know that.

*Arms outstretched, Norton heads for icebox.*

COURTESY
SAMUEL LOWE
COMPANY.

ALICE: He's going to the icebox.

*Norton opens icebox and takes out several plates and puts them on table. Ralph does a silent burn. He can't give vent to it.*

ALICE: Poor guy. Trixie defrosted the refrigerator. He must be starved. That's why he came down.

*Forgetting the act in spite of himself, Ralph speaks out loud.*

RALPH: I don't mind sleepwalking, but sleepeating, that's another thing!

ALICE: Shh.

*Norton sits and begins to feast. Ralph glares at him.*

RALPH: Yeah, I forgot.

ALICE: As soon as he's finished, he'll probably go upstairs again.

RALPH: Yeah, but he's been lucky so far—he could fall down the stairs or step out a window or sumpthin'. I better follow him and stay with him so I can keep an eye on him. Don't you think?

ALICE: By all means. I'll get your slippers.

*Alice exits. As soon as he's assured she's out of earshot, Ralph walks up behind Norton and gives him a shove. Norton, in a flurry, recovers from blow.*

NORTON: Don't you know it's dangerous to wake a sleepwalker?

RALPH: What's the idea? You know I gotta get out of here!

NORTON: If I ever came down here, awake or asleep, and I didn't go to the icebox, Alice would know there's somethin' fishy.

RALPH: Get up.

*Ralph pulls him out of chair. Lets go just as Alice returns. Norton rises and extends his hands just as Alice comes into room.*

RALPH: Er, he's finished.

*Norton turns in direction of door. Alice looks at dishes.*

ALICE: Well, one thing, asleep he doesn't eat as much as when he's awake.

*Norton has door open and Ralph is behind him. He left a chicken leg.*

*Norton doesn't go through door. He turns left and goes downstage. As he passes table he picks up chicken leg and continues around table and goes out door with chicken leg as we DISSOLVE.*

133

"One of the reasons I enjoyed playing Norton was that he was that type of guy," says Carney of Norton's propensity to do things like raid the Kramdens' icebox. "I used to think, Why can't I be more like Norton? He's such fun to play.

"I'm basically introverted. I'm not good with crowds, or big gatherings, or interviews. I'm always groping for words. All of a sudden, I'm not articulate at all.

"I can remember thinking, I wish I was more like Norton. Norton could come into a place and take over. Nothing bothers him. 'Yeah, I'll have some of that. Sure, put it on here.'" (Carney mimics building a Norton-sized sandwich.) "He'd eat. Go in the refrigerator."

28. What does Alice have in the icebox for Ralph's lunch?
29. Who helps Ralph home from the bowling match, and later brings him his bowling trophy?
30. What is the trophy for?

*As curtains part, Alice, alone on stage, is at stove, stirring contents of pot. Door opens and a cheerful Ralph enters.*

RALPH: Hello, honey.

ALICE (*anxiously*): Ralph, how did it go?

RALPH (*kisses Alice*): Fine. Fine. I passed the physical with flying colors.

ALICE: Oh, I'm so glad. Now tell the truth. Aren't you happy that you stayed home and rested last night instead of going bowling?

RALPH: Of course I am.

ALICE: I'm glad to hear you admit it. I know you enjoy bowling, but after all, it's just a game. Driving a bus is your livelihood.

RALPH (*doll of the world*): Alice, I'm not hard to convince. When you come up with a piece of logic like that, I always listen. Alice, after supper you and me are gonna take in a movie.

*Ralph goes into bedroom, closing door after him. Alice hums as she sets table. Knock on door. Alice opens door. Wilson and Mulloy enter. Mulloy is carrying something in paper bag.*

ALICE (*surprised*): Oh, hello. Come in.

BOTH MEN: Hello, Mrs. Kramden.

WILSON: Ralph here?

ALICE: He's washing up. He just got home from work.

MULLOY: Oh, then he was able to go to work today.

ALICE: Of course.

WILSON (*to Mulloy*): His back must be all better.

ALICE: His back???

*Ralph enters from bedroom, speaks while drying face with towel.*

RALPH: Alice, on the way home I passed that movie house on Pitkin Avenue and. . . .

*At this point he takes towel away from face and as he sees the two men he is speechless.*

MULLOY: I guess you're surprised to see us, Ralph. We know it's suppertime, so we'll make it short and quick. Ralph, in recognition of your courage and the way you came through for us last night, all the brothers feel that the championship trophy does not belong to the lodge. It rightfully belongs to you. So in behalf of the Racoons it gives me great pleasure to present you with this trophy.

*Mulloy takes trophy with a bowler atop and gives it to Ralph. Ralph takes it in silence. Mulloy mistakes Ralph's silence for deep sentiment.*

MULLOY: That's all right, Ralph. You needn't say anything. Good night, Mrs. Kramden.

WILSON: S'long. And Ralph, take care of that back.

*They exit. Ralph remains in same position with trophy in hand. Alice keeps her position and doesn't say a word. Ralph finally speaks weakly.*

RALPH: It'll look nice on the dresser, won't it?

ALICE (*disregards his words*): You went bowling and you hurt your back.

RALPH: Alice, I didn't want to go. Schultz couldn't bowl instead of me so I hadda show up. I had to do it for the guys.

ALICE: You were willing to risk losing your job.

RALPH: But I passed the exam, didn't I? And I asked the company doctor about my back and he said it don't have to come from bowling. It coulda been a cold in the back. That's all it is—just a cold in the back.

ALICE: Do you expect me to believe that? Ralph, it's not from a cold. It's from bowling.

RALPH: Alice, I'm gonna make you sorry you said that. I'll prove to you it's from a cold and not from bowling!

*He picks up bowling ball in case from alongside bureau. Unzippers case, takes out ball, and places it on floor as he speaks.*

RALPH: I'll prove it by doing everything you have to do with a bowling ball and show you that nothing happens. First I reach down and pick the ball up off the floor . . . no pain in the back . . . it's from a cold. I pull my arm back as far as it will go . . . no pain in the back. And then I run up to the foul line . . . (*takes three steps*) let the ball go, and there's no . . . ooooooooooh!

*Ralph is unable to straighten. He is in shape he was last night. Eye bulge, and he cannot straighten up.*

ALICE: Well, I guess it is a cold. Gesundheit!

*FADE-OUT.*

# THE BABYSITTER

January 21, 1956 · Leonard Stern and Sydney Zelinka

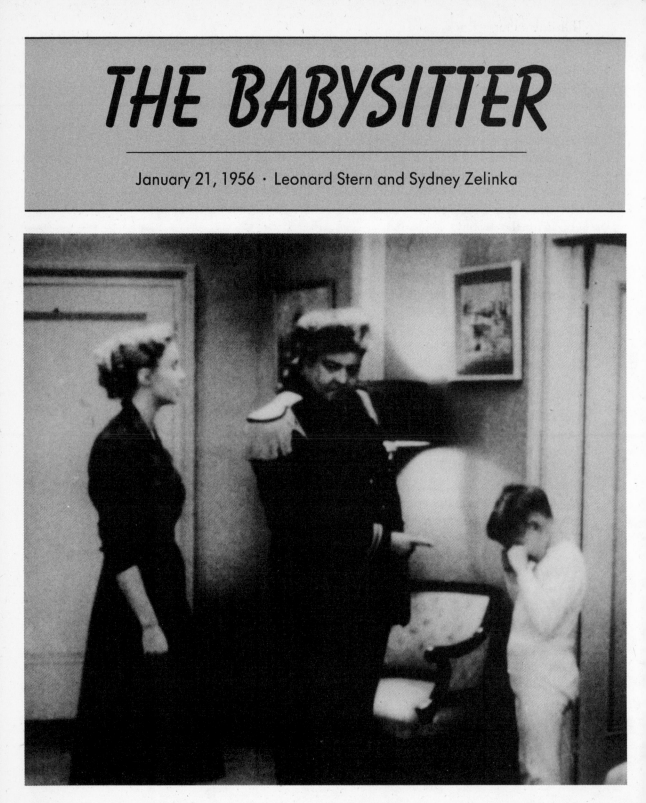

1. Alice has a telephone installed. What's the telephone number?
2. Who's the first person Alice calls on the telephone?
3. One of the reasons Alice gets a phone is to keep in touch with her mother, who's moved to:
   A. Canarsie.
   B. Bensonhurst.
   C. Astoria.
   D. New Zealand.
4. Alice hides the telephone so Ralph won't see it when he comes home. Where does she put it?
5. Who's always making stale jokes about Ralph being slightly over-weight?
6. When a bus driver calls in sick to the bus company, Ralph is next on the list as a substitute driver. Why doesn't Ralph take the shift? Who does?
7. What's the big reason Ralph doesn't want a telephone?

RALPH: You got no consideration for me at all. You're a selfish woman. Instead of finding ways of cutting down, you figure ways of spending more money. Can't you realize that I'm carrying a big enough load on my mind right now?

ALICE: You're carrying a big enough load all right—but it's not on your mind! *Ralph puts fist under Alice's face.*

RALPH: There's no telephone on the moon, Alice.

8. Ralph's mother's been yelling out the window for _____ years.
9. Before Ralph's mother lost her voice from yelling out the window, there were more people listening to her than to:
   A. Captain Video.
   B. Charlie Chan.
   C. Amos 'n' Andy.
   D. Herb Norris.
10. Who's the first person to telephone Ralph, and why does he call?
11. A man's home is like a ship. On the Kramden ship, Ralph's the captain. What's Alice?
12. What are Alice's three jobs on the Kramden ship?
13. Norton uses the Kramdens' phone. Whom does he call?
14. How much of a phone bill has Ralph rung up on Norton's phone over fifteen years?
15. Alice takes a babysitting job. It pays:
   A. 65¢ per hour.
   B. 50¢ per hour.
   C. $12.83.
   D. $62 per week.

NORTON: Ralph, a phone's a good thing. I got one as soon as I moved in here.

RALPH: What was so important about you having a phone?

NORTON: Well, it wasn't exactly the phone. I was more interested in the phone book.

RALPH: The phone book???

NORTON: Yeah. I've always been a sucker for seeing my name in print!

16. Who comes to the Kramden apartment looking for a babysitter?
17. Whom does Alice babysit for, and where do they live?
18. Ralph ducks out to a pay phone to call his own number to see if Alice is using the phone. When he gets home, he tells Alice that if he dialed Bensonhurst 0–7740 once, he called it _____ times, and each time it was busy.

Look carefully at the scene where Ralph and Alice are arguing about the telephone being busy when Ralph called what he thought was the Kramdens' telephone number—their voices are overdubbed when they mention the telephone numbers. In the script, originally titled "Bensonhurst 3-7741," the writers used a working number. When the mistake was discovered after the show was filmed, the title of the show was changed to "The Babysitter," and Gleason and Audrey had to dub in references to two nonworking numbers—Bensonhurst 0-7740 and Bensonhurst 0-7741.

RALPH: Norton, you're looking at a fool. A first-class fool. Alice didn't use the phone at all.

NORTON: But the line was busy!

RALPH: Yeah, but I was dialing Bensonhurst 4–7741. This number is Bensonhurst 3–7741.

NORTON: Eeeeeeeeeeeeeeee!

RALPH: Alice won't talk to me. I don't blame her. I don't blame her if she never forgives me.

NORTON: Ralph, don't worry. Everything'll turn out all right. Besides, there's a bright side to this dark cloud, and you've got to look at the bright side. Just think how lucky you are.

RALPH: Lucky?

NORTON: Sure. Think of how big the phone bill'd be if you were married to Bensonhurst 4–7741!

19. Who's the barber who prepares Ralph for a shave?
    A. Frank.
    B. Bill.
    C. Pete.
    D. George.

20. Whose hair does Ralph's barber cut before Ralph arrives at the barbershop?
21. Ralph wants to make up with Alice after blowing his top over the telephone. What does he buy her as a peace offering, and where does he plan to take her for dinner?
22. What magazine does Norton read in the barbershop?
23. What nights of the week is Ralph usually out of the house?
24. What time does Ralph usually get home from work?

Alice has another babysitting job, and she has to get there right away. Ralph comes home from work, suspicious of Alice because he overheard her name mentioned in the barbershop. When Alice tries to rush Ralph through his dinner, she only adds to his apprehension:

ALICE: **What would you like for dessert, dear?**
   *Ralph has just speared a piece of meat with fork, and he holds that position as he speaks.*
RALPH: **How about some cornflakes and cream? That way you'll be finished for tomorrow, too! Alice, why are you rushing me?**
ALICE (*wide-eyed*): **Was I rushing you?**
RALPH: **Rushing me! You're making history! This will be remembered as the year when Roger Bannister broke the four-minute mile and Alice Kramden broke the four-minute meal!**

25. Alice gets a second babysitting job. Whom does she sit for, where do they live, and what night of the week is it?
26. True or false: Alice doesn't want Ralph to know she's babysitting, so she says she's going to visit her mother.
27. The couple Alice babysits for are celebrating an anniversary. How long have they been married?

# $99,000 ANSWER

January 28, 1956 · Leonard Stern and Sydney Zelinka

1. Who is the host of the *$99,000 Answer?*
2. Who is the first contestant on the *$99,000 Answer,* and how much money has he won?
3. How much money is his question worth, and who prepared it?
4. What is his question, and what is the answer?
5. What does Ralph tell Herb Norris he does for a living?

Jay Jackson, who played Herb Norris, is so convincing in the role because he actually *was* a quiz show host during the fifties, on programs such as *Twenty Questions* and *Tic Tac Dough.* He recalls his work on *The Honeymooners* as one of his most *uncommon* jobs.

"It was a unique rehearsal experience," he says. "I went into the studio—my call was for two-thirty—so I went to Carney's dressing room. Carney was an old friend of mine; I knew Gleason too but there was no Gleason in evidence so I went up to Carney's dressing room.

"I said, 'What's the rehearsal schedule? How do we do this?' And he said, 'Before I tell you, have a drink.' He had a pint bottle of brandy and we worked on that a little bit, and he told me and I couldn't believe it.

"About an hour and a half later was the first rehearsal, and Jack Hurdle stood in for Gleason. He stood beside me on the stage and kind of mumbled the lines, and I'm trying to get some action up for a performance, but there's nothing coming from him; he's not acting.

"And they're stopping every twenty seconds. Satenstein's [the late Frank Satenstein, the director] saying, 'Hold it, we've got to move the camera here. You stand back. Turn your head a little this way.' We did it all again about an hour later, with the producer and no Gleason, and that was it.

"I said, 'When do we get with Gleason?' and they said 'A little later.' So about seven-thirty—I think we taped about eight in the evening—I'm summoned into Gleason's dressing room. Now remember, all the other people that were involved in this—Audrey, Art, Joyce, Mrs. Manicotti, McGarrity—all these people individually were led into Gleason's dressing room, where he was lying on a chaise longue with a robe wrapped around him.

"He says, 'Hiya pal, good to see ya. Now let's see, in the first scene you say bah-bah-bah and I say boo-boo-boo and you say. . . .' And I start to say my line and he says, 'I know what it is, don't worry about it. And I say. . . .' And this ran for about three minutes and that was it, that was all the rehearsal there was—just mumbling—and then you go out on stage and try to make some sense out of it. It was a terrifying experience, and I wouldn't have traded any of it for a million dollars!"

"We didn't rehearse much," says Carney. "Gleason didn't like to rehearse at all. He even had Jack Hurdle stand in for him in the so-called dress rehearsal. Gleason'd be upstairs looking over his lines.

*Herb Norris, alias Jay Jackson, at RALPH's first convention.* COURTESY LUIGI PEL-LETIERI AND RALPH.

"I remember one actor, when we got through the dress—'Is this the dress rehearsal?' he said to me. 'Yeah, this is it,' I said. 'When do I get to see Gleason?' he said. This poor guy. Then when we got on the air, he was one of these actors th-th-th-that sh-sh-shook a little. Gleason said, 'Don't hire him again.' The poor guy, he wasn't used to this operation."

6. Where was Herb Norris when Ralph drove his bus by him and splashed him with mud?
7. What are the ten categories Ralph has to choose from on the *$99,000 Answer?*
8. Why does Ralph stand under a streetlight after his appearance on the *$99,000 Answer?*

ALICE: He decided to stay downstairs. He's waiting for people to go by and recognize him.
TRIXIE: Who can recognize him at this hour? It's dark out.
ALICE: He thought of that. *Points out window.* There he is standing under the streetlight with his hat off! I'll bet he's waiting to give out his autograph.
TRIXIE: Now I know you're kidding!
*Ralph calls up from street.*
RALPH: Oh, Alice.

ALICE: What do you want?

RALPH: Throw down a pencil!

*Alice gives Trixie an I-told-you-so look. She gets pencil off top of icebox. She throws it out window. She waits.*

RALPH: You broke the point!

9. True or false: Norton watches Ralph on TV at the Racoon Lodge.

RALPH: Well, Alice, I've finally learned a lesson. This house is filled with nothing but jealous people.

ALICE: What are you talking about?

RALPH: There wasn't one person in this house, not one, waiting downstairs to congratulate me!

ALICE: Waiting downstairs! Ralph, it took us a long time to get home. It's after twelve and they've gone to bed. Besides, maybe some of them didn't know you were on the program.

RALPH: Don't make excuses for them, Alice. They knew, all right. Didn't I go to the trouble to make this sign? In big letters.

*Ralph turns homemade sign and reads what it says.*

RALPH: "Tonight! Don't miss Ralph Kramden on the *$88,000 Answer* tonight." And I hung it downstairs in the hall myself. They don't want to admit I'm a celebrity.

10. When he was a kid, where was Ralph every night while the bums in the neighborhood were in a poolroom or hanging out on the corner?

11. Alice says she'd be proud of Ralph if he won ＿＿＿＿ on the show.

12. How old was the kid who answered a $16,000 question on a quiz show?

13. Spell antidisestablishmentarianism.

RALPH: There you go, tearing me down and upsetting me at a time like this. Mrs. Edward R. Murrow wouldn't act this way!

ALICE: What's Mrs. Edward R. Murrow got to do with this?

RALPH: Her husband's got a television show, too!

14. What is Ralph going to do to cram for the *$99,000 Answer*?

15. Mrs. Gibson drops in to see Alice. What does she bring her?

16. What is Ralph studying with Mrs. Manicotti?

17. Why does Mrs. Gibson want Ralph to go for the *$99,000 Answer*?

18. "Don't Fence Me In": Who wrote it? What year? For what film? Who produced the film?

19. What song does Norton play on the piano to warm up?

20. "Shuffle Off to Buffalo" was written for a little picture called:
    A. *Rhythm on Ice.*
    B. *Dead Men Tell No Tales.*
    C. *Hollywood Canteen.*
    D. *Forty-Second Street.*
21. "Shuffle Off to Buffalo" was written by _____ in _____.
22. "Too Marvelous for Words": Who wrote it? What year? For what film?
23. Which song is Ralph puzzling over when jealous McGarrity comes in?
24. Give the title, the year it was written, and the author of the song Mrs. Manicotti sings for Ralph.
25. What is McGarrity's (Garrity in script) picture going to appear on the front page of every newspaper in the country for?

RALPH: For the last time, I'm goin' for the 88 thousand dollars!

ALICE: For the last time, I'd be very proud of you if you won 500.

RALPH: 500 bucks is peanuts! Peanuts! What am I gonna do with peanuts?

GARRITY'S VOICE: Eat them—like any other elephant!

*Ralph charges the window.*

RALPH: When I move to Park Avenue, you'll be singing a different tune.

GARRITY'S VOICE: Yeah. "Happy Days Are Here Again," written by Yellen and Ager, 1929!

NORTON: He's right, Ralph.

RALPH: Shut up.

ALICE: Ralph, the smartest thing for you to do would be to go to bed.

RALPH: I ain't goin' to bed until I brush up on the songs that come from the movies!

ALICE: But there are thousands of them! You can't hope to know them all.

RALPH: Oh, no? There are ten times as many popular songs, and I know them all!

ALICE: Ralph, don't kid yourself. Out of all those songs there's got to be some you overlooked.

RALPH: I know them all! Just because you can't do it is no reason why I can't!

ALICE: I'll be out of your way in a minute, genius!

*Alice goes to icebox and gets milk. Pours herself a glass of the white stuff and returns milk. As she does this, she hums aloud da-te-da-style. Song she hums is chorus of "Sweet Georgia Brown." She goes into bedroom, closing door behind her.*

RALPH: What's she singing about?

NORTON: Hey, Ralph, what was that song she was humming there?

RALPH: It's called . . . the name of it is . . . the title is. . . . That's why she did it!

NORTON: You better ask her what it is.

RALPH: Oh, no, that's what she wants me to do. I'll figure it out myself. Can you play that on the piano, Norton?

NORTON: I'll try.

*He starts in with "Swanee River."*

RALPH: Will you stop that!

NORTON: Ralph, I told you—

RALPH: Come on!

*Norton plays "Swanee River" a mile a minute into pickup, and "Sweet Georgia Brown."*

RALPH: Play it again.

*Norton does. Ralph looks terrified when he can't recognize tune.*

RALPH: Norton, I don't know it.

NORTON: Forget it, Ralph. It's just one out of a million.

RALPH: Oh, no. You can bet your life that's the song they're goin' to stick me with tomorrow on the show. I know her! She's a voodoo woman. She's putting the whammy on me! Play it again. I'm gonna get that song. I'm gonna get it by sheer concentration.

*Norton plays and Ralph listens. After a split of silence, Ralph strides to bedroom door and calls in.*

RALPH: Alice, what's the name of that song? You gotta tell me!

*Alice appears in door.*

ALICE: If you go to bed now, I'll tell you tomorrow.

*She goes in. He glares at her back and then slams door.*

RALPH: I gotta get it. I gotta get it. Play it again.

*Norton plays again. On last notes we hear . . .*

GARRITY'S VOICE: I'm warnin' you, Kramden. I'm comin' down and chopping up that piano if you don't stop playin' that "Sweet Georgia Brown"!

RALPH (*at window*): Shut up!

*Slams window. As he starts back to Norton he realizes what's been said. So does Norton.*

RALPH AND NORTON: "Sweet Georgia Brown."

RALPH (*to window*): Thanks, Garrity. *He runs across room to bedroom door.* Alice, Alice!

*Alice opens door and stands in doorway.*

ALICE: "Sweet Georgia Brown."

*He sticks his tongue out at her as we DISSOLVE.*


26. What is the last song Norton plays on the piano?

27. Who are the announcer and the pianist on the *$99,000 Answer*?

28. What are the first, second, fourth, and fifth hurdles worth on the *$99,000 Answer*?

29. What is the first question Ralph is asked? What does Ralph answer?
30. Who were the authors of the following songs, and when were they written: "I'll Be Seeing You" and "It's All Over Now."
31. Who wrote "Goodnight, Irene" and "Goodnight, Sweetheart"?
32. Who sang "Please," a song written by Robins and Rainger for *The Big Broadcast of 1933*?

"The idea of pie in the sky, the get-rich-quick scheme that was going to take Ralph out of his imprisonment in the social structure, was the basis of about ninety percent of the Honeymooners scripts," says Leonard Stern, who wrote with the late Syd Zelinka. "You recognize that when you come from a background like Ralph's, your only hope is a get-rich-quick scheme, striking gold, a miracle. Ralph doesn't have the education or the connections to do it any other way. So it's always fantasy, entering someone else's world."

Stern and Zelinka wrote two undisputed Honeymooners classics: "Alice and the Blonde" and "$99,000 Answer," which won a Writers Guild award. Both were born and raised in New York, and both were Hollywood screenwriters before joining Gleason; it was in Hollywood, when Gleason was doing small movie roles in the late forties, where Gleason first met both writers.

Zelinka, whom A. J. Russell affectionately calls "The Master," was the most experienced of the Honeymooners writers: Before Gleason he'd written for Groucho Marx and Jimmy Durante. Stern worked for Gleason on two occasions—first on *Cavalcade of Stars*, and later after Gleason moved to CBS. The first go-round, he wrote with Zelinka, Marx, Stone, and a writer named Howard Harris; later, with Marx, Stone, and Zelinka.

"Four of us worked together for a year," Stern recalls, "and then that became self-defeating. When we first started writing the Honeymooners, we would alternate an hour-long Honeymooners with three variety shows. Then, as the Honeymooners got more popular, we would do them every other show. Then we started to do three out of four. So as we did more and more Honeymooners, we realized we'd better split up. It wasn't possible to turn them out as we were working. We needed some breathing time.

"Remember, to do a live show every week, you had to begin on Monday, and you didn't finish writing, usually, until the day of the show, which was Saturday. That lead to those apocryphal stories of slipping the script under Jackie's door. We had no choice. We slipped it under when we were finished, because Jackie had total recall, a photographic memory. Everybody else— Art, Audrey, Joyce—siphoned off the pages as fast as they could come out. Invariably, we didn't finish before Friday night, late.

"I always, optimistically, thought we'd finish and I'd be able to go to the theater, and then was constantly canceling theater tickets, because we never finished. Once I was canceling tickets and I heard a thump. I turned around

. . . Marvin had fainted, from sheer exhaustion." (Marvin's widow, Doreen, recalls that Gleason once found Marx working late in the office on a script. Gleason said, "It's not my fault you've got integrity.")

"The following year, we needed sustenance and help, and each team got a new writer, which introduced Andy Russell and Herb Finn. Then we went to the thirty-nine, and we split into three teams."

Stern and Zelinka were the "lone wolves" of the Honeymooners writers: While the other writers worked at Gleason Enterprises' offices at the Park Sheraton Hotel, Stern and Zelinka wrote their scripts at Stern's apartment on Central Park South—much to Gleason's dismay, says Stern.

"One day he called us in and said, 'I have a lovely office here. Why don't you use it? You get stuck for an idea, you can go for a walk in the park.' We answered, 'When we get stuck for an idea, we don't go for walks in the park. We never leave the apartment.' He said, 'Okay, you get an idea, you work it out, then you go for a walk in the park.'

"It got to where we were shouting at each other. We told him, 'We don't go for walks in the park!' Finally he said, 'Okay, okay, I believe you. But I *think* you go for walks in the park.'"

Stern and Zelinka won the battle but lost the war: They ended up working at the Park Sheraton, but not before living through a Kramden-and-Norton–like experience.

"Syd and I were working in the apartment, and it was cold," says Stern. "We had a fireplace, and we lit a fire and went back to work. Syd was smoking a pipe—and to show you the intensity with which we worked—there was a banging on the door. It was the fire department. What happened was, we never opened the flue, and the apartment was filled with smoke. I wrote it off as Syd's pipe, he was totally ignorant of it, and it caused an alarm to go off in the building.

"There we were working on *The Honeymooners*, with all our other senses dulled completely."

# RALPH KRAMDEN, INC.

February 4, 1956 · A. J. Russell and Herbert Finn

1. What bird does Norton the ornithologist spot in Central Park?
2. Norton once spotted a robin with a wishbone in its mouth. What kind of bird did he think it was?
3. Why does Norton watch birds?
4. What does Norton have for lunch?
5. Ralph gives the wrong change to someone on the bus. How does he do it?

RALPH: Well, Norton, there comes a time in every man's life when he has to turn to a friend for help. I need twenty bucks, and so I'm turning to you.

NORTON: Boy, did you just make a wrong turn!

RALPH: Norton, I gotta have it! I'm in terrible trouble. I made a mistake givin' change on the bus this mornin'. I musta given somebody a twenty-dollar bill instead of a single. And at five o'clock tonight I gotta turn in my receipts to the cashier. What am I gonna tell him?

NORTON: Tell 'im the truth. Tell 'im you gave away a twenty instead of a single.

RALPH: I can't do that. This's happened before. Last week I was short five dollars, and the week before I was short eight dollars. I don't want them thinkin' I'm careless with money.

NORTON: Five dollars one week, eight dollars the next, twenty dollars today. You ain't drivin' your passengers—you're supportin' them!

6. Norton doesn't want to lend Ralph money because of what Ralph *doesn't* do with the money. What *doesn't* Ralph do?
7. According to Norton, what happens to people who become big shots?
8. What's Norton's definition of a corporation?
9. What investment firm has an office outside a downtown sewer Norton works at?
10. What does Norton like on his liverwurst sandwiches?
    A. Mustard.
    B. Piccalilli.
    C. Ketchup
    D. Chowchow.
11. What percentage of Ralph Kramden, Inc. does Ralph want to sell Norton, and what office in the corporation does he offer him?

RALPH: What's the matter? Don't that appeal to ya?

NORTON: Of course not! How can I eat liverwurst without Tabasco!

RALPH: Norton, will ya listen to me! You don't know what you're passin' up! Twenty percent of everything I make over and above my salary'll be yours! I own a uranium mine in Asbury Park. If they find uranium on it, twenty percent'll be yours! And that formula I got for shoe polish that glows in the dark. When I put it on the market, twenty percent of the profits'll be yours! You'll be makin' money every time I turn around. Say I shoot a game of pool with Joe Cassidy and I beat him for a buck. Twenty cents of that is yours! Don't you see, Norton? You can't lose!

12. Norton sees two yellow-bellied sapsuckers. How does he know what kind of birds they are, and where is he going to tell the birdwatcher's society he saw them?

13. Alice burns her finger on the stove and doesn't cook supper. What does Ralph make for himself?

14. Norton's hungry and he'd like a piece of fruit. He'd like an _____, an _____, or a _____.

15. Norton wants a larger percentage of Ralph Kramden, Inc. How much does he squeeze out of Ralph?

16. Who's the old lady Ralph used to help on and off his bus?

17. When is her will going to be read? What's the value of her estate?

18. Who is Frederick Carson?

ALICE: He's still her only living relative, her own flesh and blood. He might contest the will.

RALPH: Contest it? What grounds would he have to contest it? Did he help her on and off the bus? No sir, Alice. From what I read in the paper he ain't gettin' a dime! Boy, oh boy, do you know what this means? We're rich! Wait'll your Uncle Matt hears about this. You know how he's always accusing me of bein' nice to him just because I hope to be mentioned in his will? Well, now I don't have to be nice to him!

19. True or false: Ralph is so nervous about his inheritance that he puts shoe polish on his socks.

20. Where does Alice keep the shoe polish?

RALPH: Norton, what're you doin' here? I thought you went to work.

NORTON: Work! Nobody's workin' in the sewer today, Ralph. They declared a holiday.

RALPH: A holiday? What for?

NORTON: For me! Because I'm comin' into thirty-five percent of forty million dollars! Hee, hee, hee. It ain't every day that a sewer worker falls into somethin' like that!

21. What small detail does Norton think of prior to the reading of the Monahan will?

RALPH: Norton, I got some very disappointin' news for ya. Looks like you went through a lot of trouble cuttin' up that paper for nothin'.

NORTON: Oh, cuttin' up the paper was no trouble, Ralph. It was countin' forty million dollars that kept me up all night!

RALPH: Well, anyway, it was all for nothin'. Norton, the fact of the matter is, we ain't gettin' one cent! Not one cent!

NORTON: Whattaya mean?

RALPH: Well, look at the facts. Here we are spendin' Mrs. Monahan's money and forgettin' all about her nephew!

NORTON: We don't have to worry about him, Ralph. She didn't like him.

RALPH: Sure, that's what it said in the papers. But he was her own flesh and blood. And blood is thicker than water, Norton.

NORTON: Yeah, but you helped her on and off the bus!

RALPH: Sure. But I'm still only water! And even if by some miracle she left me the money, the nephew is gonna contest the will. He'll start a legal battle that'll take years to settle. And in the end, I may wind up with nothin'. But there's no reason why you should lose out too, Norton. You bought that stock in my corporation in good faith, and I ain't gonna let you down. I'm gonna give you back every cent you invested plus a nice profit.

NORTON: How much profit?

RALPH (*casually*): Oh . . . say . . . twenty thousand dollars.

NORTON: Twenty thousand! If you ain't gettin' any money from the will, where you gonna get twenty thousand dollars?

RALPH (*trapped*): I'll raise it somehow, Norton. Even if I have to mortgage my furniture!

NORTON (*sincerely*): No, Ralph. I can't let ya make that sacrifice. But I'm glad you made the offer, because it proves somethin' to me. It proves what a friend you are. It proves that you'd go to any lengths to take care of me. And it proves that you're a bigger crook than I thought you were.

22. Where did the Nortons go on their honeymoon, and how did they get there?

23. What's the one thing Norton wants to do now that he's "getting into the millions"?

24. What's the name of Mary Monahan's bird, and what kind of bird is it?

BASCOM: Mr. Carson and the others have been waiting. I'll tell them you're here.

RALPH (*clam-style*): Thank you, sir. Thank you.

NORTON: Just a moment, my good man.

*Norton reaches into his pocket, gets a coin, hands it to the bewildered butler.*

NORTON: Split this with the upstairs maid.

BASCOM (*coldly*): Thank you, sir. *The butler exits.*

RALPH: What'd you do that for?

NORTON: What's the matter? Ain't I supposed to tip him?

RALPH: Sure! But you coulda given him more than a dime!

NORTON: Okay, I'll catch him on the way out.

> *Norton turns into room and sees parrot in cage.*

NORTON: Hey, Ralph! Look! *He takes notebook and pencil out of pocket, starts to write.* "Today I saw a parrot. . . ."

> *Ralph gives him a shot.*

RALPH: Will ya cut it out, Norton! Don't do anything to embarrass me. You ain't even supposed to be here. Now sit down and be quiet.

NORTON: Can't I even look around?

RALPH: All right, but don't touch nothin'.

NORTON: Eeeee, what a grouch!

> *Norton turns to bird cage, pokes his finger in.*

NORTON: Hello there! Polly wanna cracker? *Norton turns to Ralph.* Hey, Ralph. Say hello to the parrot. He's a cute little fella.

RALPH: Nothin' doin'. I'm allergic to parrots. Every time I go near one they make me sneeze.

25. Ralph figures Mary Monahan must have spent at least _____ on the furniture in her den.

26. Who is Robert Hilliard Bradley?

27. Who are Mary Monahan's butler and maid, and how much does she leave each in her will?

28. What habit has Norton picked up watching quiz shows on TV?

29. How much did Mary Monahan leave her nephew, and what did she expect he'd do with it? What does Ralph hope he'll do with it?

30. What does Mary Monahan bequeath to Ralph?

CARSON: Let's see, where was I? Oh, yes. "To such a man and only such a man would I entrust my Fortune. I therefore direct that immediately upon the reading of this will, Ralph Kramden take possession of my Fortune, together with a lifetime supply of Doctor Tweedles' special parrot biscuits."

RALPH (*leaps out of his chair again*): I'm rich! I'm rich!

> *He and Norton start dance again. Suddenly Ralph does a take, freezes with one foot in the air and arms in awkward position. He does a skull toward parrot cage. He points to cage and looks at Mr. Carson.*

RALPH: Buh, buh, buh, himmmmma, hmmmmmma. . . .

> *Carson unhooks cage from stand.*

CARSON: That's right, Mr. Kramden. This is Fortune. And according to the will you take immediate possession.

*He hands cage to Ralph, who takes it.*

RALPH: Buh, buh, buh. . . .

NORTON: Who gets all the money?

CARSON: The bulk of the estate, some forty million dollars, goes to Doctor
Tweedles' Animal Hospital.

*The butler walks over to Norton, taking coin out of his pocket. He hands it
to Norton.*

BASCOM: Here you are, my good man! Split this with your friend.

PARROT (*voice offstage*): I'm rich! I'm rich! I'm rich!

*Ralph starts to sneeze.*

DISSOLVE.

© PRESTON BLAIR PRODUCTIONS.

# YOUNG AT HEART

February 11, 1956 · Marvin Marx and Walter Stone

1. Who is "super atomic passion," Judy Connors' latest love? Who is Judy's former boyfriend, and why did she dump him?
2. How old are Judy and "super atomic passion"?
3. Why is Judy meeting her boyfriend at the Kramdens' apartment?
4. Where are Judy and her boyfriend going on their date?
5. Ralph comes home and wants to eat right away because:
    A. He's going bowling.
    B. He's going to the pool hall.
    C. There's a meeting at the Racoon Lodge.
    D. He wants to take a bath and go to bed.
6. Where does Alice want Ralph to take her, and what does she want to do there?
7. Why doesn't Ralph have to go to the amusement park to see the crazy house?
8. How long have Ralph and Alice been past the age for roller skating?
9. Ralph: "Let's face it: Our youth is passed, the golden years are gone. We've hit the _____."
10. What is Norton's definition of "icky"?
11. When was Norton last in the Tunnel of Love? What is his response when he hears that Alice wants Ralph to take her there?
12. When Wallace, a.k.a. "super atomic passion," comes to the Kramden apartment, what does Ralph think he wants?
13. Who is "angel cake"?
14. What does Wallace have waiting in front of the apartment building?
15. What's the matter with Ralph? Isn't he hep? Doesn't he dig?
16. True or false: Judy Connors lives on the same floor as the Nortons.
17. Why is this a big night for Wallace and Judy?
18. What custom in the sewer is akin to giving a girl your pin?
19. What is Wallace and Judy's special greeting to one another?
20. Alice thinks she's fourteen; look at Ralph, he's _____.
21. Ralph says, "Get dressed, we gotta go to _____."
    A. The junior prom.
    B. The senior prom.
    C. Fred's Landing.
    D. Fred's gasoline station.
22. What dances and expressions does Ralph want to learn to prove to Alice that he wants to stay young?
23. Norton about Ralph: "How can anyone so _____ be so _____?"
24. When Norton sees Ralph in his outfit, he says it's like seeing:
    A. Niagara Falls for the first time.
    B. Yucca Flats after the blast.
    C. Boulder Dam for the first time.
    D. Somebody kissing a potato.

*Judy and Wallace.*
COURTESY HOWARD
BENDER. COPYRIGHT
© 1985 HOWARD
BENDER.

25. Ralph dresses up like a hepcat. Describe his outfit.
26. Norton says Ralph isn't exactly:
    A. The Grand High Exalted Mystic Ruler.
    B. A Ding Dong Daddy from Dumas.
    C. Pierre François de la Briosche.
    D. Johnny Mercer and Richard Whiting.

*Ralph is dressed in his conception of being young. He is wearing brown and white saddle shoes, Thom McAn–style, loud argyle socks, white duck pants. He is wearing school sweater with large football letter over football on it. On top of this he is wearing candy-striped blazer. He is also wearing old-style straw hat. He is carrying a ukulele.*

RALPH (*expectantly*): Well, Norton, do I look young enough?
*Norton without answering just circles Ralph, surveying-style. Ralph, a little impatiently, speaks again.*

RALPH (*impatiently*): Well, how do I look?
NORTON: Wait a minute, Ralph. Gimme a chance. Let me drink this whole thing in. This is sorta like seein' the Grand Canyon for the first time!
RALPH (*a little annoyed as Norton continues surveying*): Well, what do you think?

156

NORTON (*so-so-style*): Well, I guess it's all right. Of course you ain't exactly no Ding Dong Daddy from Dumas!

RALPH: What do you mean? Ain't this the way college kids dress?

NORTON: I'll tell you, Ralph. I think the last college kid that dressed like that was the original William of William and Mary!

## 27. What dance is Norton going to teach Ralph?

Imagine, if you can, Marx—who would imitate Kramden—and Stone—who would assume the identity of Norton—choreographing this scene where Norton tries to teach Ralph the Hucklebuck. The references to Ralph dancing "Reggie-style" are to Gleason's Reggie Van Gleason III character. Other Gleason characters, like Fenwick Babbitt and The Poor Soul, often appear in the writers' stage directions in the scripts.

Marx and Stone were not only script writers, they were choreographers as well. Their stage directions were always explicit and detailed, much more so than any of Gleason's other writers.

Michael Drury, writing in *Collier's* magazine in 1955, said the pair was "dedicated to the word 'style,' meaning 'in a certain fashion.' Directions in their scripts are full of the word: Ralph stamps his feet baby-style; Norton looks at Ralph scared-style; Trixie comes in wearing hat and coat having-been-downtown-style and carrying many packages not-grocery-style."

NORTON: Okay, Ralph. I got a great one here for you. It's called "The Hucklebuck." Now I'll put it on and you just watch me.

*Norton turns and puts needle on phonograph and starts it. During intro to verse Norton snaps fingers and taps his foot rhythmically. On first line of verse Norton bends at waist and grabs pants at knees with thumb and forefinger. At the end of line, still holding knees of pants, he does a hop forward. He holds this position and at end of second line—He does a second hop. He still holds position and at end of third line—Does another hop. At conclusion of verse he releases pants and stands erect. Through following lines of chorus he does Norton-style jitterbug steps fast and crazy. For the rest of the song he does fancy and hep movements, which follow directions given in lyrics of song.*

*At conclusion of this, music to Hucklebuck continues without lyrics and Norton goes into fast and fancy jitterbug moves. Ralph is watching all this in utter amazement, I'll-never-be-able-to-do-that-style. As Norton gets wilder and wilder, Ralph reaches over and takes arm off phonograph, and music stops. Norton, slowing-down-style, stops, too. Ralph, grabbing Norton, speaks.*

RALPH: Wait a minute. Wait a minute. You don't expect me to do that, do you? I could never learn that.

NORTON: It's very simple, Ralph. Just listen to me and I'll tell you exactly what to do. Now durin' the first line of the song—you grab your pants at the knees and you do a little hop like I did. Now try it.

*Ralph bends, grabs his pants at the knees, and with great effort and stiffly, takes a broad-jump kind of hop, but a very short distance.*

RALPH: Well, how was it, Norton?

NORTON (*not too enthusiastic*): Well, now I know how Orville Wright felt when they kept yellin', "You'll never get it off the ground!"

RALPH (*disgusted*): Look, Norton, we better forget it. I'll never learn.

NORTON: Don't worry, Ralph, you'll learn. Just give yourself a little time. Now for the next two lines of the song you just do that hop again, then we get into the chorus. Now for the first couple of lines of the chorus, you just act hep. Move around a little. Do any kind of steps. But just act gay, like you're havin' a good time. You know, get in the groove!

*Ralph tries this. He puts on forced smile and moves around clam-style, gay jitterbug. It is basically Reggie dance moves as done by stilted clam. Norton watches this, shaking head a little.*

NORTON: I said get in the groove, not in the grave. Be gay!

*Ralph continues for a few more seconds, then stops.*

NORTON: All right, I think you're learnin' there, Ralph. Now for the rest of the song, the words tell you exactly what you gotta do. Just listen to the words and do whatever they say. Push. . . .

*Ralph gives motion as giving somebody a shove.*

NORTON: Hunch. . . . *Ralph hunches back.* Move your sacroiliac. . . .

*From shoulders down, Ralph tries to shimmy.*

NORTON: Wiggle. . . .

*Ralph goes from shimmy into wiggling his rear end. Norton watches this, then comments.*

NORTON: Like a snake, Ralph—not an elephant.

*Ralph extenuates wiggle, trying to get with it. Ralph completes wiggle.*

NORTON: Now waddle!

RALPH (*hesitating*): How do you waddle? Like a duck?

NORTON: Well, you, ah, ah . . . you ah . . . it should be easy for you, Ralph. Just walk the way you always do.

*Ralph just gives him a look.*

NORTON: Now look, Ralph, I'll put the record on again and we'll try it. Now get with it. Be gay. Watch me and do whatever I do.

*Norton crosses, puts needle onto record, then crosses back and he and Ralph face audience and stand beside each other. As music comes in and during intro to verse, Norton does crazy jitterbug steps and Ralph, trying to be gay, does clam version of Reggie-style dance steps. Then, on first line of verse, both do forward hop with pants grabbed at knees. They repeat hop on each of next two lines of verse. During following lines of chorus, they go back into Norton's jiggerbug and Ralph's Reggie-style-but-clam dance.*

*After they get into dancing to instrumental chorus, door opens and Alice enters. She stands there watching them in amazement for a few seconds. As Ralph does a turn he sees her. He freezes a-little-embarrassed-style. Then he crosses and turns phonograph off. Norton slows down gradually after phonograph is off. As Norton is slowing down, Ralph gives him a shot with elbow.*

"That wasn't rehearsed. I had an idea what I was gonna do," says Carney of his Hucklebuck dance, one of the funniest scenes in all the *The Honeymooners* episodes. "Years ago I used to do a little bit of eccentric dancing. I've got an ear for music and rhythm and I just improvised those dance steps. Anything to make it look ridiculous, to give the impression that Norton thought he knew what he was doing."

28. Ralph is taking Alice:
    A. Dancing and roller skating.
    B. To the Crazy House.
    C. Dancing at the Hong Kong Gardens.
    D. To see Spade Cooley at the Sons of Italy hall.
29. What does Ralph "pin" Alice with?
30. At the skating rink, Ralph's worried he'll lose his _____ instead of recapturing his youth.
31. Norton leaves Ralph, Alice, and Trixie at the skating rink to:
    A. Get the skate key from his Handy Housewife Helper.
    B. Get a wheel on his skate oiled.
    C. Get coffee for everybody.
    D. Play a Basil Fomeen record on the jukebox.
32. What do Alice and Trixie want from the snack bar?
33. When Ralph and Alice were dating as kids, where did they go to eat at the end of the evening, what did they order, and how much did it cost?
34. The waiter at the restaurant Ralph and Alice ate at said he had no:
    A. Bread.
    B. Fortune cookies.
    C. Sweet and sour lichee nuts.
    D. Pigs' knuckles and sauerkraut.
35. Ralph and Alice used to go to dances at the Sons of Italy hall. What bands played there?

NORTON: Hey, remember Hal Kemp? He used to have that singer with him. Hey, Trixie, what was the name of that singer?

TRIXIE: Don't you remember? It was Skinny Ennis.

NORTON: Yeah, that Skinny Ennis. He used to always sing that song. . . . *Sings, à la Skinny Ennis, "Got a Date with an Angel."*

RALPH: Yeah, they don't write songs like them anymore. Remember? . . . *Sings "Did You Ever See a Dream Walking?" and "You Oughta Be in Pictures."*

NORTON: Hey, Ralph, how about the night we snuck into the Arcadia Ballroom. Nick Lucas was there. *Sings "Tip Toe Thru the Tulips with Me."*

## 36. Who said, "It's a shame youth has to be wasted on young people"?

"That speech at the end of the show, where Gleason did it straight— where he apologized, told Alice he loved her, where he summed up—it was called 'the walking speech,'" says Stone. "It was Gleason's idea, and it was a great device. It was perfect, because you couldn't go off with people thinking that he was still feeling the way he did when he abused her. It took the curse off.

"If he didn't have that at the end, I don't think women would like the show at all. If he didn't have that thing, I don't think the Honeymooners would have been acceptable. People don't want to watch a guy who's unlikable all the time.

"Gleason knew instinctively you can't have that. You're going to hate him. He said, 'You've got to bring him back.' That was his way of doing it, which was a really good way."

# A DOG'S LIFE

February 18, 1956 · Leonard Stern and Sydney Zelinka

"I remember the dog show because it was based on fact," says Stern. "My mother-in-law and father-in-law on a Thursday night decided to stay home instead of going out, and my mother-in-law looked to see what was in the icebox. She made him hamburgers, forgetting she'd put the dog food in there.

"He told her the hamburgers tasted funny. She told him she bought only the best meat, and then realized it was dog food. Jimmy, my father-in-law, told me the story, and he said 'Don't tell Bianca.' Then I got the idea of using it.

"When we finished writing it, we invited Bianca and Jimmy and two of their friends to the show. I told Jimmy what we'd done. As the story unfolded, my mother-in-law, still not realizing, turned to her friend and said, 'That could happen to anyone.' Then Jimmy said to her, 'Why do you think we're here?"

1. True or false: Alice went to the dog pound with Mrs. Manicotti.
2. What kind of dog does Alice get?
3. What does Alice feed the dog?
    A. Trixie's potato salad.
    B. Lettuce for his teeth.
    C. Horsemeat.
    D. Neapolitan knockwurst.
4. Who's going to take Alice's dog to get his shots?
5. Why don't the Nortons have a dog?
6. The Manicottis live:
    A. Upstairs from the Kramdens.
    B. Downstairs from the Kramdens.
    C. On Himrod Street.
    D. Behind Fred's gasoline station.
7. The Racoons have more emergency meetings than the _____. They've had _____ during the last week.
8. What meeting at the lodge is really a poker game?
9. Norton unknowingly eats the dog food Alice has in the icebox. He eats it:
    A. With chowchow.
    B. On a hero.
    C. On crackers.
    D. With spaghetti.
10. What's Norton's weight?
11. True or false: Anything Trixie fixes for Norton is strictly out of the wood.

NORTON: You're a lucky guy, Ralph. The only things Trixie serves me come out of a can. If they put stuff like this in cans, I wouldn't mind.

*Ralph's eyes light up.*

RALPH: Norton. You just gave me a million-dollar idea! Why can't I put this stuff in cans?

NORTON (*impressed*): Ralph, you're sitting on a gold mine! First thing you gotta do is get the recipe from Alice.

RALPH: That's the last thing I do. If I tell Alice about this, she'll just pooh-pooh the idea. She still keeps throwing up to me the money I lost on the one mistake I ever made—that shoe polish that glows in the dark.

NORTON: Then there was the electric zipper . . . I went for a little bundle on that one. And how about that permanent indelible lipstick formula you bought?

RALPH: Wait a minute—wait a minute. A permanent lipstick could make a fortune, and every test we made proved it was a permanent lipstick. How about the model we tested it on? After she put it on her lips it didn't come off on the coffee cup, it didn't come off on cigarettes. You couldn't get it off on a handkerchief, and you couldn't smear it, right?

NORTON: Yeah, I gotta admit it was permanent all right. If only it coulda been made in some other color but green.

RALPH: I still say we gave up too soon on that. Remember, Norton, Paris wasn't built in a day.

NORTON: I think you mean Rome. Rome wasn't built in a day.

RALPH: Was Paris?

12. Who invented the wrench-lock?
13. What does Norton want to call Alice's "appetizer"?

RALPH: Norton, you've been in with me on a couple of losing propositions, but now you're in on a winner. When we get this business started, you've got a lifetime job with us.

NORTON: It's hard to believe, Ralph. After twenty years working in the sewer, I'll finally have a job where I can take home samples!

14. What name for the appetizer does Ralph suggest?

RALPH: Norton, I promised you a job. And I'm gonna keep that promise. But you ain't working in the advertising department. Now, keep quiet and lemme think. Simple. A combination of both names: I'll call it KranMar.

NORTON: KranMar . . . KranMar's what?

RALPH: KranMar's Mystery Appetizer.

NORTON: That's good, Ralph. Very good. Now what you need is a little slogan to put across the can. Something catchy. How about this? Just one taste, and none'll go to waste.

RALPH: Not bad, Norton. But it's too long. What you gotta have is something short and right to the point. *Snaps fingers.* I've got it. KranMar's Mystery Appetizer . . . It's dog-gone good.

15. Who does Ralph ask to finance his scheme to sell KranMar's?
16. Mr. Marshall's secretary is:
    A. Miss Wilson.
    B. Gloria.
    C. Miss Evans.
    D. Shirley.
17. Who does Mr. Marshall ask to taste Ralph's delicious mystery appetizer?
18. Ralph wouldn't give anything his mother-in-law cooks to a _____.
19. Who suspects that Ralph's appetizer is really dog food?
20. What employee at the Gotham Bus Company raises dogs?
21. What kind of name does Trixie want Alice to give her dog?
22. Why has Norton been going to work an hour early all week?
23. Norton calls Trixie the _____ of _____.
24. Why doesn't Ralph want Alice to have a dog?

RALPH: Well, keeping a dog costs money. You gotta get a license, collars, a leash, sweaters. It gets sick and you gotta take it to the doctor. Them veterans are expensive. We ain't got that kinda money to spare.
NORTON: Alice'll manage. She'll find things to cut down on.
RALPH: Yeah, and I know just what she'll cut down on. Well, I'm not letting that dog take the food outta my mouth!
    *Norton points to bowl.*
NORTON: Up till now the shoe's been on the other foot. Besides, Ralph, it's nice to have a pet.
RALPH: I got nothing against pets if they're of some use. Take a horse—a horse works for you. A cow gives milk. A chicken gives eggs. And a cat gets rid of mice. But a dog is useless.
NORTON: Hold on. They use dogs to take care of sheep.
RALPH: All right. The next time I have a flock of sheep in this apartment, I'll get a dog!

25. What time does Ralph go to bed?
26. Who's the clerk at the dog pound?
    A. Mr. Peck.
    B. Mr. Faversham.
    C. Mr. MacGregor.
    D. Charlie.

27. How long does the dog pound keep dogs before they're "over the limit"?

"The ending of the dog show was sort of a backward real-life story of ours," says Cora Zelinka, Syd's widow. "When we came to New York we had a dog and Syd didn't know what to do with it, so he took the dog to the pound. When he came home he said, 'Cora, did I see a dog there!' He would have brought it home if he could have."

28. How many dogs does Ralph take home from the dog pound?

ALICE: What are you doing with my pup? And those other dogs?
RALPH: Honey, would it be too much trouble for you if we had three dogs in the house? I love this one—and you see, these two have been here past the limit, and if nobody takes them, well. . . .
ALICE: Ralph, after all these years I should have known—your bark is much worse than your bite.

© PRESTON BLAIR PRODUCTIONS.

"There was a show—Jackie discovers some new food in the refrigerator which he thinks is a wonderful hors d'oeuvre and it turns out to be dog food— I remember when we were doing it," says George Petrie, who played more characters on *The Honeymooners* than any other supporting actor. "Jackie had a funny line. He stopped the rehearsal and said, 'I think Norton should have that line.' He'd never say Art; he'd say Norton. He thought it would be a bigger laugh if Norton did it.

"You've got to give him credit, because Jackie was smart. They changed it and it was a very big laugh. How big it would have been the other way, I don't know. Jackie was smart enough—like Jack Benny and all the great comics—he knew the value of the people around him. He knew what Carney contributed to the show. He did that on several occasions, saying something should be Norton's line."

# HERE COMES THE BRIDE

February 25, 1956 · Marvin Marx and Walter Stone

1. Who are the Racoons throwing a bachelor party for, and who is he marrying?
2. What night is the party being held?
3. What is Norton's toast to the prospective groom?
4. How long did the Kramdens live with Alice's parents when Ralph and Alice were first married?
5. Who seems like a nice guy when he's dancing on the Red Skelton show?
6. Stanley Saxon doesn't want to argue with his bride-to-be about moving in with her parents. Norton: "If you don't want to argue, _____."

STANLEY: It's too late now, Ralph. Agnes has made up her mind.

RALPH (*shocked*): Agnes has already made up her mind! Agnes has already made up her mind! Who cares if she made up her mind! This is the United States. The twentieth century. A man's home is his castle. And in that castle he is king. You, Stanley, are the king of your castle!

NORTON: Here, here!

STANLEY: But Agnes was very definite about it, Ralph. I don't want to argue.

NORTON: You don't want to argue? Then what are you gettin' married for? Believe me, Stanley, Ralph has the right idea. Let 'em know who's boss right away. That's the way I started Trixie out. I let her know that I was king of my castle. In fact, when we got married, we had an argument about the very same thing. You know, about us livin' with her family. Boy, she started an awful row. But I put my foot down. I said, "Trixie, we're movin' in with your folks!"

*Stanley Saxon.*
COURTESY JIM ENGEL.

167

A moment later:

RALPH: I now propose a toast to the new Stanley . . . the king of his castle!
*They all drink their beer and put their glasses back on table. Stanley has a lot more confidence now.*
RALPH: Well, Stanley, now what'da'ya say?
*Stanley looks up at Ralph I'm-a-changed-man-style. He then tilts his head back, but looking straight forward, and starts beating his chest and howling Tarzan-style. As Stanley yells in this Tarzanlike manner, Ralph and Norton exchange glances and nod heads as if to say, "Well, we convinced him."*

7. Who thinks Ralph rented his tuxedo and top hat from an undertaker?

"I can remember when we were going to the wedding," Audrey says. "We discussed what kind of dress I'd wear and I told the costume designer [the late Peggy Morrison]. She was a very nice woman, but she had a little problem of belting brandy.

"Jackie said he wanted something that looked like I was going to a Polish wedding, a skirt that stuck straight out with tulle, the fabric everybody wore years ago. Peggy got the perfect dress, but it was miles too long.

"I tried it on and took the skirt and held it up as far as it should go and put safety pins in it. Tulle you can cut. You don't have to hem it. So I said, 'Peggy, if you just cut this off it'll be perfect, right where these pins are.' She disappeared with the dress.

"I didn't see it again until it was time to put it on to walk through the door. She had belted just enough brandy that she had cut it so short that it was ridiculous. I looked like Shirley Temple doing 'Good Ship Lollipop' or something. I said, 'Jack, what am I going to do?'

"He said, 'Stay behind the table.'"

8. How long has Alice's sister Agnes been "practicing" for her wedding day?
9. Name three people other than Stanley Saxon who wanted Agnes to get married.
10. What did Agnes do at the reception after she threw her bouquet?
11. Where did Ralph rent his tuxedo?

RALPH: By the way, Alice, make sure you get this suit back to McCardle's first thing in the morning. I'm renting it by the day and my time's up at noon.
ALICE: All right, Ralph.
*Ralph now opens box, which is empty, and then removes tuxedo jacket. Underneath tuxedo jacket Ralph is wearing top part of long underwear and*

*instead of a shirt is merely wearing a stiff shirt-front dickey and bow tie, which only covers space between lapels. And instead of sleeves he is just wearing fake celluloid cuffs. He starts to fold jacket and put it in box. As he is putting it in box, he speaks.*

RALPH: Boy, Alice, this formal dressin' is murder. Imagine! A guy like the Duke of Windsor has to dress like this all the time!

ALICE (*sarcastically*): Yeah, I wonder where he gets his long underwear!

12. When did the newlywed Kramdens have their first fight?
13. Agnes thinks Stanley's a:
    A. Simp.
    B. Bum.
    C. Beast.
    D. Moax.
14. Who's the fixer of marriage problems?
    A. Mammy Yokum.
    B. Jane Russell.
    C. Martha Washington.
    D. Dorothy Dix.
15. True or false: Agnes borrows Alice's green dress.

Every time a *Honeymooners* episode ends and the credits roll, viewers are reminded that Alice's house, or daytime, dresses were from the "Pat Perkins" line. Pat Perkins was not the name of the dresses' designer, however; in real life there was no Pat Perkins.

Pat Perkins was the name of a line of moderately priced dresses manufactured by Sunnyvale, Inc., a dress manufacturing company owned by the late Mac Kaplan. Kaplan was a marketing genius: When he heard that Gleason was turning the Honeymooners into a half-hour sitcom, he realized there would be no better way to promote his dresses than through what was expected to be one of the hottest shows on television. What he did, says his son, Charles, was offer Gleason all the dresses Audrey Meadows would need for the show, in exchange for a credit at the end of each program.

"This looked like it could be a forever thing, if he could get the credit line on *The Honeymooners*, which would put the Pat Perkins name in front of

*Audrey Meadows and Mac Kaplan* COURTESY CHARLES KAPLAN.

more people than any other name in the history of the garment business," says Kaplan's brother, Seymour.

"It sounded like a marvelous fashion setup for an inexpensive garment, because what wouldn't look great on an Audrey Meadows.

"The only thing was, Mac spent the rest of the time trying to get that apron off her."

16. Where were Stanley and Agnes supposed to spend their honeymoon?

**RALPH:** Boy, she kills me, Norton. Agnes really kills me. She's spent the last twenty years of her life tryin' to catch a husband, and now that she's caught one, she leaves him.

**NORTON:** Yeah . . . women are funny, Ralph. I had a cousin like Agnes. Boy, was she out to hook a husband. She was really desperate. Then when she finally married, she has a fight with her husband on their honeymoon, and runs home to her mother. And believe me, Ralph, here was a girl who tried everything to get married. Love potions! Witchcraft! Loaded fortune cookies! Everything! I'm tellin' you, this girl was on a manhunt longer than Sergeant Friday! In fact, when they were gettin' married and she walked down the aisle, they didn't play (*"Here-Comes-the-Bride"-style*) dum dum de dum. They played (*"Dragnet"-style*) dum de dum dum!

17. Ralph tells Alice to invite Stanley over for supper. What's on the menu?
18. Where has Norton heard the phrase "king of the castle," and who said it?
19. Ralph decides the best way to get Agnes and Stanley back together is to convince Agnes that all men are "beasts." So he tells Alice that when he comes home from work he'll bawl her out in front of Agnes about something she was supposed to have done and didn't do. What was Alice supposed to do, and what is it Trixie can't do because Norton is playing boss of his house, too?

ALICE (*steaming*): Ralph Kramden, how could you dare interfere in their marriage. Putting those crazy ideas in Stanley's head. He told me everything you told him at that bachelor party.
*Ralph becomes sheepish and looks at her macaroni-style. They all start pounding him now.*
AGNES: I might have known this was all your fault, Ralph!
STANLEY: I shouldn't have listened to him, sweetheart.
AGNES: Oh, it wasn't your fault, Stanley. He's been a troublemaker ever since he's been in the family.
ALICE: Well, Ralph, I hope you're satisfied.
*Suddenly Ralph explodes.*
RALPH (*exploding*): Wait a minute! Stop! Hold everything! Are you finished?! Done?! Through?! Now I got somethin' to say. All right, I admit I was wrong about a few things. I shouldn'ta told Stanley that he should set himself up as the ruler of the family. All right, there ain't no ruler. Marriage is a fifty-fifty proposition. I admit I was wrong about that. But I wasn't wrong about the thing that made me say it—about them movin' in with your mother. That ain't no way for people to start married life and you know it, Alice. When you're startin' out, you got to make your own decisions. And if they move in with your mother, they won't be allowed to make one. Maybe I went about it the wrong way, Alice, but what I told them, I meant for their own good. So if you still think I'm wrong, go ahead and think it!
*With this, Ralph wheels and storms into bedroom, slamming door behind him. Alice looks after him, a little thoughtfully. After a split, Agnes speaks.*
AGNES (*told-you-so-style*): You see, Alice, he's nothing but a beast!
ALICE (*defending Ralph's argument*): Now wait a minute, Agnes. I don't agree with everything Ralph told Stanley, but he was right about one thing.
AGNES (*shocked*): You don't mean you're defending him, Alice!

ALICE (*awkwardly*): Well, after all, Agnes, you and Stanley are just starting out in your married life now and you should be able to make your own decisions. And, well, I love Mother as much as you do, Agnes, but if you live with her in her house. . . . *Pauses very awkwardly.* Remember, Ralph and I went through this.

AGNES (*ponders for second and then speaks*): But Alice, we don't have our own apartment and we can't afford to go to a hotel until we find one.

STANLEY (*love-will-find-a-way-style*): Don't worry, Agnes. I'll figure something out.

AGNES (*sweetie-pie-style*): Oh, Stanley, you're so masterful!

The next week:

RALPH: There's a postcard from Agnes and Stanley. It's from Niagara Falls. It says that they're just leavin' and headin' back from their honeymoon.

ALICE: Oh, they're back already, Ralph.

RALPH: Yeah. Soon as they get settled, we oughta take an evening and go over and visit them.
*Ralph puts mail down and starts for bedroom door. Alice stops him by speaking.*

ALICE (*a little awkwardly*): Uh, Ralph, just a minute before you go in the bedroom.

RALPH (*pauses and turns, bewildered*): What's the matter?

ALICE (*not knowing how to break it*): Well, Ralph. . . . Uh, you remember how you told Agnes and Stanley that they shouldn't move in with Mom and Dad to start out their married life?

RALPH (*a little warily*): Yeah.

ALICE: Well, they decided you were right, and they couldn't afford a hotel or anything, and. . . .

RALPH (*exploding*): Alice, don't tell me. Don't tell me that both of 'em, both Stanley and Agnes, are livin' here now!

ALICE: Well, no, Ralph . . . not Agnes and Stanley. . . . You see. . . .
*At this point bedroom door opens and Alice's mother appears.*

MOTHER: Hello, Sonny.
*Ralph turns and look of panic comes on face.*

ALICE: You see, Mom and Dad agreed with you, too. They gave the kids their apartment and they're gonna live here with us!
*Ralph reacts ready-to-cry-style.*

MOTHER: Well, Alice, is supper ready yet?

ALICE: In a minute, Mom.

RALPH (*weakly*): Never mind supper for me, Alice. I just lost my appetite. Besides, I'm gonna turn in early. I just had a terrible shock!
*Mother and Alice just look at Ralph as he takes two chairs and starts putting them together sadly, making his little bed. APPLAUSE UP AND OUT.*

# MAMA LOVES MAMBO

March 3, 1956 · Marvin Marx and Walter Stone

1. Carlos Sanchez has just moved into the Kramdens' building and Alice has made him Ralph's favorite dessert. What is it?
2. What does Carlos do for a living?
3. Who used to live in the apartment Carlos now occupies?
4. What are the Kramdens having for dinner that evening?
5. Alice leaves the apartment for a few minutes to go where, and to do what?
6. What does Trixie make as a welcoming gift for Carlos?
7. Why does Ralph think the new neighbor is an old guy?
8. Norton tells Ralph about an uncle he once had who was a bachelor. What line of work was the uncle in?
9. Carlos is a bachelor, but Norton tells Ralph that after he eats Trixie's potato salad, he won't be alone anymore. Why?
10. True or false: Ralph suggests to Norton that after supper they visit the old guy and play a game of chess with him.
11. Carlos stops by the Kramdens' apartment before Ralph and Norton have a chance to visit him. What does he want?

How did Marx and Stone envision Carlos when they wrote "Mama Loves Mambo"?

*He is Cesar Romero or Cesar Romero type. He is Spanish Latin-lover type with graying temples. He is dressed in gray pants with black gaucho-style sweater and loafers with tassels on them. In short, he looks pretty good and is very suave.*

12. Norton to Ralph, when he gets a look at Carlos: "For an old guy _____."
13. Ralph warns Carlos about the noisy neighborhood, but Carlos tells Ralph the noise won't bother him because he works nights. What is Norton's response?
14. Ralph gives Carlos the hammer he wanted to borrow, and then tells him, "And if you don't mind, _____."
15. As Carlos leaves the Kramden apartment, Ralph uses a Spanish phrase and Norton a Latin expression to bid him goodbye. What does each one say?

ALICE: Isn't he nice, Ralph? Such a gentleman.
RALPH: What do you mean, gentleman. I'm just as much a gentleman as he'll ever be.
*Alice gives him an oh-brother look.*
ALICE: All right, gentleman. This basket of wash has to go into the bedroom.
RALPH: Okay . . . I'll show you that I'm a gentleman. *Ralph crosses quickly and opens bedroom door.* There, I opened the door for you. Well, what are you waitin' for? Carry 'em in!

16. Who does Norton say he looked like before he began eating Trixie's cooking?
17. How many women are taking mambo lessons in the Kramdens' apartment? Who asked Carlos to teach the women the mambo?

Carlos Sanchez was played by Charles Korvin, an East European heartthrob of the fifties. Korvin was considered a good actor in his day, but he had one problem when it came time to do *The Honeymooners*: He couldn't dance. The people casting the show didn't know that, though, because Korvin wanted the role, and lied when asked if he could dance the mambo.

As soon as he was sure he had the part, Korvin went to Dale's, a dance studio on Fifth Avenue in Manhattan, where Roberta Weir, a former Rockette and an instructor at the studio, spent a week trying to teach him how to dance.

"I recognized him as soon as he came in," Weir recalls. "He had that dimple on the chin. When he walked in he said, 'I'm in a panic and you have to help me. . . .' He told me he had the audition and he was given the part, and when they asked him 'Do you mambo?' he said, 'Of course.'

"We worked the basic introduction step where we went forward, and we worked on the crossover thing. I don't think I ever got him to turn. I tried to because that's one of your two basic steps. But he had a problem. He was a very good actor, but he was not a dancer.

"He was a charming man, but before he left I told him, 'I'm surprised you can walk.' He was so uncoordinated. I remember when that show was on the first time and I looked to see what he did, I was embarrassed. I didn't want anyone to know I taught him."

18. Name the artist and the song he recorded that Carlos uses to teach the women the mambo.
19. Which woman asks Carlos if she's got the right hip movement?
20. Ralph comes home in the middle of the lesson and, in a rage, kicks the women out of the apartment. What does he call Carlos as he gives him the boot?
21. How long has Carlos been giving the women mambo lessons?
22. Alice wants to know what's so terrible about learning the mambo. "Everybody does the mambo," she tells Ralph. "Everybody does it?" he questions. "I don't know anybody who does it. I don't do it. Norton doesn't do it. My _____ never did it!"

RALPH: Everybody does it, Alice? Everybody?
ALICE: Well, Ralph, I didn't mean everybody. I just meant that. . . .
RALPH (*not letting her get out of it*): You said everybody, Alice. Well, let me tell you . . . I can name a lot of people who don't do the mambo. For one, I

don't do it . . . and Norton don't do it . . . and I'll tell you somethin' else, Alice. I'll bet you that not once in his entire life has Anthony Eden come home and found his wife doin' this! *On word "this," Ralph gives big wiggle.*

23. The mambo lesson ran late so Alice didn't have time to fix Ralph a hot meal. What does she decide to prepare instead?
24. Alice admonishes Ralph for not treating her like a woman. What are the four things Ralph says he lets her do that prove he recognizes her womanhood?
25. How long does Ralph say Alice was satisfied with him before Carlos arrived with his fancy manners?

ALICE (*exasperated*): Ralph, you're nothing but a . . . but a . . . but a grouchy old crab!

RALPH: I'm a what?

ALICE: A grouchy old crab.

RALPH: (*smug-style*): Sticks and stones may break my bones, but names'll never hurt me.

ALICE: Neither will sticks and stones. They couldn't get through the blubber!

26. Who comes to the Kramden apartment looking for his wife, and why does he think he'll find her there?
27. This distraught neighbor's wife has been practicing the mambo all day. What happens when she practices that drives him crazy?

*The Manicottis.*
COURTESY
JOHN F. LANGTON, JR.

176

NORTON: You mind if I stay down here with you for a while? I got to get out of the house. That Trixie's drivin' me crazy.

RALPH: What's the matter?

NORTON: I don't know. Everything I do Trixie picks on me. Pick, pick, pick. She started in on me as soon as I got home. She says, "Why don't you take off your boots out in the hall? . . . Do you have to wear that hat in the house? . . . Why don't you wear a jacket when you come to the table? . . . Can't you be a gentleman?" What's the matter with her, anyway? Don't she know that old saying? You can't make a silk purse out of a sow's ear!

RALPH: I know what you're goin' through, Norton. Alice is startin' in on me now, too.

NORTON: Alice is startin' in on you? *Chuckles.* Boy, that's a case of you can't make a silk purse out of a sow!

28. As the three husbands are griping about Carlos and the effect he's had on their wives, Carlos returns to the Kramden apartment. Why?

29. Ralph to Carlos: "It's easy for you to play _____. You don't do any work. When you go to work you dance."

30. Ralph says his dirty hands are proof that what he does for a living is "real work." He tells Carlos to note the difference between his hands, and Ralph's and Norton's. Why does Norton say it's not fair to compare his hands to Carlos's?

31. Ralph tells Carlos to stop causing trouble. Carlos responds by lecturing the husbands on how lucky they are to have caring wives. As usual, Ralph swallows his pride and admits he's been a moax. His final gesture of repentance is to ask Carlos a favor. What is it?

32. Ralph decides he's going to be a gentleman. To prove his sincerity to Alice, he offers to serve Alice breakfast in bed. What does he cook?

33. Ralph tells Alice to stay in bed late because they don't have to be where, until when?

34. Name the things Alice has to get for Ralph while he's preparing her breakfast.

35. Ralph wants to make the bed. What can't he find in the bedroom?

36. Trixie is as worn out as Alice is by having a fuss made over her. In trying to prove that he too can be a gentleman, what silly thing did Norton do the night before that has Trixie in a frazzle?

37. Ralph serves breakfast to both Alice and Trixie. What is his playful instruction as he slops the food into their bowls?

38. Aghast at what Ralph has served, Trixie offers the food to Norton. What is his response?

39. The wives finally admit they like the old Ralph and Norton better than the new Ralph and Norton. What does Norton have Trixie do as a symbol of his "reinstatement" as king of his castle?

# PLEASE LEAVE THE PREMISES

March 10, 1956 · Marvin Marx and Walter Stone

1. Ralph visits his doctor because he's nervous. What's causing Ralph's nervousness?
2. What's Ralph's doctor's cure for nervousness?
3. What's the Aberdeen Proving Grounds for nervousness cures?
4. What four things aggravate Ralph from the time he's in the doctor's office until he gets home?

RALPH: . . . I already had a couple of aggravations and I tried it out.

ALICE: You mean you tried it out already?

RALPH: Already? The first aggravation was when the doctor gave me the bill! Then I gave it the supreme test. I came home from the doctor's office on the subway. And if you wanna test a cure for aggravation, the subway is the Aberdeen Proving Grounds. Well, I get on the subway and naturally I can't get no seat. Well, right away this old lady gets on. And she's carryin' an umbrella. Where does she stand? Right next to me. She starts pokin' me with the umbrella.

*As Ralph starts telling this story he gets steamed and worked up just remembering it.*

RALPH: First she's pokin' me in the back. Then she starts givin' it to me in the arm. Once I got it in the eye. . . .

*Ralph has now worked himself into a little bit of a pitch. From talking about it, he's ready to blow his top. He stops abruptly and starts reciting.*

RALPH: Pins and needles, needles and pins, a happy man is a man who grins. Now what was I mad about? Oh yeah, I was tellin' you what happened on the subway. Well, now you know what the old Ralph would have done to that old lady and her umbrella.

NORTON: Well, you woulda grabbed her umbrella. Broken it in a million pieces. Thrown it on the floor and jumped up and down on it a few times. Then you woulda pulled the emergency cord and stopped the train. You'd force the doors open, and then you'd push the old lady off the train somewhere about twenty blocks from the nearest station!

RALPH: Exactly! But instead I repeated this little sayin', calmed myself down and ignored the whole thing. Well, the old lady finally gets off on Thirty-fourth Street. But don't worry, they send in a substitute! It's a little guy with a rose bush. He holds it over his head, right in my kisser. The thorns are stickin' me in the face and the neck. So I says to him, "Why don't you hold it in front of your own face?" And he says, "I can't, I got rose fever." *Ralph gets steamed just at remembering what the guy said.*

RALPH (*steamed*): I can't, he says, I got rose fever! *Ralph realizes he's getting steamed and goes into saying.* Pins and needles, needles and pins, a happy man is a man who grins. *Forces a sickly smile.* Now, what was I mad about? Oh, yeah, the guy with the rose bush. Well, just when I was ready to blow my top, I start repeatin' the sayin' again. So instead of gettin' mad, I just move away from him. I force my way down to the end of the car. Now, there's a guy standing there with a big board. He don't hold it up straight in front of him. No, he's got it on his shoulder. Every time he turns he hits me right in the back of the neck. I said, "Couldn't you have that thing sent?" He said, "Don't blame me. Some guy is havin' it sent. I'm deliverin' it!" Well, I start with the sayin' again. Pins and needles, needles and pins. . . .

NORTON: It worked again, huh, Ralph?

RALPH (*hesitantly*): Well, I didn't quite make it this time. I broke the board over his head on "A happy man is a man who grins." But it worked them other times, Alice. And it almost worked the last time. If I just keep practicin' I know I'll be fine.

5. If Ralph's doctor's cure for nervousness works on Ralph, what does Norton think should be done with it?

6. Mr. Johnson gets permission from the rent commission to raise the tenants' rent at 328 Chauncey Street. What percentage does he raise it, and how much does it amount to in dollars and cents?

7. Ralph refuses to pay the rent increase, and locks himself and Alice in their apartment. What historical figure does he liken himself to?
   A. Abraham Lincoln.
   B. General Custer.
   C. George Washington.
   D. Alf Landon.

8. What does Alice say is the big difference between George Washington at Valley Forge, and her and Ralph in their apartment?

9. In Kramden's "army" he's the _____, Norton's the _____, and Alice is a _____.

*Mr. Johnson.* COURTESY JOHN F. LANGTON, JR.

10. Other wives stand behind their husbands when they try to accomplish something. Why won't Alice stand behind Ralph?
11. What is Alice saving for Sunday dinner?

RALPH: Boy, it's freezin'. I need some more clothes, Alice. Where's my other pair of long underwear?

ALICE: I washed them the other day. They're hangin' in the bathroom.

*Ralph exits into bedroom. . . . Ralph comes in from bedroom. He is holding long underwear by sides. It is frozen stiff in standing-up position. Underwear is very large size. The arms are over head like man in holdup. Ralph just stands there looking up toward ceiling. Alice is intent on heating water and doesn't notice him. She is intent on waving candle under pan.*

RALPH: When you're done with the candle, you can thaw these out, Liberace!
*Alice sees long underwear stiff and breaks into gales of laughter.*

RALPH: Go ahead, Alice, laugh! Laugh! Sure, it's easy for you to laugh. You're wearin' my other pair!

12. How long have the Kramdens and the Nortons been locked in their apartments? What is Norton's biggest complaint about being locked up?
13. Alice, Ralph, and Norton have a last meal. What does Alice serve?
14. Ralph once read about two men stranded on an island who had to eat the same thing every day. What did they eat?
15. Norton doesn't like celery. What does he imagine he's eating instead?
16. How many hot-water bottles is Norton wearing to keep warm?
17. Ralph decides to climb out the bedroom window in search of food. Where is he going to get it?
18. Where has the sheriff posted guards to prevent Ralph from sneaking out of his apartment?
19. Why does Ralph finally decide to pay the rent increase?

*Ralph puts newspaper up in front of his face. Alice now starts closing suitcase. Just as she is doing this there is a loud clap of thunder. Ralph slowly pulls newspaper down and slowly looks up. As he is looking up it starts to rain. Alice looks at him what-are-you-gonna-do-now-brave-man-style. Ralph looks at her a little macaroni-style. He then gets up slowly and folds newspaper deliberately.*

RALPH (*pulling-victory-out-of-defeat-style*): All right, Alice. I'm gonna give up and pay that increase. But not for the reason you figure. Not because it's rainin'. I'm gonna pay that increase 'cause I just realized I can use it as a weapon. By payin' that increase I can force that landlord into givin' us a new shade in the bathroom!

# PARDON MY GLOVE

March 17, 1956 · A. J. Russell and Herbert Finn

1. Alice is planning a surprise party for Ralph, and she's given Trixie a list of people to call. Who on the list hasn't she been able to reach?
2. Who was Trixie supposed to warn not to say anything about the party to Ralph?
   A. Cassidy.
   B. Reilly.
   C. Fensterblau.
   D. Harper.
3. What time is the party supposed to start, and what night of the week is it scheduled for?
4. What's on Alice's food list for the party?
5. What is Alice giving Ralph for his birthday?
6. Ralph and Norton return from a meeting at the Racoon Lodge with a pizza. Alice tells Ralph not to eat pizza because she's already made him something to eat.
   A. Knockwurst.
   B. Hot dogs, lima beans, mashed potatoes, and spaghetti.
   C. Salad.
   D. Tuna.
7. What are the ingredients in the dish Alice has prepared for Ralph, and what are they good for?
8. Norton: "If _____ were manhole covers, the _____ would be a paradise."

*They eat silently for a moment, with Ralph eyeing the pizza out of the corner of his eye. Finally he can stand it no longer.*

RALPH (*suggestively*): Er . . . Norton, would ya like some of my salad?

NORTON: Not now, Ralph. Maybe after I finish my pizza.

RALPH: Norton, haven't you got any manners? In polite society, if somebody offers you something they got, you're supposed to offer them something you got!

NORTON: I know that! But you said you didn't want any pizza.

RALPH: It don't make any difference! Politeness is politeness. You should offer me some even if I don't want any.

NORTON: All right. You want some pizza?

RALPH (*flatly*): Yes!

NORTON: Well, ya ain't gettin' any.

9. What size piece of pizza would Ralph like?
10. How does Ralph find the guest list for his surprise party?
11. Norton doesn't think Ralph's invited to his own party. Why?
12. Who is Andre?

*Andre.*

13. Why is Andre going to redecorate the Kramdens' apartment for free? What color is he going to paint it?

Andre, as well as Herbert J. Whiteside, "the big Hollywood producer" in "On Stage," was played by Alexander Clark, a stage actor who, like so many of the actors who worked in *The Honeymooners*, was hired by Jack Hurdle. Clark, now in his eighties, is retired from the stage and lives in New York.

"You know, I've imagined these past years what Andre would have had to do in order to put some interior decorating into that apartment," Clark told a gathering of Honeymooners fans at one of RALPH's Honeymooners conventions. "After one quick glance at the apartment, I said, 'Let's concentrate on the outside.' I looked outside the window and I saw that it looked like Sanitation Boulevard.

"I said, 'Well, you can have some gunnysack curtains.' And that icebox—that was from the Middle Ages, the days when the iceman used to come with tongs and drop a big piece of ice in it. I didn't know what to do about the table so I just left it.

"Now that bureau where the glove was put, I figured that should be a highboy, or a lowboy, and I finally said, 'Oh boy!'

"I figured I wouldn't bother about getting curtains for the bathroom, because if the neighbors saw Ralph taking a shower, they'd buy the curtains."

14. What was Alice doing in Morgan's department store that day?
15. Where are before and after photos of the Kramdens' apartment supposed to appear?
    A. *American Weekly.*
    B. The paper that dropped *Little Orphan Annie.*
    C. The Sunday paper.
    D. *Universal* magazine.
16. How long will it take to redecorate the Kramdens' apartment? When was it last decorated?

ANDRE: We have no time to lose, my dear. Now, as to the color scheme for the bedroom. I always try to choose colors that suit one's personality. I had in mind robin's-egg blue trimmed with seashell pink.
ALICE (*dubiously*): Gee, I like it, but I'm wondering about my husband.
ANDRE: You don't think robin's-egg blue and seashell pink suit his personality?
ALICE: I'm not sure. But if you want to play it safe, make it pool-table green and bowling-ball black!

17. Alice wants Andre to come back at _____ o'clock to discuss the redecorating plans.

18. Alice has rescheduled Ralph's party for what day?
19. Alice and Trixie are impressed with Andre's sophistication and manners. What happened to Ralph's and Norton's manners?
20. Andre leaves one of his gloves behind. Where does Alice hide it?
21. Ralph comes home and there's no party. Norton says Alice made up lists of guests and food for the party, and then let Ralph find the lists. So what's the surprise?

RALPH: So it's upstairs in your apartment, huh?
NORTON: What's upstairs?
RALPH: The party! It's upstairs in your apartment!
NORTON: Party? If there was a party upstairs, would I be down here dancin' with you?
RALPH: Don't kid me, Norton. I know what's goin' on. Alice sent you down to keep me here until everything is ready!
NORTON: Ralph, there ain't nothin' goin' on in my apartment. Trixie's fixin' the hem on her skirt, and then she's gonna go visit her mother in Passaic!
RALPH: Are you sure of that?
NORTON: Course I'm sure! I oughta know where my mother-in-law lives!
RALPH: I mean about the party. There's gotta be a party! If it isn't upstairs, then it's down here!
NORTON: It is? Well, I don't wanna be a wet blanket, but this is the deadest party I ever went to!
RALPH: I don't understand this, Norton. You saw the list of food and guests. And Alice is all dressed up. That adds up to a party, don't it? But where is it? What's the answer, Norton? Think! Think!
*Ralph begins to pace thoughtfully; Norton gets an apple from fruit bowl on table, bites it, frowns thinking-style.*
NORTON: How about this, Ralph? She makes a list of the food she's gonna serve, and she makes a list of the people she's gonna invite. She gets everything ready for a real surprise party! Only here's the surprise. It ain't for this year, it's for next year! *Ralph stares him down.* Whattaya lookin' at me like that for? You're the one that asked me to think!

22. Which neighbor does Ralph visit to ask about the party?
23. Norton spots Andre's glove while Ralph is rummaging through a drawer looking for his birthday gift. Which has Andre left behind, the right-hand or left-hand glove?
24. Andre's glove makes Ralph suspicious of Alice. She's dressed up, too, and that fans the flames of Ralph's suspicions. What's Alice's explanation for being dressed up?
25. What does Alice have to do for Trixie before she can make Ralph's supper?

26. What night of the week does Ralph always go bowling?
27. Why does Ralph think Alice called off his party?
28. True or false: Ralph's going bowling, but he's not going bowling.

NORTON: Look, Ralph, whattaya torturin' yourself for? If I were in your place I'd call Alice out here and demand an explanation!

RALPH: What good's that gonna do? You don't think she'll admit it, do ya? Besides, I'll take care of her later. Right now, all I wanna do is get my hands on that guy. And when I do—pow!

NORTON: Well, it ain't like we don't know nothin' about the guy. Let's see what we got. He wears gloves and he smokes cigars. That ain't much to go on, but I got an idea.

RALPH: What is it?

NORTON: Put an ad in the paper. To wit: Found, one glove. Owner can have same by identifying, et cetera, et cetera. . . . When he shows up to claim it, you got him!

RALPH: What kind of an idea is that? He wouldn't come to claim it. He's got a guilty conscience!

NORTON: Now we're gettin' somewhere, Ralph. He wears gloves, smokes cigars, and he's got a guilty conscience!

29. Ralph wants to spy on Alice and her "paramour" from the fire escape; Norton says it's uncivilized for a man to spy on his wife like that. What does he want Ralph to do?
30. What time does Ralph usually leave for work?
31. When Ralph threatens to take off Andre's head, Andre dashes for the door. On his way out he calls Alice:
    A. Alice.
    B. Killer, because she slays him.
    C. Sweetums.
    D. Mrs. Kranston.
32. True or false: Morgan's was going to give the Kramdens new drapes, new rugs, and new furniture.
33. When Ralph realizes he's just cost the Kramdens a newly decorated apartment, he admits he's a:
    A. Clam.
    B. Stupid moax.
    C. Stupidhead.
    D. Moax.

# *YOUNG MAN WITH A HORN*

March 24, 1956 · A. J. Russell and Herbert Finn

1. How long has Ralph been promising to clean out the bedroom closet?
2. Where does Alice want to put the junk she's cleaned out of the closet?
3. Norton didn't show up for a lunch date he had with Ralph. Where was he?
4. Norton's going to take a test for a new job. What is it?
5. What transit authority job does Norton want Ralph to try for?
6. Alice wants to throw out Ralph's cornet with the other junk from the closet. Where did Ralph get the cornet?
7. Name two things Ralph hasn't touched in years.
8. Ralph tries to play the cornet but can't because something's stuck in it. What is it?

*Ralph looks at the cornet and smiles retrospectively.*

RALPH: Yessir, there are a lotta memories attached to this. I can still see myself—a little bit of a kid, standing in the parlor practicing—and my father standing in the doorway, watching—making sure I didn't sneak out to play baseball!

NORTON: How about a little tune, Ralph? Beat out a chorus of rock and roll!

RALPH: Well, it's been a long time, Norton. My lip ain't in shape. But I'll give it a try.

A minute later, after Ralph pulls a sock out of the cornet:

*Ralph starts to play. Ralph does all right until he reaches the high note. Then he hits a real clinker.*

ALICE: I liked it better with the sock in it!

RALPH: I never could hit that high note! I tried and tried and tried but I never could hit that high note!

*Ralph puts the cornet to his lips and plays. He does all right until he comes to the high note. Then he hits the clinker again.*

ALICE: Nobody's watching. Why don't you sneak out and play baseball!

9. True or false: Norton thinks Ralph has a high-frequency cornet that only dogs can hear.
10. What song does Ralph play on the cornet?
11. True or false: Ralph figures that if he'd stuck with his cornet lessons when he was a kid, he could've been another Horace Heidt.
12. Who tried to teach the young Ralph Kramden architecture, and why did Ralph eventually give it up?
13. If Ralph had continued to study architecture, he might've been the guy who built:
    A. The pool hall.
    B. The Racoon Lodge.
    C. The Empire State Building.
    D. The sewers of Paris.

14. The Gunthers once lived in the Kramdens' apartment, and now they've come for a visit on their anniversary. How long ago did they live at 328 Chauncey Street?
15. What is August Gunther known for?
16. What's the view from the Kramdens' bedroom window, and what was it the Gunthers saw when they lived in the apartment?
17. What business is August Gunther's brother-in-law in?

RALPH (*surprised*): August Gunther? You ain't the Gunther that makes Gunther's Doughnuts, are you?

GUNTHER: I am.

RALPH: Well, I'll be darned. Your doughnuts are known all over the country. We eat 'em all the time. As a matter of fact, we got some in the icebox right now. Don't we, Alice?

ALICE (*uncomfortable*): No, Ralph, I don't think so.

RALPH: Whattaya talkin' about! We had a whole boxful this morning!
*He opens the icebox and gets a box of doughnuts.*

RALPH: See, Mr. Gunther?
*He holds up the box, and now he gets a good look at them himself. He laughs weakly.*

RALPH: That's funny. These are Bender's Doughnuts.

ALICE (*covering up*): The . . . er . . . the store was out of yours, Mr. Gunther.

Later, after Gunther has given Ralph his formula for success:

RALPH (*impressed*): To think it all started in this very room. You took stock of yourself, you made a list, and from then on you didn't make any mistakes!

GUNTHER: Well . . . I made one mistake. I loaned my brother-in-law money to go into business.

RALPH: Yeah? What business did he go in?

GUNTHER: The doughnut business! His name is Bender!

18. Ralph decides to list his weak and strong points. What's the first weak point he lists?
19. Norton's granddaddy used to say "There's always hope _____."

One of the great moments in "Young Man with a Horn" is watching Norton blow the cornet in Ralph's ear while Ralph is trying to list his good and bad points. Gleason's timing is impeccable. Just when you think he can't possibly tolerate the noise any longer, he holds his blow-up a few beats longer—and then explodes. But Russell and Finn's original idea for this scene was somewhat different. We pick up their stage directions just after Norton has cleaned the cornet in the sink:

*Norton makes the cover!* REPRINTED WITH PERMISSION FROM TV GUIDE® MAGAZINE. COPYRIGHT © 1955 BY TRIANGLE PUBLICATIONS, INC., RADNOR, PENNSYLVANIA.

*He removes the mouthpiece and blows through it cleaning-style. Then, without replacing mouthpiece, he blows through cornet similarly. He is amazed to see a shower of bubbles come out of the cornet. Recovering from his amazement he realizes he's got a good thing, and starts blowing bubbles gleefully. Ralph, intent on his list, does not notice what is going on until bubbles start falling all around him. He is too stunned to speak as he watches Norton blowing bubbles.*

NORTON: Wanna blow a few?

RALPH: Gimme that! Of all the stupid, childish things to do! A grown man blowing bubbles! Ain't you got no consideration for me? I'm trying to rearrange my life and you blow bubbles! It's not easy, what I'm doing, you know—taking stock of myself, holding a mirror up to myself. It ain't easy to put myself under a microscope this way!

NORTON: You're tellin' me. You'd have a hard time puttin' yourself under the Mount Palomar telescope!

20. Norton cleans up the cornet and then plays it to hear how it sounds. What does he play?
21. Who said, "A person don't look at himself like others see him"?
22. According to Norton, what are five of Ralph's bad points, and what is his good point?

*Ralph reaches onto bureau, picks up cornet and runs his hand fondly over it.*

RALPH: Y'know, Norton, I tried a lot of ways of getting ahead, but the fickle finger of fate always interfered.

NORTON: Don't tell me about the fickle finger of fate, Ralph. I know what you mean. If it hadn't been for the interfering fickle finger of fate, you know what I'd be today?

RALPH: What?

NORTON: Today I'd be the world's foremost dress designer!

RALPH: You? A dress designer?

NORTON: Sure! I studied it when I was in vocational school! I was a genius at it! I entered a competition for a scholarship. And I won, too!

RALPH: No kidding?

NORTON: Sure! Then a big dress designer from New York called me and told me to get right down to his office. He had a job for me! Boy, was I excited! I ran all the way!

RALPH: Well, what happened? How come you wound up in the sewer?

NORTON: Because while I was running up Forty-sixth Street I fell into an open manhole. By the time I found my way out I had two weeks' salary coming! *Ralph watches him a moment, then quietly and calmly opens door.*

RALPH (*oversweetly*): Good night, Norton.

**NORTON** (*cheerily*): Good night, Ralph!

*Norton exits. Ralph shakes head poor-nut-style. He is about to sit and resume work when he spots the cornet and mouthpiece. He inserts mouthpiece into instrument, puts it down. Again he is about to sit when again he blows tentatively into it. Bubbles come out. He smiles an amused smile. Then, after looking around sneaky-Pete-style, he starts blowing bubbles.*

23. Ralph has owed Norton money for a month. How much?
24. List in order the five good points and the twenty-two bad points that appear on Ralph's wall chart.
25. Why does Alice have Trixie buy only eggs for her at the grocery?
26. True or false: Ralph got Alice out of bed at half past three so he could make the bed.
27. Who did Ralph have a disagreement with at the bus company over the population of New York, and what population figure did each quote?
28. How did Norton answer this question on the civil service test: "If you were heating your own home, and oil was 12 cents a gallon and it went up 7 percent, and coal at the same time was $14 a ton and it went up 9 percent, what would you do?"
29. Did Norton pass the test for sewer inspector?
30. True or false: Ralph and Norton are just a couple of hangnails on the fickle finger of fate.
31. Ralph actually did hit the high note once in his life. When?

© PRESTON BLAIR PRODUCTIONS.

# HEAD OF THE HOUSE

March 31, 1956 · Leonard Stern and Sydney Zelinka

1. Who is Dick Prescott?
2. How often does Prescott's column appear in the paper?
3. Norton remarks that a question Prescott asked the previous week must have caused a lot of controversy. Which question did Prescott think it was? Which question did Norton have in mind?
4. What does Norton give as his full name and as his job title?
5. What question does Prescott ask Norton?
6. When Norton retracts his answer, Ralph accuses him of being afraid of Trixie, and goes on to boast that he's the boss in his house. What two things did Ralph say the day he married Alice?
7. Prescott copies down what Ralph says to Norton, and says he's going to print it. When are Ralph's remarks going to appear in the paper?
8. When Prescott leaves, Norton begins to laugh. Why?
9. Norton tells Ralph to call the paper and tell them not to print his statement. Ralph refuses, saying the difference between him and Norton is that he is a boss and Norton is a _____.

Alice has already read Ralph's remarks as scene two opens in the original Stern/Zelinka script. Alice is enraged, and Ralph comes home hoping to head off a confrontation:

*Alice, newspaper in her hand, is angrily pacing up and down. She refers to newspaper once or twice and grimaces at what she sees. Door opens and Ralph enters carrying bouquet of flowers. He's as sweet as sugar and most anxious to smooth things over quickly.*

RALPH: Hello, dear, I brought you some flowers.
*He extends flowers. Alice just glowers at him.*
RALPH: Honey, do you want me to put these flowers in water?
ALICE: No. But you can put your head in water three times and take it out twice! . . . Ralph Kramden, did you realize how ridiculous those flowers make you look?
RALPH: Ridiculous? I was just bein' nice.
ALICE: Nice! You were scared stiff to come home without a peace offering! Some big boss!
RALPH: I wasn't scared, Alice. I wasn't scared!
ALICE: You didn't even have enough nerve to come home right after work!
RALPH: I had to work overtime.

10. Ralph goes home that night without the evening paper; Alice asks to see it. Why?
11. Ralph tells Alice the evening paper is never entering their house again. Why not?
12. How many men are quoted in the questioning photographer's column?

13. Alice asks Ralph why he was the only man to make the idiotic statement he did. He says \_\_\_\_\_.
14. According to Ralph, men are leaders, women are \_\_\_\_\_.
15. Ralph decides to celebrate his "emancipation" as boss of the house by doing what?
16. What happened to Ralph the time he and Alice ate at a Hungarian restaurant?

RALPH: I'm going upstairs and get Norton. Him and me are drinking this wine! And when I get back it better be right here where I put it!
*Puts it down on table to emphasize point.*
ALICE: I'm not going to let you do it!
RALPH: Alice, for the last time—what I wanna do, I do! And nobody stops me. Remember this—I wear the pants around this house!
ALICE: Believe me, they'd fit around this house!

"I remember one of Jackie's greatest skills was reaction," says Stern. "I remember once saying to Jackie, 'You don't have any of the punch lines.' He said, 'I react?' I said yes. He said, 'Then I'll take care of myself.'"

17. Alice pours out the wine Ralph wants to drink and replaces it with grape juice. She's sure Ralph won't suspect a thing, but she's worried Norton might notice. Trixie tells her not to worry because \_\_\_\_\_.

"I remember one of my favorite scenes was the wine and the grape juice," says Carney. "We really were laughing at each other—he broke me up and I'm sure I broke him up. But it was part of the thing, because we were supposed to be laughing . . . crocked and everything. Funny scene."

RALPH: Well, how about getting down to business.
NORTON: Nice-looking bottle of wine, Ralph.
RALPH: Yeah. Norton, you gotta be pretty careful when you're buying wine. When I went in the store, the guy tried to talk me into buying a stale bottle of 1939 stuff. But I was too smart for him. I made him give me a bottle of fresh wine—1956!
NORTON: Guess they have a tough time getting rid of that old stuff.
*Ralph pours into Norton's water glass till it's half full.*
NORTON: That's enough, Ralph. I'd rather start with a short one.
RALPH: Well, let's drink to all the poor souls in the world who're afraid of their wives.
NORTON: As we say in the sewer, Ralph, here's mud in your eye!
*They drink bottoms up. After drink, Norton considers the taste a moment.*
NORTON: An amusing little wine.
RALPH: Sure goes down smooth . . . but when it gets down—what a kick!
NORTON: Va va va voom!

RALPH: That first one might be lonesome down there. How about giving it a little company?

NORTON: Pour away, mine host.

*Ralph refills glasses. Clink glasses and drink. As drink hits bottom, shudder from effect.*

NORTON: Ralph, I'm proud to be sitting here drinking with you because you proved to me that you're a man who backs up his words with his deeds!

RALPH: And that's the way I've always been. And the next time you see that no-good Joe Fensterblau, you can tell him about me.

NORTON: You mean that bus driver? What've you got against him?

*Ralph refills glasses as he answers.*

RALPH: Plenty. Ever since that poker game where I hadda quit early, he keeps accusing me of being afraid of Alice. And that's not all . . . every time I bump into him down at the bus company, he's always telling me I'm a bigmouth and four-flusher!

NORTON (*comforting*): Ralphy-boy. How can you get upset over what that Fensterblau tells you. He ain't got a mind of his own—he just repeats what everybody else says. Anyway, you're too big a man to carry a grudge. How about a drink to that poor misguided soul, Joe Fensterblau.

*They both raise glasses. This time they have a little trouble getting the two glasses to meet. They do and they drink. Norton coughs when it gets down.*

RALPH: Boy. When you've had a few'a those you know you've had something.

NORTON: You said it . . . but you know, I was just thinking it might be smart if we had a little something to eat with this.

RALPH: Okay. I'll see what's in the icebox.

*Ralph rises. He is unsteady. Heads in direction of bureau.*

NORTON: Hey, pal. It's over this way.

*Ralph turns and makes his way to icebox.*

RALPH: That Alice. She's always moving the furniture!

*Ralph misses door handle a few times.*

NORTON: Looks like she's still moving it.

*Ralph opens icebox. Takes out a plate with something on it and puts it on the table with two spoons. He sits down.*

RALPH: Tuna fish.

NORTON: Take it away.

RALPH: But pal, tuna is one of your favorites.

NORTON: Yeah. But fish with red wine is unthinkable.

RALPH: I don't like tuna fish anyway.

NORTON: With your kind permission, Ralph, I'll get something else.

*Ralph, hand on Norton's shoulder, stops him from rising.*

RALPH: It's kind'a you pal, but before you start out for the icebox there's something I wanna do. I wanna drink one drink alone—to you.

*Norton sits. Ralph pours himself a short drink. Lifts glass.*

RALPH: To you! *Drinks.*

NORTON: And now, pal, I wanna drink one to you.

> *Norton pours himself a big drink. As he keeps pouring, Ralph stops him.*

RALPH: Wait a minute! What's the idea? When I drank to you I only took that much. *Ralph indicates small amount.*

NORTON: Well, there's much more of you to drink to!

RALPH: Drink hearty!

> *Norton drinks. After he finishes he picks up tuna plate and rises. He is unsteady and after taking one step away from table he turns back and leans on it. Ralph sees his trouble.*

RALPH: What'sa matter, pal?

NORTON (*holding head*): Ooooh . . . I don't know how I'm gonna get home tonight.

RALPH: You'll make it.

NORTON: Yeah. If there's some way'a falling upstairs.

> *Norton gets to icebox after a struggle. He puts plate of tuna fish on top shelf. He remains there looking for something else.*

RALPH (*sings*): Oh, Nellie dear!

NORTON: I always did love the way you sing that.

RALPH: Thanks, pal.

> *He continues with song. As Ralph sings, Norton searches in icebox.*

NORTON: Aha!

> *Takes out plate and comes back to table.*

NORTON: Ralph, I got us something.

RALPH (*interrupts his singing*): What is it?

NORTON: Tuna fish.

RALPH: Good. I love it.

> *They both dig into tuna fish with spoons. As they do this, Ralph picks up song again. Norton joins in harmony as curtain closes.*

18. Ralph pours drinks for himself and Norton. Who makes the first toast, and what is it?

19. How does Ralph characterize the "wine"?

20. What is the second toast, and to whom is it made?

21. In the middle of their bender Ralph begins laughing hysterically, and Norton asks what he's laughing at. What is Ralph laughing at?

22. Norton wants to sing a song, but Ralph says no; he's "feeling beautiful," he says, because he can't wait to get to work the next day to see the expression on Joe Fensterblau's face after Fensterblau has read Ralph's quote in the paper. Why is Ralph so eager for Fensterblau to know that he's boss of his house?

23. As Ralph gets progressively "drunker," what does he say he feels on his face?

24. Norton pours another round, and spills some "wine" on the table. Ralph says "Either that's wine on the table or _____."
25. What song do Ralph and Norton decide to sing?
26. Ralph wants to get something in the bedroom before he and Norton begin singing. What is it?
27. Ralph never makes it to the bedroom; he winds up in the hallway instead. What does he say when he returns?
28. Ralph and Norton pass out, and the wives return. In what order do they give their toasts, and what are they?
29. True or false: Ralph and Norton work half a day on Saturday.
30. Fred, one of the bus drivers, is impressed with Ralph's boasting, and tells Ralph he's twice the man he is. "Yeah," Norton agrees, "with about _____ pounds left over."
    A. 20.
    B. 50.
    C. 100.
    D. 111.
31. What did Ralph take the morning after to recover from his "hangover"?
32. What does Norton usually do on Saturday afternoons?
33. Norton tells Trixie he's playing pool with Ralph and she can either like it or lump it. What does she do?
34. What is Joe Fensterblau's nickname for Ralph?
35. Fensterblau reads Ralph's remarks in the paper, but he's still not convinced Ralph's boss of his house. What does he want Ralph to do to prove he's boss, and how much does he bet Ralph and Norton that Ralph can't do it?
36. Fensterblau's not a fussy man. What does he want for dinner at the Kramdens'?
37. What time does Ralph tell Fensterblau to come over for dinner?
38. Where is Alice that afternoon?
39. Alice refuses to cook the dinner for Fensterblau, and even more than losing the bet, Ralph is afraid of losing face. What scheme does he devise to ensure that Fensterblau doesn't find out Alice refused to cook?
40. Norton says men are the best chefs. Who does he name to illustrate his point?
41. Why does Norton include Grace Kelly's father among the chefs?

*Joe Fensterblau.*
*What an*
*expression!*
COURTESY
JIM ENGEL.

NORTON: How about the chicken? How's it comin'?
RALPH: This nutty cookbook must have been written by a dressmaker. First of all it's gotta be a dressed chicken, then you gotta sew it. After that you gotta baste it every five minutes. If there's one word about embroidery, I give up!

42. How much rice does Ralph tell Norton to cook?

43. Ralph accidentally sews the chicken to his shirt. What is Norton's jest?

44. Ralph puts the chicken in the oven and "turns it up full," saying that it will cook in _____.

45. How long does it take Ralph and Norton to shop, prepare the food, and get it cooking?

RALPH: How's the soup?

NORTON: I can't figure out what's wrong with it. You better taste it.
*Ralph tastes and makes face.*

RALPH: It's terrible.

NORTON: That's what's wrong with it!

RALPH: I told you we shoulda got canned soup.

NORTON: No, Ralph. One taste'a canned soup and Fensterblau woulda got suspicious.

RALPH: Yeah. But what's he gonna think when he tastes this stuff?!

NORTON: He'll think it's rotten homemade soup!

46. What does Norton say when the rice begins boiling over?

47. Alice comes home from her mother's to find Ralph and Norton have turned her kitchen into a shambles. Fensterblau walks in and Ralph tells him there won't be any supper. How does Alice pull Ralph's fat out of the fire?

48. What night does Fensterblau finally have dinner with the Kramdens?

49. Does Fensterblau pay off on the bet he has with Ralph?

FENSTERBLAU: Oh, hello, Mrs. Kramden.

ALICE: I certianly owe you an apology. I planned to have dinner ready by now, but when I was in the midst of cooking, that crazy stove went blooey and everything turned out to be a mess. So all I can do is offer you a rain check for tomorrow night and I'll make you the greatest meal you ever had.

FENSTERBLAU: Gee, that's awful nice of you, Mrs. Kramden. I'll be here. Ralph, I guess I owe you some money.

RALPH: No, you don't. Let's call it even. Alice's having you over for supper don't prove I'm the boss. It was a stupid bet anyway, because in the right kind of marriage there is no boss in the house.

FENSTERBLAU (*after a pause*): Yeah . . . I think I understand. See you tomorrow night, folks.
*Fensterblau leaves. Ralph turns to Alice.*

RALPH: Thanks for what you did, Alice.

ALICE: Thanks for what you said.

RALPH: Baby, you're the greatest.
*KISSVILLE CITY.*

# THE WORRY WART

April 7, 1956 · Marvin Marx and Walter Stone

1. Ralph once took Alice, Norton, and Trixie to:
   A. The Davis Cup.
   B. The World Series.
   C. The U.S. Open.
   D. The three-legged race at the Racoon Lodge picnic.
2. Norton wants to reciprocate. Where does he want to take Ralph and Alice?
3. How did Norton get the tickets for the event?
4. The tickets Norton gets are scarcer than _____.

ALICE: Thanks for the invitation, Ed. *Alice then looks around room as she speaks.* But I don't have to go to Madison Square Garden to look at antiques!
   *Norton then looks around room and speaks knowingly.*
NORTON (*knowingly*): I dig you there, Alice. Of course, I wouldn't take this antique stuff too lightly, you know. If some of this stuff you got here really was antique, it could be worth a fortune. You know, there's a lot of money in antiques. I know. I had an old Chinese back scratcher. I didn't think it was worth anything. I was ready to throw it away. But instead I took it to a dealer. I got twenty-nine cents for it!
ALICE (*mock-serious*): You're kidding!
NORTON (*not digging*): Word of honor! Of course, I was lucky that I just hit him at the right moment. You see, his back was itchin' at the time.
ALICE: Oh.
NORTON: By the way, Alice, if you'd like me to examine any of this stuff here, I could tell you if it was worth anything. No charge, of course.
ALICE (*uninterested-style*): Go ahead. Although I doubt if you'll find anything here worth twenty-nine cents!
   *Norton shrugs his shoulders we'll-see-style. . . .*

5. Norton once sent away for a four-legged Chippendale. What did he think he was getting?
6. Norton thinks he's an antiques appraiser. In his opinion, what vintage is the Kramdens' icebox?
7. What TV crime drama does Norton mention when Ralph comes home and finds him raiding the icebox? What medical show does Ralph mention?
8. Who sends its bill to Ralph on a postcard, and how much is it for?
9. Who at 328 Chauncey Street yakety-yak-yaks to the other tenants about Ralph's bill?
10. Whose all-time low gas bill record does Ralph break, and when was the original record set?

NORTON: Oh, it's that blabbermouth we got for a mailman. He reads all the postcards and then he goes yakkity-yakkin' all over the building.

RALPH: You're kiddin'.

NORTON: I'm kiddin', huh? You know what your bill is? Ninety-three cents!

*Ralph looks at postcard and then looks at Norton agreement-style.*

RALPH (*a little amazed*): Yeah.

NORTON: He told Trixie. In fact, congratulations on that ninety-three-cent bill, Ralph. The mailman told us that you just broke the low gas bill record set by the Collier Brothers in 1931.

*Ralph looks a little sheepish at this.*

NORTON: He tells us your gas bill every month. Boy, you been hittin' in the low nineties for quite a while now! In fact, four months ago when your bill went way up to two dollars and eighty-five cents, the mailman got scared. He thought you took the gas pipe and committed suicide.

*Ralph reacts sheepishly to this and then speaks, remembering what happened four months ago.*

RALPH: Oh, yeah . . . four months ago. That's when we were doing a lot of bakin' up here. Remember . . . you and me went into the no-cal pizza business!

NORTON: How can I forget it? Boy, that was a great business, Ralph. Everything just broke right for us. In fact, that was the best business you ever got me into. We only lost about eighty dollars!

RALPH: You know, I thought we'd make a lot of money in that business, Norton. I can't figure what went wrong.

NORTON: Well, I think our first mistake was when we wanted to advertise our no-cal pizza, and we used you for the model! Remember, with them before-and-after pictures.

RALPH (*forget-it-style*): All right, Norton.

NORTON: The only trouble was, the afters kept getting bigger than the befores!

11. What are the Kramdens having for dinner?
12. Who warms up in the bullpen, but still pitches?
13. How much is Ralph's tax refund, and what does he plan to spend it on?
14. Ralph gets a letter from the IRS asking him to report to their office. Who is he supposed to see, and when?
15. Ralph panics over his letter from the IRS; Norton's only concerned about eating. What condiments does he ask Ralph for?
16. Where did Alice want Ralph to go to find somebody to make out the Kramdens' tax return?
17. Ralph needs forty-two dollars to go to Fred's Landing. If the IRS takes back some of his refund, what economy measure does Alice advise Ralph to take?

18. Alice tells Ralph lots of people have their tax returns investigated. Norton agrees and says "You're darn right. The _____ are full of them."

RALPH (*controlling temper*): Norton, I'm gonna count to five, and when I finish counting, you better be out of here.
*Norton crosses to door a little fearfully.*
RALPH: Get ready, Norton. I'm countin' to five!
*Norton opens door, then turns and addresses Ralph smugly.*
NORTON (*smugly*): Countin' to five. If you could count, they wouldn't be investigatin' your taxes!
*Ralph's eyes bulge, and Norton scoots out door quickly. Ralph then turns to Alice, eyes still bulging.*
RALPH: Alice, you got to promise me one thing. If I do go to jail, don't tell him what the visiting days are!

© PRESTON BLAIR
PRODUCTIONS.

19. Alice is awakened by Ralph, who is poring over his tax return. What time is it?
    A. Midnight.
    B. Eleven o'clock.
    C. Two in the morning.
    D. About half past three.
20. Alice wants Ralph to get some sleep; he'd rather stay awake worrying. Ralph: "Their job is taxes. They're not gonna send me to jail for _____."
21. Ralph says if Alice went on *The $64,000 Question*, her category would be:
    A. Sleep.
    B. Taxes.
    C. Jail.
    D. Everything.

RALPH: Look, Alice, you seem to be taking this whole investigation pretty lightly. Well, now let me tell you something. I didn't want to mention this before, 'cause I wanted to spare you. But now I'm gonna tell you. We made out a joint return, Alice! Do you know what that means? That's the government's sneaky way of making sure that the husband and wife go to prison together!

22. What is Alice going to make for Ralph to help him relax?
23. Ralph reads the newspaper to take his mind off his taxes. He reads an item about a new highway. What two countries will it connect, and how many hours will it save people who travel on it?

24. According to Norton, what's the worst thing the government can do to Ralph for cheating on his taxes?
25. What was Norton's major in vocational school?
26. What is Ralph's social security number?
27. When Norton sees Ralph's social security number on the tax form, he thinks the number is Ralph's:
    A. Weight.
    B. Bank account.
    C. Interest on his bank account.
    D. The number of Ralph's chattel.
28. What are Ralph's and Norton's business deductions?
29. Who does Ralph wine and dine every time there's an opening at the bus company for traffic manager?
30. Why does Norton deduct 25 percent of his rent for tax purposes?
31. What does Norton think chattel is?
32. How much money does Ralph have in the bank, and how much interest has it earned?
33. What did Ralph get from his boss in lieu of a bonus, and what is it worth?
34. What or how much did Ralph win gambling, and how did he win it?

RALPH: You think they found out about all this?

NORTON (*with authority*): They find out about everything.

RALPH (*getting really worried*): You think they found out about the five dollars I won at the fat-man's race?

NORTON (*writing and speaking*): Fat-man's race, five dollars!
*Suddenly Ralph snaps his fingers realization-style.*

RALPH: Wait a minute, Norton. Remember that big poker game we had up here about six months ago? It lasted all night. I won about eighty-five bucks in that game.

NORTON (*whoops-style*): Eighty-five bucks! That must be it, Ralph. That's a lot of money. They found out about it, and that's why they're investigatin' you.

RALPH (*worried*): But how could they find out about it? The only ones who knew I won that much were the guys playin' in the game.

NORTON: Yeah. And none of them guys would squeal on you. Let's see. Who all was there that night?

RALPH: Well, there was you, me, Fogarty, Grogan, Brady, Manicotti, Maloney, and, uh, that other guy Maloney brought with him. I don't know who he was.
*Suddenly realization hits both of them, and they look at each other knowingly.*

NORTON: That's it, Ralph. He was a revenue agent! They get around, you

**know. Come to think of it, I also remember seein' him at the fat-man's race!**

35. What is the penalty for failing to report income?
36. What last-ditch strategy does Norton give Ralph to help bail him out of his predicament?
37. True or false: If they get anything out of Ralph, it won't be out of Ralph that they get it.
38. Norton to Mr. Puder: "He's Kramden, I'm _____."
39. Why does the IRS want to see Ralph?
40. What does Norton confess to Mr. Puder?
41. What can Ralph Kramden never be accused of?

© PRESTON BLAIR PRODUCTIONS.

# TRAPPED

April 14, 1956 · Leonard Stern and Sydney Zelinka

1. What's the house record for consecutive balls sunk at Harry's pool-room?
2. What did the bride say to the groom when she took the burnt steak out of the oven?
   A. Leave it there, the cat'll get it.
   B. Well, Norton, our goose is cooked.
   C. It's as good as done.
   D. I'll kiss you later, I'm eatin' a potato.
3. Ralph shoots pool like a champ one day a week. Which day?

"Pool playing became classic; both Gleason and Art played pool," Stern says. "The courage they had to play it live, in front of an audience, and make the shots that were required so that the jokes would work, was astounding."

"The writers couldn't tell us what to do in situations like that," says Carney. "We just had to work it out ourselves, and trust that everything would work out okay. But Gleason knew how to handle himself with a cue, and so did I, although I did it very broadly, waving the thing around."

4. One of Norton's fellow sewer workers had a "blessed event." Who was it, and what was the event?
5. True or false: Ralph and Norton usually shoot pool for a penny a ball, but Norton wants to raise the ante to five cents a ball and a crack across the knuckles for every scratch.
6. Ralph and Norton flip a coin to see who breaks. Who wins, and how does the coin land?
7. Ralph tries to sink the _____ ball in the corner pocket and misses.
   A. Two.
   B. Three.
   C. Four.
   D. Bowling.
8. How many shots are fired during the holdup of the bank?
9. Who gets knocked off during the bank robbery?
10. True or false: The bank robbers shoot one hole through Ralph's Racoon cap.
11. Back at the apartment, there's trouble with the water pipes. Who comes to check Alice's sink?
12. Who's happy he won't have to take a bath because the water's not running?
    A. Tommy Mullins.
    B. Old man Grogan.
    C. Johnny Bennett.
    D. Tommy Manicotti.

13. Trixie's away at her sister's, so Norton invites Ralph over for dinner, and to play pinochle and watch a movie. What's playing that night on *The Late, Late Show*?
14. Who's having a TV antenna installed at 328 Chauncey Street?

> . . . *Ralph peers in. He steps in quickly, closes door and locks it in one motion. He carries window shade. Puts it down on table, his back to bedroom as Alice reenters.*

ALICE: Oh, Ralph.

*Ralph is given a start and jumps at unexpected sound of Alice's voice.*

ALICE: What's the matter, Ralph?

RALPH (*trying to cover*): I—er, nothing. You surprised me, Alice.

ALICE: I just want to finish putting a hem on a dress and then I'll be in and give you your— *Alice notices window shade on table.* A window shade! What's that doing here?

RALPH: I bought it on the way home. We need one. I don't like people being able to look into the window.

*Alice looks at shade, shaking her head, wonderingly.*

RALPH: Well, don't look so surprised. You always wanted me to get a window shade.

ALICE: I know, but I gave up asking you seven years ago.

RALPH: I hope you learn from this, Alice. When you stop nagging me I always get you what you want. . . .

"One woman sent me curtains for the window," says Audrey. "I had to write back and explain why there were no curtains in the window. People would write back and say, 'But the Nortons' apartment is so good.'

"The woman who sent the curtains attached a dime with Scotch tape. She said that was so I could go to Woolworth's and buy a curtain rod, because it was too difficult for her to wrap it up."

"There were never any curtains or draperies on the windows, no shades, because this was the way Jackie lived when he was young," says Phil Cuoco, set decorator for *The Honeymooners*. "Anything you see on the set was very definitely the way Jackie lived.

"God help you if you put a 'Home Sweet Home' sign up. The CBS brass couldn't understand it."

ALICE: Ralph, you've got to go to the police. If you don't it's only going to get worse. You won't be able to walk down a dark street without being frightened by every shadow. A car'll backfire and you'll think you're shot. You'll think every passenger on your bus is there to kill you. Ralph, you can't live the rest of your life in fear.

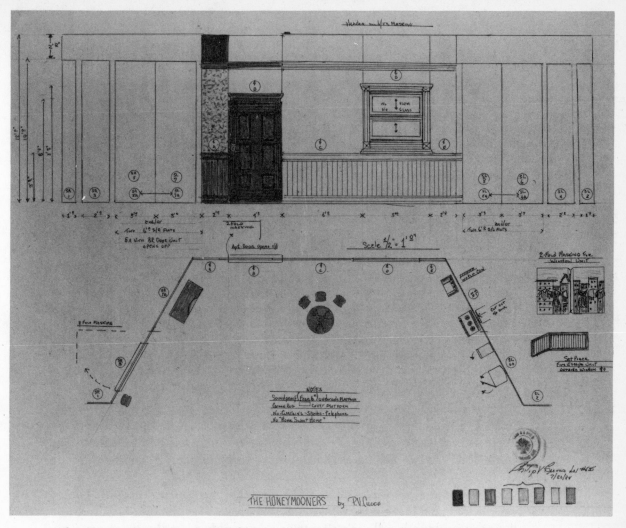

The Honeymooners *set, as created by set designer Phil Cuoco.* COURTESY PHIL CUOCO.

**RALPH:** Alice, you've convinced me. I'll never leave the house again!
**ALICE:** How will you make a living?
**RALPH:** I'll . . . I'll, I'll take in washing!

15. True or false: The Manicottis live on the same floor as the Nortons.
16. Who are the bank robbers, and who's driving their getaway car?

George Petrie and Frank Marth play the thugs in this episode. Both had been working with Gleason for several years, and were at the top of the list of "Gleason Actors"—actors who were versatile, dependable, and most of all, unflappable. Outside of the show's four stars, Petrie and Marth played in more episodes of *The Honeymooners* than any other actors.

Petrie remembers how Marth had to switch roles—from the police de-

*George Petrie, one of Gleason's versatile character actors.*
COURTESY GEORGE PETRIE.

tective who comes to question Ralph, to Bibbo—just hours before "Trapped" was filmed.

"We were doing a dress rehearsal, the last rehearsal, and the guy playing the part Frank played, when he came up to Jackie and played the scene—'All right, I've had enough out of you,' whatever the line is—the guy was twitching. His face was twitching. Very nervous. Well, that's the last thing in the world Jackie needs. He hates that, because that's insecurity, and he doesn't need that.

"Now the actor was a good actor, but they had an expression: 'There were actors, and there were Gleason Actors.' Not to say the others were bad; they just couldn't handle the situation, they couldn't handle the stress.

"After the rehearsal, Jackie walked over to Jack Hurdle and he did the finger across the throat, meaning 'Cut. Get rid of him.' And they let him go, and they put Frank Marth in his part. We then had to call another rehearsal before we went on. We had a read-through: 'This is where you move, this is where you move. . . .'"

Marth's first appearance on a Jackie Gleason show was also as a hoodlum.

"I had been an actor about a year or so, and they called me up and wanted to know if I wanted to work on the Gleason show," he recalls. "I went in there and they had a room full of guys with broken noses—'dese, dose, and dem' types; they all looked like killers and murderers—and a bunch of us looked like high school kids. So Jackie came along and said, 'You over there, and you, and you,' and he lined up all the guys with the broken noses on one side and all the young-looking guys on the other.

"We did a skit called 'The Last Mile and a Half,' and all the innocent-looking guys played the rough guys. I was in a cell next to Art Carney, and my name was Monk Meyers.

"The next week they were doing a sketch where they needed a cop, and Gleason said get the guy who was Monk. That was me, and from that time on I worked the show fairly regularly."

Petrie and Marth are still acting. Petrie appeared in the television movie *The Day After*, and has a recurring role as Harve Smithfield in *Dallas*. Petrie had his name added to the list of Gleason Actors when, during one of his early appearances on a Gleason show, he helped Gleason out of a jam in a Reggie Van Gleason III skit.

"We walked backstage after the skit and all he did was tap me on the shoulder and say, 'Thanks, pal,' and that's all. That's the way Jackie was. Half the time I don't think he knew anyone's name.

"Once Jackie was out of town. I got called late Friday night. Usually you were called on Wednesday and told you were working Saturday. But late Friday I got the call. The next day I said to the producer, 'What happened? Get a new script or something?' He said, 'No, I had the part of a priest, and I didn't want to put just anyone in it. I thought maybe Jackie wanted a Catholic to play the part. But he's a funny guy, so I gave him a choice. He called me from Boston and I asked him about the priest. He said, "What are you asking me for? Give it to that Petrie guy. I like to work with him. As a matter of fact, anytime he's right for a part, you use him."'

"So the producer had carte blanche on me, and that's one reason I did a lot.

"In the episode where they're being held hostage after he's seen a murder, I was the head of the gang. After we'd finished dress rehearsal, Jackie came over and gave me a nudge. He didn't say much, but when he said something it was worth it. He said, 'Get a scar.' In the sleepwalker one, where I was the psychiatrist, he said, 'Get a hairpiece.'

"You know, in a situation comedy, no one appears more than once. If you're on, it's once a year, and that's all, unless you're a regular playing the same character. I was playing different characters. He said, 'I don't want the audience to recognize that you're the same guy.'

"Let's face it: After enough times, everybody knows I'm the same guy. I tried to do everything a little differently, but what can you do after twenty episodes. Not a whole lot.

"When we were reading 'The Sleepwalker,' I said, 'How about a little Viennese accent here?' He said, 'Good.' Later he said, 'Get a hairpiece.' So I got a little thing.

"From that moment on I used to drive the makeup man crazy."

*Bibbo and Danny.* COURTESY JOHN F. LANGTON, JR.

17. Ralph tries to bluff the crooks with a water pistol. Whose is it?
18. Norton comes down to fix Ralph's pipes. How many pipes in the bedroom need fixing?

"Being on *The Honeymooners* was a very pleasurable experience for me, because it was very much like a little family," says Ralph Robertson, who played Tommy Manicotti in this episode, and Johnny Bennett in "A Matter of Record."

"Art Carney was very funny off-camera as well as on; Joyce was a lovely lady, as was Audrey, and it really made it pleasant to be a kid actor on the set. Jackie, of course, supervised the actors on the set during the run-throughs.

"I remember we met at his hotel room at the Park Sheraton, and when I got home from the hotel I went over to my mother and said, 'Mommy, can I have what Mr. Gleason drank?' And she said, 'Sure, what was it?' And I said, 'Three fingers.' It took me a few years to figure what that was all about.

"Being on the show affected my life. You may remember in a few episodes there was a pool table. Gleason was a fantastic pool player, and Carney was not too bad, either. And that pool table led to a wasted life in the poolrooms of Washington Heights. I was also arrested on two occasions in Washington Heights on charges of starting a riot with a water gun."

Ralph eventually relinquished his title as "fastest water gun in the East" and now works as a therapist and psychiatric social worker in New York City. He's still searching New York's hall of records to determine whether he was Mrs. Manicotti's son or grandson.

19. True or false: When Ralph won't allow Bibbo to tie him up, Bibbo takes him into the bedroom and works him over.

# THE LOUDSPEAKER

April 21, 1956 · Marvin Marx and Walter Stone

1. Ralph comes home with big news. What is it?
2. True or false: The Racoon of the Year is elected.
3. Who does Norton think is Racoon of the Year?
   A. Havemeyer.
   B. Woodruff.
   C. Himself.
   D. Cassidy.
4. What happened to Norton when the United States won the Davis Cup?
5. Where did the Racoons get the idea that only the Grand High Exalted Mystic Ruler should know the identity of the Racoon of the Year until the winner is announced?
6. Why does Ralph think he's going to be Racoon of the Year?
7. The Grand High Exalted Mystic Ruler is the:
   A. Leader of the Bayonne Bunch.
   B. Owner of Salvatore's Pizzeria.
   C. Convention manager.
   D. Emperor of all Racoondom.
8. Who is the Grand High Exalted Mystic Ruler, and where does he work?
9. When one is named Racoon of the Year, the gold braid on his uniform is changed to _____.
10. What happened to Frank Brady when he won Racoon of the Year?
11. What material is Norton's vest made of, and where did he get it?
12. True or false: The Kramdens missed Alice's mother's birthday party because Ralph had a meeting at the lodge.

RALPH: Tuesday night happened to have been a pretty important night at the Racoons, too, Alice.

NORTON: Darn right it was. It was Morris Fink's birthday and they were servin' free beer and pretzels! The only thing that put a little damper on the party was Morris didn't show up! He phoned to say he couldn't make it. You see, it was his mother-in-law's anniversary and he had to go over there!
*Ralph gives Norton a shot with his elbow.*

RALPH: Now look, Alice. Being named Racoon of the Year is a pretty big honor. And you won't think the Racoons are so silly after you hear all the great things I get with this award. First of all, my dues will be paid up for the rest of my life! They'll present me with a stuffed raccoon . . . it's a beautiful thing, Alice. It's really a clock. The eyes go back and forth! Also, from now on I get to wear a gold stripe on my pants and an extra tail on my hat. Not only that, but they're gonna hang a picture of me in the assembly hall of the Racoon Old-Age Home. But most important of all, Alice—most important of all, both you and I will be entitled to free burial privileges in the Racoons' national cemetery in Bismarck, North Dakota!

13. What are the "fine, wonderful, and distinctive honors" one receives upon being named Racoon of the Year?

14. Alice is a wisenheimer. What honor does she think Ralph has coming at the convention?

RALPH: That's not the one I was thinkin' about. What I was gonna say is that if any of the Racoons ever get sick, it'll be my responsibility to go and visit them.

ALICE: Oh, that is a very important responsibility, Ralph. You better start now and find out what the visiting hours are at Bellevue!

RALPH (*livid*): That did it, Alice—that did it! You have just broken the camel's back with that straw. You have ridiculed my brother Racoons. You have just made fun of something very big that's close to my heart.

ALICE: The only thing big that's close to your heart is your stomach!
*Ralph's eyes bulge full akimbo-style.*

RALPH: Just for that, Alice . . . just for that . . . your father ain't gettin' my old overcoat.

15. Where is the Racoon National Cemetery?
    A. Weehawken.
    B. Canarsie.
    C. Albuquerque.
    D. Bismarck.
16. For what office is the Racoon of the Year eligible to run?
17. What's the primary duty of the Grand High Exalted Mystic Ruler?
18. When he becomes Grand High Exalted Mystic Ruler, what does Ralph promise to do for Norton?
19. Alice says the Racoons won't hear a word of Ralph's acceptance speech as Racoon of the Year. Why not?
    A. They'll be full of beer.
    B. They'll be listening to Basil Fomeen.
    C. Norton'll be playing "Swanee River."
    D. They'll be full of cold grape juice.
20. Ralph came home from a lodge meeting one night and thought there was a cat in the apartment. Whose cat did he think it was, and what was really happening?
21. Trixie and Alice want to play cards while Ralph and Norton are at the lodge. Which of their friends can't make the game?
22. Ralph gets the hiccups. What remedies do Alice and Norton suggest?

COURTESY
SAMUEL LOWE
COMPANY.

Norton thought a "foreign sound" would cure Ralph's hiccups in the episode as it was filmed; in the script he has an even better idea. Marx and Stone set it up this way: Alice is having something to eat before going to play cards with the girls. For dessert she's having cream pie, which she sets on the table. Norton is eating rock candy; the bag rips and candy spills all over the floor. While Ralph is in the bathroom looking for something to cure his hiccups, Alice begins sweeping up the rock candy. While she's doing this, Norton grabs a paper bag and leaves the apartment.

Before Alice can sweep up all the candy, Ralph comes out of the bedroom in his bare feet and steps on a piece of it. He begins "hopping about and yipping." He begins screaming at Alice, who notices Ralph's hiccups have disappeared. Ralph's anger subsides, and he sits down at the table to continue rehearsing his speech.

*At this point front door opens noiselessly and Norton pokes his head in. Ralph continues with speech. Norton, seeing Ralph seated at table with back to him, sneaks up behind him tippy-toe-style. He is carrying paper bag which is now inflated fully with air.*

RALPH: And your imperial majesty, Grand High Exalted Mystic Ruler. It brings a tear to my eye and a lump to my throat when I think that all you Racoons came here tonight just to pay honor to me. I am humble.

*At this point Norton is standing right next to Ralph with paper bag poised for smashing against other hand.*

NORTON (*shouting in Ralph's ear*): Look out, Ralph! The ceiling's falling!

*On this he smashes paper bag with loud bang. Ralph, panicky, reacts by flinging arms over top of head and burying face on table protective-style. It goes right smack into the cream pie. Ralph holds it down there for a moment as Norton speaks jovial-style.*

NORTON (*chuckling*): Okay, Ralph . . . I bet you're rid of your hiccups now. How'd it work?

*Ralph lifts his head slowly out of pie. There is cream all over face and upper part of uniform. He just stares at Norton this way more sad than mad.*

NORTON: Boy, Ralph. You better clean yourself up if you're gonna speak at that dinner tonight!

*Ralph turns and looks straight ahead mournfully, poor-soul-style. He then lets out one big hiccup. This is followed by a series of hiccups as we BLACK-OUT of scene.*

23. Why does Ralph want Alice to steam his Racoon cap?
24. Alice's only winter coat is made of:
    A. Imitation dyed rabbit fur.
    B. Corduroy.
    C. Crinoline.
    D. Fur.
25. What has Ralph learned by "associating" with politicians and important men?

26. Who are the two characters in the joke Ralph makes up to tell at the lodge?
27. What's the punch line to Ralph's joke?

"We were trying to get a real bad joke, and Marvin remembered that one from somewhere," says Stone. "He had used it in a similar circumstance somewhere. We just built it up more.

"Gleason didn't do it the way we envisioned it. We didn't want it done that badly. Just do it. Maybe in his mind he thought it was more in character that Ralph couldn't tell a joke."

28. How many tails does Morris Fink have on his Racoon cap?
29. Ralph tells his joke to one of the tenants in the building. Who is it?
30. True or false: Alice doesn't have a sense of humor.

"A lot of the stuff on *The Honeymooners* was taken from our own home life," says Doreen Marx. "Like some of the names of the characters: Morris Fink—the Grand High Exalted Mystic Ruler—was the name of the boy-friend of my husband's sister. Mr. Puder [from the IRS] was Richard Puder, co-owner of a CPA firm in downtown Newark. He did Marvin's books. Marvin had an Uncle Leo. Marvin loved the name Bayonne; both he and Walter loved New Jersey."

Here is Marvin's description of Morris Fink's grand entrance into the Kramdens' apartment:

*Door opens and Grand High Exalted Mystic Ruler enters. He is a short chubby man, Joe Besser–style. He is dressed in very fine Racoon uniform like Ralph's, only it is white. White jacket, white pants with gold stripe, white shoes, and white Racoon hat with three tails. He has campaign ribbons on chest. Ralph stands there for a second in amazed awe. Then in daze he reaches back and waves raccoon tail and emits howl.*

RALPH: Owwwwwwww!
*Grand High Ruler returns Ralph's salute waving three tails individually and giving howl for each tail.*
GRAND RULER: Ooooowwwwww! Ooowwwww! Ooowwwwww!
RALPH (*in awe*): Alice, do you know who this is? I want you to meet the Grand High Exalted Mystic Ruler. It's an honor to have him in our house.
ALICE: I am humble!

*Morris Fink.*
COURTESY
JOHN F.
LANGTON, JR.

31. Who is Racoon of the Year?
32. True or false: Ralph will always be Racoon of the Year in his house.

# ON STAGE

April 28, 1956 · Leonard Stern and Sydney Zelinka

1. What office does Ralph hold in the Racoon Lodge?
2. The women's auxiliary of the Racoon Lodge has an idea on how to raise money. What is it?

RALPH: Hiya Norton, whattaya you doin' here?

NORTON: I promised Trixie I'd pick her up. Is the ladies' auxiliary finished with their meeting yet?

RALPH: No, they're still at it. That dramatic coach Faversham is in there lecturing on acting again.

NORTON: Boy oh boy, those dames are sure goin' in for culture. First it was that dance instructor from Arthur Murray's teachin' them to mambo, and then that German chef teachin' them how to cook.

RALPH: Yeah.

NORTON: Trixie took to it real good, though. She's been practicin' for two weeks and you oughta see her now. She cooks like Arthur Murray and mambos like a German chef.

3. What does Ralph think is the only way the lodge could make money putting on a play?
4. Who wants to stage the play for the lodge?
5. What has the Acme Finance Co. repossessed from the lodge?

RALPH: It all boils down to one thing. The members don't pay their dues. Just let me read this list to you. Joe Gordon, eleven months behind in his dues. Henry Frankel, eight months behind. Jim Brooks, seven months behind. Howard Phillips, nine months behind. Jack Diamond, ten months behind. Why can't they all be like Frank Ryan? Our lodge would be in good shape if they all paid their dues like he does.

NORTON: Frank Ryan?

RALPH: Yeah. He's only three months behind in his dues!

NORTON: Well, Frank happens to be married to a very wealthy girl!

6. Norton says he can type faster than Ralph with _____ on.
7. In which branch of the armed forces did Norton serve?
   A. Army.
   B. Navy.
   C. Air Force.
   D. Marines.
8. How did Norton learn to type?
9. Being such a good typist, why didn't Norton take an office job?

10. What salutation does Norton suggest for the letter Ralph's sending to the Racoons whose dues are in arrears?
    A. Hello, Bill!
    B. Oh, hello there!
    C. Greetings!
    D. Hello, Bunny, this is old Buttercup!
11. Ralph decides not to send letters to the Racoons. Instead he:
    A. Calls them on the telephone.
    B. Calls them on the house phone.
    C. Yells out in the hall.
    D. Calls them on Norton's phone.
12. Give Ralph a party and a room full of people, and he's the first person to do what?
13. When has Ralph appeared on stage, what did he do, and what was he wearing?
14. Norton wants a part in the Racoons' play. What actor does he impersonate to prove to Mr. Faversham that he can act?
15. What were Gregory Peck and Kirk Douglas doing for a living when they were "discovered" by Hollywood?
16. In his first movie, Clark Gable played a:
    A. Sewer worker.
    B. Mambo dancer.
    C. Man from space.
    D. Bus driver.
17. What old adage has Ralph always followed?
18. True or false: The Racoons' play is a sell-out.
19. Which big Hollywood producer is going to attend the Racoons' play?
20. Norton auditions for every part in the play. Which one would he have gotten if he'd had nicer knees?
21. Alice is worried that if Ralph acts well in the play, he's going to drive his bus straight to:
    A. Canarsie.
    B. Bismarck.
    C. Hollywood.
    D. Minneapolis.
22. What does Earl Wilson write in his column the day of the Racoons' play?
23. Who gets the flu and can't be in the play?
24. Norton doesn't fit Hannigan's part, but he fits his _____.
25. Which characters do Ralph, Alice, and Norton play?
26. Ralph's character collects expensive furnishings and works of art to impress the woman he loves. Where does he get them?

27. Ralph's character owns:
    A. A bowling alley.
    B. The Hong Kong Gardens.
    C. A mansion, a villa in France, a yacht, and a string of poloponies.
    D. Fatrack's Factory.

No episode of *The Honeymooners* had a more unusual origin than "On Stage." It actually began, says Leonard Stern, with one word: 'poloponies.'

"That one word came first, and we built a whole sketch around it. When the word 'poloponies' came up, we started to devise a character who would be rich enough to have polo ponies. Then we came up with the play, and who he would rehearse with. The whole thing was worked backwards, just to justify having 'poloponies' in a speech."

28. Which is Norton's best profile, the left side or the right side?

NORTON: I want to know which do you think is my better profile. When I'm on stage I want to make sure the audience sees my best side.

RALPH: Why don't you stand with your back to them?

ALICE: Ralph! Ed, it's your left side.

NORTON: Just as I thought. Thank you, very much. Now I'll go and brush up on my lines. *He exits.*

RALPH: How do you like that, Alice? How do you like that? If there's anything I hate more than anything else in this world it's a guy who becomes a ham! *Alice rolls her eyes heavenward.*

29. Who's chairman of the lodge's entertainment committee?
30. How many years has the lodge been in the red?
31. What does Ralph promise to do for the lodge if he signs a Hollywood contract?
32. True or false: Herbert J. Whiteside wants to cast Alice as a jelly doughnut taster in his next movie.
33. Where's the gang going for dinner after the play?
34. What will you miss out on if you get to the Hong Kong Gardens too late?
    A. The floor show.
    B. The sixty-cent dinner.
    C. Fortune cookies.
    D. Chicken chow mein and potato pancakes.
35. Which scene in the play did Whiteside and Faversham like best?

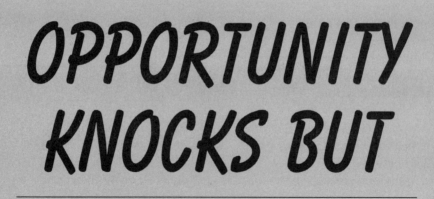

# OPPORTUNITY KNOCKS BUT

May 5, 1956 · Leonard Stern and Sydney Zelinka

1. Who does Freddie Muller usually ride home from work with? Why can't he ride with him this day?
2. What doesn't Mr. Marshall like about the Gotham Bus Company's new buses?
3. Who tells Mr. Marshall that Ralph's the best pool player at the bus company?
4. What did Mrs. Marshall give her husband as an anniversary present?
5. As a boy, where did Mr. Marshall go after graduating from school?
   A. Around the world.
   B. From Mongolia to Tibet.
   C. Straight to Hollywood.
   D. To the floor show at the Hong Kong Gardens.
6. Norton is late meeting Ralph after work. Why?
7. Norton has heard Mr. Marshall's name mentioned often in the Kramden household. When did Ralph talk about Marshall constantly?
8. Kramden's his name, _____ is his game.
9. Mr. Marshall invites Ralph and Norton to his house to play pool. What time does he tell them to come, and what's his address?
10. How did Norton earn a buck during the Depression?
11. Who was Norton caddying for the day he got his job in the sewer?
    A. Morris Fink.
    B. A sewer official.
    C. Pierre François de la Briosche.
    D. A wholesale butcher.
12. How did Norton get his job in the sewer?
13. True or false: Ralph suggests Norton send *Esquire* the story of how he got his job in the sewer.
14. What's Norton having for dinner that night?
15. Ralph figures that after playing pool with Mr. Marshall, it won't be long before he owns his own pool table. According to Norton, where will Ralph have to stand to make a shot if he puts a pool table in his apartment?
    A. With his head in the stove and his feet in the icebox.
    B. On the fire escape.
    C. In the sink.
    D. In Fogarty's old flat.
16. Mr. Marshall has a fish mounted on his wall. What kind of fish is it, and when and where did he catch it?
17. Norton's boss has the same type fish on the wall in his living room. Where did he get it?
18. Mrs. Marshall has a trophy on the mantel in the Marshalls' den. What did she win it for?
19. What is Mr. Marshall's butler's name?

*Freddie Muller.*
COURTESY
JIM ENGEL.

223

20. How many men at the bus company does Ralph estimate play pool?
21. What phrase about bus drivers does Norton coin?
22. Norton works for the city. In what capacity?
23. What are the three suggestions Norton gives Mr. Marshall about the bus company?
24. What job does Mr. Marshall offer Norton?
25. Trixie and Alice are waiting for Ralph and Norton to come home from Mr. Marshall's. Trixie reads in the newspaper about a sale on men's shorts. How much are they, and what sizes are on sale?

*Mr. Marshall.*
COURTESY
HOWARD BENDER.
COPYRIGHT © 1985
HOWARD BENDER.

ALICE: Isn't it strange, Trix? All these years I've been telling Ralph he's been wasting his time shooting pool. And why does he get invited to the boss's house? He's a good pool shooter!

TRIXIE: Funny how things work out.

ALICE: Yes. A cousin of mine had a brother-in-law named Bob, who spent all his spare time fishing. His boss suddenly wanted to learn how to fish. Bob taught him all he knew and today he's vice-president of the company. It just proves that if you're good at something, regardless of what it is, it can pay off.

TRIXIE: Well, that gives me some hope for Ed. He can become a big man in the sewer if his boss ever decides he wants to learn how to play punchball!

ALICE: Don't you worry about Ed. He'll do all right.

TRIXIE: I can't help worrying. The trouble with Ed is that he just doesn't speak up! He can do more for somebody else than he can for himself! Like tonight, I'm sure he's being a big help to Ralph.

26. True or false: Ralph and Norton eat lunch at a restaurant.
27. What is Trixie going to make for Norton to eat on the way to lunch at the restaurant?
28. If Norton takes the job at the bus company, what does he want Ralph to call him?
29. Ralph is jealous of four things he thinks Norton will have or do if he takes the job at the bus company. What are they?
30. How long has Ralph worked for the bus company?
31. Ralph was angry when _____ was laid off at the bus company.
    A. Reilly.
    B. Cassidy.
    C. Fensterblau.
    D. Havemeyer.
32. Norton's idea for odd and even buses was based on a similar idea of Ralph's. What was Ralph's proposal to keep the buses moving along?

# UNCONVENTIONAL BEHAVIOR

May 12, 1956 · Marvin Marx and Walter Stone

1. Trixie has been shopping at Krauss's. What did she buy for Alice?
2. How much is chopped meat at Krauss's?
3. Where is Alice planning to stay while Ralph's away at the Racoon convention?
    A. Trixie's.
    B. Her mother's.
    C. Fred's gasoline station.
    D. Fred's Landing.
4. Where is the convention being held?
5. How much money have Ralph and Norton saved to bring to the convention?
6. Whom does Trixie have to call about the card game that night?
7. Norton sets his watch by the Chinese restaurant across the street from the apartment house. What time does the restaurant open, and what time do they start cooking the egg foo young and the moo goo gai pan?
8. What time do the first whiffs of the egg foo young reach Ralph's window and Norton's window?
9. The aroma of egg foo young rises at the rate of _____ feet per second.
10. True or false: Moo goo gai pan's aroma rises at a faster rate than that of egg foo young.
11. True or false: Norton doesn't know what time it is when somebody orders chicken chow mein and potato pancakes at the restaurant.
12. Who's Norton going to write a letter to about his busted watch?

RALPH: Wouldn't it be a lot easier just to buy a new watch, Norton?
NORTON: I don't need a new watch, Ralph. There's nothin' wrong with this one. It just needs a new mainspring, that's all. I'll have to find out where to get it repaired. I think I'll write a letter to Walt Disney about it tonight.
RALPH: Norton, if a man in a white coat ever knocks on your door, don't ask for tutti-frutti, 'cause he ain't the Good Humor man!

13. Name all the novelties Ralph's bringing to the convention.
14. Norton borrows Ralph's caveman false face to wear in the sewer. Why doesn't he want to wear the other one?
15. At last year's convention, the cops were cracking down on people throwing bags of water out of the hotel windows. That didn't stop Norton: 1–2–3, he let it ride. What happened?
16. What happened on May 3, 1953?
17. What's Ralph's supreme sacrifice?
18. Norton was away with Trixie once, and he couldn't go bowling, he couldn't shoot pool, he couldn't do anything. When was that?
19. True or false: Norton wants to make Ralph poster boy for the nut-of-the-month club.

20. What berth do Ralph and Norton have on the train to the convention?
21. What time does the train Ralph and Norton are aboard leave the station?
22. What coats are Alice and Trixie wearing to the convention?

NORTON: Boy, Ralph, this is gonna be some convention draggin' our wives along. On accounta you askin' Alice I'm stuck with Trixie.

RALPH: All right, Norton, what could I do? I'm stuck with Alice, ain't I?

NORTON: Well, at least Alice ain't no Trixie. Boy, what a personality that girl's got. She's grumblin' all the time. Believe me, if the Marx Brothers had a sister, she'd be it . . . Complain-o.

23. How long is the Racoon convention supposed to last?
24. What three items does Norton buy at the novelty counter in the train station?

A first draft of "Unconventional Behavior"—the second half of which is included at the end of this chapter—had Ralph, Norton, the wives, and a Racoon dignitary on the train to Minneapolis. As usual, Ralph is scheming: This time he's trying to impress a Racoon muckety-muck. Meanwhile, Norton amuses himself by filling up bags with water.

A revised script eliminated everyone but Kramden, Norton, the conductor, and twin brothers, played by the late Jack Norton, an actor famous in the golden days of Hollywood for his drunk act. Humphrey Davis, the actor who played the conductor, recalls the rehearsal at which Jack Norton appeared, and why his "twin" roles were written out of the final script.

"Jack Norton, who always played a dapper drunk, was a favorite of Jackie's. He would use him whenever he could. Jackie did a lot of nice things for a lot of people that not many people know about, and Jack Norton was one of those cases.

"Jack was suffering from emphysema, and he was at the Will Rogers Hospital in upstate New York. Jackie would bring him in every once in a while to do a bit, so he could make some spending money and get a change from being in the sanatorium.

"In this particular show, Jack was supposed to play twin brothers—one of them was a drunk, like he always played, and the other was a sort of prissy, confident type. In the Pullman sleeper, the drunk was in one end of the car and the other brother was in the other end. There was room in the back so that Jack could slip out and run from one end to the other so that he could play both parts.

"Well, the stage at the Adelphi was a pretty wide stage and the car was slightly shorter than a regular Pullman car, and it had bunk sections and curtains. But during the afternoon when we were doing the camera run-through, Jack started to struggle with the going back and forth. The exertion got to be too much for him, and Jackie, as soon as he sensed this, took him offstage, gave him his money, put him in a cab, and sent him back to Saratoga.

"That left approximately five minutes of air time with nothing to do, because Jack had been involved for that length of time. So Jackie and Art went on the air and filled in with absolutely hilarious pantomime by using trick handcuffs that Art was going to be a riot with at the convention. They played this incredible off-the-cuff comedy routine of trying to sleep in the upper and lower berths with their hands locked together in these handcuffs. And five minutes was used up just like that, with absolutely incredible comic invention."

CONDUCTOR (*offstage*): All aboard!
> *Sound: Train pulling out of station. Ralph and Norton react lurch-style.*

RALPH: Hey Norton, the train's leavin'. Maybe they did miss it.

NORTON: So what. The worst that can happen is they'll catch the next train to Minneapolis. They got their own tickets.

RALPH: Yeah. What are we worryin' about?
> *Curtain on upper stage-left berth parts and Jack, dressed in tails, night hat, etc., sticks his head out.*

JACK: Pardon me. Would you mind keeping it a little quiet down there? I'm trying to get some sleep."
> *They look up at him and then Ralph speaks.*

RALPH: I'm very sorry, sir.

JACK: Don't get nasty!
> *Jack then pulls his head in and closes flaps.*

RALPH: Come on, Norton. Maybe we better get to bed.
> *Ralph starts to remove pj's from suitcase and Norton digs into trick store baggage. He pulls out eyeglasses with Ping-Pong eyeballs and fake nose. He puts them on.*

NORTON: Hey, get a load of these, Ralph. I got them in the novelty store in the station.

RALPH: Hey, they're a riot, Norton.

NORTON: Boy, you can have a lot of fun with these, Ralph. When we get to Minneapolis, I sneak up on someone on the street, tap him on the shoulder, and then when he turns around I go "Boo!"
> *Ralph chuckles like what'll-they-think-of-next-style as Norton removes glasses. Jack sticks head out again.*

JACK: I'm telling you for the last time to keep it quiet. I've got to get my sleep. I've got a very early appointment in the morning. The club car opens at eight o'clock!

RALPH (*annoyed*): All right, all right.

228

JACK: You be careful how you talk to me. My brother happens to own this railroad.

RALPH: Don't give me any of that stuff about your brother owns this railroad!

JACK: He certainly does. It's the only reason they let me ride the train!

A little while later, after Norton and Ralph have become handcuffed together and have tried to boomph their way out of the handcuffs:

NORTON: All right, Ralph. Put your hand down and I'll try and stamp it off. *They both bend down and hold chain a few inches from floor. Norton lifts his leg to stamp on chain but misses it. Norton straightens up and gets his hand caught in back of Jackie's knee.*

NORTON: I guess that ain't gonna work, Ralph.

RALPH: I know it ain't gonna work.
    *At this point Jack Norton sticks his head out.*

JACK: Maybe you better go back to the boomph.

RALPH: You keep out of this.

25. What's the magic word for getting out of Norton's trick handcuffs?
26. Why doesn't Norton want to sleep against the wall of the berth?

NORTON: Why doesn't one of us sleep in the upper berth and one of us in the lower berth?

RALPH: How can we do that when we're handcuffed?

NORTON: Well, we could sleep with our arms hangin' out of the sides.

RALPH: That is the stupidest thing I ever heard of . . . we'll do it! All right, Norton, you get in the upper and I'll get in the lower.

NORTON: Okay, Ralph.
    *Ralph helps Norton get into the upper berth, then gets into lower himself. As a result Norton in the upper berth is on his back with his right arm dangling down. Ralph is on his stomach with his left arm sticking up.*

RALPH: Goodnight!
    *Norton tries to get comfortable. Can't succeed, then speaks.*

NORTON: Ralph! . . .

RALPH (*exasperated*): What now?

NORTON: I can't sleep on my back.

RALPH: Then roll over and go to sleep.
    *Norton tries to roll over, almost pulling Ralph out of berth. Ralph leaps out of bed.*

RALPH: Get down here. I'll sleep in the upper berth.
    *Norton scrambles down.*

RALPH: All right, boost me up.
    *Norton tries to boost Ralph up and can't. After a few futile attempts he speaks.*

NORTON: Now I know where Tennessee Ernie got the inspiration for "Sixteen Tons."

RALPH: Just get me up there.

*Now after a struggle Ralph succeeds in getting into upper berth. He is on his stomach with his left hand hanging down. Norton in the lower berth is on his back with his right arm hanging up.*

NORTON: Ralph. . . .

RALPH: What do you want now?

NORTON: Remember, Ralph, when I was in the upper berth and you were in the lower berth and I said I couldn't sleep on my back, so you got out of the lower and I got out of the upper and I got into the lower and you got into the upper?

RALPH: Yeah.

NORTON: Well, I'm on my back again.

RALPH: That's impossible.

NORTON: Maybe the train turned over.

RALPH: Go to sleep!

NORTON: But I can't sleep on my back.

Ralph and Norton maneuver around the berths awhile, until Norton finally is on his stomach:

NORTON: Ralph. . . .

RALPH: Whattaya want now?

NORTON: I can't sleep on my stomach, either. I gotta sleep on my side.

A few seconds later:

NORTON: I wonder where the girls are now?

RALPH: Well, if they missed the train, they probably went home.

NORTON: Boy, I'm glad they ain't along, Ralph. They'd be causin' us nuthin' but trouble.

RALPH: Only if you'd brought along handcuffs for four.

27. Ralph asks Norton if he's hungry or thirsty. What does he forget to ask him?

28. Ralph and Norton think they're going to Minneapolis, but the train they're riding is going to:
A. Richmond, Va.
B. Albuquerque, N.M.
C. Bismarck, N.D.
D. Norfolk, Va.

*At this point Jack sticks his head out of upper stage-right berth. This is the upper berth on opposite side of stage from where he has been sticking his head out.*

JACK: Will you please keep it quiet there. I'm trying to get some sleep!
*Ralph and Norton both look at him in amazement. Then look at each other in amazement, and then look back at him.*

RALPH (*amazed*): How did you get over there?

JACK (*bewildered*): What are you talking about? I've been here all the time. And don't get so fresh with me, young man. It so happens that I own this railroad!
*Ralph and Norton exchange amazed glances as we BLACKOUT of scene!*

The following are scenes two and three of the first draft of "Unconventional Behavior," which Doreen Marx found in a collection of Marvin's Honeymooners scripts. You won't find any boomphs, handcuffs, or bulging eyes here, but Ralph and Norton—along with the wives—do make it to Minneapolis. And all along the way it's good, clean fun.

SCENE TWO

*As travelers part, camera holds on establishing shot of inside of pullman train. There are six pullman berths, three uppers and three lowers. On stage-right side of Pullman car is an archway which leads into another section of same car. On stage-left side of car is doorway leading to next car. Set is bare for a split when Alice and Trixie enter through archway. They are dressed in nightgowns, robes, slippers, etc., ready-for-bed-style. Their hair is in curlers and they are carrying towels, toothbrushes, etc., coming-from-washroom-style. As they enter, Trixie is grumbling. They cross toward center upper and lower berths.*

TRIXIE (*grumbling*): Well, I still don't like it, Alice.

ALICE: Neither do I, Trix. But what can we do? We're lucky they took us along with them.

TRIXIE: It burns me up. They've got that beautiful compartment in the next car, and we have to sleep in these things.

ALICE (*resigned*): Well, it's only for a night. Look, we better get some sleep.
*Norton and Ralph enter. They are also dressed for bed, with robes covering nightclothes. They are also wearing Racoon hats.*

RALPH: Oh, here they are, Norton.
*Ralph and Norton cross to girls and as they do, Ralph speaks.*

RALPH: Well, girls, I see you're all ready for beddy-bye. We just dropped in to say goodnight. *He then touches mattress bouncy-style.* My, don't these look comfy.

NORTON (*let's-get-out-of-here-style*): Yeah. Well, goodnight, girls. Come on, Ralph. Enough of this slummin'. Let's get back to our compartment.

RALPH: Okay, Norton. Goodnight, girls.

*Ralph and Norton start for door when Trixie stops them by speaking.*

TRIXIE: Wait a minute, Daniel Boone and Davy Crockett! How come you two don't sleep out here and let us take the compartment?

*Ralph and Norton exchange apprehensive looks.*

RALPH: Look, I told you before. Norton and me are officers in the Racoons. The lodge paid for that compartment for us. We have to pay for these.

ALICE: Well, I can't see what difference it makes to the Racoons who sleeps where.

RALPH: So you can't understand what difference it makes who sleeps where. Well, that shows how little you know, Miss Know-It-All. There happens to be a very good reason why you're sleepin' out here and we're sleepin' in there.

ALICE: Well, what is it?

*Ralph hesitates, trying to think of reason, and then speaks.*

RALPH: Uh, uh, go ahead. Tell her, Norton!

NORTON: It's very simple. It's much more comfortable in there!

*Ralph gives Norton a steamed look and shot with elbow.*

TRIXIE: Well, that settles it. Ed, get our bags and take them into the compartment.

NORTON: What for? What do you care how comfortable your bags are?

TRIXIE: We're going with them.

RALPH: Oh, no you ain't! You might as well get that through your head right now!

*Ralph and Trixie stand glaring at each other for a second, and then curtain on upper stage-left berth parts and Jack, dressed in tails, night hat, etc., sticks his head out. He is right above where they are speaking.*

JACK: Pardon me. Would you mind keeping it a little quiet down there. I'm trying to get some sleep.

*They all look up at him and then Ralph speaks.*

RALPH: I'm very sorry, sir.

JACK: Don't get nasty!

*Jack then pulls his head in and closes flaps.*

RALPH: Well, you satisfied? You're gonna wake up the whole train.

TRIXIE: I just want to know why we have to sleep out here when you've got a compartment. Remember, we're your wives!

NORTON: Please, Trixie, don't bring that up. I feel bad enough as it is!

RALPH: Do you girls have to be so unreasonable? We're takin' you to the convention, ain't we?

*At this point Jack sticks his head out of curtain again.*

JACK: I'm telling you for the last time to keep it quiet. I've got to get my sleep. I've got an early appointment in the morning. The club car opens at eight o'clock!

*Jack does not pull head in this time, but continues looking at group like he's sober and they're drunk. Ralph realizes that he can't win.*

RALPH: All right. If we keep this up all night, we'll be in Minneapolis and none of us'll get any sleep. You girls go in and take the compartment!

JACK (*to girls*): Don't let him talk to you that way, honey. If you don't want to take the compartment, don't take the compartment!

RALPH (*steamed, to Jack*): You keep out of this!

JACK: You be careful how you talk to me. My brother happens to own this railroad.

RALPH: Don't give me any of that stuff about your brother owns this railroad!

JACK: He certainly does. It's the only reason they let me ride the train!

RALPH (*exasperated*): Norton, will you take their bags and get them into the compartment?

NORTON (*protesting*): But, Ralph. . . .

RALPH: Get them into the compartment so we can get some sleep.

*Norton, disgruntled, but doing it, reaches under middle bunk and pulls out two suitcases. Ralph just looks angrily at the girls as Norton does this. Norton gets bags and then speaks.*

NORTON (*to girls, disgruntled*): All right. Go ahead.

*Trixie gives Alice a we-won look and girls go off. . . . Norton follows . . . and turns and speaks to Ralph.*

NORTON: Boy, Ralph, if this is any sample of what the rest of the convention is gonna be like, we shoulda stayed at home.

*Norton exits. Ralph pulls down covers on bottom berth, punches up pillow, softening it, etc. As he is doing this, train conductor enters through archway. At this point another Racoon enters through door. He is very distinguishable man, as audience must recognize him again without hesitation when he comes back in. He speaks to conductor. He is dressed high-Racoon-officer-style.*

STEINHARDT: Oh, pardon me, conductor, can you direct me to my compartment? I seem to have forgotten the number.

CONDUCTOR (*pulls out roster book*): Certainly, sir. What is your name?

STEINHARDT: Julius Steinhardt.

*Ralph immediately reacts to this. Conductor speaks.*

CONDUCTOR: Oh, you're in compartment 3B. That's right down at the end of this car, Mr. Steinhardt.

STEINHARDT: Thank you.

*Conductor and Steinhardt cross each other, conductor heading for door and Steinhardt for archway. Ralph stops Steinhardt by speaking. Conductor exits.*

RALPH: Oh, Mr. Steinhardt. *Steinhardt turns.* I'd like to introduce myself. My name is Brother Kramden—Ralph Kramden. *Points to Racoon hat on his head.* I'm with the Racoons, too . . . Bensonhurst Lodge.

STEINHARDT (*not impressed*): Oh, really?

RALPH: That's right. Say, at this convention you're pickin' the Rovin' Racoon, ain't you?

STEINHARDT (*what-are-you-driving-at-style*): Yes.

RALPH: Well, I wish you'd keep me in mind, Mr. Steinhardt. I think I'd be very good for the job.

STEINHARDT (*brushing-him-style*): Well, we'll see when the time comes, Mr. Kramden. Now if you don't mind, I'd like to get to my compartment. Good night.

*Steinhardt turns and goes through archway and Ralph calls after him.*

RALPH: Good night, Mr. Steinhardt. See you at the convention.

*Ralph looks after him for a second, and then Ed Norton comes in through doorway. He is carrying two different suitcases from those he left with.*

NORTON: Well, Ralph. I hope you're satisfied. You had to ask Alice to come along to the convention. On account of that I'm stuck with Trixie.

RALPH: All right, Norton. What could I do?

NORTON: At least Alice ain't no Trixie. Boy, what a personality that girl's got. She's grumblin' all the time. Believe me, if the Marx Brothers had a sister, she'd be it . . . Complain-o!

*Norton now crosses over to berths and starts putting suitcases under lower berth. As he does, Ralph speaks.*

RALPH: Well, we better get some sleep, Norton. We got a big day ahead of us tomorrow.

NORTON: Okay, Ralph.

*Both boys take their robes off, and slip out of slippers.*

RALPH (*indicating upper berth*): All right, Norton. Up you go.

NORTON: (*belligerently*): What do you mean, up I go? How come automatically I got to take the upper berth? Why don't you take it?

RALPH: All right, crybaby. I'll take the upper.

*Ralph grabs the side of the upper berth and then speaks to Norton.*

RALPH: Okay, Norton, help boost me up.

*Norton takes his hands, and without touching Ralph, moves his hands around behind Ralph like he's trying to find a good place for a grip. Suddenly he stops hand motions and speaks.*

NORTON: On second thought, I'll take the upper!

*Ralph just gives him a look. Norton pushes Ralph aside two-finger-style and scurries into upper berth. Ralph then gets into lower. Ralph pulls covers over him and then looks up and speaks.*

RALPH: Good night, Norton.

NORTON: Good night, Ralph.

*Ralph now pulls his curtain shut. Norton goes through motions of getting comfortable and then sits up. He looks down toward floor I-forgot-something-style. He then swings over the side and by stepping obviously into Ralph's berth by stepping into curtains, gets down to floor. He immediately reaches under Ralph's berth for one of the suitcases. Ralph whisks his curtains open, steamed-style, and speaks angrily.*

RALPH (*steamed*): What are you doin'?

NORTON: I got to get something out of my suitcase, Ralph.

RALPH: Well, hurry up.

*Norton throws his suitcase into upper berth and climbs up after it, stepping all over Ralph. After he is up there, Ralph just looks up, annoyed-style. Norton looks down as though nothing happened and speaks.*

NORTON: Good night, Ralph.

RALPH (*annoyed*): Good night!

*Ralph again closes his curtains. Norton, sitting up in berth, opens suitcase and takes out hero sandwich. He takes bite and as he's munching on it, he closes suitcase. He then puts hero sandwich down and starts climbing down from berth again. Again he puts his feet into Ralph's berth while leaning over into his berth. Ralph opens half of curtain up by his head. Norton's feet are down at other end. Ralph speaks, steamed.*

RALPH: What are you doin' now?

NORTON: I just wanted to put my suitcase back.

RALPH (*steamed shouting*): Get back up there.

NORTON: But, Ralph. . . .

RALPH (*steamed shouting*): Get back up there!

*Norton, scared-style, tries to scramble up quickly and flails feet in air into Ralph's berth. He finally gets up.*

RALPH: Now good night.

*Ralph again closes his curtain. Norton takes another bite out of hero sandwich. He then feels breast pocket of his nightshirt. After that he looks quickly into suitcase. Not finding what he sought, he leans over and calls.*

NORTON: Ralph. . . .

*Ralph, annoyed, opens curtains and looks up.*

RALPH (*annoyed*): What is it?

NORTON: Do you have a cigarette? I left mine in the compartment.

RALPH: Go to sleep!

*Ralph shuts curtain. Norton sits thinking a second and then speaks.*

NORTON: Look, Ralph, I don't have to disturb you. I'll just climb down, go into the next car and wake up the girls and get mine.

*Norton sticks one foot over edge of his berth preparatory to getting down. Ralph whisks open his curtain, takes a steamed swipe at Norton's foot as he speaks.*

RALPH (*steamed*): Get back up there! *Norton pulls his foot in quickly.* If you wake up those girls now, they'll want the compartment and the berths and everything!

*At this point, Jack sticks his head out of curtain.*

JACK: Well, they can't have the engine. That belongs to my brother!

RALPH (*steamed*): You keep out of this. I don't care if your brother does own the railroad.

*Jack pulls head back in. Ralph, steamed, closes curtain on his berth.*

NORTON (*sulking-style*): I still didn't get my cigarette. . . .

*Ralph, ready to explode, whisks his curtain open, and gets out.*

RALPH: If you have your cigarette, will you leave me alone?

NORTON: Sure, Ralph.

RALPH: All right, then I'll get you a cigarette.

*Ralph bends down and pulls own suitcase out. He opens it and rifles around in it after placing it on floor. He releases trigger on cigar box which is in suitcase, and suddenly three snakes fly up in air. Ralph does fright reaction. Ralph then picks up cigar box and flings it across car steamed-style. Norton laughs at this. Ralph crosses to him and waves threatening fist in his face.*

RALPH: You keep this up, Norton, and you'll get to Minneapolis before tomorrow morning!!

JACK (*same big take*): Minneapolis?

RALPH (*pointing and steamed*): You shut up!

*Jack pulls his head back in. Ralph bends down again and rummages through suitcase quickly. He pulls out pack of cigarettes, straightens up, and gives them to Norton.*

RALPH: All right, Norton, now I don't want to hear another word!

NORTON: Thanks, Ralph. Good night.

*Ralph just nods good night angry-style, shuts suitcase quickly, and slides it under berth. All during this, Norton is feeling pockets, looking through suitcase, etc., looking for matches. Just as Ralph is getting comfortable and is pulling blankets up over him, but before Ralph closes curtains, Norton leans over and speaks.*

NORTON: Ralph. . . .

*At sound of Norton's voice, Ralph leaps up in bunk, livid-style. By sitting straight up, he hits top of his head on top of his berth. He winces painfully, then livid-style looks out of berth and up at Norton and speaks.*

RALPH: What do you want now?

NORTON: I don't have any matches.

*Ralph, too livid to even speak, gets out of bed, pulls out suitcase, goes through it quickly, pulls out matches, then straightens up and shoves matches at Norton.*

RALPH: Now will you please leave me alone.

NORTON: Okay, Ralph. I know you're pretty steamed. Sure is a pain in the neck havin' the girls along, ain't it?

RALPH: I forgot all about the girls!

*Ralph then leans down and all in one steamed move shuts suitcase and shoves it under berth. As Ralph is doing this, Norton shoves cigarettes and matches into breast pocket of nightclothes. At same time, Jack sticks his head out between curtains and calls down to Ralph.*

JACK: Pardon me. As long as you're up, would you mind giving me my suitcase? It's the green one underneath here.

*Ralph gives him an annoyed look, but to avoid argument, reaches under berth below Jack and takes out suitcase. As he pulls it out and as he lifts it, there is a great rattling of glasses, bottles, etc. Ralph stops lifting, looks strangely at suitcase and then up at Jack.*

JACK: You'll have to excuse the noise. You see, my brother gives me a very small allowance and I have to bring back the empties!

*Ralph just gives a ceilingward glance and hands bag to Jack, who sticks hand out of berth, takes suitcase, goes back into berth. By this time, Norton has laid down and is ready to go to sleep. Ralph, who is about to get in his own berth, notices this.*

RALPH: Norton!

NORTON (*props himself up on elbow*): What do you want, Ralph?

RALPH: How come you ain't smokin' your cigarette?

NORTON: Oh, I didn't want it for now. I just wanted to have it handy for the first thing in the mornin'!

RALPH (*eyes bulge livid-style*): Smoke it now!!

NORTON: But, Ralph. . . .

RALPH: Smoke it now!

*Norton, intimidated-style, takes cigarette out of pack, lights it, and takes a few puffs. Ralph just nods at him don't-stop-until-I-tell-you-style. Ralph then gets back into his berth and closes curtains. A split after Ralph closes curtains, Norton looks down and speaks.*

NORTON (*timidly*): Ralph. . . .

RALPH: Shut up! I'm goin' to sleep.

*Norton then nods to himself like then-I'll-get-rid-of-this-style, and throws cigarette down on floor on side of berth toward archway. Norton then lies down, but after a split sits up again.*

NORTON: Ralph, I'm thirsty. Can I come down and get a glass of water?

RALPH: No! Now go to sleep!

NORTON: But I'm thirsty. I can't sleep unless I have a glass of water.

*Ralph opens curtains slowly and steps out slow-burn-trying-to-control-self-style.*

RALPH: All right, Norton! I'm goin' to get you the water, but I don't want to hear another word out of you!

*Ralph turns toward archway, but before he can even take a step Norton speaks.*

NORTON: Ralph, I threw my cigarette—

RALPH (*wheeling and exploding*): I said, not another word!

*Ralph then turns and starts toward archway. He gets to approximate spot where Norton threw cigarette. He supposedly steps on it and does yelp of pain. He then dances around, grabbing foot as he howls in pain. At conclusion, Norton speaks.*

NORTON: That's what I was tryin' to tell you, Ralph. You see, I. . . .

*As Norton spoke, Ralph crossed to him, menacing-style.*

RALPH (*interrupting, menacing-style*): Get down here!

NORTON (*fearfully*): But, Ralph.

RALPH: I said, get down here.

*Norton, fearful but intimidated, gets down.*

RALPH: All right, you take the lower. I'll take the upper.

*Ralph puts one foot on lower berth and hands on upper.*

RALPH: All right, Norton. Gimme a boost.

*Norton gets behind Ralph and starts pushing with much grunting and exertion. He stops, spits on his hands and continues. Then as he continues pushing and grunting he speaks.*

NORTON: Boy, now I know where Tennessee Ernie got the inspiration for "Sixteen Tons."

RALPH: Just get me up there!

*After a little more grunting and pushing, Norton gets Ralph into upper berth. Immediately on seeing Norton's suitcase, Ralph throws it down on floor, steamed. As Ralph starts straightening himself out in upper berth, Norton starts picking up spilled things from suitcase on floor and starts putting them back in suitcase. There were some of the water bags in suitcase. On picking up some of these, he looks up at Ralph and speaks.*

NORTON: Hey, Ralph.

RALPH (*leaning out of berth*): What?

NORTON: I just got an idea. I got a couple of these water bags in my suitcase. Why don't we fill one up and try it out?

RALPH: What do you mean?

NORTON: Well, you could take the bag up there with you, and I could be the lookout. When I see somebody comin' I give you the signal, you stick your hand out, and drop it right on their head. *Norton laughs in anticipation.*

RALPH: Not now, Norton. It's late. We gotta get some sleep.

NORTON: We can sleep after the convention, Ralph. I thought we were goin' on this thing to have some fun.

*Ralph thinks for a minute and then speaks.*

RALPH (*smiling*): Well, I guess it would be fun. . . .

NORTON (*jumping at chance*): I'll fill it up, Ralph.

*Norton takes one of the water bags and goes off through archway. He chuckles mischievously as he goes. Ralph looks after him for a second and then goes back to straightening out berth. He finds Norton's hero sandwich and is about to throw it on floor, steamed-style, when he hesitates, looks at it affectionately, and then takes a bite out of it. He chews it for a second and then Norton returns with filled bag. He speaks.*

NORTON: Here you are, Ralph. Boy, this is gonna be fun.

RALPH: Now, look, Norton. As soon as you see somebody comin', let me know so I can get ready. Then in order to stop 'em, you call him over by sayin' somethin' like, uh, pardon me, do you have a match? Then he'll come over to give it to you. Then when he's right in position, you say, uh, my, what a lovely day. That'll be my cue to stick the bag out and drop it right on his head.

*Norton chuckles. Ralph pulls back into berth and closes curtains. Norton sits on edge of lower berth tapping knees nervously and looking in both directions. Suddenly, as he's looking down archway, he perks up.*

NORTON: Hey, Ralph, here comes the pigeon! Get ready.

*Norton continues looking at archway with anticipation. After a split, Julius Steinhardt enters through archway. He is now dressed in nightclothes and bathrobe, carrying towel over arm. A few steps after he gets through archway, he stops and tightens belt on robe for audience identification. He then continues a couple of steps, when Norton speaks.*

NORTON: Uh, pardon me. Do you have a match?

STEINHARDT: Oh, uh, certainly.

*He crosses toward Norton. As he does, Norton looks upward to see if he's getting in right position. Before Steinhardt can pull out matches, Norton speaks.*

NORTON: Would you mind standing a little more to the right, please?

*Steinhardt looks a little bewildered as Norton edges him over a little with hand. Getting him in right position, he speaks out-of-the-blue-style.*

NORTON: My, what a lovely day!

*Steinhardt looks a little more bewildered than ever. Ralph's hand comes out through slit in curtain with bag of water. He drops it right on Steinhardt's head. Norton breaks up. Steinhardt splutters. And Ralph pokes his head out of berth good-time-Charley-style.*

RALPH (*good-time-Charley-style*): Who'd we get, Norton?

*Ralph laughs as Steinhardt looks up at him. Ralph's laughter dies down as he realizes who he's hit. His eyes bulge in panic as Steinhardt speaks.*

STEINHARDT (*spluttering-style*): Kramden, what's the meaning of this?

RALPH (*petrified*): Mr. Steinhardt! I didn't mean to. . . . I mean I didn't know. . . . I mean hamma hemma hamma humma!

STEINHARDT: All right, Kramden. You wanted me to keep you in mind. I'll keep you in mind, you, you idiot!

*Steinhardt storms back through archway, brushing-himself-with-towel-style and spluttering. Ralph looks out of berth in direction of archway and calls after him.*

RALPH (*pleading*): Mr. Steinhardt. . . .

*As Ralph keeps looking in that direction pleading-style, and Norton looks at Ralph what's-the-matter-style, Jack sticks his head out of upper stage-right berth. This is the upper berth on opposite side of stage from where he has been sticking his head out.*

JACK THE SECOND: Will you please keep it quiet there. I'm trying to get some sleep!

*Ralph and Norton both look at him in amazement, then look at each other in amazement, and then look back at him.*

RALPH (*amazed*): How did you get over there?

JACK THE SECOND (*bewildered*): What are you talking about? I've been here all the time. And don't get so fresh with me, young man. It so happens that I own this railroad!

*Ralph and Norton exchange amazed glances as we BLACKOUT of scene.*

SCENE THREE

*As travelers part, camera holds on establishing shot of hotel lobby. There is an archway on stage-left wall leading to main lobby, and there is another archway on stage-right wall with sign over it reading: "To main dining room." Along back wall are several club chairs, end tables, magazine racks, floor lamps, pictures, coffee tables, etc. Along sides of room are letter-writing tables, club chairs, etc. This is not the main lobby, but small reading and letter-writing room set aside from main lobby. As scene opens, Ralph and Norton are seated in club chairs center stage. Their faces can't be seen, as both are holding open newspapers up in front of their faces. After a split, bellhop enters from stage-left archway. As he crosses and exits through stage-right archway, he calls:*

BELLHOP (*call-for-Philip-Morris-style*): Call for Morris Fink. . . . Call for Morris Fink!

*Ralph pulls newspaper down and watches bellhop. Ralph is disgruntled.*

RALPH (*not looking at Norton*): Maybe we ought to have that guy page the girls, Norton. We been waitin' here over an hour.

*Norton pulls newspaper down from in front of his face, revealing that he is wearing horror mask from first scene. Both boys are wearing Racoon uniforms and Norton is wearing his Racoon hat on top of mask.*

NORTON: What did you say, Ralph?

RALPH (*still looking in direction bellhop went and away from Norton*): I said, maybe we ought to have that guy page the. . . .

*At this point Ralph turns and sees Norton and does big fright reaction. After reaction he yells at Norton.*

RALPH: Will you take that thing off!

*Norton just shrugs, and as he takes mask off, Ralph shakes his head can't-you-ever-be-sensible-style.*

RALPH: What's the matter with you, Norton? Do you always have to act like a two-year-old kid?

NORTON (*disgruntled*): That's what I thought we come to the convention for. To have a little fun. All you done for the past two days is grumble.

RALPH (*sour-grapes-style*): Fun? A lot of fun this convention's been for me. Ever since I dropped that bag of water on Steinhardt's head, he won't even talk to me, much less consider me for Rovin' Racoon. And the only other thing I've done at this convention is wait for the girls. Anytime we want to go anyplace, they're out shoppin' or somethin'.

NORTON: Yeah, I know what you mean, Ralph. But you got to admit they picked up some nice souvenirs. You ought to see the lampshade Trixie bought. It's beautiful. It's all decorated with scenes from the life of Harold Stassen!

RALPH: Who's Harold Stassen?

NORTON: I don't know. But he must be pretty important if they do his life on a lampshade!

RALPH: Well, I don't care what they're buyin'. I wish they'd get here. Believe me, Norton, the next time we take our wives on a convention with us, we're leavin' them home!

NORTON: You can say that again!

RALPH (*impatient*): What time is it, anyway?

*Norton looks at his watch and registers same expression as before—it's-not-working-style. He hits his wrist a couple of times trying to get it started like before.*

NORTON: It stopped again, Ralph.

RALPH: Well, find out from somebody.

*Norton looks around and at this point bellhop enters through archway stage right. As he passes Norton, Norton stops him by speaking.*

NORTON: Oh, pardon me, there.

BELLHOP (*he stops*): Yes, sir?

NORTON: Can you tell me if there are any Chinese restaurants in the neighborhood?

*Ralph explodes and gives Norton a shot.*

RALPH (*exploding*): Just ask him the time!

*Norton reacts cowering-style. Ralph looks up at bewildered bellhop and speaks.*

RALPH: Can you tell me the time, please?

BELLHOP (*looking at watch*): It's four-fifteen, sir.

RALPH: Thank you.

*Bellhop . . . exits.*

RALPH (*sarcastic*): Are there any Chinese restaurants in the neighborhood!

NORTON: Look, Ralph, when you got a gift you want to use it. . . .

*At this point, Ralph gives Norton a look and starts lifting his newspaper to read it again. Then Julius Steinhardt enters through stage-right archway and crosses to stage-left writing table. He is dressed Racoon-uniform-style. Ralph watches him cross and sit down at writing table. As Steinhardt takes paper and pen, preparing to write, Ralph speaks to Norton.*

RALPH: Hey, Norton, there's Steinhardt. Do you think if I go over and try to be friendly, he'd let bygones be bygones?

NORTON: Well, it ain't gonna do you any harm to try, Ralph.

*Ralph gets up and approaches Steinhardt with trepidation, like let's-start-friendship-all-over-again-style.*

RALPH (*false-hearty-style*): Well, if it isn't my old friend, Mr. Steinhardt. How are you there, Mr. Steinhardt?

STEINHARDT (*looks up, extremely cold*): Oh, it's you, Kramden.

RALPH (*weak but trying*): Say, Mr. Steinhardt, I was wonderin' if you and the wife would care to join me and my missus for supper tonight?

STEINHARDT (*very cold*): No, thank you, Kramden.

RALPH (*still trying*): Maybe tomorrow night?

STEINHARDT (*thirty below zero*): I'm afraid not, Kramden. I have a very important dinner engagement tomorrow. I'm eating alone.

RALPH: Well, maybe sometime when you're not so tied up maybe?

STEINHARDT (*coldsville*): Never!!

*Giving Ralph complete brush, Steinhardt turns back and starts writing. Ralph stands there for a second, sheepish, but knowing he's defeated, crosses back to Norton.*

NORTON: How did it go, Ralph?

RALPH: I think he's softenin' up a little. He was a lot nicer to me now than when I saw him at lunch!

NORTON: You know what I really think put you in his bad book, Ralph? It wasn't so much that water bag you hit him with on the train . . . it was that second one you dropped on his head this mornin'!

RALPH: Well, how did I know he was goin' to be the next one to come in the washroom!

NORTON: Well, as they say in France, Ralph, c'est ce bon!

RALPH: Yeah, I guess you're right, Norton. That's life. I don't stand a chance of becomin' Rovin' Racoon now!

NORTON: Then forget about it and enjoy the convention. Come on. Sit down.

*Boys pick up papers and start reading again. After a split a woman enters from stage-left archway, followed by Alice and Trixie. She looks around quickly for a second and spots her husband. She is Mrs. Steinhardt. As she crosses to him, she speaks.*

WOMAN: Oh, there you are, Julius.

STEINHARDT (*looking up from writing, speaks*): Oh, hello, Cynthia. I see you're back from shopping.

WOMAN: Yes, Julius, and I want you to meet these women. I met them while I was shopping and they're the loveliest girls.

*Steinhardt gets up to meet girls.*

WOMAN: I asked them to have dinner with us one evening. Their husbands are here with the convention, too.

STEINHARDT (*friendly-style*): Oh, really. Well, I'd be delighted to have dinner with them.

WOMAN: This is my husband, girls. Julius, this is Mrs. Norton and Mrs. Kramden.

STEINHARDT (*reacting*): Kramden?

*On hearing his name mentioned so loudly, Ralph looks up from newspaper in that direction.*

RALPH (*exclaiming*): Alice!

*They all look in his direction. Ralph gets up and crosses, followed by Norton. As Norton crosses, he speaks.*

NORTON: Boy, I thought they'd never show up.

WOMAN (*bewildered at husband's reaction*): You know Mr. Kramden, Julius?

STEINHARDT: Know him? He's the imbecile who dropped those two water bags on my head. And I certainly don't intend to have dinner with him. No offense to you ladies.

WOMAN: Oh, Julius. He was just having fun on the convention.

STEINHARDT: You call that fun?

WOMAN: Well, I seem to remember something you did on your first convention, Julius. Remember that fire hydrant in Washington, and how the water went all over President Harding's shoes!

STEINHARDT: Well, you see that was different. That was. . . .

*He breaks out of stern mood and starts laughing at his own misspent youth.*

STEINHARDT: I guess it was pretty funny at that.

WOMAN: Compared to that, dropping a couple of water bags was child's play.

STEINHARDT (*forgiving*): I guess you're right, Cynthia. And to show you that there are no hard feelings, Kramden, we'll all have dinner tomorrow night.

RALPH (*beaming*): Oh, thank you, sir.

NORTON: Wait a minute, Mr. Steinhardt. I guess you forgot. You can't have dinner with us tomorrow night. You got an important engagement. Remember? You're eatin' alone!

*Ralph gives Norton shot with elbow. Ralph picks it up quickly.*

RALPH: Uh, don't worry, Mr. Steinhardt. We'll be there.

STEINHARDT: Fine. We'll meet here in the lobby tomorrow night at eight o'clock. And incidentally, Kramden (*sly-old-fox-style*), maybe at dinner we can discuss that Roving Racoon appointment.

RALPH: Gee, that'd be just swell, Mr. Steinhardt.

WOMAN: Wonderful. And I'll be looking forward to seeing you girls again, too.

STEINHARDT: Well, come along, Cynthia.

*They start to leave, but Ralph stops them.*

RALPH: Here, Mr. Steinhardt. Have a cigar.

*Ralph reaches for his pocket and fumbles, not being able to find cigar. Norton quickly pulls one out of his pocket and extends it to Ralph.*

NORTON: Here, Ralph. Here's one of mine.

RALPH (*taking it and extending it to Steinhardt*): Thanks, Norton. Here, Mr. Steinhardt.

STEINHARDT: Well, thank you.

*As Steinhardt opens it and sniffs it, Ralph lights match and then lights cigar. After a few puffs Steinhardt speaks.*

STEINHARDT: Well, see you tomorrow. And don't be so formal. Call me Julius.

RALPH (*awkwardly*): Okay (*then awkwardly*), Julius.

*Steinhardt and wife exit through stage-left archway.*

RALPH: Oh, boy. That job is as good as mine.

ALICE: I'm sorry I kept you waiting so long, Ralph. But you see, when we met Mrs. Steinhardt. . . .

RALPH (*interrupting*): Don't apologize, Alice. Your meeting Mrs. Steinhardt was the greatest thing that could have happened to me. And you know somethin', sweetie, I was right the first time. Never go on a convention without takin' your wife.

*They all smile at each other, when we hear loud explosion offstage left. They all look up in that direction quizzically. Steinhardt reappears through archway. His face is blackened, there is short spread-eagle cigar in his mouth, and his Racoon hat is on sideways. After standing glaring at Ralph for a second, he takes cigar out of his mouth and speaks.*

STEINHARDT: The dinner is off!

RALPH (*panicky*): But, Julius.

STEINHARDT: And don't call me Julius!

*Steinhardt turns irate-style and exits. Ralph wheels on Norton and gives him a shot.*

RALPH (*exploding*): What did you give me one of those cigars for!

*Norton reacts to shot and as Ralph turns and looks at girls with ready-to-cry expression, we BLACKOUT of show.*

# THE SAFETY AWARD

May 19, 1956 · Leonard Stern and Sydney Zelinka

1. Who are the reporter and the photographer from *Universal* magazine, the magazine that's doing a three-page spread on Ralph for being voted the city's safest bus driver?
2. What does Ralph have to do if he wants his picture on the cover of *Universal* magazine?
3. Where and at what time is Ralph supposed to be presented with his award?

RALPH: This is a special award. Happens once in a blue moon. But take policemen and firemen, they're gettin' awards all the time, and I think bus drivers, in a way, are public servants just like them guys.

INTERVIEWER: They get most of their awards for bravery in the face of extreme danger. When does a bus driver have to show bravery in the face of extreme danger?

RALPH: When he opens the door for a mob of howlin' women on their way to a Janaury white sale at Macy's!

4. What did Ralph say to the woman who wanted to bring her pedigreed French poodle worth $10,000 onto his bus?

INTERVIEWER: I guess you run into all kinds.

RALPH: All women are the same. The bus is crowded—there might be an empty one right behind—but they push, they shove, they fight to get on the bus. And then when they're all on and I finally get the door closed, that's the signal for them to start askin', 'Does this bus go up Madison Avenue?' But that's nothin'. Did you ever see a woman on a crowded bus go lookin' through her pocketbook for change? If they dig deep enough, they come up with everything. A gas bill from 1932, a hockey puck, even burnt-out electric light bulbs. But the right change? Hah!

INTERVIEWER: Didn't you ever have even one woman who got on the bus calmly, knew where she wanted to go, and had the right change in her hand?

RALPH: Are you kiddin'! I've only been drivin' a bus for sixteen years!

5. How long ago did Ralph and Norton meet?
6. True or false: Norton works for the city, in a white-collar job.
7. Why does Norton ride Ralph's bus?
8. What angle will Mr. Martin use in his story about Ralph?
9. Norton, on the relationship between the Kramdens and the Nortons: "The four of us get along like _____."
10. Whose car does Ralph want to borrow so he can drive to the award presentation? Who's going to give Ralph's friend a ride home so he can lend Ralph the car?
11. How long has Ralph driven his bus without having an accident?

*Original bus driver's union pin, worn by Ralph Kramden.*
COURTESY RALPH.

NORTON: Ralph, I've been meanin' to ask you—there are other good drivers in the company but they all get into scrapes, little accidents and things. You're the only one able to go this length of time with a perfect record. How do you account for it?

RALPH: Simple, Norton, very simple. All you gotta do is follow one rule. And that rule is—look where you're going and go where you're looking!

*As Ralph speaks these last words he starts to walk off and comes in contact with stout woman who's crossing. She takes a step backward and speaks indignantly.*

WOMAN: Why don't you look where you're going!

12. Ralph wants to wear a pair of shoes that are at the shoemaker's. He says he could be wearing them if the shoemaker paid more attention to shoes and less attention to _____.

13. Norton borrows one of Ralph's new handkerchiefs. Ralph tells him, "That's for showin', _____."

14. True or false: Alice and Trixie wear identical dresses to the award ceremony.

15. Norton says Alice and Trixie look like:
    A. The Collier Brothers.
    B. The simp and the blimp.
    C. Boss and Ziggy.
    D. The Bobbsey Twins.

16. Alice bought her new dress at:
    A. Freitag's.
    B. Morgan's.
    C. Bloomgarten's.
    D. The Racoons' old-clothes drive.

17. What famous poem does Norton quote on his way upstairs to tell Trixie not to wear her dress to the award ceremony?

18. Alice and Trixie have been friends for _____ years.

19. True or false: Trixie wears an imitation dyed rabbit fur coat over her dress.

20. True or false: Ralph and Norton wear identical jackets to the award ceremony.

*As curtains part, camera holds on establishing shot of exterior of Kramden house. After a split, our foursome come out through front door. Norton is wearing a different jacket. One that does not resemble Ralph's. Ralph talks to Norton.*

RALPH: All right, all right, I heard you!

NORTON: Okay, Ralph, as long as it's clearly understood that if the store refuses to exchange my jacket, you pay for the torn sleeve!

21. What happens to Trixie on the way to the car?
22. Who wanted to put a "safe bus driver" plaque in Ralph's bus?
23. Ralph has an accident on the way to City Hall. Who are the occupants in the other car?
24. What part of Freddie Muller's car is damaged in the accident?
    A. The headlight.
    B. The bumper.
    C. The fender.
    D. The radiator.

RALPH: What burns me is it wasn't my fault. I'm pulling away from the curb and he comes barreling into me.

ALICE: Did you put your hand out?

RALPH: I musta. I always do.

*His reply is met with silence from Alice.*

*Hollerin' Hurdle.* COURTESY JIM ENGEL.

The Honeymooners. *Notice Kramden's mug. This is another photo taken during the session of the autographed photo that appears in the introduction of this book.* COURTESY PERSONALITY PHOTOS, INC.

RALPH: I'm tellin' you, I always do!

ALICE: Well, you still get the award.

RALPH: Hey! Let's go.

NORTON: Say, Ralph, I know how you feel about these things. . . . I, er, don't know how to say it to you but, er. . . .

RALPH (*grudgingly*): Okay, you drive!

25. Why isn't the commissioner present to give Ralph his award?
26. Who gives Ralph the award instead, and what is he famous for?
27. True or false: Ralph's accident happened because he didn't give a turn signal.
28. According to Ralph, what's the uppermost thing on a bus driver's mind?

JUDGE: Mr. Kramden, it gives me great pleasure to present you with this award as the safest bus driver of the year.

*Judge hands cup to Ralph, who takes it and keels over.*

INTERVIEWER: Get a picture of him, Charlie. This one ought to make the cover! *APPLAUSE.*

# *MIND YOUR OWN BUSINESS*

May 26, 1956 · Leonard Stern and Sydney Zelinka

1. True or false: Ralph and Norton are playing gin rummy.
2. In the card game, Norton has "runs" of _____ and _____, and he's thrown down two _____.
3. Ralph plays cards "scientifically." What card does he throw out because he's deduced Norton doesn't need it?
4. How many points does Norton have in the game?
5. Who does Norton think is going to beat him out of a promotion in the sewer?

RALPH: You're just looking for excuses. If you want that promotion, you can get it. You've got to go in and sell yourself. You've got to remind them how important you are to the organization!

NORTON: I don't have to do that, Ralph. I think they appreciate what I'm doing.

RALPH: Appreciate? You walk into a bank and try to deposit all that appreciation, and see how much interest they give you on it. I watched my father give the best years of his life to the Frobish Packing Company. He worked hard and he worked long, and when he was with them thirty-five years, they finally gave him a big testimonial dinner. They had a big spread, as much liquor as you could drink. All in honor of my old man, who slaved for them for thirty-five years. And do you know what happened to my father at his testimonial dinner? They fired him for getting loaded!

6. How long has Cassidy been with the sanitation department, and where has he been working the last six months?
7. How long has Norton worked in the sewer?

How did the writers decide that Norton would be a sewer worker? Actually, they didn't. Just as the writers never intended for Norton to become a regular in the early Honeymooners sketches at Dumont, neither was any thought given to what Norton's occupation would be. He wound up in the sewer because of a joke written for Trixie.

"Norton comes home from work, complaining about dinner or something," says Stone. "She says he has some case complaining about dinner. 'I've been slaving over a hot stove all day, and you've been down in a nice cool sewer.' One joke led to the whole thing."

8. Ralph plays Norton double or nothing in the last hand of cards. How much does he lose to Norton?

RALPH: Now that I've straightened you out and you've got no more problems, let's get back to our gin game.

NORTON: I'd better not. I wanna go upstairs and go over all this in my mind a couple of times. And look, Ralph, I want you to forget about the fourteen cents you owe me.

RALPH: Oh, no. I lost it playing cards, and all I want is a chance to win it back.

NORTON: I'm telling you, forget the fourteen cents.

RALPH: One hand. Double or nothing. Just one hand.

NORTON: Okay, but I'd just as leave forget the fourteen cents.

*Ralph shuffles and deals cards to Norton, who picks them up as he receives them.*

RALPH: You'd better play this one carefully, Norton. I'm out to get you this time!

*As Ralph gathers all his cards together, Norton lays down his hand.*

NORTON: Gin!

*Ralph does eye bulge.*

RALPH: All right, have it your way. Let's forget the fourteen cents!

9. Norton demands his promotion in the sewer and gets fired instead. He gets so depressed he loses his appetite. What food does Alice offer Norton that he turns down?

NORTON: I laid it right on the line. I either get the promotion or else! Well, it turned out to be else.

ALICE: I'm awfully sorry. How about Trixie?

NORTON: I'm scared to tell her. Look, Alice, you and she been pretty close for a long time, and I thought you might go up and break it to her.

ALICE: Ed, you're the one who has to do it. You've got to tell Trixie.

NORTON: Yeah, I guess so. There's no other way. If only I didn't have to tell her I got fired. Hey, maybe I can tell her we went out of business and had to close down—the sewer went bankrupt.

*Norton looks hopefully at Alice, who shakes her head negatively.*

NORTON: No, huh? How about this? I'll make believe I'm still working, only each day I'll come home a little earlier. First I'll come home at five o'clock. Then three o'clock, one o'clock, then eleven o'clock in the morning. It'll be so gradual, that when I'm finally stayin' home all the time she won't think anything of it.

ALICE: Ed, there's no way of getting around it. You've got to go up and tell her.

*Norton goes reluctantly to door before he stops and turns.*

NORTON: You know, a guy's better off if he ain't got a job. If he's a bum. If he don't do a day's work in his whole life. That way, he never has to come home and tell his wife he got fired.

10. Ralph says nothing will stop him from going down into the sewer to get Norton his job back. Alice disagrees. Why?

RALPH: I got faith in Norton. He'll be able to do something.

ALICE: Sure. He'll go into business for himself. He can open his own little sewer in the Bronx! Ralph, all his experience is in the sewer. What else can he do? He can be out of work for months.

RALPH: Wait a minute, Alice, now you're goin' overboard. He'll get work. There are plenty of jobs around for a man of Norton's ability. Don't forget he had no trouble fifteen years ago.

ALICE: Fifteen years ago?

RALPH: Yeah. When he left the sewer for another job. And he didn't have to go looking for that job. They came looking for him. They wanted him and they made sure they got him. And in no time at all he was one of the best men in the navy!

ALICE: The navy! Fifteen years ago they were taking everyone.

RALPH: But Norton was the only one ever decorated for working a bilge pump!

11. How long is Norton out of work before he gets another job? Who does he go to work for? What type of work is he doing?

12. Trixie: "You can take the _____ out of the _____, but you can't take the _____ out of the _____."

13. Since Norton got fired, how many times have the Nortons had dinner with the Kramdens?

14. Where do Trixie and Norton eat dinner the day Norton starts his new job?

15. How many prospects does Norton visit his first day on the job? Whom does he finally sell an iron to?

16. Why is a sewer worker like a brain surgeon?

17. How much money does Norton tell Ralph he earned the first day of his new job?

18. Norton tells Ralph he stopped working at _____ PM because he didn't want to push himself into a higher tax bracket.

19. Name two dishes the Nortons ate at the Kramdens' during Norton's unemployment.

RALPH: I'm glad all this happened, because now I'm wise to that four-flusher.

ALICE: What are you talking about?

RALPH: I found out he don't want me to get a job with the Jiffy Iron Company. He don't want me to make forty dollars a day like he's doing. He don't want to share anything. He wants to keep it all to himself. Well, it ain't gonna work. I'm getting myself a job with the Jiffy Iron Company first thing in the morning, and then I'm quittin' the bus company!

ALICE: You'll do no such thing.

RALPH: You got nothing to say about this. This is war. Ralph Kramden is declaring war on Ed Norton! I'm gettin' a job with that company, I'm movin' into his territory, I'm gonna wipe him out! And I'm doin' it right away. Like that Civil War general said, 'You got to get there firstest with the mostest.' And that's what I'm doin, I'm gettin' there firstest with the mostest!

ALICE: You may not get there firstest, but you'll sure get there with the mostest!

20. Ralph was once a salesman; he sold _____ in front of his house when he was six years old.
    A. Knockwurst.
    B. Snow shovels.
    C. Lemonade.
    D. Raccoon caps.
21. What's Ralph's plan to get his promotion and raise at the bus company?

RALPH: I ain't gonna threaten to quit. I'm just gonna tell him about the other job. And you know as well as I do, when your boss knows someone else wants you, that's when he wants you the most!

ALICE: Ralph, I wish you luck.

RALPH: Thanks, Alice. And I wanna thank you for talking me outta quitting my job. This way is much better. Alice, tomorrow I get my promotion. And tomorrow night you're not cooking supper. You ain't going near that stove. We're going out.

ALICE: Ralph, that's wonderful.

RALPH: Yep. We're gonna eat at your mother's!

22. True or false: Norton is finally promoted to foreman.

*As curtains part, camera holds on establishing shot of Kramden kitchen. Alice, wearing a housecoat, is seated at table having breakfast. The toaster is on table. She is drinking coffee as Ralph enters. He carries a small inexpensive zipper bag.*

ALICE: Ralph, why are you home so early? What happened?

RALPH: Alice, you certainly hit the nail on the head when you said the boss likes me.

ALICE: You've seen him already?

RALPH: Sure. I move fast. First thing I went over to the Spiffy Company and made sure they had an opening for me. Then over to the bus company, right into the boss's office and I spoke my piece. Boy, were you right about the boss liking me.

ALICE: He gave you the promotion.

RALPH: He said to me—Ralph, he called me—"Ralph, I think very highly of you. You're one of our best men and we'd hate to lose you. Unfortunately, there's no chance for your promotion right now, but because I'm so fond of you I'm not going to stand in your way. You take that job with the Spiffy Iron Company and good luck!" How about that?

ALICE: Ralph, he let you go!

RALPH: That ain't all he did for me. He said he was gonna buy my first iron. Then he called in all the guys from the office—I got four orders from them. And in the locker room I got seven orders from drivers. And they all bought it because of my salesmanship. They said, "Ralph, if that iron's as good as you say it is, we'll take it." I didn't even have a sample to show and I sold twelve irons.

ALICE: That's very good, Ralph.

RALPH: Good? I made almost twenty-five dollars and I haven't even started. Boy, am I goin' to make a bum out of that Norton!

ALICE (*points to bag*): Have you got the sample iron in there?

RALPH: Yeah, I just picked one up.

RALPH (*opens bag and takes out iron*): What do you think of it? Isn't it a beauty?

ALICE: It looks great. How much do they sell for?

RALPH: Seven ninety-five.

ALICE: That's very little. A plain iron costs that much. Can I try it, Ralph?

RALPH: Sure, go ahead.

*Alice takes ironing board that is against wall next to icebox and sets it up. Ralph unwinds iron cord and makes sure one end is attached to iron. He speaks as he does this.*

RALPH: Alice, tomorrow I'm bringin' one home for you. The company gives the salesmen a break. I get a two-percent discount.

*Alice has board set up. Ralph puts iron on board.*

ALICE: That's very nice. Plug it in, will you, Ralph?

*Ralph takes cord and goes to wall socket. He speaks as he walks and bends.*

RALPH: I can't wait until I start sellin' these irons. I'm gonna set this town on fire.

*He plugs in iron. In rapid succession the toaster, radio on bureau, and broiler on top of icebox explode. Ralph stands transfixed. Alice rushes to his side and pulls out plug.*

ALICE: You'll set the town on fire all right. Ralph, there's something wrong with the iron.

RALPH: It can't be the iron, Alice. It must be the outlet. You know this broken-down house.

ALICE: This has never happened before. Ralph, I'm afraid it's the iron.

RALPH: There's nothin' wrong with that iron. I'll try it in this outlet.

*Takes iron to downstage side of bureau.*

ALICE: Ralph, maybe you better not.

RALPH: Stop worryin'. It says right here on this tag—"This product unconditionally guaranteed by the Spiffy Corporation." That means they stand behind the iron.

ALICE: They know what they're doing. That's the only safe place to stand.

RALPH: You'll see. You'll see. *Plugs in iron. Nothing happens. There.*
*Offstage comes sound of explosion. They both stand wondering what happened. Loud voice from offstage cries out.*

MAN: Helen, the television set exploded!
*Frightened, quickly Ralph pulls out plug.*

ALICE: Ralph, you can't go out and sell those irons.

RALPH: Alice, maybe it's just this one iron that's no good.

ALICE: I've heard of these gyp outfits. They undersell everyone else. They only use door-to-door salesmen and if something goes wrong with the product the customer's stuck with it.

RALPH: You're wrong, Alice. You're wrong. Norton sold a bunch of them yesterday, didn't he? I just happened to get a bad iron.

Later Norton tells Ralph and Alice he's back working in the sewer, and that he lied to them about making forty dollars a day selling irons so Ralph and Alice wouldn't worry about him. Here's what happens next:

RALPH: Alice, I don't think I've ever felt as bad as this in my whole life. I think the worst things of Norton, my best friend. A guy who always thinks of me first. And to top that I go and blow a steady job and a pension. Alice, I'm a failure.

ALICE: Ralph, you couldn't help what happened with your job and you're not a failure. Your boss likes you. He told you so himself.

RALPH: That's all fine, Alice, but I ain't with the bus company anymore. I'm a salesman with nothing to sell.

ALICE: You're wrong. You're going to get your job back, because you've got something to sell. And I'm sure your boss is gonna buy it because this time you're selling a good product . . . you.

RALPH: Alice, do you think I can do it?

ALICE: Of course you can. You sold yourself to me a long time ago, and I know I got a bargain.

RALPH: Baby . . . you're the greatest!
*KISSVILLE.*

© PRESTON BLAIR PRODUCTIONS.

# *ALICE AND THE BLONDE*

June 2, 1956 · Leonard Stern and Sydney Zelinka

NORTON: I can't get in upstairs. Trixie's got the chain on the door.

RALPH: That's your problem.

NORTON: It's your problem, too. If Trixie finds out I came in at two AM, it means that Alice'll find out you came in at the same time. We're in this together.

RALPH: Yeah.

NORTON: I figured I'd go out your window and up the fire escape. The only chance I got is if Trixie left the window open.

RALPH: Okay. But I'm warnin' ya . . . not a sound!

*They tiptoe across to window. Norton attempts to open it. He can't. He tries to work latch and fails to turn it.*

NORTON: The latch is stuck.

RALPH (*impatiently*): Lemme do it.

*Ralph shoves Norton aside and tries to twist lock open.*

NORTON: Careful. I once caught my finger in one a them and, boy, did it. . . .

*At this moment Ralph's finger is squeezed in latch. He turns with eye bulge. He is in pain. Norton tries to prevent Ralph's bellow of pain.*

NORTON: Shhh. . . .

*As silent pain continues, Norton does his best to prevent sound from Ralph. Finally, Ralph regains control. Norton heaves sigh of relief.*

NORTON: Whewww. If I wasn't here you'da woke the whole house.

RALPH: If you wasn't here I wouldn'ta hurt my finger.


"His pain bits were always wonderful to me," says Carney. "I still break out in laughter when I see them. Nobody does it like him. He is a very funny man, a great physical comic."


1. True or false: Ralph is treasurer of the Racoon Lodge.
2. According to Alice, what will happen if the Bensonhurst chapter of the Racoon Lodge folds?
3. Alice says the Racoons threw their money away on their "Admiral Dewey sport jackets." How much did they cost?


RALPH: Be careful, Alice. Be careful how you talk about that jacket. Every decoration on it is a symbol sacred to the order of Racoons. This epaulet on the left indicates the wisdom of the East. This epaulet on the right indicates the wisdom of the West. These buttons stand for the seven pledges of brotherhood. And these gold stripes tell a complete history of my career in the Racoons. This stripe indicates a neophyte of the third order. This stripe indicates a junior Racoon of the second order. This stripe indicates a senior Racoon of the first order.

ALICE: And this stain indicates a bowl of spaghetti of the sixty-cent order!

RALPH: You're jealous, Alice. You're jealous. Because when I wear this uniform and you're with me, nobody notices you. This uniform makes me look distinguished and important!

ALICE: Then how come the time you passed the Hotel Dixie, a man slipped you a dime and said, "Boy, get me a taxi!"

RALPH: What do those out-of-towners know!

4. Norton tries to sneak into his apartment through a window. Trixie catches him and tries to slam the window on his head. Norton says she's a regular _____.

NORTON: Psst, Ralph.

RALPH: You don't have to whisper. Alice woke up and we just had a big fight.

NORTON: What about?

*Ralph gives him a skull.*

RALPH: What about? Whether the tall skinny one is really the father of the Mills Brothers! . . . What do you think it was about? Comin' home late.

5. It's rumored that Bert Weedemeyer is going to be the new _____ at the Gotham Bus Company.
   A. Traffic manager.
   B. General manager.
   C. Bus dispatcher.
   D. Bus drivers' supervisor.
6. True or false: Bert Weedemeyer asked Ralph to play pool with him.
7. What night do the Kramdens and the Nortons visit the Weedemeyers?
8. What color dresses do Alice and Trixie plan to wear to the Weedemeyers'?
9. Who sat in the two empty seats on the bus on the way to the Weedemeyers'?
   A. Ralph and Norton.
   B. Ralph and Alice.
   C. Alice and Trixie.
   D. Ralph.
10. How much does Trixie bet Alice their husbands won't notice their new dresses? What does Ralph notice instead of Alice's dress?
11. True or false: The Weedemeyers have a vase of artificial rosebuds in their living room.

TRIXIE: A fine decorator! I can't even figure out what design or period it's supposed to be.

ALICE: I'll tell you what it is. It's authentic early Halloween!

12. Where does Rita Weedemeyer shop for her husband?

*The Weedemeyers.*
COURTESY HOWARD BENDER.
COPYRIGHT © 1985
HOWARD BENDER.

Here's Stern and Zelinka's description of Rita Weedemeyer, as she makes her entrance.

*She has platinum blond hair and wears a black satin dress. You get a feeling that her taste has been strongly influenced by the photos of glamorous movie stars. She has a throaty voice.*

**RALPH:** Mrs. Weedemeyer, that's a lovely dress.
**RITA:** Why, thank you.
**RALPH:** I noticed it the minute you came into the room.
**NORTON:** There's a French word that describes that dress—chick! Mrs. Weedemeyer, that's the kind of dress that'll never go out of style.

13. What are the Weedemeyers' pet names for each other?
    A. Atomic Passion and Angel Cake.
    B. The simp and the blimp.
    C. Johnny Mercer and Richard Whiting.
    D. Twinkles and Kitten.
14. Does Alice have certain names she likes to call Ralph?
15. Alice gives Ralph a pet name: "Tubby." Rita likes it; who's going to love it?
16. The Weedemeyers skipped their dessert at dinner. Bert: "We thought you might like to have it with us." Norton: "_____."
17. What do the Weedemeyers serve for dessert?
18. True or false: All the Weedemeyers' friends say they live on pot roast.

19. True or false: Alice and Trixie want to go home, so Alice says she must leave because she has arterial monochromia.
20. Bert and Rita have a _____ kitchen and a _____ refrigerator.
21. Bert's serving dessert, and while doing so he kicks the coffee table. Nothing falls, but Norton says anyway, _____.

"Leave it there, the cat'll get it" has become a part of every Honeymooners fan's lexicon. But, as with many of the classic Norton bits, the phrase was a Carney ad-lib.

"I still use that line," he says. "During a rehearsal or during the taping of a show or something, even though it's not the Norton character, if something falls off the table I'll just throw it in, and very often they'll keep it in."

"What Art did was deflect the fact that the actor who played Bert kicked the table, by turning it into something funny," says Freda Rosen, the actress who played Rita Weedemeyer. "It's called a 'save.' Art was great at saving.

"But the unusual thing is that when somebody comes out with an ad-lib to save something, then usually that's it, they go back to the script. With the Honeymooners, the unusual thing is that you ad-lib, and then the other guy picks up on it, and they really turn it into something funny. You'd never know it was an ad-lib if you didn't study this stuff and get it under your skin.

"Gleason picked up on it and repeated it twice to Alice. Then Audrey picks up on it, and it's like a whole new process. They played together so beautifully, and it really is comedic genius."

"We didn't do a *lot* of ad-libbing," Carney says. "We had to sometimes, when something went wrong. Gleason knew that I wasn't out to upstage him or steal his thunder, and he let me do and say anything I wanted to, because he trusted me.

"But we stuck to the script pretty closely. I think a lot of people don't realize it was an acting job. You're creating characters that become believable. If it doesn't look like we're acting, or working, that's a compliment. But that's what it was, an acting job.

"One of our neighbors' fathers said to me one day, 'You mean you get paid for doing what you did last night?' I said, 'Yes, and handsomely too.' He didn't realize that I'm a professional, and I have been since 1937. I wanted to say to him, 'You want to try it?'"

22. True or false: Bert made dessert because Rita was at the Millman Shop all day.
23. The Kramdens and the Nortons are going home. Rita: "We'll have to do this again real soon." Ralph: _____.
24. Norton wants one for the road. What?

BERT: Good night. I hope you folks don't have a long wait for the bus. They don't run very often this time of night.

NORTON: Hey, Ralph, seeing's how Alice's got a headache, maybe we oughta take a cab.

RALPH: A cab? That'd cost at least two bucks!

NORTON: So what? It'll come to only fifty cents a piece.

RALPH: Yeah, that's right.

25. Norton likes a _____ cookie.

This segment of a short exchange between Ralph and Norton in the Kramdens' apartment appears in the script between the time the Kramdens and the Nortons leave the Weedemeyers, and the time Alice stuns Ralph with her alluring outfit:

NORTON: Hey, Ralph, I seen you get off the bus. Didn't you hear me whistle after ya?

RALPH: No.

NORTON: There's something I want to talk to you about. . . . *He looks significantly toward the bedroom and draws Ralph away.* Confidential. You know how the girls didn't talk to us all the way home last night?

RALPH: Yeah.

NORTON: Well, how did Alice act after you got her here?

RALPH: Nothing. Absolute silence.

NORTON: I can't take much more of this, Ralph. I don't mind when we have a nice normal fight. Trixie throwin' things, yellin' and shoutin' and screamin' at me. I go right to sleep. But this time, she was so quiet I was awake all night.

26. Alice thinks Ralph is infatuated with Rita, so she dresses up in a sexy outfit. Ralph doesn't suspect jealousy; he figures she's been:
    A. Eating pizza.
    B. Eating salad.
    C. Eating rum cake.
    D. Eating rum candy.

"I loved the Rita Weedemeyer show," says Audrey, "because it's so typical of the way women feel when the husband tries to be nice to another woman. He didn't mean anything with Rita Weedemeyer, but he didn't notice we had dresses, too. It was truth, a situation everybody can understand."

27. True or false: Alice asks Ralph if he can compare her kisses to pot roast.

28. Why does Alice call Ralph "killer"?

> *She kisses hand and blows kiss to Ralph and exits. Ralph gets up and paces. The door opens and a wide-eyed Norton rushes in. His face is smeared with lipstick. He looks as bewildered and puzzled as Ralph.*

NORTON: Hey, Ralph. Look at me. Look at me! *He points to face with both hands.* Lipstick. I walk into the house, Trixie throws her arms around me and starts huggin' and kissin' me like crazy!

RALPH: What'd you do?

NORTON: I ran out. I thought I was in the wrong apartment!

TRIXIE'S VOICE: Poodles? Where's my Poodles?

NORTON: That's Trixie. I gotta beat it. She's out looking for me.

RALPH (*pointing at Norton*): Poodles?

NORTON: Yeah. She calls me Poodles because when I come home from work I always have a cold nose!

29. What's Ralph's answer for never making Alice feel like his sweetheart, or noticing how she looks?

RALPH: I have—I've got an explanation. A perfect one. I'm a dope. Not a run-of-the-mill dope. The world's champ. For years I've been taking for granted the most wonderful thing that's ever happened to me—you! I've never shown you the appreciation you deserve, Alice. You could walk outta that door right now and I wouldn't blame you. You deserve something better than me. There are a million guys who'd give you anything if they could have a girl like you.

ALICE: **Ralph, I don't want a million. There's just one guy I want . . . you!**
RALPH: **Baby, you're the greatest!**
  *Dissolve on KISSVILLE.*

There isn't a Honeymooners fan in the world who doesn't think of Rita Weedemeyer when he sees a cigarette holder. What he doesn't know is that Freda had to learn how to smoke and how to use a cigarette holder to play the part of Rita, the blond, curvaceous, childlike sexpot wife of Bert Weedemeyer, a Gotham Bus Company executive.

Freda was the wife of the late Arnie Rosen, an award-winning comedy writer who, with Coleman Jacoby, wrote for Gleason in the fifties. He and Jacoby were responsible for teaming Gleason with Carney. Freda, though, takes pride in the fact that she was hired to play Rita without anyone on the Gleason show knowing she was Arnie's wife.

"I loved it that Arnie came for the show," says Freda. "Everybody said, 'Gee, what are you doing here?' He was so smug . . . he said, 'That's my wife!' And they said, 'Ohhhh.'"

"Alice and the Blonde" was the last of the Honeymooners episodes to air (June 2, 1956) before the show went into reruns for the summer. The script had been written long before the show was staged, but the episode kept getting pushed back on the schedule because the casting people could not find a suitable Rita.

"I don't know why, because it was so easy," says Freda. "I think everybody was playing it too sexily. They wanted somebody kind of shallow and dumb, but not really anything heavier than that. Innocent, nonthreatening, just a dumb broad. I don't know if dumb broad is really the right term. Rita had an endearing quality, even though she spent all her time in the beauty parlor and her husband did all the cooking. Nobody ever told her she shouldn't. Simple as that.

"Just a dingy broad, which was actually me. It was really typecasting."

Freda remembers that on the day she auditioned, nineteen other actresses were there to read for the part.

"We all sat around in a room and they called us in one at a time. You couldn't hear what the other girls were doing, and you didn't know how anybody else did. It's very disheartening to be in a room with nineteen other girls, all of whom are better looking, with better figures and better everything, and you think, 'What am I doing here with nineteen gorgeous girls?'

"But that was the role I wanted the most. That show, as far as I was concerned, was the best show going at the time."

Freda was hired—"They said, 'That's fine. Don't change anything'"—and the first thing she did was run out and buy three cigarette holders so she could practice the part of the scene where she has to light up a cigarette.

"I practiced at home," she says. "The first three times I put it in, the cigarette fell out of the holder and burned me, my shoe, and the carpet. Once I was outside on the corner, and it fell out on the street. The holder was obscenely long, but I finally learned how to hold a cigarette in it."

Next came a typical Honeymooners rehearsal, and the same trauma most actors who played *The Honeymooners* experienced.

"We went through it once with Jack Hurdle reading Jackie's lines. We walked through what was called a dress rehearsal, and then Jackie got there and said hello, and 'We're gonna do it right.' Everybody said, 'Right,' and he said, 'Okay, we're gonna go out there and do it,' and we said 'Huh?!'

"Would you settle for panic? It was going out live!"

Because there was no real rehearsal, and because Freda had no contact with Gleason until just before filming, she had no idea that in the scene Gleason was going to slap her on the arm on his way into the Weedemeyer kitchen to help Bert serve dessert. Freda's dress—"It was blue velvet, the kind of velvet that shows fingerprints"—was so tight that when Gleason whacked her she lost her balance and almost fell.

"If you noticed, I always took very tiny steps. When he pushed me, I took those little steps backwards, because otherwise it was right on my fanny.

"They sewed me into that dress. I was supposed to sit on the sofa, but I realized I couldn't sit, so I leaned on the arm of the sofa and hoped the stitches wouldn't . . .

"It was great fun, and scary!"

*Rita Weedemeyer, alias Freda Rosen.* COUR-TESY RALPH.

# THE BENSONHURST BOMBER

## BOMBER

September 8, 1956 · Marvin Marx and Walter Stone

1. What pool table do Harvey and George choose to play on, and where are they when Ralph and Norton arrive at the poolroom?
2. What is Norton eating when he comes into the poolroom with Ralph, and where did he get it?

RALPH: Boy, you kill me, Norton. You just finished eatin' your supper. Then we walk four blocks to get here. And you got to stop for popcorn, candy, chestnuts, pretzels. . . . There's one thing I'll never understand. How come you're always eatin' and you never gain an ounce. I just look at food and I put on weight.

NORTON: Well, you see, I'm able to keep my figure by doin' a lot of exercise.

RALPH: Exercise? What kind of exercise?

NORTON: Walkin' . . . you see, I eat so much durin' the day I get indigestion . . . then I got to walk the floor all night!

*Ralph stands there thinking about this for a second.*

RALPH: Wait a minute . . . did it ever occur to you that if you didn't eat so much, you wouldn't get indigestion, and you wouldn't have to walk the floor all night . . . so why do you eat so much?

NORTON: I gotta . . . that walkin' the floor all night makes me hungry!

*Ralph just stares at him like he's out of his mind.*

NORTON: Let's face it, Ralph. It's a vicious cycle. Walkin' makes me eat. And eatin' makes me walk. As we say in the sewer, one hand washes the other!

RALPH: Well, I got news for you, one-hand-washes-the-other. You been comin' up through too many manholes where they forgot to take off the cover!

3. What does Ralph want to get to eat on the way home from the pool hall?
4. Who broke the last time Ralph and Norton played pool, and how did they decide who it would be?
5. Ralph and Norton decide to toss a coin to see who will break. Who wants heads? Who finally breaks?
6. How much does it cost to shoot pool?
7. True or false: Norton sinks the eight ball on his first shot.
8. What shot does Ralph call?
9. Norton calls his second shot. What is supposed to happen?

RALPH: Wait a minute. You expect to make all them balls?

NORTON: Of course not. But just in case anything drops, I want to make sure I called it!

10. George returns and finds Ralph and Norton playing on the table he and Harvey were supposed to play on. He tells Ralph he had the table first, but went to get a cold drink. Ralph says: "I hope it was very cold, and I hope it was _____."

*George and Harvey, alias Leslie Barrett and George Mathews.* COURTESY LUIGI PELLETIERI AND RALPH.

11. Which of Ralph's friends is bigger than George?
    A. Bert Weedemeyer.
    B. Harvey Wohlstetter, Jr.
    C. Muriel.
    D. Shirley.

"The faces and names in Aristophanes' comedies are lost forever, but thanks to television, my image will probably be repeated on into eternity," says Leslie Barrett, the stage actor who played George.

"I was really grateful that when I got on the show, Mr. Satenstein and Mr. Gleason allowed me to create that character. Of course, I didn't get a job after that for two years, because everybody thought I talked like that," he says of George's squeaky whine.

12. What does Ralph threaten to do to George and Harvey if they start trouble?
13. When Ralph's in the right, _____.
14. What does Ralph tell Norton he'll do to Harvey if Harvey tries to start something?

HARVEY: So you're gonna twist me into a pretzel? Did you hear that, George? He's gonna twist me into a pretzel.
    *As Ralph speaks he picks up bag of pretzels.*
RALPH: I didn't say that. I said, "Here, have a pretzel!"

*Ralph offers bag to Harvey. Harvey just knocks it out of Ralph's hands to floor.*

RALPH (*trying awfully hard to get in good*): Look, I tell you what. I got a great idea, Harvey. Harvey. Gee, that's a nice name! Look. Why don't we all play pool together. You know, partners. You three against me. Loser pays! That's except if you three lose. Then I'll pay!

15. True or false: Harvey's even bigger than Ralph's friend Shirley.
16. What excuse does Ralph give Harvey for not fighting him?
17. When and where does Harvey tell Ralph to meet him for a fight?
18. Harvey decides not to play pool after all. What does he want to do instead?

NORTON: Boy, Ralph, what do you want to go pickin' a fight with a big guy like that for?
RALPH (*exploding*): What did you have to say 'I'm gonna twist him into a pretzel' for? Did you get a load of the size of that guy?
NORTON: All right, so what are ya worried about, Ralph? I got a feeling that guy's gonna chicken out. He ain't gonna fight ya. I heard a few things about him. He'll be too scared to fight.
RALPH (*amazed*): He'll be scared to fight me!?
NORTON: Darn right he will. He's got two assault and battery raps against him now. He ain't gonna take a chance on being a three-time loser!
*Ralph does a big eye bulge as we BLACKOUT of scene.*

19. Norton's excited about Ralph's showdown with Harvey. As he mimics a sportscaster, what nicknames does Norton give to himself and Ralph?
20. Word comes in from the candy store about some late money bet on Ralph in the fight. How does the bet affect the odds?
21. True or false: The guys in the neighborhood are betting that Ralph loses the fight.
22. What's closing so the boys can watch Ralph fight?
    A. The Racoon Lodge.
    B. The pool hall.
    C. The bowling alley.
    D. The Gotham Bus Company.
23. Ralph doesn't want to fight; Norton says he has to or he'll let his friends down. Which ones?
    A. Shifty, Red, and Nutsy.
    B. Reilly, Cassidy, and Freddie Muller.
    C. Peck, Tebbets, and Harper.
    D. Stanley Saxon, Jerry Shor, and Frank MacGillicuddy.

24. Which of Ralph's friends hasn't missed a night in the poolroom in his entire life and even played pool on his wedding night?
25. If they close the pool hall to watch Ralph fight Harvey on Friday, why will they close it again Saturday?
26. How does everybody in the neighborhood know about Ralph's fight with Harvey?
27. Ralph's not the type that _____ in the crowd.

Norton gives Ralph a pep talk about how he's got to stand up to Harvey, or live in fear. And just when he's got Ralph convinced he's got to fight Harvey:

NORTON: All you got to do is show Harvey you ain't scared of him . . . that he don't frighten you just because he can take horseshoes and straighten them out with his bare hands.
*As Norton continues, Ralph's eyes bulge wider and wider fear-style.*
NORTON: Lift pool tables over his head. Punch holes in brick walls just for laughs. Crush coconuts by squeezin' 'em in his hand. Tear telephone books in half. . . .
RALPH (*exploding*): Will you keep quiet! *He gives Norton a shot as he does this.*

28. Who's the one person that doesn't know about the fight?
29. Compared to a clam, Norton's an _____.
30. What famous World War II expression does Norton quote?
    A. *C'est la guerre.*
    B. Leave it there, the cat'll get it.
    C. A slip of a lip can sink a ship.
    D. Mambo, anyone?
31. What famous robbery would still be a secret if Norton was connected with it?
32. Ralph tells Alice he's gonna be gone for a couple of weeks. Where?
33. If they ever institute a nut-of-the-month club, who's going to be January and February?
34. Norton figures when Harvey sees Ralph's boxing stance he'll:
    A. Die.
    B. Die laughing.
    C. Quit the Racoons and join the Elks.
    D. Shuffle off to Buffalo.

NORTON: Don't get discouraged, Ralph. Now, enough of your offense. Let's concentrate on your defense. Do you know how to dodge and feint?
RALPH: Don't worry. If that Harvey comes up here after me, I'll faint all right!

35. Ralph and Norton are practicing boxing. Why does Norton tell Ralph to cover his face, and then hit him in the stomach?

NORTON: . . . Let me teach you a few things.

RALPH: But Norton. . . .

NORTON: It ain't gonna hurt you to learn—and I can teach you a lot, Ralph. I did a lot of boxin' in the Navy. I was middleweight champ.

RALPH (*amazed*): You were middleweight champ of the Navy?

NORTON: Not of the Navy. I was middleweight champ of my P.T. boat! There were five of us on board. Two fat guys, two skinny guys, and myself.

36. Norton devises a scheme to trick Harvey into thinking Ralph's a tough guy. What code phrase is supposed to set the scheme into motion?
37. Sewer workers stick together. What's their motto?
38. Ralph knocks a guy out at Kelsey's Gym with his "bad hand." Which hand is it?
39. Harvey wants to back out of the fight. Ralph calls him:
    A. A blabbermouth.
    B. A yellow-bellied sapsucker.
    C. A mope.
    D. A yellowbelly.

The late George Mathews played Harvey and many other tough-guy roles in films, on Broadway, and in TV series such as *The Untouchables* and *The Phil Silvers Show*. He didn't own a television set during the fifties, and didn't see himself in "The Bensonhurst Bomber" until twenty-eight years after it was filmed, when he watched the episode with 2,300 Honeymooners enthusiasts at one of RALPH's Honeymooners conventions.

"The salary was $750 or $1000, which was a lot of money in the days I'm talking about," Mathews told the audience at the convention. "I'd just gotten out of Phil Silvers' show—I was called 'The Beast.' I was a tough sergeant who was going to straighten Bilko out, and he straightens me out—and when they called my agent I said, 'Well, I got so-and-so on *The Phil Silvers Show* and I want that on the Gleason show.' And they gave it to me."

40. Norton's friend was supposed to show up at Kelsey's and let Ralph knock him out. Why didn't he make it?
41. Why did the guy Ralph knocks out say, "Hey, Fatso, get outta the way"?

# DIAL J FOR JANITOR

September 15, 1956 · A. J. Russell and Herbert Finn

1. Why does Norton need a monkey wrench?
2. Norton: "I never thought I'd live to see the day when I'd work eight hours in the sewer and want to come home and see _____."
3. Something is bothering Ralph when he comes home from work. He has:
   A. Six months to live.
   B. Arterial monochromia.
   C. 111° temperature.
   D. A headache.
4. What does Norton advise Ralph to do?
5. While Norton was in the service he suffered from a bad headache. What caused it?
6. Why did Norton take a lot of kidding from his pals in the service?
7. What does Alice offer to do to help Ralph? Ralph tells her not to bother and asks her to _____.
8. Name three things in the Kramden apartment the janitor is supposed to fix.
9. What was Ralph's Christmas present to the janitor?
10. Ralph is too lenient with the janitor. How many times has he been down to see him during the week?
11. Norton is banging on his pipes because he needs water to take a bath. The noise bothers Ralph. He asks Norton to _____.
12. Norton comes down to Ralph's to borrow _____. How does he carry it back to his own apartment, and why does he need it?
13. Headaches and who go together?
14. Norton hasn't had water in so long he's beginning to see _____.
15. Why does the janitor quit? How many janitors have quit so far?
16. What remuneration do the janitors at 328 Chauncey Street get?
17. Janitors wouldn't stay in the same building with Ralph and Norton if Johnson paid them:
    A. $12.83.
    B. $40 million.
    C. $62 a week.
    D. $1000 a month.
18. What does Johnson threaten to do to Ralph and Norton?
19. Johnson says he's going to get a lawyer; Norton says he'll fight fire with fire. Who will he get?
20. What kind of cases does Norton's lawyer specialize in?
21. Why can't Norton contact his lawyer friend?
22. Who becomes the fifth janitor of the building?

Russell and Finn wrote two versions of "Dial J For Janitor": the one that was filmed, and another in which the Kramdens move out of their apartment and into a basement apartment. Alice, in the first draft, eventually talks

Ralph into quitting the job. But before he does, Ralph decides to renovate his old apartment and then move back into it after he quits as janitor. What he doesn't know is that Mr. Johnson has in the meantime given the apartment to the Nortons. The original draft doesn't have Ralph getting stuck in the steam pipes, but he gets plenty "steamed" nonetheless.

"We thought we would get a lot more fun in the basement," says Russell, "but Jackie or someone thought it was too much of a hassle. Jackie didn't like to change little things like that. He wanted the table, the bureau, the chairs, the icebox, period. Every time you tried to take him out of there, unless there was a very good reason, he wouldn't do it.

"Jackie wanted the immediate recognition. He didn't want the basic concept of the show disturbed. Occasionally we would try to get something past him—we figured 'This is funny, he'll go for it,' but he didn't. He also considered budget, because we worked on such short notice. This guy didn't really look at the script until the last minute, and that left the builders with very little time to build the set. So if you had to build a whole big set, the guys needed at least a day.

"But because Jackie was always so late reading the script, the safest thing to do was not rock the boat."

*The janitor's apartment. This is below street level. The entrance door and the door to the bedroom are situated exactly as in the Kramden apartment. But instead of a regular-size window a small one is set up high at the street level, with bars on the outside. The Kramden furniture is arranged as in the Kramden apartment. Along the back wall, up high, run some basement-type pipes. It is unmistakably a cellar apartment. . . .*

ALICE: What are you doing?

RALPH: I'm installing a house phone, Alice. It's in line with my new system of efficiency. When I get this connected all a tenant has to do when he wants me is to press the buzzer in his apartment and it'll ring down here. Like this.

*Ralph presses a button on a panel. We hear a loud raucous buzz.*

ALICE: Isn't that kind of loud?

RALPH: It's gotta be loud. So I can hear it in case I'm in the bedroom or out in the cellar.

ALICE: In this apartment when you're in the bedroom you are in the cellar!

RALPH: Now don't start that again, Alice. There's nothing wrong with this apartment. Just remember that we're getting a hundred and fifty dollars a month and we're saving forty-five dollars on rent. For that kind of money you can put up with a few little inconveniences. Sure, it may be a little dark in here and maybe we're cramped for space, but it's dry in winter and cool in summer!

ALICE: So's a coal mine!

RALPH: This is just like you, Alice. Always looking on the bad side of things. Instead of knocking this apartment, why don't you concentrate on the good points? There are lots of them, y'know.

ALICE: Maybe you're right, Ralph. Maybe I haven't been fair to this apartment. As you say, it may be a little dark in here, but who wants sunshine? Sunshine gives me freckles! And those quaint bars on the window. They give me such a feeling of security. It's so nice to know I don't have to worry about falling up out of the window! And there's nothing like having a furnace just outside your door. That's very handy for toasting marshmallows and barbecuing hamburgers. We ought to throw a big weenie roast and invite all our friends. But we must be sure to tell them, 'Don't use the cellar stairs, we've got our own private coal chute!' And this floor! This wonderful concrete floor! It's such a boon to a housewife! I never have to sweep it! All I have to do is hose it down!

RALPH: Are ya through, Alice? Are ya through?

ALICE: Not quite, Ralph. I forgot to mention the most attractive feature of this apartment. It's so close to the subway. No one could be closer than us. In fact, the subway tunnel is just on the other side of that wall! *She points to back wall.* And it's so much fun when the train goes by! *She looks at her watch.* Oh goody, goody! There's one due in about twenty seconds!

RALPH: You can stop right there, Alice! It's not as bad as you say. I admit that for the first couple of nights the train disturbed me, too. But you get used to it. As a matter of fact, last night it lulled me to sleep. It was like having a babbling brook outside my window.

*From the distance we hear the low rumbling sound of a subway train approaching.*

ALICE: Here it comes! Man your battle stations.

*Alice clutches the table in hang-on-for-dear-life style. The rumble of the approaching train gets louder and louder. As the train thunders by on the other side of the wall, the entire place shakes. As the train moves into the distance the quaking subsides, and the rumble becomes a low hum, then fades. Throughout, Ralph and Alice shake like jelly.*

RALPH: There! That wasn't so bad, was it?

ALICE: That was the local babbling brook! Wait till the express goes by! . . . A few weeks of this and we'll either be nervous wrecks or the best mambo dancers in the country!

23. Ralph says a janitor should be treated with _____ because he's not a _____ or a _____.

24. What does Ralph say the tenants should do when the janitor does them a favor?

25. Ralph suggests the janitor get how many bonuses a year, and when?

26. What is Ralph's first job as janitor?

27. As part of his efficiency system as janitor, what does Ralph install in his apartment?
28. Alice says she has a few items to test Ralph's efficiency system. What are they?
29. Why is Ralph behind in his janitor's work, and what did Alice have to do because of it?
30. Alice tells Ralph he'd be able to keep up with his janitor's jobs if he quit going bowling. Why won't Ralph do it?
31. Ralph orders Alice to fix his supper. She says she'd be happy to, if only to prove _____.
32. How does Ralph notify the tenants in the building about the new house phone?

RALPH: Attention all tenants! Now hear this! The buzzer system is officially installed. From now on if you want me just press the buzzer and speak into the mouthpiece! This means that there'll be no more yelling even from the second floor. This means you, Garrity!
GARRITY (*offstage*): Oh, yeah?
RALPH: Yeah!
GARRITY (*offstage*): Oh, yeah?
*We hear a loud door-slam offstage. Garrity has gone inside. Ralph, steamed, comes in and shuts the door. He gets an idea. He goes to the buzzer system, presses a buzzer. After a beat he speaks into mouthpiece.*
RALPH: *Yeah!*

33. Which tenants call Ralph on the house phone, and what are their complaints?
34. Who tries to use the house phone to get an outside line?
    A. Grogan the cop calling the station house.
    B. Norton calling for the correct time.
    C. Mrs. Schwartz trying to get Jersey.
    D. Mr. Johnson calling his lawyer.

ALICE: Ralph, you can't leave the receiver off the hook. You told the tenants to call you when they wanted you!
RALPH: Sure, but I didn't tell them to call me every second on the second! Boy, oh boy, I don't blame those other janitors for quitting!
ALICE (*leaping on this*): You mean you're sorry you took the job?
RALPH (*not giving in*): No, I am not sorry! You'd like me to quit, wouldn't you! I'm really disappointed in you, Alice. You oughta be proud that I had the character and ambition to take on two jobs!
*There is a knock on the door. A coal-truck driver enters appropriately dressed.*

COAL MAN: Hey, bud, I got a load of coal for ya. Where do ya want it?

RALPH (*still steamed*): Whattaya mean, where do I want it? In the coal bin, of course! Just drop your chute through the alley window!

COAL MAN: I'm new on the job. Ya wanna show me where it is?

RALPH: What's the matter with you? Can't you find a window in an alley?

COAL MAN: Okay, okay, don't get sore!

*The coal man leaves. Ralph shuts the door.*

RALPH: What a dope! *Mimicking coal man.* I got a load of coal for you. Where do you want it? Where does he think I want it? In my living room? In my bedroom?


*From offstage on the bedroom side we hear the loud noise of coal coming down a chute. Everyone freezes for a moment and remains still in wondering-what-is-going-on style.*

ALICE: What's that?

*She goes to bedroom door and opens it. She stands there aghast as pieces of coal come rolling into the living room and coal dust wafts out.*

ALICE: Oh, no!

RALPH: They're dumping coal in the bedroom! Hey, you—cut it out! Hold it!

*The noise stops. Norton looks over Ralph's shoulder into bedroom.*

NORTON: Well, this is right in line with your new system of efficiency. Now all you have to do is move the furnace in there, and you can stoke it without getting outta bed!


Ralph decides to quit as janitor. He can't break the bad news to Mr. Johnson until Monday, though, because Johnson's away for the weekend. Ralph has a brainstorm: He'll work on his old apartment all weekend so it'll be in tip-top shape when he moves back in:


ALICE (*calling out*): Ralph? . . .

RALPH (*from bedroom*): Be right out, hon!

*Ralph enters from bedroom. His new overalls are smeared with paint and torn at the knee. One of his hands is crudely bandaged. He has been working like a dog and is dead tired.*

ALICE: Ralph, you must be dead tired. Why don't you call it quits?

RALPH: I'm just about through, Alice. What a weekend this has been! Boy, oh boy, I never worked so hard in my life. I'm really beat. I nearly busted my hand when that wrench slipped, my knees'll be black and blue for months to come, and my foot still hurts from that nail I stepped on. But it was worth it, Alice! This apartment is now in perfect condition! Look, I'll show ya!

*He goes to window and opens it.*

ALICE (*happily*): Ralph, it stays up!

RALPH: You bet your life it stays up! I worked on it for three hours. I hadda put in a new frame, new sash cords . . . everything! And look, Alice! *He points to sink.* That faucet doesn't leak anymore. And I fixed that floor, too. I filled in all the cracks so it won't squeak when you walk on it!

ALICE: Ralph, I didn't know you had it in you!

RALPH: Wait'll you see the bedroom! I fixed the closet door, I put in more shelves, I painted it, and I even varnished the floor! Come on, I'll show you. I'm tellin' ya, when we get our furniture back in here, this apartment'll be the showplace of the building.

In come Norton and Johnson:

RALPH: Oh, hello, Mr. Johnson. I've been trying to get you on the telephone all morning. I'm afraid this is my last day as janitor here. Y'see, I found out that I just can't do two jobs at once so I gotta ask you to accept my resignation.

JOHNSON: Resignation, on such short notice? Gee, I don't know. . . .

NORTON: Look, Mr. Johnson. If you're reluctant about accepting his resignation, I believe I can get a petition from all the tenants urging you to do so! *Ralph shoots Norton a look, then turns to Johnson.*

RALPH: Don't worry, Mr. Johnson. I've got a very good man to replace me. He'll start working after lunch.

JOHNSON: Oh, well, in that case I guess it's all right.

RALPH: Thanks. Well, now that the status is quo again, I'll be moving back to this apartment.

JOHNSON: Moving back? I'm afraid you can't do that.

RALPH: Why not?

JOHNSON: Because I've already rented it. You know, I've had a lot of trouble with the water on the top floor. It's going to be a big job fixing those pipes. It'll probably take weeks. So I told Mr. Norton he could have this apartment.

RALPH: Norton!

NORTON: Yup! Well, I guess I better start moving in. *Norton opens the door and calls into hall.* Okay, fellas! Start bringing down the furniture! *As Norton shuts the door the window falls with a terrific bang.* Okay, Ralph, you've still got a few hours of being janitor. How about fixing that window!

35. How long does Ralph work on the Manicottis' kitchen sink? What does he tell Mrs. Manicotti when she complains about the job?
36. Norton comes down to Ralph's, choking and gagging. What's the matter with him?

37. How long has Norton been waiting for Ralph to fix his pipes?

38. True or false: Norton is so mad he says Ralph won't get his vote for Racoon of the Year.

39. What else is Norton upset about?

40. Why didn't Ralph pick up Norton's garbage?

41. Ralph promises to fix Norton's pipes in the morning. Why can't he do it that night?

42. Where has Norton been bathing while he's had no water?

43. What does Alice serve for supper?

44. Norton calls Ralph a janitor. What title does Ralph prefer?

45. What is Ralph's diagnosis of Norton's water problem?

46. What is Ralph trying to do when he gets stuck between the pipes?

47. Norton sees Ralph jammed between the pipes. He proclaims this a case where "the spirit is willing, _____."

48. Who comes into the basement, sees Ralph stuck in the pipes, and runs out screaming for help?

49. Who does Norton suggest they call upon to rescue Ralph? What silly examples does he use to convince Ralph it's a good idea?

50. It wasn't Ralph's fault he got stuck between the pipes, says Alice. He was just doing his impersonation of:
    A. Rita Weedemeyer.
    B. A wrench-lock.
    C. Two pounds of baloney in a one-pound bag.
    D. A knight out on a dog.

51. Ralph resigns as janitor. Because he's incapable or because the salary isn't enough?

52. Johnson tells Ralph he's already found a new janitor. What jobs does Ralph have for him?

53. Alice figures now that Ralph isn't janitor, he'll go bowling with Norton. Ralph says if he lives to be a hundred years old he wouldn't go bowling with Norton. Why?

54. Who succeeds Ralph as janitor?

# A MAN'S PRIDE

September 22, 1956 · Leonard Stern and Sydney Zelinka

1. Ralph and Norton are at the fights. Ralph sees Bill Davis, a rival from his school days. Why doesn't Ralph like him?

Bill Davis was played by the late Dick Bernie, as was Joe Fensterblau—an adversary of Ralph's at the bus company. Bernie played small-time braggarts like Davis and Fensterblau to perfection. He was "a ham, and he liked Bill Davis the best because it was his biggest role," says his daughter, Fredrica Stalter. As a young girl, Fredrica rehearsed the Honeymooners scripts with her father.

"I used to learn all the lines and then drill him," she says. "I'd learn the script as well as he would. I would play all the other parts so he could rehearse where to come in and what to say. I missed out on doing a lot of homework because of that. But when I watched him on TV I really felt as if I was a part of it."

2. Who does Norton want to visit backstage at Madison Square Garden?
3. Ralph and Norton got their tickets to the fights from:
    A. Bill Davis.
    B. Slugger Simpson.
    C. Basil Fomeen.
    D. The Grand High Exalted Mystic Ruler.
4. True or false: Slugger Simpson knocked out his opponent in the first round.
5. Norton saw Slugger Simpson fight three weeks earlier. Where did the fight take place, whom did he fight, and what was the outcome?
6. What did Bill Davis write in Ralph's school autograph book?
7. Where does Bill Davis live, and what does he tell Ralph he does for a living?
8. Bill Davis' headquarters are in _____ and his plants are in _____.
9. Ralph tells Bill Davis he:
    A. Is assistant traffic manager at the bus company.
    B. Is the bus dispatcher.
    C. Is a bus drivers' supervisor.
    D. Runs things at the bus company.
10. When does Ralph see loads of people?
11. Bill Davis wants to visit Ralph at the bus company at _____ o'clock, but Ralph wants him to come at _____ instead.
12. Ralph's middle name is:
    A. Trouble.
    B. Buttercup.
    C. Fatso.
    D. Icky.

NORTON: You know, Ralph, when I was a kid there was a guy named Houdini. He had a great act. They handcuffed him, they put him in a big packing case. They nailed down the cover. Tied ropes around it. Attached a big rock and then they dropped the whole thing in the middle of the East River.

RALPH: What about it?

NORTON: Well, getting outta that was a cinch compared to what you got yourself locked into.

13. Match the fighters with their opponents:
    A. Digilio       E. Dilenger
    B. Sandler      F. Malanga
    C. Andrews     G. Wilding
    D. Brady        H. Gioseffe

14. Where is the Gotham Bus Company located?
15. A few months earlier, Norton met one of Trixie's old flames. What did he do for a living?
16. Whose office does Ralph use to impress Bill Davis?

RALPH: Norton, if you were a stranger and you walked in here and saw me sitting in this chair, what would you think?

NORTON: I'd think you needed a larger chair.

17. Norton cautions Ralph not to say anything that will tip Bill Davis off that he's a bus driver. What shouldn't Ralph say?
18. Mr. Monahan catches Ralph in his office. What lame excuse does Ralph give for being there?
19. Who's in charge of promotions at the bus company?
20. Who telephones Monahan while he's talking to Ralph?
    A. Freddie Muller.
    B. Cassidy.
    C. Mr. Harper.
    D. Reilly.

BILL: Ralph, you're all wound up. Why don't you call this Marshall character and cancel your appointment?

RALPH: I can't. The phones are shut off.

*Phone on desk rings. They all look at it.*

BILL: I thought the phone was shut off.

RALPH: I—I meant the outgoing phone.

*Phone keeps ringing.*

BILL: Aren't you going to answer it?

RALPH: No. It must be a business call and I'm taking your advice. I'm not gonna burn myself out.

*Phone stops.*

BILL: Now you're talking. Relax.

NORTON: R.K. Tempus Fugits! *Indicates watch.*

    *As Ralph looks toward Norton, Bill picks up framed picture from desk.*

BILL: Hey, whose picture is this you got on your desk?

RALPH: A . . . buh . . . buh.

BILL: It isn't Alice. What's it doing on your desk?

    *Trapped, Ralph looks to Norton to get him out.*

RALPH (*to Norton*): Buh . . . buh . . . what's this doing on my desk?

NORTON: It's the company contest. She's Miss Madison Avenue Bus Line of the Month!

RALPH: Oh, yeah.

BILL: She's an elderly woman!

RALPH: She was our first winner—1923! That'll show you how busy I am. I even forget what's on my desk.

21. What's Norton's phone number?
22. Bill Davis invites the Kramdens to have dinner with him and his wife at:
    A. The Hong Kong Gardens at eight o'clock.
    B. Salvatore's Pizzeria at eight-thirty.
    C. Freitag the delicatessen's at nine o'clock.
    D. The Colonnade Room at nine-thirty.

ALICE: He must be doing very well.

RALPH: He says he's doing well.

ALICE: Well, he can't be doin' bad if he flies to New York on a business trip and brings his wife along.

RALPH: May I point out to you that they came in the middle of the week.

ALICE: What about it?

RALPH: On weekdays wives travel half-fare.

ALICE: Oh, Ralph.

RALPH: I'll believe he's doin' well when he comes in on a weekend!

23. What's the most expensive restaurant in the whole world, and how much does it cost to eat there?
24. Ralph doesn't want to go to the Colonnade. Where does he offer to take Alice instead?
25. What's Alice's favorite Chinese appetizer?

RALPH: Er, er, do you know what kind of place that Colonnade Room is?

ALICE: I've read about it for years. It's supposed to be a very fine, exclusive restaurant.

RALPH: It's the most expensive restaurant in New York! It's on Park Avenue. Do you know what it costs to eat there? If it costs a cent, it's gotta cost you at least three dollars a person! On top of that, it's probably the kind of place you gotta check your coat . . . and I ain't spending that kind of money!

ALICE: Ralph, Bill invited us. He certainly doesn't expect you to pay for it. He was down at the company—he knows you're a bus driver.

RALPH: Er, er, nothin' doin'. I ain't going!

ALICE: He was nice enough to invite us and I accepted the invitation. We have to go. Besides, we never get a chance to go to a place like that. It's been years since we danced together.

RALPH: Okay. Tonight I'm takin' you dancin' at the Hong Kong Gardens. And how about this—we'll have the number-three dinner.

ALICE: Ralph.

RALPH: You can even have the sweet and sour lichee nuts—and they're à la carte!

26. What's Ralph's reason for not wanting to eat at the Colonnade? What evidence does he give Alice to support his claim?

27. Norton wants Ralph to tell Bill Davis he can't have dinner with him because he just took the job as:
    A. Janitor at 328 Chauncey Street.
    B. Captain of the *Ile de France.*
    C. Captain of the *Queen Mary.*
    D. President of Ralph Kramden, Inc.

RALPH: Norton, I'm in trouble! Big trouble! Bill Davis phoned and spoke to Alice.

NORTON: Oh, oh! She knows about the boss's office?

RALPH: No, but she's bound to find out. He invited us to dinner and Alice insists we go. Norton, what am I gonna do?! When Bill finds out I'm a bus driver how am I gonna look?

NORTON: About the same way you're gonna look when Alice finds out you're the boss of the Gotham Bus Company.

28. What does Alice have for dinner at the Colonnade?
29. What do each of the Kramdens and the Davises order to drink after dinner?
30. What does Bill Davis really do for a living?
31. Ralph can dance a fox-trot, but when they play _____ or _____ music, he's out.
32. How did Bill and Millie Davis get to New York from Chicago?
33. How much money do Alice, Ralph, Bill, and Millie each contribute to help pay the check?

# APPENDIX I

## Famous Last Words, Wisecracks, and Punch Lines

*A rare photo of the production crew on* The Honeymooners. COURTESY LEO F. O'FARRELL.

285

## TV OR NOT TV

1. Alice is buttering Ralph up because she wants a television set. She offers him a cold drink—lemonade, milk, or juice—while he's waiting for his supper. Ralph says: _____.

## FUNNY MONEY

1. Ralph comes in with a suitcase. Alice's mother looks at it and says: _____.
2. Alice asks what's in the suitcase. Ralph says he doesn't know, but there can't be anything of value inside or someone would have claimed it. Mrs. Gibson: _____.
3. Ralph reaches the boiling point with Alice's mother and throws her out of the apartment, telling her there isn't room enough in it for the both of them. What is her parting shot?
4. Alice refuses to give Ralph money to pay his lodge dues. She's saving it to buy furniture. "We already got furniture," he says. "You call this junk furniture?" Alice replies. Ralph answers: _____.
5. Norton: "Oh Ralph, it's me, Norton. Want me to put the car in the garage?" Ralph: _____.

## THE GOLFER

1. Ralph wants to surprise Alice with news that he's being promoted to assistant traffic manager. He starts by telling her he won't be needing his lunch box any more. Alice: _____.
2. Ralph can't wait to have his own office and telephone. When Alice calls him at work the switchboard operator will buzz him, he'll pick up the telephone and say, "Hello, this is Mr. Kramden. What can I do for you?" To which Alice will answer: _____.
3. Alice tells Ralph he can't learn to play golf overnight. Ralph thinks Alice is trying to discourage him. He doesn't care, though, because he's got enough confidence in him for both of them. Alice: _____. Ralph growls back: _____.

## A WOMAN'S WORK IS NEVER DONE

1. Ralph and Alice go to hire a maid. Out walks Thelma, a real battle-ax. Ralph is stunned by her appearance; he thinks all maids wear short skirts and black silk stockings. Thelma sizes him up as a troublemaker and says: _____.
2. Ralph brings Thelma back to the apartment. She walks in, takes one look around, and says: _____.
3. Ralph is ringing for Thelma. He wants her to prepare coffee and cake for him and Norton. When Thelma finally answers the summons, she declares: _____.
4. Norton leaves a hot iron on Ralph's bowling shirt. When Ralph discovers his shirt's been burned, right where it says "Hurricanes," he asks Norton if that's his idea of a joke. Norton answers: _____.

## A MATTER OF LIFE AND DEATH

1. Ralph thinks he's dying of arterial monochromia, and tells Norton he's going to leave him his bowling shoes. Sad because he thinks Ralph's dying, but thrilled at this windfall, Norton blurts out: _____.
2. Ralph discovers he's not dying from arterial monochromia. He asks Norton to pose as a doctor who can cure the disease so he can get out of his obligation to *American Weekly* magazine. What does Norton tell the secretary at the magazine when she touches him on the shoulder?

COURTESY RALPH. COPYRIGHT
© 1984 JOHN LANGTON.

## BETTER LIVING THROUGH TV

1. Ralph wants money from Alice to invest in Handy Housewife Helpers; she won't part with a dime. Ralph pleads with her to envision a $2000 payoff. "This is probably the biggest thing I ever got into," he says. Alice looks at him with disbelieving eyes and counters: _____.
2. Ralph threatens to leave Alice if she doesn't give him money for the Handy Housewife Helper. "Just remember, you can't put your arms around a memory." Alice: _____.

"Gleason always screamed about that—'No more fat jokes!' But you couldn't not," says Stone, who wrote his share. "Certain people . . . like Jack Benny was cheap. You play on things. I see shows where we overdid it. I mean, wait a minute, give him a break. But it was such a sure laugh."

3. Ralph and Norton are about to do a commercial on live television. Norton tells Ralph they've rehearsed enough; all they have to do is wait for their cue, and do their spot as millions of people watch. Ralph turns to Norton and says: _____.

## PAL O' MINE

1. Norton buys a ring for Jim McKeever. Ralph thinks it's for him and gets it stuck on his finger. Alice gives him some butter to help slide the ring off. Ralph won't use it; he asks if there's any lard around. Alice tells him: _____.

## BROTHER RALPH

1. Ralph berates Alice because they only have $12.83 in savings. Alice reminds Ralph his $62-a-week salary doesn't go very far. Ralph tells Alice to keep her voice down; he doesn't want his salary to "leak out." Alice counters: _____.
2. Ralph has just learned that Alice is the only girl in the office where she works. He becomes instantly jealous, and says: _____.

## THE DECIDING VOTE

1. Ralph gives Alice a secondhand vacuum cleaner as an anniversary present. It doesn't work, and it roars like a motorboat with three propellers. Norton says it sounds as if the engine needs a drop of oil, and Ralph readily agrees. How does Alice respond?
2. Alice tells Ralph the vacuum cleaner is a piece of junk. Ralph: "What are you, an authority on vacuum cleaners?" Alice: _____.
3. Alice is sweeping the floor after the vacuum cleaner fails the "oatmeal test." She tells Ralph that having a vacuum has lightened her housework. He says: _____.
4. Norton talks with Frank MacGillicuddy at the Racoon Lodge the night of the vote for convention manager. He says he hasn't been smoking cigars lately because it's too much trouble to light the wet end. "The wet end? You're supposed to light the dry end," says Frank. Norton replies: _____.
5. Ralph is bitter after losing the vote for convention manager, mostly because he thinks Norton voted for MacGillicuddy. As usual, Ralph overdramatizes the situation: "Well, that's how it goes. History repeats itself. _____."
6. Ralph assassinates Norton's character in a letter of reference to Morgan's. He asks Alice for a stamp so he can mail it, but she says she's not going to help him make an idiot out of himself. Ralph: _____.
7. Alice seconds Ralph's conviction that Norton didn't vote for him. Norton is as hurt by this as Ralph was at thinking Norton double-crossed him. Once again, Norton reverts to Shakespeare for an answer: _____.

## SOMETHING FISHY

1. Ralph: "What do you know about fishing in the first place? When did you ever catch anything?" Alice: _____.
2. Ralph can't get the car started. Alice inserts one of Trixie's hairpins in the engine and it starts right up. But when Ralph tells her she can't go on

the fishing trip, she takes the hairpin out. Ralph: "Do you think that stops me? If you can do it I can do it." Norton: \_\_\_\_.

## 'TWAS THE NIGHT BEFORE CHRISTMAS

1. Ralph buys Alice a present, and then discovers a neighbor has bought her the same thing. He decides to hock his bowling ball to get money to buy Alice another gift. Ralph: "When there's an emergency, I come out of it. When they made me, they threw away the mold." Norton: \_\_\_\_.
2. Christmas morning Ralph discovers Alice has given him a bowling ball bag. What is Ralph's startled response?

## THE MAN FROM SPACE

1. Ralph declares war because Norton rents a costume for the Racoon Lodge's costume party. Ralph warns Norton to get on the other side when he sees him walking down the street. Norton snaps back: \_\_\_\_.
2. Alice doesn't recognize Ralph as the "man from space." He criticizes her for not being up on current events and not knowing the latest developments. What does Alice answer back to prove she's up-to-date?
3. Alice: "A twelve-year-old girl's knees are supposed to show." Ralph: \_\_\_\_.

## A MATTER OF RECORD

1. Norton's second baseman gets the measles on the eve of a big stickball game. Johnny Bennett to Ralph: "Do you think you could cover second base?" Norton: \_\_\_\_.

## OH MY ACHING BACK

1. Alice wants to go to her mother's. Ralph wants to go bowling, so he tells Alice he doesn't want to go with her because he's too tired. Alice says they can go, have supper, and then leave. Ralph: "You know I'm not the kind of man that

eats and runs." Alice: "Eats and runs? The way you eat, \_\_\_\_."

## THE BABYSITTER

1. Alice has a telephone installed, and Ralph is mad because he thinks it'll cost too much. Alice says she'll cut down on something in order to pay for it, and Ralph thinks she'll cut down on his food. "I'll start losing weight. Then do you know what I'll look like?" he moans. Alice: \_\_\_\_.
2. Ralph bursts in on Alice while she's babysitting at the Wohlstetters'. Ralph thinks Harvey Wohlstetter is in the bedroom, but instead Harvey Jr. walks out. He gets a look at Ralph in his Racoon uniform and says: \_\_\_\_.

## $99,000 ANSWER

1. Ralph: "Yessir, this is the time I'm gonna get my pot of gold." Alice: "Just go for the gold, \_\_\_\_."
2. Alice will be happy if Ralph wins $600. Six hundred bucks? "Peanuts. Peanuts," says Ralph. "What am I gonna do with peanuts?" Alice: \_\_\_\_.

*Herb Norris.* COURTESY HOWARD BENDER. COPYRIGHT © 1985 HOWARD BENDER.

## RALPH KRAMDEN, INC.

1. Ralph's eating a peanut butter sandwich. Norton asks Ralph if it's the crunchy kind. Ralph: "Yes, it's the crunchy kind, and I can prove it to you. _____."

## YOUNG AT HEART

1. Wallace and Judy Connors plan a big night at the amusement park. Norton says they remind him of the silly things he used to do when he was a kid, before he grew older and matured. Ralph: _____.

## A DOG'S LIFE

1. Ralph is disgusted because Norton eats and eats and never gains a pound. Norton says it's his metabolism, and tells Ralph he's weighed 165 pounds for as long as he can remember. Ralph: "Did you ever see a picture of me when I weighed 165 pounds?" Norton: _____.

## MAMA LOVES MAMBO

1. Alice enters the apartment carrying a heavy load of laundry. Ralph looks on as Carlos Sanchez takes it from her and carries it to the table. He tells her she shouldn't carry such heavy things, and Alice, looking over her shoulder at Ralph, says she wishes *he* would be as concerned about her. Ralph answers: _____.
2. Norton is leaving the Kramdens' apartment to give Carlos some of Trixie's potato salad. Ralph says, "Norton, you're beautiful." Norton: _____.
3. Ralph is incensed at Alice when he comes home from work and finds the apartment full of mambo dancers: "You want to wiggle, _____."
4. Alice wants to give Ralph tuna salad for supper because the mambo lesson ran late and she didn't have time to cook. What is his reaction?
5. Alice likes Carlos because he treats her like a

*Carlos Sanchez.* COURTESY HOWARD BENDER. COPYRIGHT © 1985 HOWARD BENDER.

woman. She tells Ralph he seems to have forgotten she's a woman. Ralph: _____.
6. Alice refuses to cook Ralph's supper and storms into the bedroom. Ralph follows her as far as the doorway, cocks his fist, and bellows: _____.
7. Ralph tells Norton Alice has been satisfied with him for fifteen years, but now that Carlos has moved into the building with his "fancy manners," she wants to change him. Norton: _____.

## PLEASE LEAVE THE PREMISES

1. Ralph, Alice, and Norton are locked in the Kramdens' apartment because Ralph won't pay a rent increase. They're about to dine on a stalk of celery. Alice asks Ralph to arrange the silverware, because he has "fingers" in his gloves. Ralph: _____.

## PARDON MY GLOVE

1. Ralph and Norton come home from the lodge with a pizza. Alice gives Ralph salad instead. Ralph runs through the ingredients of the salad to convince himself and Norton he'll enjoy the salad as much as Norton will enjoy the pizza. He tells Norton, "Everything's good for some-

*Andre, alias Alexander Clark, at* RALPH's *Christmas party.* COURTESY BRUCE BENNETT/BRIAN WINKLER AND RALPH.

thing on this plate." Norton grabs the whole pizza and says: _____.
2. Ralph finds Andre's glove and thinks Alice is having an affair. Norton comes down to pick up Ralph to go bowling. Ralph is distraught: "Here my home is being broken up, my happiness destroyed, and you want to know if I'm ready to go bowling." Norton, remorsefully: _____.

## YOUNG MAN WITH A HORN

1. Ralph: "What is a sock doing in my cornet?" Alice: _____.
2. Ralph plays "Carnival of Venice" on his cornet to Alice's dismay. Alice: "I liked it better with a sock in it." Ralph: _____.

## HEAD OF THE HOUSE

1. Ralph boasts to Norton how he's boss of his house, and now he's going to be quoted in the newspaper. Norton tells him he should retract the statement. Ralph calls Norton a mouse. Always the pragmatist, Norton replies: _____.
2. Ralph thinks Alice is jealous of men because they're "leaders" and women are "followers." "Men have done it all," he brags, and gives Alice a classic example of the male species' accomplishments: "There'd be no America if it wasn't for Christopher Columbus." Quick-witted Alice says: _____.
3. Ralph burns to a crisp the chicken he prepares for Fensterblau's dinner. Ralph: "Well, Norton, our goose is cooked." Norton: _____.

## THE WORRY WART

1. Ralph thinks the IRS is investigating him. While Ralph stews, Norton eats spaghetti and meatballs. In the middle of Ralph's fit, Norton asks for bread. Ralph: "When I finish with you _____."
2. Ralph: "Norton, I'm gonna count to five. And when I get to five you better be out that door." Norton: "I'm not a-scared of you; _____."
3. Ralph tries to calm himself at the IRS office by remembering that he's an American citizen and a taxpayer. Norton says: _____.

## ON STAGE

1. Ralph, Alice, and Norton rehearse for the Racoons' play. Ralph, who is playing a millionaire, points out the Kramdens' window and promises Alice's character, Rachel, everything she sees. Norton bursts out laughing. Ralph asks him why. Norton: _____.

## OPPORTUNITY KNOCKS BUT

1. Norton makes suggestions about the bus company to Mr. Marshall, who offers him a job. Later, Norton realizes he'd told Mr. Marshall

ideas he'd gotten from Ralph. Norton: "I thought I had a wonderful head on my shoulders, _____."

## UNCONVENTIONAL BEHAVIOR

1. Norton and Ralph are handcuffed together on a train they think is taking them to the Racoon Convention in Minneapolis. Norton's in the upper berth, Ralph the lower. Norton: "Ralph, do you mind if I smoke?" Ralph: _____.

## THE SAFETY AWARD

1. Mr. Martin from *Universal* magazine interviews Ralph and Norton for his story about Ralph's appointment as New York's safest bus driver. He asks if Norton and Ralph are close friends. Norton: _____.
2. Ralph is proud of himself for winning the safety award, and he compares himself to great men who stand out among their peers. Norton: _____.
3. What "little ode" of the sewer does Norton recite to Ralph to help him calm down?
4. Judge Hurdle crashed into Ralph's car because he was wearing the wrong glasses and didn't see Ralph's turn signal. To keep the record straight, he fines himself $50. Norton adds: _____.

## MIND YOUR OWN BUSINESS

1. Ralph wants a promotion and raise, so he's going to pull the "ol' squeeze play" on Mr. Marshall. Ralph: "I'm going to squeeze Mr. Marshall; he's in no position to squeeze me." Alice: "Of course not, _____."

## ALICE AND THE BLONDE

1. Rita Weedemeyer tells Alice if she wants a pet name to call Ralph, all she has to do is find Ralph's outstanding feature and find a name that fits it. Alice says to Ralph: _____.
2. Rita: "What a husband you have. He certainly is

a treas-ure." Alice: "If he keeps this up much longer, _____."
3. Alice: "I call you 'killer' because you slay me." Ralph: _____.

## THE BENSONHURST BOMBER

1. Harvey challenges Ralph to a fight, then leaves the poolroom with his friend George to go home and "punch the bag." What does Norton yell after him?
2. Ralph tells Alice he's going "outta town"; she needn't worry about him because he can take care of himself. Norton: "If you knew how to take care of yourself _____."

## DIAL J FOR JANITOR

1. Alice tells Ralph he should quit bowling so his janitor's work doesn't pile up. Ralph refuses, and explains to Alice that in addition to bowling helping him to relax, it also helps him keep down his weight. Alice counters: _____.
2. Ralph still hasn't fixed Norton's water pipes. To make a point, Norton comes down to Ralph's and pretends he's choking. Concerned, Ralph asks him what's the matter. Norton pleads for water. Ralph: _____.
3. Ralph finally decides Norton isn't getting water because of low water pressure. It's a scientific fact, he tells Norton, water always seeks its level. Norton answers: _____.
4. Ralph is stuck between the pipes in the basement and he's getting hot. He sends Norton into the furnace room to turn a wheel that will shut off the steam. When Norton turns it, steam pours into the basement. Ralph screams, "Turn it toward the wall!" Norton: _____.

## A MAN'S PRIDE

1. Ralph gets himself into a fix by bragging to Bill Davis that he's boss of the Gotham Bus Company. He regrets what he's done, and promises Norton from here on in he's going to swallow his pride. Norton says: _____.

# APPENDIX II

## MEMBERS OF THE INTERNATIONAL ORDER OF FRIENDLY RACOONS

Andrews
Bowden (named after Stage Manager Hal Bowden)
Frank Brady
Bud
Carlyle
Cassidy
Charlie
Dribbin
Morris Fink
Herman Gruber
Hanley (named after actor Eddie Hanley, who played Pete Woodruff, a stagehand in "Better Living Through TV," and several other roles)
Joe Hannigan
Havemeyer
Ralph Kramden
Lou
Frank MacGillicuddy
Freddie Muller
Eddie Mulloy
Joe Munsey (Rumsey)
Muldoon
Ed Norton
Philbin (named after Jack Philbin, executive producer of the *Honeymooners*)
The President
Reilly
Stanley Saxon
Schultz
Jerry Shor (named after Gleason's pal, restauranteur Toots Shor)
Pete Woodruff

## MEMBERS OF THE HURRICANES, THE RACOONS BOWLING TEAM

Charlie
Herman Gruber
Ralph Kramden
Freddie Muller
Eddie Mulloy
Ed Norton
Schultz

## GOTHAM BUS COMPANY EMPLOYEES

Bradstetter
Cassidy
Charlie
Clemmins
Mr. Douglas
Miss Evans
Herman Fatrack
Joe Fensterblau
Mr. Gordon
Harry
Mr. Harper
(Poor Old) Havemeyer
John
Ralph Kramden
Joe Lustig
Mr. Marshall
Mr. Monahan
Freddie Muller
Mr. Muller
Mr. Peck
Pete
Reilly
Mr. Tebbets
Bert Weedemeyer

## SEWER WORKERS

Nat Birnbaum
Cassidy
Morris Fink
Flaherty
Haggerty
Jim McKeever
Ed Norton
The Ugliest Woman That Ever Lived

## 328 AND/OR 728 CHAUNCEY STREET RESIDENTS

Johnny Bennett and Family
Cassidy
Collier Brothers
Judy Connors and Family
Tommy Doyle and Family
Old Man Fogarty (sometimes spelled Fogerty)
Mrs. Gallagher
Garrity and family (or McGarrity, who was played by radio and TV actor Bill Zuckert)
Grogan the Cop
The Gunthers
Mrs. Helprin
Mrs. Hannan
Mr. Johnson, the Landlord
The Kramdens
The Manicottis
Tommy Mullins and Family
The Nortons
Mrs. Olsen
Mr. Reilly
Carlos Sanchez
Mrs. Schwartz
Mrs. Stevens

## ALICE'S BOYFRIENDS

Chester Barnes
Fred Beatty
Bill Davis
Jack Townsend

## WHILE THE SAME SET WAS USED IN ALL THIRTY-NINE EPISODES, THE SLIDE LOCK ON THE KITCHEN DOOR WAS MISSING IN THREE:

A Matter of Life and Death
The Deciding Vote
The Babysitter

## THREE DIFFERENT SETS OF KITCHEN TABLE AND CHAIRS WERE USED:

*Set 1*
TV or Not TV
Funny Money
The Sleepwalker
The Deciding Vote

*Set 2*
A Woman's Work Is Never Done
A Matter of Life and Death
Pal O' Mine
Something Fishy
The Babysitter

*Set 3*
was used in all other episodes

## RALPH DOES NOT WEAR HIS BUS DRIVER'S UNIFORM IN THREE EPISODES:

$99,000 Answer
Trapped
On Stage

## RALPH WEARS A UNION PIN ON HIS BUS DRIVER'S UNIFORM IN SEVEN EPISODES:

Opportunity Knocks But
Unconventional Behavior
The Safety Award
Mind Your Own Business
The Bensonhurst Bomber
Dial J for Janitor
A Man's Pride

## RALPH AND NORTON WEAR TWO DIFFERENT RACOON JACKETS (ADMIRAL DEWEY SPORT COATS):

The light-color jacket is double-breasted and has four buttons on the front.
The dark-color jacket is also double-breasted, but Ralph has eight buttons on his while all the other Racoons have only six buttons.

## RALPH USES THE EXPRESSION "A MERE BAG OF SHELLS" IN FOUR EPISODES:

Trapped
Dial J for Janitor
$99,000 Answer
Funny Money

## RALPH SAYS "ONE OF THESE DAYS, POW! RIGHT IN THE KISSER" IN ONLY ONE EPISODE:

Mind Your Own Business (This expression was a favorite of Gleason's in the "lost" Honeymooners skits that were part of the Gleason show from 1952 to 1955.)

## RALPH SAYS "BANG-ZOOM" IN SEVEN EPISODES:

Alice and the Blonde
Dial J for Janitor
The Loudspeaker
Young at Heart
Please Leave the Premises
Here Comes the Bride
$99,000 Answer
(Ralph never said "Bang-Zoom, to the Moon.")

## GET OUT

Ralph was always throwing Norton out of the Kramden apartment, and on occasion, he threw out other people as well. In the course of thirty-nine episodes, Ralph threw out Norton twenty-one times. Trixie, Alice's mother, and Carlos Sanchez were thrown out twice each. Tony Amico, Jim McKeever and three other sewer workers, Mrs. Manicotti, Mrs. Stevens, and an unnamed mambo dancer were also given the old heave-ho by Ralph.

## "BABY, YOU'RE THE GREATEST" (KISSVILLE) ENDED NINE EPISODES:

Alice and the Blonde
Head of the House
On Stage
Opportunity Knocks But
Young at Heart
The Babysitter
Brother Ralph
Pardon My Glove
Here Comes the Bride

# APPENDIX III

And More Honeymooners . . .

Add to the Classic 39 the "Lost 75." The "Lost 75"?

These are Honeymooners skits and episodes first performed on the hour-long *Jackie Gleason Show* that aired on CBS from 1952 to 1955 and 1956 to 1957. The earliest skits ran only six or seven minutes, but many of the later ones went as long as forty-five. None of the Lost 75 have been seen on television in their entirety since they first aired live—until now.

Where have these shows been all these years? Were they really lost? Not literally. Gleason, announcing the "discovery" of the Lost 75 to reporters at a press conference, told them that he had copies of all his old shows "stacked up in an air-conditioned room . . . waiting for the phone to ring."

But for the last thirty years, as far as the public was concerned, the Honeymooners skits that preceded the Classic 39 were gone. If you didn't see them the first time around, tough luck.

Tough luck, that is, until RALPH came along. At RALPH's Honeymooners Convention in March 1984, Honeymooners episodes from April and June 1955 were shown for the first time in twenty-nine years. David Margolick, a reporter who covered the convention for the *New York Times*, said of the screenings: "For most Honeymooners fans, the experience was akin to the discovery of a tenth Beethoven symphony or a lost manuscript by F. Scott Fitzgerald."

The twenty-five hundred Honeymooners fans who attended the convention thought they were living through a once-in-a-lifetime experience. They were among the chosen few who got an exclusive look at the pre-39 Kramdens and Nortons. The audience was spellbound by the two episodes: In one Ralph and Norton become astrology buffs, and in the other Ralph is a look-alike for a gangster. Fans even attempted to stifle their laughter so not one precious word of dialogue would go unheard.

Later in the day, Frank Satenstein, director of *The Jackie Gleason Show* and *The Honeymooners,* brought the house down when he told the audience: "We did many, many hour-long shows as well as the well-known thirty-nine, and it's my hope that someday we're going to be able to get them out of the vault at CBS. And I think if all you fans write in to CBS and make enough of a stink, they'll release them. The word is, 'Open the vault.'"

Thunderous applause.

Shortly after the convention, RALPH was approached by the Museum of Broadcasting in New York City. The Museum wanted to obtain copies of the "lost" episodes for its archives. RALPH was unable to give the museum the prints it wanted but suggested CBS as a possible source for them. When museum officials contacted CBS, they struck gold: four "lost" shows. The episodes did SRO business when the museum screened them later that summer.

Meanwhile, RALPH began a letter-writing campaign to CBS Entertainment in Los Angeles, asking for the release of the Honeymooners segments Frank Satenstein had mentioned. The campaign was such a success, CBS asked RALPH to call off its members. We're getting too many letters, they said, and added that CBS didn't own the rights to the old Gleason shows— Gleason did.

*Joan Canale and Frank Satenstein.* COURTESY BRUCE BENNETT/BRIAN WINKLER AND RALPH.

Gleason was aware of the brouhaha started by the RALPH and Museum of Broadcasting screenings of several "lost" episodes. He waited for the phone to ring. When it rang it was Viacom Enterprises, syndicator of the half-hour shows. Soon a deal was negotiated that would bring the "lost" Honeymooners back to television.

So what's in the Lost 75?

These episodes are similar to—and different from—the Classic 39. The cast, of course, is the same. The Kramdens and the Nortons still live in Bensonhurst. Ralph and Norton love to bowl and shoot pool. Ralph is cheap, Alice is practical. Norton is loyal and Ralph takes advantage of him. Ralph and Norton belong to the Racoon Lodge. And, of course, Ralph hates Alice's mother.

The differences are as obvious as the similarities. Ralph, though it does seem impossible, is even louder and more obnoxious than he is in the half-hour shows. In the Lost 75, he wears a variety of bus driver's uniforms. Alice is often more shrill and combative than the Alice of the Classic 39. On occasion she looks different: Her hairstyle changes a lot, and she frequently wears nicer-looking clothes. The "lost" Norton is still the nicest guy in the world. But the Norton in the early fifties skits is dopier than the later Norton who would suggest to Ralph that a bureau would be easier to move if he took the drawers out, put them on top of the bureau, and then moved it. Trixie, like Alice, yells more. In the longer episodes, she has more on-camera time.

There are lots of fat jokes, sewer jokes, fights about you-name-it, crazy harebrained schemes, insults, dumb Nortonisms, and the like. These older Honeymooners, though, seem to rely much more on visual humor—pies in the face, ovens and sinks exploding, water pipes bursting, Ralph careening around the set in agony, Ralph throwing things, and so on. There's even one scene where Ralph and Norton do Laurel and Hardy impersonations. Yet another classic bit.

Will the Lost 75 Honeymooners become as popular as the Classic 39? Maybe, but it will be years before anyone can really answer that question. In the meantime, all the new information in the Lost 75 should keep Honeymooners trivia buffs busy for the *next* thirty years. . . . .

# ANSWERS

## The Honeymooners

Executive Producer
**Jack Philbin**

Producer
**Jack Hurdle**

Director
**Frank Satenstein**

Musical Director
**Sammy Spear**

Film Editor
**Leonard Anderson**

Scenic Designer
**Richard Rychtarik**

Assistant Producer
**Stanley Poss**

Writers
**Marvin Marx**
**Walter Stone**

Costumes
**Peggy Morrison**

Daytime Dresses by
*Pat Perkins*

Writers
**Leonard Stern**
**Sydney Zelinka**

Entire Production
Supervised by
**Jackie Gleason**

Filmed on the
DuMONT
**ELECTRONICAM**
T·V Film System

Writers
**A. J. Russell**
**Herbert Finn**

Director of Photography
**Jack Etra**

Jackie Gleason
Enterprises Inc. Productions

Park Sheraton Hotel
New York City

COPYRIGHT MCMLVI by
JACKIE GLEASON ENTERPRISES INC
PRODUCTIONS

298

## TV OR NOT TV

1. The old pipe-and-slippers routine.
2. Nuts.
3. Lemonade.
4. He's waiting for 3-D television.
5. False—$62.
6. Washing machine, vacuum cleaner, television, electric stove.
7. $75
8. D
9. Ten years.
10. A
11. Fourteen years.
12. C
13. Nineteen; water softener.
14. Tails; Norton loses.
15. Kern (or coin, if you don't live in Brooklyn).
16. False—space helmets and disintegrator guns.
17. Pluto and the moon.
18. I, _____, Ranger third class in the Captain Video Space Academy, do solemnly pledge to obey my mommy and daddy, be kind to dumb animals and old ladies in and out of space, not to tease my little brothers and sisters, and to brush my teeth twice a day and drink milk after every meal.
19. Ranger third class.
20. Space shows, westerns, cartoon frolics, and puppet shows.
21. Air supply.
22. Julia and Harry.
23. Kenny Baker, Jane Frazee, Buddy Ebsen, Jerry Colonna, and Frankie Darrow.
24. A
25. Maxie Rosenbloom and King-fish Lavinsky.
26. D

## FUNNY MONEY

1. The paper is no good.
2. Fifty grand.
3. Ziggy leaves it on the bus.

4. C
5. He's got to go down to the depot, identify the article, and describe the contents; then the clerk opens it to see if the description matches.
6. The person who finds it, usually the bus driver.
7. ". . . doesn't mean you have to live in a stable."
8. "Hello stupids."
9. Mammy Yokum.
10. $15; he's behind in his lodge dues.
11. False—a bulldozer.
12. A job at the laundry.
13. A
14. They'll throw him out.
15. Sure. It's pretty embarrassing just to be in it.
16. Furniture.
17. False—from Ralph's grandfather to Ralph's grandmother.
18. Sell the suitcase he found on the bus.
19. Pizza.
20. B
21. He's collecting for the annual children's party.
22. A buck.
23. $100—and there's more where that came from!
24. A cashmere bowling bag.
25. Four; living room, bedroom, bathroom, fire escape.
26. For when he sleeps there in the summertime.
27. That Ralph call the fire escape.
28. Mr. Marshall, his boss; Ralph tells Marshall he's quitting and calls him a bum.
29. A slight clicking noise.
30. $100
31. "It pays to buy the best."
32. All the salesmen and executives.
33. Merrill Lynch, Pierce, Fenner & Ziggy.
34. Sonny Boy.
35. $200; go to Florida with her husband.
36. Three propellers.

37. Tommy Doyle; $100; he's arrested for passing counterfeit money.
38. Burn it.
39. "My wife is taking a bath in the sink."
40. Two days.
41. Just as fast.
42. His suits.

## THE GOLFER

1. Reilly; Pete.
2. Cassidy.
3. Cigars; beer.
4. "No profane language."
5. Freddie.
6. Ralph told him.
7. Mr. Harper.
8. Mr. Harper doesn't know Ralph's alive.
9. That Mr. Harper knows he's alive.
10. C
11. "Tell him you're smart, but you got no good connections."
12. A
13. Talk about something they're interested in.
14. D
15. D
16. All around.
17. Silver Oaks.
18. Sunday.
19. He plays with his regular partner on Sundays.
20. Four weeks from Saturday at 10 AM.
21. Left field.
22. Nothing, but he's an expert on holes.
23. Ten years. (In other episodes, he's worked in the sewer longer.)
24. Take out the garbage.
25. She thinks he's going on a diet.
26. "Oh, I'm dreaming. Oh, I don't know what I'm doing. Oh, I'm jumping to conclusions."
27. A
28. He's going tiger hunting with Ali Khan.

29. She runs down to Madison Avenue and Forty-second Street and hands a note to the cop on duty to give to Ralph.

30. He wants Ralph to play on Sunday because his regular partner was called out of town.

31. Dee-vine!

32. A pin cushion.

33. Chicken noodles.

34. Scientific.

35. Two days.

36. "To Emily, whose slice inspired me to write this book."

37. Step up, plant your feet firmly, and address the ball.

38. D

39. "Hello, ball."

40. If you ain't got that swing.

41. Telling Mr. Harper he could play golf.

42. Forget about the ball.

43. A mountain goat.

44. Football, because his backfield was in motion.

45. To get away from their wives.

46. Relaxation.

47. Sign an affidavit with a "notary republic."

48. Because he has a big mouth.

49. Mr. Douglas, a vice-president at the Gotham Bus Company. He tells Ralph that Mr. Harper can't play golf because he chipped a bone in his ankle.

50. Mr. Douglas.

## A WOMAN'S WORK IS NEVER DONE

1. Wash and iron his bowling shirt.

2. Hurricanes.

3. Alice tells him to just open his mouth.

4. May be your own.

5. Sew his socks.

6. C

7. Wash the breakfast dishes, scrub the kitchen floor, wash the windows, do the marketing, cook the pot roast, clean the bedroom closet.

8. Yucca Flats after the blast.

9. Twenty-four hours; fourteen years ago.

10. "Man works from sun to sun, but a woman's work is never done."

11. Because she's got the toughest boss in the world—a husband.

12. "You marry us!"

13. Stellar Employment Agency.

14. Act important.

15. B

16. False—Alice's lunch hour.

17. Mr. Wilson.

18. To an estate on Long Island.

19. What's your address? (Most everyone thinks Gleason goofed when he gave the address as 728 Chauncey Street, when all along it'd been 328 Chauncey Street. Not so: Someone, possibly associate producer Jack Hurdle, made the change in the script, and wrote next to it, "There is a place by this address in Bklyn.")

20. Stuffing jelly into doughnuts; Krausmeyer's Bakery. (Also changed in the script was the name of the bakery. Marx and Stone wrote "Steinhardt's," but because there was actually a bakery in Brooklyn by that name, it was changed to Krausmeyer's.)

21. Miss Reynolds.

22. Short skirt, white hat, and black silk stockings.

23. Sickly.

24. She won't do heavy work or scrub floors; the Kramdens can't have pets; she gets time-and-a-half pay for working parties, and the next day off; she's off Thursdays and Sundays; her work is through the minute the supper dishes are done; she doesn't clean up the morning after late-night snacks.

25. A

26. Carry her suitcase.

27. From Norton.

28. At the burlesque show; helping Lily St. Cyr into a bathtub full of wine.

29. She looks more like the person who installed the bathtub.

30. At the stables, talking to the groom.

31. "How do you do. This is Mr. Kramden's residence."

32. "This is Mr. Norton's residence," because Ralph uses Norton's telephone.

33. "Very good, sir."

34. The Four Hundred.

35. One lump.

36. One lump.

37. Simp; blimp.

38. Her union card.

39. He rings the bell.

40. Three; the agency won't send him any more.

41. One walked in Ralph's bedroom, saw a mop, got scared, and ran out.

42. A buck an hour; wash the dishes.

43. 1–2–3 lift.

44. Ralph didn't heave-ho.

45. He takes out the drawers and places them on top of the bureau.

46. Ralph's bowling shirt.

47. A left hook; flattery.

48. Little Buttercup.

49. A

50. Marilyn Monroe.

51. She's a jelly doughnut taster.

52. To get part of her uniform she left behind.

53. The Nortons.

## A MATTER OF LIFE AND DEATH

1. Collie; Ginger.

2. $10

3. $3

4. She's tired and he's been in the sewer all day.

5. A

6. Kept him alive until his wife caught up on the insurance payments.

7. B

8. "Your hand is very dirty."

9. Arterial monochromia; hair falling out, irritability, tongue turning blue, tiring easily, chills.

10. Boxer; scratching for fleas.

11. True.

12. Eight.

13. Delivering newspapers, delivering groceries for the A&P, shoveling snow for the WPA.

14. Alice handed out the shovels at the WPA.

15. With a bald head, blue tongue, and a saucer of warm milk.

16. If they pay by the pound, Alice'll be a millionaire.

17. He had hiccups for three weeks; *American Weekly*; $5,000. (In the original script, Ralph was going to sell his story to *Confidential*.)

18. "Doomed Man Has Only Six Months to Go"

19. "In Six Months, Blimp Takes Off"

20. Dick Gersh; 1623.

21. D

22. False—"I Was a Mambo Dancer for the FBI."

23. Have him thrown in jail for twenty years for fraud.

24. $5,000; he puts it in the bank in Alice's name.

25. Merry widow.

26. Dr. Morton.

27. D

28. The Paradise Express.

29. P.S. 31, Oyster Bay; Oxford.

30. It was so foggy over there, he never knew where it was.

31. He doesn't have to practice, he knows it.

32. It's not sterile.

33. Permission to publish the story as it turned out.

34. Blueberry pie.

## THE SLEEPWALKER

1. Four.

2. D

3. A banana.

4. False—Ralph slips.

5. He says Norton's nervous and upset; take two weeks' sick leave.

6. Chicken chow mein and potato pancakes. (Had the first draft of the script not been changed, Norton's usual Wednesday night fare would have been chicken chow mein with spaghetti sauce!)

7. False—tacks.

8. Eats, sleeps, and exercises.

9. Six-letter word for hunting dog.

10. D

11. Going through Australia.

12. $3.31

13. Three.

14. A

15. The Kosciuszko Street sewer.

16. Red; eenie, meenie, minie, moe.

17. Apples, bananas, kumquats, and popcorn.

18. In the top bureau drawer.

19. *Esquire.*

20. A painting of an Oriental dragon.

21. Dick Tracy.

22. 11:45 PM.

23. 3 AM; a banana.

24. False—the bump in his head.

25. Pentathol (truth serum).

26. 100, 99, 98, 97, 96, . . . 3.

27. He couldn't go to college because he hadn't finished grammar school.

28. She jumped out of a boat in the Tunnel of Love at Coney Island and went after a cocker spaniel.

29. A dog.

30. Eggs.

31. D

## BETTER LIVING THROUGH TV

1. Crinoline.

2. He's going broke.

3. "Over that hill, I think they're friendly Indians."

4. Open cans, remove corks from bottles, core apples, scale fish, sharpen scissors, remove corns, cut glass, and has a screwdriver attachment.

5. From a coworker's brother.

6. 2,000; 10¢ each; $1 each.

7. A parking lot . . . next to a drive-in movie.

8. By doing a TV commercial.

9. $100

10. A

11. False—his brother.

12. *Life Begins at Eighty*

13. A

14. B

15. D

16. Bellevue.

17. About a minute, if Ralph's was the first door he knocked on.

18. He proposed.

19. Fourteen years. (In other episodes it's fifteen. However, if you consider that the Kramdens have lived in their apartment fourteen years, as Alice once stated, and that they lived with Alice's parents the first six years they were married, then they've been married at least twenty years!)

20. TV set, vacuum cleaner, washing machine.

21. Wallpaper that glows in the dark, uranium mine in Asbury Park, no-cal pizza.

22. She was in love with his uniform.

23. Fifteen.

24. Ralph, Chef of the Future; Norton, Chef of the Past.

25. Cheese grater, corkscrew, knife sharpener, apple corer, can opener.

26. "The hair never had a chance!"

27. A happier life through television.

28. Spearfishing.

29. Skate key.

30. Third.

31. Ohhhhhh, it can core a apple.

32. Bensonhurst 5-6698. (This is not the telephone number found in the script. Just as the writers had the habit of using names of real people and places in the scripts, they may also have used working telephone numbers. In every instance, the numbers were changed, probably by Jack Hurdle or Stanley Poss, by showtime.)

33. Belt her in the mouth.

34. B

## PAL O' MINE

1. Orange juice.

2. Jim McKeever; Norton's co-workers.

3. D

4. White tie and black boots.

5. False—neither one is invited.

6. T-shirt.

7. False—60 percent cotton, 40 percent dacron.

8. A chair.

9. A ring; "To a great pal. From Ed Norton."

10. Suspenders.

11. D

12. The store doesn't gift-wrap items under $3.

13. True.

14. He's been working double-time.

15. False—Jane Russell. (If Stern

and Zelinka had had their way, the correct answer would have been Lana Turner.)

16. Pizza.

17. Butter.

18. 89 cents a pound.

19. Like King Farouk getting into Gary Cooper's bathing suit.

20. Houdini.

21. B

22. Twenty years.

23. Punch bowl, cups, tablecloth, chair.

24. Teddy Oberman.

25. Washes cars.

26. Teddy uses the water before it gets to Norton.

27. Number 3.

28. A

29. C

30. C

31. B

32. A manhole cover falls on his head; Bushwick Hospital, Room 317.

33. How I feel about him is another.

34. Manhole cover falling on his head.

35. D

36. Dr. Hyman.

37. Dr. Seefer.

38. Type A; Dr. MacDonald.

39. His watch.

40. C

41. Get the ring off his finger.

## BROTHER RALPH

1. Hire a traffic expert; with a $10 bonus.

2. Built.

3. Ten.

4. Fifteen.

5. Because the mailman rides with Ralph.

6. False—he's been laid off at least two times, maybe three.

7. Straitjacket.

8. B

9. $186.32

10. $12.83

11. Three Indian-head pennies and a two-cent stamp.

12. She never had any practice!

13. $62 a week.

14. She took a commercial course in school.

15. Spaghetti, lima beans, mashed potatoes, and hot dogs.

16. Three.

17. Alice is going back to work to make out inventory sheets; Ralph wants to go to the movies.

18. Mr. Amico, Alice's boss. (Marx and Stone envisioned Tony as "a suave John Wayne, only better looking and broader shoulders. He is dressed very-good-Madison-Avenue-style." That must have caused a good laugh around the set because the real Tony Amico, who worked as Gleason's valet/Man Friday, was a stout, stocky second-generation Italian whom author Jim Bishop, in his book *The Golden Ham*, described as "a youth with beautiful teeth, dimples, and a fist about the size of a Calais ham.")

19. Tony, Frank, Bill, Pete, and George.

20. True.

21. D

22. C

23. An hour and a half.

24. And I'm bringing Norton.

25. B

26. Nothing.

27. Freddie.

28. False—he'll be driving a crosstown bus.

29. Fifteen years.

## HELLO, MOM

1. Cream chipped beef; in a movie magazine; Ricardo Cortez.

2. Making a bedspread.

3. A

4. Quicker than a cat can wink its eye.

5. H-o-s-e (house).

6. Do you think it could mean sickness?

7. Wednesday.

8. She arrived on New Year's and stayed 'til Christmas!

9. Washing machine, electric stove, vacuum cleaner.

10. Poor Alice hasn't got a phone, either.

11. False—like a boa constrictor and a mongoose.

12. "I'm not losing a daughter, I'm gaining a ton."

13. N-a-t (gnat); ant; Norton's friend in the sewer, Nat Birnbaum, doesn't spell his name with a *g*.

14. Jack Townsend would've given her a fur coat and Fred Beatty would've bought her a home on Long Island.

15. Alice: "They wanted to sit in the shade!"

16. Exit.

17. Fantasyland—old man Grogan's underwear hanging out the window, garbage cans in the alley, the back of a Chinese restaurant; Adventureland—the sink; Frontierland—the stove and the icebox.

18. The World of Tomorrow; he's going to send her to the moon!

19. D

20. Cassidy. (Why else would he be saying goodbye to Ralph and Norton outside of Norton's apartment?)

21. Serve pizza after the meetings. (Of course!)

22. Happy marriages. (Of course!)

23. Norton's mother-in-law coming for a visit. (Of course!)

24. The invasion of locusts.

25. Trixie's mother.

26. Like Ralph from the back.

27. B

28. Nasty.

29. Alice's mother.

30. He joined the circus.

31. Emmett Kelly; the big red nose.

32. Ralph's!

33. A

34. Ralph; fifteen years ago, on his honeymoon.

## THE DECIDING VOTE

1. A dining room set; Morgan's Furniture Store; on time.

2. Icing; starch.

3. A vacuum cleaner; Dowser's; $4.95.

4. Clean rugs, upholstered furniture, and drapes, and pick up dirt.

5. Rugs, furniture, and drapes.

6. The oatmeal test; a drop of oil.

7. Try corn flakes.

8. No; return it.

9. "The armature sprocket is causing interference, which in turn causes the combustion line to interfere with the flow in the dynaflow."

10. Joe Munsey.

11. Frank MacGillicuddy.

12. The seven executive members; Joe Munsey's, Jerry Shor's, and Norton's.

13. Chicago; use of a car at the convention and meeting the big shots.

14. Bowling with Frank MacGillicuddy.

15. Egg foo young.

16. Steak; Frank MacGillicuddy.

17. He's been working in an air-conditioned Park Avenue sewer.

18. B

19. The hippiest critic I've ever seen.

20. Ralph, across the board.

21. Sergeant-at-Arms.

22. Norton.

23. Kramden, Hanley, Philbin, Shor.

24. Frank MacGillicuddy.

25. Drink beer.

26. A. "How long have you known the applicant?" "Too long."

B. "Do you consider the applicant trustworthy?" "Don't make me laugh."

C. "In your opinion, is the applicant of good character?" "The applicant is a bum!"

27. Soap.

28. You couldn't.

29. Joe Rumsey (a.k.a. Munsey in the opening scene); he bought his wife a vacuum cleaner on Ralph's recommendation, and his didn't pass the oatmeal test either!

## SOMETHING FISHY

1. 19 to 2, Norton; a dime.

2. Three.

3. Pelt.

4. It's the only game they can play with a ball that floats.

5. False—recruitment drive.

6. Kramden, Hanley, Philbin, Shor, and Bowden.

7. Fifty.

8. C

9. The applicant must have earned a public school diploma, he must have resided in the United States for the past six months, he must pay a $1.50 initiation fee; Section Two of the rules and bylaws.

10. Anthony Eden.

11. B

12. He's an undertaker.

13. Sunday.

14. Muldoon, Havemeyer.

15. All of them; seven.

16. Independence.

17. C

18. The president.

19. Ninety.

20. Alice told him to be home by 10:30.

21. They're for men only.

22. Catch, cook, eat.

23. Freddie Muller's; 6 AM.

24. True.

25. Every poolroom in Bensonhurst.

26. She didn't go to the beauty parlor for three months.

27. 4 AM.

28. About half past three.

29. Worms.

30. A hairpin.

## 'TWAS THE NIGHT BEFORE CHRISTMAS

1. The bureau drawer and the oven.

2. A paper bell.

3. The Nortons on Christmas Eve, the Kramdens on Christmas morning.

4. An orange juice squeezer that looks like a statue of Napoleon.

5. D

6. In the bedroom closet, behind the hat box on the shelf; a mousetrap.

7. Norton gives Ralph spats and Ralph gives Norton a tie.

8. Fat Man's Shop.

9. D

10. A hairpin box made of 2,000 matchsticks.

11. A

12. The Emperor of Japan's spies.

13. Mrs. Stevens; to Bayonne, to visit her sister.

14. Mrs. Stevens gives Alice a hairpin box made of 2,000 matchsticks and Alice gives her a kitchen thermometer.

15. In the novelty store near the subway.

16. Scrooge. (In the script, Norton also says: "Boy, for a guy who's built like Santa Claus, you sure ain't got much Christmas spirit!")

17. $22; a bowling ball.

18. Put it on Alice's gift, and then give her the gift the day after Christmas.

19. Alice's Uncle Leo; a $25 gift certificate from Wallace's Department Store.

20. Tommy Mullins.

21. Hock his bowling ball; $10 or $15.

22. Pajamas.

23. Alice gives Ralph a bowling ball bag and Ralph gives Alice an orange juice squeezer that looks like a statue of Napoleon.

## THE MAN FROM SPACE

1. D

2. He dropped it in the sewer. And if he's any judge of currents, it's probably in Brooklyn!

3. Either Ralph has tuna fish or he wants to borrow money.

4. Ham.

5. $50

6. Cassidy goes as Tugboat Annie and Reilly goes as Julius Caesar.

7. B

8. $10; to rent a costume.

9. Because Ralph thinks like he does.

10. Flaherty.

11. Norton's idea for a kid's cereal—pablum on pizza.

12. King Henry VIII, $10; Billy the Kid, $5.

13. A tin can so he can go as Billy the goat.

14. Because he wants to win first prize.

15. Pierre François de la Briosche, the man Norton thinks designed and built the sewers of Paris.

16. "Wait until tomorrow night and see who the judges pick as winner at the costume ball."

17. Junkman.

18. A

19. A flashlight.

20. Icebox door, knobs from the bureau, pot, and chair.

21. B

22. Because Ralph is using the faucet, the radio tube, and the sash cord.

23. The denaturizer. (This bit isn't in the script. Again, Gleason's genius as an ad-libber is evident.)

24. A

25. He didn't build the sewers of Paris—he condemned them!

26. Alice as a twelve-year-old girl and Trixie as a sailor.

27. He's called to an emergency in the sewer.

28. False—the Peabody.

29. D

30. Pete Woodruff, who's dressed as a playboy of the Roaring Twenties.

31. First prize in the contest!

## A MATTER OF RECORD

1. The Cougars; Johnny Bennett.

2. An apple.

3. C

4. Norton hit two and Johnny hit one.

5. Thursday, Aug. 5, 1942.

6. Ralph's boss gave him tickets to *Murder Strikes Out*.

7. D

8. Mother; Bensonhurst.

9. He wants to watch Captain Video on TV.

10. Blabbermouth.

11. Three.

12. Three blocks.

13. False—half a block.

14. Chester Barnes.

15. Mrs. Findley.

16. D

17. False—Norton goes.

18. Five days.

19. "Swanee River." (Playing "Swanee River" must have been Art

Carney's idea; Russell and Finn wrote "Hearts and Flowers" in the script.) He plays a harmonica.

20. Heart, liver.

21. Ralph calls Alice "Bunny" and Alice calls Ralph "Buttercup."

22. When he's communing with his thoughts, when he's being tender with his wife, and when he's in the isolation booth of *The $64,000 Question*.

23. Say hello to your mama.

24. Gibson.

25. 33 Kosciuszko St. (Original address: 31 Beeber St.)

26. He crossed out where it's printed on the envelope "If not delivered in five days . . . ," and wrote "Deliver it!"

27. Wandering around Bayonne with swollen eyes.

28. Steve Austin; he can't play because he has the measles.

29. Beer, skittles.

30. False—he wants him to tape the handle of his bat.

31. You are a stupid head.

32. C

33. C

34. Manicotti, Garrity, Bennett, Austin.

35. True.

36. A. (If that's so, why did Norton wait over two weeks after Alice heard the wrong record to bring her the right one?!)

37. Measles.

## OH MY ACHING BACK

1. Overnight; her brother-in-law Harvey is picking her up.

2. Trixie wants Alice to defrost the refrigerator. Norton can't do it because he cries when he looks into an empty refrigerator.

3. She's going to her mother's house because Uncle Leo's in town.

4. Fifteen.

5. He says it's the worst day he's ever had driving a bus, he collapses in a chair, and he says he can't go with Alice.

6. Take a bus company physical.

7. The Racoon Lodge bowling tournament; the Bayonne bunch.

8. The National Racoon Mambo Championship; somebody slipped in a Spade Cooley record. (In the original script, Norton says, ". . . and they would never have won if at the last minute they hadn'ta slipped in a Pupi Campo record on us!")

9. Ralph and Norton played pool against Trixie and her mother.

10. Front, four bowling pins; back, a bowling ball and four pins.

11. It looked like rain.

12. He'll hurt his back.

13. Schultz; he has to work.

14. Eddie Mulloy.

15. Herman Gruber; he's serving three kinds of pizza, pigs' knuckles and sauerkraut, and Neapolitan knockwurst.

16. His eighty-year-old mother from Canarsie.

17. The Neapolitan knockwurst.

18. Sleep with a heating pad on his back.

19. A cigarette lighter.

20. 111°

21. He tells Norton to fake a sleepwalking attack, so he'll have to sleep upstairs with him.

22. An airplane spotter and the Leaning Tower of Pizza.

23. "It looks like rain."

24. About a year.

25. D

26. A

27. Feeding time at the zoo.

28. Fried chicken.

29. Freddie and Charlie.

30. Player of the Year, for Ralph's outstanding achievement in the tournament.

## THE BABYSITTER

1. Bensonhurst 0-7741.

2. Trixie.

3. C

4. In the top bureau drawer.

5. Joe Lustig.

6. The bus company can't reach Ralph to offer him the shift because he doesn't have a telephone. Joe Lustig gets the job.

7. He can't afford it.

8. Eighty.

9. C

10. Norton calls to congratulate Ralph on getting a telephone.

11. A lowly third-class seaman.

12. Get the mess, swab the deck, and see that the captain feels good.

13. The correct time.

14. $176.30

15. B

16. Mrs. Simpson.

17. The Bartfelds; 383 Himrod St., Apt. 4D.

18. Four hundred.

19. A

20. Mr. Bartfeld.

21. Flowers and candy; the Hong Kong Gardens, to see the floor show.

22. *Esquire*

23. Monday, Thursday, and Friday.

24. 6 PM.

25. The Wohlstetters; 465 Van Buren St., Apt. 3C; Friday.

26. False—she says she's going to the movies.

27. Ten years.

## $99,000 ANSWER

1. Herb Norris.

2. Mr. Parker; $27,450.

3. $49,500; Prof. Walter Newman.

4. How many times does the numeral or word "one" appear on a dol-

lar bill? Twenty-five—the word sixteen times and the numeral nine times.

5. Brive a dus.

6. On Madison Avenue.

7. Poetry, Currencies of the World, Popular Songs, Table Tennis, Women Behind the Men, History, Chinese Cooking, Famous Quotations, Bridge Builders, Rare Tropical Birds.

8. So people will recognize him.

9. False—at the bowling alley.

10. In a ballroom listening to a dance band.

11. $600

12. Twelve years old.

13. Yeah, we know, you'll spell it when we give you $16,000 for spelling it.

14. Stay home every night and study sheet music and records, and rent a piano for Norton to play "every song he's every heard."

15. Dress material.

16. Popular songs taken from Italian classics.

17. She wants to see the expression on his face when he misses it.

18. Cole Porter; 1944; *Hollywood Canteen*; Warner Bros.

19. "Swanee River." (Leonard Stern says Norton's warming up on the piano by playing "Swanee River" was introduced in a Honeymooners skit from an early hour-long Gleason show. In that one, Ralph and Norton try to write a song to win a contest. "He did it incessantly, every time they tried to write the song," Stern says. "When we had the chance to use a piano again, two or three years later, we incorporated it.")

20. D

21. Warren and Dubin; 1932.

22. Johnny Mercer and Richard Whiting; 1937; *Ready, Willing and Able*. (In the script, Ralph also names "As Time Goes By," written by Herman Huffeld for the film *Casablanca*.)

23. "Melancholy Serenade." (Gleason wrote it, and it was the theme song for *The Jackie Gleason Show*.)

24. "Take Me Back to Sorrento"; 1898; Ernesto DeQuista. (Stern and Zelinka wanted Mrs. Manicotti to sing "The Butcher Boy," written by Lew Brown and Rudy Vallee in 1938.)

25. Killing Ralph.

26. "Sweet Georgia Brown"

27. Tom and José.

28. First, $100; second, $600; fourth, $6,187.50; fifth, $12,375.

29. Who is the composer of "Swanee River?" (Stephen Foster.) Ralph says Ed Norton wrote it!

30. Irving Kahal and Sammy Fain, 1938; Bazzy Simon, 1927.

31. John Lomax and Huddie Ledbetter; Rudy Vallee and Ray Noble.

32. Bing Crosby.

## RALPH KRAMDEN, INC.

1. Yellow-bellied sapsucker.

2. A chickenhawk.

3. Because they watch him.

4. A string of knockwurst and a liverwurst sandwich.

5. He gives a twenty-dollar bill for a dollar bill.

6. Pay Norton back!

7. They forget their relatives.

8. "When a person or group of persons duly authorized to sell or distribute shares, become avowed with the intention of the stockholders grouping about together with those shares, with the intention of selling the shares comes to an equal interest there."

9. Merrill Lynch, Fierce, Pierce & Bean.

10. C

11. 20 percent; the vice-presidency.

12. They had yellow bellies and they were sucking sap; Albuquerque, New Mexico.

13. A peanut butter sandwich.

14. Apple, orange, banana.

15. Thirty-five percent.

16. Mary Monahan.

17. Friday at 10 AM; $40 million.

18. Mary Monahan's attorney.

19. True.

20. Top left-hand drawer of the bureau.

21. Bringing a suitcase to carry home the $40 million.

22. Niagara Falls; they hitchhiked!

23. Take a second honeymoon to Niagara Falls. (Russell and Finn originally wrote that Norton and Trixie had always wanted to "take one of them sightseein' buses through Chinatown!")

24. Fortune; a parrot.

25. $100

26. Mary Monahan's nephew.

27. Herbert Bascom, $50,000, and Mary O'Donnell, $25,000.

28. Clapping when people are awarded money.

29. One dollar; deposit it with his bookie; pick a winner.

30. Fortune, the parrot.

## YOUNG AT HEART

1. Wallace; Freddie—he was a termite, strictly out of the wood.

2. Judy's fourteen years old. Wallace is almost eighteen.

3. Judy doesn't want Wallace to meet her father.

4. The amusement park, roller skating, a bop dance contest, and the Tunnel of Love.

5. D

6. To the amusement park; she wants to go roller skating, enter the bop dance contest, and go through the Tunnel of Love—and the Crazy House.

7. He's got one at home.

8. Since Alf Landon stopped being presidential timber.

9. Second plateau.

10. Must mean fat.

11. When he was fixing a leak in one of the pipes; "What do you and Alice know about fixing leaks?"

12. Ralph thinks he's selling magazines.

13. Judy Connors.

14. A frantic hot rod that's ready to percolate.

15. No, no. Norton's the one that digs—he works in the sewer.

16. False—she lives downstairs from them.

17. Wallace is giving Judy his pin.

18. Carving your best girl's initials on a shovel.

19. They kiss their own hands one at a time, and pat each other's hands one at a time.

20. Thirteen.

21. A

22. The Big Apple, the Suzie Q, the Continental, the Hesitation Waltz; "Voh-doh-dee-oh-doh," "23 Skidoo," "I'll kiss you later, I'm eatin' a potato." (Gleason left out one dance, the Lambeth Walk, and one expression, "Chicken Inspector," written in the script.)

23. Round, square.

24. C

25. Straw hat, sweater with football emblem and large letter V, striped jacket, white pants, saddle shoes.

26. B

27. The Hucklebuck.

28. A

29. His bus driver's badge.

30. Old age.

31. B

32. Coffee.

33. Chinese restaurant; chop suey and fried rice; sixty cents.

34. A

35. Isham Jones, Ted Fio Rito, Little Jack Little, Basil Fomeen, Johnny Messler and his toy piano.

36. Bernard Shaw. (The actual quote from George Bernard Shaw is, "Youth is a wonderful thing: what a crime to waste it on children.")

## A DOG'S LIFE

1. True.

2. Cocker-poodle.

3. C

4. Mrs. Manicotti.

5. Norton's allergic to fur. (Except Lulu's!)

6. A. (In other episodes they live downstairs from the Kramdens and next to the Kramdens.)

7. U.N.; four.

8. The executive meeting.

9. C

10. 165 pounds.

11. False—out of the can.

12. Herman Fatrack. (Stern and Zelinka never heard of Herman Fatrack; they thought Herman Bartfeld invented the wrench-lock.)

13. Kramden's Delicious Marshall.

14. KranMar's Delicious Mystery Appetizer.

15. Mr. Marshall, his boss.

16. C

17. Messrs. Peck and Tebbets.

18. Dog.

19. Mr. Peck.

20. Charlie.

21. A French name.

22. They're training a new man in the sewer.

23. Voice, doom.

24. Because he'll have to walk it.

25. Around midnight.

26. C

27. Five days.

28. Three.

## HERE COMES THE BRIDE

1. Stanley Saxon; Agnes Gibson, Alice's sister.

2. Saturday.

3. "May your life be rosy and bright. If you take the advice of an old married man, you will get out of town tonight."

4. Six years.

5. Boris Karloff. (The original script had Boris dancing on the Milton Berle show. Berle was on NBC, and the Skelton show was on CBS; no wonder Boris wound up dancing with Skelton.)

6. What're you gettin' married for?

7. Garrity.

8. Twenty years.

9. Her mother, her father, and the caterer.

10. She ran and caught it herself.

11. McCloud's.

12. On the train, after their wedding.

13. C

14. D

15. False—the blue dress.

16. Niagara Falls.

17. Roast beef, mashed potatoes, peas and carrots.

18. In a Robin Hood movie; Richard the Lionhearted said it to Friar Tuck.

19. Alice is supposed to have Ralph's robe and slippers out; Trixie can't go to the movies with Alice!

## MAMA LOVES MAMBO

1. Chocolate fudge cake.

2. He dances.

3. Fogarty.

4. Stew.

5. She goes up to the roof to take in the wash.

6. Potato salad.

7. He has gray hair and he lives alone.

8. He was a night watchman.

9. He'll need a nurse.

10. False—checkers.

11. A hammer.

12. This boy looks pretty well preserved.

13. "What are you, a garbage man?"

14. *Hasta la vista.*

15. Ralph, *"gasa mañana"*; Norton, *"semper fidelis."*

16. Clark Gable.

17. Five; Mrs. Stevens.

18. Tito Rodriguez, "Claris for Mambo."

19. Mrs. Manicotti.

20. Rudolph Valentino.

21. A few days.

22. Grandmother.

23. Tuna salad.

24. Sew, cook, wash the windows, and clean up.

25. Fifteen years.

26. Mr. Manicotti; she left a note saying she'd be at the Kramdens' taking mambo lessons.

27. When she swings her hips, she knocks the dishes off the table.

28. To get his phonograph.

29. Sir Galahad.

30. Because Norton has his in water all day.

31. He wants Carlos to teach him the mambo.

32. Oatmeal.

33. Church, eleven o'clock.

34. A pot, the oatmeal, and the coffee.

35. The sheets.

36. He woke up Trixie at two o'clock so he could tip his hat before getting out of bed for a glass of water.

37. "Roll that around your mouth."

38. "It's gentlemanlike to wait. I may wait till tomorrow!"

39. Open the door and follow him out of the Kramdens' apartment.

## PLEASE LEAVE THE PREMISES

1. Aggravation.

2. Repeat the dictum "Pins and needles, needles and pins, it's a happy man that grins," put on a smile, and then say "What am I mad about?"

3. The subway.

4. A doctor's bill, and being poked with an umbrella, a rose bush, and a piece of wood.

5. It should be presented to the U.N. as the greatest instrument for peace known to mankind.

6. Fifteen percent; $5 a month.

7. C

8. George Washington didn't have his wife, Martha, with him!

9. General, sergeant, private.

10. There's no room back there!

11. The water in the hot-water bottle.

12. Three days; being alone with Trixie.

13. Celery.

14. Coconuts.

15. Steak, mushroom sauce with onions, avocado salad pear, mashed potatoes and gravy.

16. Four.

17. Freitag the delicatessen's.

18. Outside the apartment door, on the fire escape, and below Ralph's bedroom window.

19. Because Alice knows Ralph knows how easy she gets virus.

## PARDON MY GLOVE

1. Joe Munsey.

2. A

3. 6 PM, Thursday.

4. Sandwiches, ice cream, coffee, punch, potato chips, peanuts, coconut cake.

5. A belt.

6. C

7. Carrots, for the eyes; beets, for the blood; lettuce, for the teeth.

8. Pizzas, sewer.

9. A teensy-weensy little piece.

10. He wipes his hand on Alice's apron and finds it in the apron pocket.

11. His name's not on the guest list.

12. The interior decorator at Morgan's Department Store. (Andre has a last name in the script: Fleming! But when Alice introduces him to Trixie, he says, "Please, my dear, call me Andre. Nobody knows me as Mr. Fleming.")

13. It's part of an advertising campaign for Morgan's Department Store; cool, pale green.

14. Looking for curtain material.

15. C

16. One day; two years ago, when Alice's nephew came in with an ice cream cone.

17. Eight.

18. Friday.

19. They swapped them for marriage licenses.

20. In the top left-hand bureau drawer.

21. There isn't going to be a party!

22. Mrs. Manicotti.

23. Right-hand glove.

24. She says Winston Churchill dropped by for tea.

25. Match up some thread.

26. Thursday.

27. She's having a rendezvous with her boyfriend at the apartment.

28. True.

29. Hide a dictaphone in the room.

30. About 7 AM.

31. D

32. True.

33. D

## YOUNG MAN WITH A HORN

1. A year.

2. In the cellar.

3. He went to City Hall, to fill out a job application.

4. Sewer inspector.

5. Senior clerk in transit authority.

6. From his father.

7. The cornet and his toes.

8. A sock.

9. True.

10. "Carnival of Venice"

11. False—Harry James.

12. His uncle taught him; he gave it up to learn the Charleston.

13. C

14. Forty years ago.

15. Doughnuts.

16. The kitchen of a Chinese restaurant; a laundry.

17. The doughnut business.

18. Oversleeping.

19. When you got water and soap.

20. Reveille.

21. You remember—Dickens.

22. Bad points—he's a rotten pool player, rotten bowler, rotten cornet player, he doesn't pay his debts, and he can't speak French; good point—he's the sweetest guy in the world.

23. Two dollars.

24. Good points—loves wife, admits mistakes, is softhearted, has good intentions, is basically honest when pinned down.

Bad points—is late for work, oversleeps, snores, loses temper, doesn't pay debts, too fat, brags, connives, daydreams, shirks responsibility, is stubborn, too fat, overeats, neglects wife, spends foolishly, is gullible, is sloppy dresser, treats wife like workhorse, is generally untidy, too fat, talks too much, argues too much.

25. Ralph is shopping for dinner.

26. False—5:30 AM.

27. Joe Cassidy; Cassidy, nine million people, Ralph, seven million people.

28. "Pack up and move to Florida."

29. No . . . he washed out.

30. True.

31. The day he married Alice.

## HEAD OF THE HOUSE

1. The Questioning Photographer.

2. Nightly.

3. Whether or not the U.N. should outlaw the H-bomb; which is more authentic, the Canarsie or the Weehawken style of mambo?

4. Edward L. Norton; he's an engineer in subterranean sanitation.

5. "In your house, who is the boss—you or your wife?"

6. "I do" and "I'm the boss!"

7. Friday night.

8. He's wondering how Ralph will look in a Foreign Legion uniform.

9. Mouse.

10. She's following a puzzle contest.

11. He doesn't like its editorial policy—they cut out *Little Orphan Annie*.

12. Five.

13. He was the only man brave enough to make that idiotic statement.

14. Followers.

15. Drinking a bottle of wine he was going to give Alice's brother for Christmas.

16. He had a two-day hangover from a slice of rum cake.

17. Norton gets tipsy just reading the label.

18. Ralph; "To my wife, who has finally found her place."

19. "A little strong but good."

20. "Here's mud in your eye;" Trixie.

21. What was he laughing at? What was he laughing at? He forgot what he was laughing at.

22. One night when they were playing poker, Fensterblau said Ralph had to leave early because of Alice.

23. Hair.

24. Someone was stabbed upstairs.

25. "I Had a Dream, Dear"

26. A pitch pipe.

27. "Somebody stole the bed."

28. Trixie, "I give you our husbands; Alice, "You can have 'em."

29. True.

30. A

31. Cold grape juice.

32. He goes shopping with Trixie.

33. She lumps it.

34. Windy.

35. Tell Alice he's bringing home a friend for supper; $10 each.

36. Soup, roast chicken with stuffing, rice, salad, dessert, and coffee.

37. 6 PM.

38. At her mother's.

39. He and Norton will cook the meal, and he'll tell Fensterblau Alice cooked it and went out.

40. Oscar at the Waldorf, Pierre at the Ritz, and Grace Kelly's father.

41. He cooked up a pretty sweet dish.

42. The whole box. (Gleason goofs and says, "If it's too much, I won't eat any.")

43. "What have you got, a new watch fob?"

44. Twice the time. (Gleason goofed again—he should have said half the time.)

45. Two hours.

46. "That is the wildest rice I've ever seen!" (Set decorator Phil Cuoco says he used dry ice in the pot to make the rice boil over and the pot lid fly off.)

47. She tells Fensterblau there's no dinner because the stove blew up while she was cooking. (There were two stoves for *The Honeymooners*: a real stove, and one with a false back panel for episodes like this one where things like a burnt chicken had to be put inside it.)

48. Sunday.

49. No—Ralph tells him to forget it.

## THE WORRY WART

1. B
2. To the antique show at Madison Square Garden.
3. From a scalper.
4. Hen's teeth.
5. A dog.
6. Early Ma and Pa Kettle.
7. *Dragnet; Medic.*
8. The gas company; 93 cents.
9. Mrs. Schwartz.
10. The Collier Brothers; 1931.
11. Spaghetti and meatballs.
12. Dizzy Dean.
13. $42; two weeks' vacation at Fred's Landing.
14. Mr. Richard Puder; 10 AM, on the 21st of the month.
15. Ketchup, piccalilli, and chow-chow.
16. The barbershop.
17. Rent a cheaper tent, with a smaller snake.
18. Jails.
19. C
20. Insomnia.
21. D
22. A glass of warm milk.
23. Mongolia and Tibet; five.
24. Send him to the federal pen.
25. Arithmetic.
26. 105–36–22.
27. A
28. Ralph's—the cost of cleaning his uniform, union dues, driver's license, and $80 entertaining Freddie Muller; Norton's—union dues, vulcanizing his rubber boots, waterproofing his lunchbox, and 25 percent of his rent.
29. Freddie Muller.
30. He practices in the bathtub.
31. Livestock.
32. $75; $2.25.
33. A skinny chicken; two dollars.
34. $25 shooting pool, a horse with a clock in the stomach for high score in pinball game at Salvatore's Pizzeria, $5 in the Racoon Lodge's three-legged race, and $85 playing poker.
35. "All persons are required under this title to pay an estimated tax or tax, or are required by this title or by regulations made under authority thereof to make a return other than a return required under authority of section 6015 or section 6016, keep any records or supply any information, and who willfully fails to pay such estimated tax or tax, make such a return, keep such records, or supply such information." (Okay, but what is the penalty for failure to report income?)
36. He tells him to stand on the 18th Amendment—and tell the IRS he was drunk when he made out his taxes.
37. True.
38. Clean.
39. He forgot to sign his tax form.
40. That during the last fiscal year he found $3 floating in the sewer.
41. Not putting down a horse with a clock in its stomach.

## TRAPPED

1. Seventeen.
2. C
3. Saturday.
4. Haggerty; his mother-in-law moved to Schenectady.
5. True.
6. Norton; tails.
7. B
8. Four.
9. The watchman.
10. False—his felt hat.
11. Tommy Manicotti.
12. D
13. *Dead Men Tell No Tales*, starring Humphrey Bogart.
14. Mrs. Helprin.
15. False—they live below the Kramdens (at least in this episode).
16. Danny and Bibbo; Marty.
17. Tommy Manicotti's.
18. One.
19. False—Bibbo's the one who gets worked over. It seems he never ran into a bus driver before.

## THE LOUDSPEAKER

1. He thinks he's being named Racoon of the Year.
2. False—appointed.
3. C
4. He was so excited, he stayed home from work for three days.
5. From the Academy Awards.
6. The Grand High Exalted Mystic Ruler told him to sit at the speaker's table and to be prepared to say a few words.
7. D
8. Morris Fink; in the sewer.
9. Platinum.
10. He got uppity and joined the Elks.
11. Cashmere; the Racoon Lodge's old-clothes drive.
12. False—they missed her anniversary!
13. He opens the first clam at the annual clambake, he steers the boat as the Racoons sail past Raccoon Point, and he gets free burial at the Racoon National Cemetery.
14. Dropping the first bag of water out of the hotel window.
15. D
16. Grand High Exalted Mystic Ruler.
17. Making speeches.
18. Use his influence to get Norton buried in the Racoon National Cemetery.
19. A
20. Mrs. Gallagher's; Ralph had his Racoon cap on backwards.
21. Mildred.
22. Alice, aspirin; Norton, to scare Ralph with an unexpected sound.

23. It makes the fur stand up.
24. B
25. If you want to make a point, do it with a joke.
26. Sir Lancelot and King Arthur.
27. "I wouldn't send a knight out on a dog like this."
28. Three.
29. Garrity.
30. False—she does . . . she married Ralph!
31. Norton.
32. True.

## ON STAGE

1. Treasurer.
2. Put on a play.
3. Let people in free, and charge them to get out.
4. Mr. Faversham.
5. The pool table, TV set, phonograph, and piano.
6. Boxing gloves.
7. B
8. He studied typing under the GI Bill.
9. He didn't want to be cooped up in an office.
10. C
11. A
12. Dance the hula with a lampshade on his head.
13. At the 1949 bus driver's frolics; Ralph did the comedy stuff, wearing a ballet dress.
14. James Cagney.
15. Gregory Peck was an usher at Radio City Music Hall and Kirk Douglas was a soda jerk.
16. D
17. "Be kind to the people you meet on the way up, because you're gonna meet the same people on the way down."
18. True.
19. Herbert J. Whiteside. (Herbert J. Whiteside was added to the show after a script rewrite. Origi-

nally, Mr. Faversham's friend was George Spelvin, a movie actor he discovered. And later, when Spelvin comes to New York to cast a movie, it's Ed Sullivan, and not Earl Wilson, who writes about it in his column.)
20. The upstairs maid.
21. C
22. That Herbert J. Whiteside was in town to cast his new movie, and that he was looking for new faces.
23. Joe Hannigan.
24. Costume.
25. Ralph, Frederick; Alice, Rachel; Norton, Hamilton Douglas.
26. From castles and palaces in Europe.
27. C
28. The left side.
29. Freddie. (If Stern and Zelinka had had their way, the entertainment committee chairman would have been a guy named Ben Hopkins.)
30. Seven.
31. Return once a year and do a play.
32. False—a teacher.
33. To the Hong Kong Gardens.
34. C
35. The love scene.

## OPPORTUNITY KNOCKS BUT

1. Bradstetter; he had to do a report for Mr. Marshall.
2. The transmissions.
3. Mr. Gordon.
4. A pool table.
5. A
6. It took him "a year" to get across town in a Gotham bus.
7. When Ralph was laid off.
8. Pool.
9. 9 PM; 1149 Park Avenue.
10. Caddying.
11. D
12. He chased a golf ball down a

sewer, and the foreman in the sewer took a liking to him and gave him a job. (In "Pal O' Mine," Norton says Jim McKeever gave him his start in the sewer. If it was a foreman who hired Norton, though, it couldn't have been McKeever because he didn't make foreman until years later.)
13. False—*Reader's Digest*.
14. Lasagna.
15. C
16. Tarpin; April 1939; Key West, Florida.
17. He killed it in self-defense in the sewer.
18. First prize for breeding at the international dog show.
19. Roberts.
20. Nine out of ten.
21. "A relaxed bus driver is a efficient bus driver."
22. About 50,000 gallons.
23. Set up a recreation room, put the right man in the right job, and schedule odd and even buses.
24. Bus driver's supervisor.
25. 89¢ a pair; 32 to 50.
26. True. (Except for all the other days when they bring lunch from home!)
27. Three corned beef sandwiches.
28. E.N.
29. Have his own office, a big desk, a secretary to dictate to, and eat lunch with Mr. Marshall.
30. Sixteen years. (It's fifteen in other episodes, but sixteen must remain the definitive answer.)
31. D
32. Alternate buses.

## UNCONVENTIONAL BEHAVIOR

1. A can of corned beef hash.
2. Fifty-eight cents a pound.
3. B

4. In Minneapolis.

5. Ralph, 50¢; Norton, $50.

6. Mildred.

7. 5 PM; 5:26; 5:37.

8. 5:27 and 56 seconds; 5:28.

9. 320

10. False.

11. False—the family dinner.

12. Walt Disney.

13. A trick camera, a box of cherry bombs, a hand buzzer, two false faces, a fake candy box, and paper bags to fill with water.

14. It looks like his boss.

15. He almost drowned—the window was closed.

16. Ralph asked Alice for money to finance his no-cal pizzeria.

17. Taking Alice to the Racoon convention.

18. On their honeymoon.

19. False—National Nut Week.

20. Number 3.

21. 11:15 PM.

22. Alice, checkered coat; Trixie, imitation dyed rabbit fur coat.

23. Five days.

24. Bulging eyes, rubber marshmallows, and trick handcuffs.

25. "Boomph."

26. He has claustrophobia.

27. If he wants a match.

28. D

## THE SAFETY AWARD

1. The reporter is Mr. Martin, the photographer is Charlie. (In the script, Charlie and Mr. Martin work for *Life* magazine.)

2. Wear a bikini.

3. 12:30 PM, at the commissioner's office.

4. "If he's worth that much, let him take a cab."

5. 150 pounds ago.

6. False—a wet-collar job.

7. He's assured of a comfortable,

smooth, safe ride . . . and Ralph lets him ride for free.

8. Ralph's steadiness.

9. The Three Musketeers.

10. Freddie Muller's; Clemmins.

11. Fourteen years.

12. The grand opera.

13. Not blowin'.

14. True.

15. D

16. C

17. "The Charge of the Light Brigade"

18. Fourteen.

19. False—a raincoat.

20. False. (But they originally dressed in identical black jackets.)

21. The heel on her shoe breaks.

22. Ralph.

23. Judge Lawrence Norton Hurdle and his wife Helen. (In the script, the judge's name is Halloran—Hollerin' Halloran.)

24. C

25. He has the flu.

26. Judge Lawrence Norton Hurdle; he's famous for $50 fines and fifty-minute lectures.

27. False—the judge didn't see Ralph's signal because he was wearing the wrong eyeglasses.

28. The safety of the public.

## MIND YOUR OWN BUSINESS

1. True.

2. Queens, clubs, sevens.

3. The seven of spades.

4. 28,000

5. Cassidy.

6. A year; in the sewer under City Hall.

7. Seventeen years. (It's only ten years in "The Golfer.")

8. Twenty-eight cents.

9. Goulash.

10. There isn't a manhole in New

York big enough for Ralph to fit through.

11. Two weeks; Spiffy Iron Company (strangely enough, in the script, the company is called both Jiffy and Spiffy); selling irons.

12. Man, sewer, sewer, man.

13. Fourteen—every night for two weeks.

14. Trixie's mother's.

15. 137. His mother. ("Mama, you just gotta buy this iron from me!")

16. They're both specialists.

17. $40

18. Two.

19. Veal chops and meat loaf.

20. C

21. The ol' squeeze play—he'll tell his boss he has another job offer, and that he'll take it unless he gets his promotion and raise.

22. True.

## ALICE AND THE BLONDE

1. True.

2. The value of real estate in Bensonhurst will go up 100 percent.

3. $35. (The jackets were even more expensive in the original script: $75!)

4. Madame Guillotine.

5. B

6. False—playing pool was Ralph's idea.

7. Monday.

8. Alice, green; Trixie, blue.

9. D

10. Twenty-five cents; her crooked stockings.

11. False—the flowers are real.

12. The Millman Shop. ("I know from being a writer's wife that using names is a writer's way of paying off," says Freda Rosen, a.k.a. Rita Weedemeyer. "It was somebody's Millman. Names are coins of the realm to writers. I remember thinking at the time

that it was an awkward phrase—the Millman Shop stands out like a neon light. There are easier names to use, but that's the way it was written. The words count. Arnie [her late husband, Arnie Rosen] once put the name of our pediatrician in a show. He was in heaven. You do that with somebody's Aunt Ethel, and Aunt Ethel remembers you in her will, she's so happy.")

13. D. (From the script—Rita: "Bert calls me Kitten because I'm so cuddly, and I call him Twinkles because his eyes sparkle like the stars.")

14. She has several she'd love to call him.

15. The boys in the poolroom.

16. I wouldn't dream of having it without you, Bert.

17. Coffee and cookies.

18. False—love.

19. False—a headache.

20. Two-tone, sensible-sized.

21. "Leave it there, the cat'll get it."

22. False—the beauty parlor.

23. "How about tomorrow night?"

24. A cookie.

25. Short.

26. D. (Stern and Zelinka described Alice in her outfit as the "Bensonhurst Sadie Thompson." Also, in the original script Ralph suspected Alice of nipping at the cooking sherry.)

27. True.

28. Because he slays her.

29. He's a mope.

## THE BENSONHURST BOMBER

1. Number 1; having a cold drink.

2. A pretzel he got at the egg-cream place.

3. Pizza.

4. Ralph; they tossed a coin.

5. Ralph; Norton breaks.

6. Sixty-five cents an hour.

7. False—he scratches.

8. The fourteen ball in the far corner.

9. The eight and the fifteen ball will go into the corner pocket, but before the eight ball goes into the corner pocket it will kiss off the three, causing the nine ball to drop into the side pocket. Before the nine ball drops into the pocket it will hit, carom off the cushion, come bouncing into a bunch of balls, causing a chain reaction making all the balls go into the corner pocket, with the exception of the four ball, which will end up in the upper left corner.

10. Strong milk.

11. D

12. Twist them into bookends.

13. He's in the right. Nobody pushes him around.

14. Bend him into a pretzel.

15. True.

16. He's wearing a new suit.

17. Eight o'clock on Friday night at Kelsey's Gym.

18. Go home and punch the bag.

19. Smiling Ed Norton and The Bensonhurst Bomber.

20. It knocks them down to 500 to 1.

21. False—they're betting that he doesn't show up.

22. B

23. A

24. Nutsy.

25. To honor Ralph's memory.

26. Norton blabbed it to everybody.

27. Melts.

28. Alice.

29. Oyster.

30. C

31. The Brinks robbery.

32. Out of town.

33. Ralph and Norton.

34. B

35. To teach him never to trust anybody in the ring.

36. "Hey, get a load of Fatso!"

37. "Water is thicker than blood."

38. The right hand.

39. D

40. He was home in bed with a cold.

41. Maybe the phrase just fits. . . .

## DIAL J FOR JANITOR

1. To fix his water pipes.

2. Water.

3. D

4. Take aspirin.

5. Pressure on the brain.

6. They asked what the doctor removed—the pressure or the brain. . . .

7. Make up an ice pack; open the window.

8. The window, the bedroom closet, and a leaky faucet.

9. A cigar.

10. Only five or six.

11. Stay dirty.

12. Water; he takes it back in a hot-water bottle; Trixie's folks came for dinner and he has to stretch the soup.

13. Mr. Johnson, the landlord.

14. Mirages.

15. Ralph and Norton drove him out; four.

16. $150 per month and free rent.

17. D

18. Evict them.

19. Sam Wiggams.

20. Evictions.

21. He was evicted from his office!

22. Ralph.

23. Respect, slave, horse.

24. Tip him a couple of bucks.

25. Two; at Christmas and at Easter.

26. Fixing Norton's pipes.

27. A house phone.

28. Mrs. Bennett complained about her radiator, Norton wants his water pipes fixed, the fire inspector wants Ralph to clean out the cellar, Norton wants his water pipes fixed, and Mrs. Olsen complained that Ralph broke her venetian blinds.

29. Ralph went bowling; Alice had to take out the ashes and bank the furnace.

30. Bowling is his only relaxation, and it helps keep his weight down.

31. That one of the Kramdens can fix something.

32. He yells in the hall.

33. Mrs. Manicotti—her bathroom sink needs fixing; Mrs. Fogarty—somebody's been taking food out of her icebox.

34. C

35. Three hours; she should have taken her dirty dishes out of the sink.

36. Water! Water! He wants water!

37. A week.

38. False—janitor of the year.

39. Ralph didn't pick up his garbage.

40. Norton's can was only half full.

41. He has to clean out the cellar.

42. Fred's gasoline station. (Russell and Finn had Norton bathing at the YMCA in the script.)

43. Roast beef.

44. Maintenance engineer.

45. Low water pressure.

46. Turn a valve.

47. But the flesh is just too much!

48. Mrs. Manicotti.

49. The fire department; firemen rescue cats from trees, and deliver babies. . . .

50. C

51. Neither—the job made too many demands on his leisure time.

52. Fixing the window and the sink.

53. Norton had the gall to circulate a petition to have Ralph fired as janitor.

54. Norton.

## A MAN'S PRIDE

1. Bill was courting Alice in school at the same time Ralph was. (Of course if anyone asks you how Ralph and Alice met, you're supposed to answer "at the WPA," ignoring that in this episode they went to the same school.)

2. Slugger Simpson.

3. B

4. False—Slugger was the one knocked out.

5. Ridgewood; McHenry; Slugger was knocked out in the second round.

6. "Some kids are small, some kids are tall. Fatso Kramden is the only kid who walks down the hall wall to wall."

7. Chicago; he says he owns a manufacturing business.

8. Chicago, Akron.

9. D

10. Between 8 and 9 in the morning.

11. Six, six-thirty.

12. A

13. A and D, B and C, E and F, G and H.

14. At 9th Avenue and 48th Street.

15. He was a garbage collector.

16. Mr. Monahan's.

17. "Step to the rear of the office."

18. He wanted to ask for a promotion to dispatcher.

19. Mr. Muller.

20. D

21. Bensonhurst 6–0098.

22. D

23. The Colonnade; if it costs a cent, it must cost three dollars a person.

24. The Hong Kong Gardens.

25. Sweet and sour lichee nuts.

26. The food is no good; no truck drivers eat there.

27. B

28. Steak.

29. Alice, demitasse; Ralph, a small cup of black coffee; Bill, coffee; Millie, demitasse.

30. He's an assistant plumber.

31. Mambo, samba.

32. By bus.

33. Alice, $7; Ralph, $16; Bill, $12; Millie, $9.

## APPENDIX I
### Famous Last Words, Wisecracks, and Punch Lines

### TV or Not TV

1. "Let me have what you're drinkin'. I wanna get loaded too."

### Funny Money

1. "What's that? Your lunch box?"

2. "There can't be anything of value in it or you wouldn't have found it."

3. "There isn't enough room in this place for you and anybody."

4. "Junk?! Junk?! Junk?!"

5. "Just fill it with gas and point it toward Mexico." (In the original script, Ralph tells Norton to point it toward Canada.)

### The Golfer

1. "Why won't you need this lunch box . . . are you getting a bigger one?"

2. "Hello, this is Mrs. Kramden. When are you going to take out the garbage?"

3. Alice: "You've got enough everything in you for the both of us." Ralph: "How'd you like to go sailing over the clubhouse, Alice!"

## A Woman's Work Is Never Done

1. "The chubby one is gonna be trouble."
2. "If these are the servant's quarters, I quit."
3. "If that's the Good Humor man, get me a popsicle."
4. "No, that's my idea of a burn."

## A Matter of Life and Death

1. "This couldn't have happened at a better time."
2. You guessed it: "Don't touch me, nurse, I'm sterile!"

## Better Living Through TV

1. "The biggest thing you ever got into was your pants."
2. "I can't even put my arms around you."
3. "I wish you would stop talking like that, nervous, you're gonna get yourself all Norton."

## Pal O' Mine

1. "Yeah, about three hundred pounds of it."

## Brother Ralph

1. "Your salary couldn't drip out."
2. "You must be a riot around the water cooler!"

## The Deciding Vote

1. "It wouldn't help if you dipped it in Texas."
2. "No. I'm an authority on junk."
3. "I hope they like those jokes on the moon, because that's where you're going."
4. "In the sewer there ain't no dry end."
5. "Brutus had his Caesar, Kramden has his Norton."
6. "I don't need your help, I'll do it myself."
7. "Et tu, Alice? Et tu?"

## Something Fishy

1. "Fifteen years ago. I caught three hundred pounds of blubber."
2. "Don't be too sure, Ralph. I ain't got no hairpin."

## 'Twas the Night Before Christmas

1. "They had to. You probably broke it."
2. "A bowling bag ball! I mean a bowling ball bag!"

## The Man from Space

1. "When you walk down the street, there ain't no other side."
2. "I don't know the latest developments? Who is it that lets your pants out every other day?"
3. "Not any twelve-year-old girl that's married to me."

## A Matter of Record

1. "You're looking at a man that could cover the infield, the outfield, and four sections of the bleachers."

## Oh My Aching Back

1. ". . . you're lucky you can walk."

## The Babysitter

1. "Yeah, a human being."
2. "Gee, I never knew Davy Crockett was so fat."

## $99,000 Answer

1. ". . . you've already got the pot."
2. "Eat 'em. Like any other elephant."

## Ralph Kramden, Inc.

1. "When this jar hits your head, you'll hear a crunch!"

## Young at Heart

1. "Yeah, now you're a full-grown nut."

## A Dog's Life

1. "No, Ralph, I never did see any of your baby pictures."

## Mama Loves Mambo

1. "If I told you once, I told you a thousand times not to carry a heavy wash like that. Now, the next time you have a heavy wash like that, make two trips!" (Ralph gets a big laugh with that line, but Walter Stone got it from someone who wasn't laughing

when he said it. "Before I was a writer, I used to work for a truck company in New Jersey. I worked with a guy in the morning who said, 'The old lady is a pain. . . . Her back is out.' He was talking about the laundry or something. He said, 'If I told that dame once, I told her a hundred times, if you have a heavy load, make two trips!'")

2. "Ralph, as long as we're neighbors, you don't have to call me Norton . . . call me Eduardo."

3. ". . . wiggle over to the stove and get my supper."

4. "Tuna fish?! What am I, a cat or something?"

5. "I forgot that you're a woman? How could I . . . you're always yappin'."

6. "You're gonna do the mambo. But it's gonna be on the moon!"

7. "She's got her nerve. She knew when she married you that she was gettin' the worst of it."

### Please Leave the Premises

1. "How would you like some fingers in your nose?"

### Pardon My Glove

1. "Poor little pizza . . . ain't good for nothin'."

2. "I'm sorry, Ralph. How about shootin' a little pool?"

### Young Man With a Horn

1. "Maybe it's one of the tender memories that's attached to it."

2. "I'd like you better with a sock in ya!"

### Head of the House

1. "I'd rather be a live mouse than a dead boss."

2. "There'd be no Christopher Columbus if it weren't for his mother."

3. "The chicken is a little well-done, too."

### The Worry Wart

1. ". . . there's gonna be piccalilli all over Bensonhurst!"

2. ". . . if you could count, they wouldn't be investigating your taxes."

3. "If you were a taxpayer, you wouldn't be down here right now."

### On Stage

1. "What does Rachel want with a Chinese restaurant and a pizzeria?"

### Opportunity Knocks But

1. ". . . till I found out it was yours."

### Unconventional Behavior

1. "I don't care if you burn."

### The Safety Award

1. "I'm as close as anyone can get to Ralph Kramden."

2. "If you stood out any more in front, you wouldn't be able to get behind the wheel of a bus."

3. "When the tides of life turn against you, and the current upsets your boat, don't waste those tears on

what might have been, just lay on your back and float."

4. "And don't forget the fifty-minute lecture."

### Mind Your Own Business

1. ". . . he couldn't even get his arms around you."

### Alice and the Blonde

1. "Isn't that a good idea, Tubby?"

2. ". . . he's gonna be a buried treas-ure."

3. "And I'm callin' Bellevue 'cause you're nuts!"

### The Bensonhurst Bomber

1. "A pox on you and all your ancestors!"

2. ". . . you wouldn't have to leave town."

### Dial J For Janitor

1. "You don't need anything to keep your weight down. You need something to hold it up."

2. "I hope there's some water on the moon, 'cause that's where you're going!"

3. "We've heard rumors to that effect down the sewer."

4. "The wall?! There's four walls!"

### A Man's Pride

1. "That ought not to be too hard. You've learned to swallow everything else."